Stored Tissue Samples

Stored Tissue Samples

Ethical, Legal, and Public Policy Implications

Edited by Robert F. Weir

University of Iowa Press Ψ Iowa City

University of Iowa Press,
Iowa City 52242
Copyright © 1998 by the
University of Iowa Press
All rights reserved
Printed in the United States of America
Design by Richard Hendel
http://www.uiowa.edu/~uipress
Printed on acid-free paper

Library of Congress
Cataloging-in-Publication Data
Stored tissue samples: ethical, legal, and public
    policy implications / edited by Robert F. Weir.
            p.   cm.
        Includes bibliographical references and index.
        ISBN 0-87745-634-8, ISBN 0-87745-635-6 (pbk.)
        1. Preservation of organs, tissues, etc.—Moral
    and ethical aspects.   2. Preservation of organs,
    tissues, etc.—Law and legislation.   3. Preservation
    of organs, tissues, etc.—Political aspects.
    4. Tissue banks.   I. Weir, Robert F., 1943–   .
    RD127.S76 1998
    362.1′783—dc21   98-11343

98   99   00   01   02   C   5   4   3   2   1
98   99   00   01   02   P   5   4   3   2   1

Contents

Preface, vii
Robert F. Weir

Part I.
Stored Tissue Samples in Specific Clinical and Research Settings

A Pilot Test of DNA-based Analysis Using Anonymized Newborn
Screening Cards in Iowa, 3
*M. Therese Lysaught, Lisa Milhollin, Ryan Peirce,
Jane Getchell, William Rhead, Jan Susanin, Jeannette
Anderson, and Jeffrey C. Murray*

An Ethical and Policy Framework for the Collection of
Umbilical Cord Blood Stem Cells, 32
Dorothy E. Vawter

Human Embryo Cryopreservation: Benefits and Adverse Consequences, 66
Amy E. T. Sparks

Use of Stored Tissue Samples for Genetic Research
in Epidemiologic Studies, 82
*Karen K. Steinberg, Eric J. Sampson, Geraldine M. McQuillan,
and Muin J. Khoury*

Informed Consent, Stored Tissue Samples, and the Human Genome
Diversity Project: Protecting the Rights of Research Participants, 89
Henry T. Greely

Part II.
Multidisciplinary Perspectives: History, Biomedical Research, Ethics, and Law

Beyond the Grave — The Use and Meaning of Human Body Parts:
A Historical Introduction, 111
Susan C. Lawrence

Negotiating Diverse Values in a Pluralist Society:
Limiting Access to Genetic Information, 143
Mary Ann G. Cutter

Researcher Obligations to Tissue and DNA Sample Sources, 160
    Curtis R. Naser

Human Biological Samples and the Laws of Property:
    The Trust as a Model for Biological Repositories, 182
    Karen Gottlieb

DNA Banking: An Empirical Study of a Proposed Consent Form, 198
    Jon F. Merz and Pamela Sankar

Human Genetic Material: Commodity or Gift? 226
    Bartha Maria Knoppers

Advance Directives for the Use of Stored Tissue Samples, 236
    Robert F. Weir

The Role of Community in Research with Stored Tissue Samples, 267
    William L. Freeman

Part III.
Special Issues in the Use of Stored Tissue Samples in Forensic and Military Settings

The Use and Development of DNA Databanks in Law Enforcement, 305
    John W. Hicks

Storing Genes to Solve Crimes:
    Legal, Ethical, and Public Policy Considerations, 311
    Jean E. McEwen

DNA Banking in the Military: An Ethical Analysis, 329
    Kenneth Kipnis

Stored Biologic Specimens for Military Identification:
    The Department of Defense DNA Registry, 345
    Victor Walter Weedn

Contributors, 359

Index, 363

Every year countless persons provide tissue samples to physicians, biomedical investigators, blood banks, DNA banks, and hospitals with little thought about what might be done with these tissue samples once they are placed in storage. Virtually all of us have at one time or other provided a blood sample, a urine sample, or a skin sample to a physician for diagnostic purposes, with no inkling that it might later be used for additional scientific purposes by biomedical researchers we have never met.

Many of us have also had parts of our bodies surgically removed, with no thought being given to what might become of the "waste" tissue that was taken from our bodies. It never occurred to us that this extra tissue might end up being stored and studied for decades in a hospital pathology lab, or that this tissue might be used later in genetics studies of our DNA, or that this tissue might subsequently be transformed in a research laboratory into an "immortalized" cell line that could be used forever by scientists anywhere in the world.

Likewise, until recently many people have not given much thought to the ethical and legal implications of other stored human tissues: sperm in sperm banks, ova and preembryos in hundreds of assisted reproduction programs, umbilical cord blood at the birth of some babies, the legally mandated neonatal blood spots that are collected on thousands of babies each year in every state, blood in blood banks, and bones and other tissues for transplantation purposes.

At the national level, three organizations in the federal government have designed and implemented programs that enable them to store tissue samples (blood, cheek cells, or urine) from thousands of citizens. One of these programs is at the Centers for Disease Control and Prevention (CDC) in Atlanta. For years the CDC has been carrying out a three-stage research project known as the National Health and Nutrition Examination Survey (NHANES). By 1994 scientists at the CDC had collected what they described as a "national treasure chest" of medical and epidemiological information about 40,000 persons in twenty-six states who had voluntarily participated in the third part of the NHANES study (NHANES III). Included in this national information base were 19,500 stored blood and urine samples from the participants in the study and 8,500 immortalized cell lines.

However, the CDC scientists faced a problem: they did not know if they could use this wealth of personal, demographic, and health information because the participants in NHANES III had not given adequately informed consent when they signed up for the scientific study. More specifically, these 40,000 people had not understood that the CDC scientists were planning to do long-term research on their banked tissue samples. The CDC's response to this ethical problem is discussed later in this book.

A second federal program using stored tissue samples has been developed by the Federal Bureau of Investigation (FBI). Authorized by the 1994 DNA Identification Act, the FBI has begun to establish a national database of DNA identification profiles for use by federal and state law enforcement agencies. Known as CODIS (the COmbined DNA Index System), the FBI's DNA database has the potential of supplementing the more conventional use of fingerprints for identification purposes; it also provides the possibility of linking previous criminal offenders by means of their DNA profile to subsequent crime scenes (e.g., to blood, hair, or other biological tissues discovered at the scene) when no fingerprint evidence is available.

When fully operational, CODIS will be linked to the DNA databases maintained by state departments of forensic science. In establishing the legal authorization for this nationwide forensic system, the 1994 federal law also permitted state legislatures to enact laws that require individuals convicted of specified offenses to submit to DNA typing. At the present time, forty-two states have enacted such legislation, with the state laws having considerable variation regarding the types of crimes for which DNA evidence can be collected, the procedures for collecting DNA samples, the protection of individual privacy, and the criminal sanctions for unauthorized use of the biological samples or the personal information derived from them. More detailed information about CODIS is provided later in this book, along with a discussion of the promises and potential problems connected with the use of forensic DNA databases.

The third federal program using stored tissue samples has been carried out by the Department of Defense (DoD) since the time of Operation Desert Storm in Kuwait and Iraq. In 1991 the DoD authorized the establishment of a DNA Registry within the Armed Forces Institute of Pathology (AFIP). The registry consisted of two parts: a DNA identification laboratory and a specimen repository for body fragments. The reason given for the establishment of this DNA Registry was both practical and important: to improve the military's ability to identify the remains of men and women killed in battle or accidents, even in circumstances when individual bodies may have been virtually destroyed by explosion, fire, or other destructive cause.

The original plan for the DNA Registry was fairly simple: (1) collect two DNA specimens (a blood stain on filter paper and an oral swab) from each member of the army, air force, navy, and marines; (2) send the DNA specimens to the AFIP in Washington, D.C., for storage, along with other means of personal identification (a fingerprint, Social Security number, identifying bar code, and personal signature); (3) enter the relevant identifying information in a DNA database; (4) retain the specimens for seventy-five years; and (5) protect individual privacy by restricting the potential use of the samples to military identification purposes, except in unspecified "extraordinary circumstances." The long-term goal was to have a complete set of DNA samples in the registry by 2002 for all men and women in the armed services.

However, the DoD's DNA Registry, while a model of technological sophistication and efficiency, ran into unexpectedly serious concerns in several quarters regarding the protocol for gathering and retaining tissue samples: the lack of informed consent, the invasion of personal privacy, and the possibility of unauthorized access by third parties to personal information about individuals in the armed forces. The concerns about consent and privacy were dramatically illustrated in 1995 by two marines stationed in Hawaii who were willing to face court-martial rather than provide the required DNA samples (a similar air force case occurred in 1996 in Illinois). The widespread concerns about unauthorized access to personal information led in 1996 to a revised policy for the DNA Registry that shortens the planned storage time to fifty years, permits the stored biological materials and data to be destroyed upon request when an individual leaves military service, and greatly reduces the chances of unauthorized access. The discussion of the DoD's DNA Registry by two authors in this book includes a defense of the registry by its central administrator, as well as assessments by both authors of the registry's merits, problems, and future possibilities.

We live, therefore, in an era in which countless tissue samples are collected voluntarily each day from patients in physicians' offices, medical clinics, and hospitals. Thousands of additional tissue samples are voluntarily given to scientific investigators each day for biomedical research purposes that the participants in that research believe to be important. In addition, each day numerous men and women in the nation's jails and prisons and in the military services are required to provide tissue samples for future purposes they hope will never be realized: conviction and imprisonment for crimes they have committed or identification of their bodies at death. And in each of these individual cases, the blood sample, cheek cells, or other types of tissue that are collected, whether voluntarily or under coercion, may be stored in biomedical laboratories in a variety of ways, for an indeterminate period, and for a variety of scientific purposes.

Neither the widespread practice of storing human tissues nor the ongoing debate about the ethical, legal, and public policy implications of these practices is limited to the United States. Rather, a variety of human tissues (especially blood) is being stored by biomedical investigators throughout the world, immortalized cell lines are commonly shared by scientists in numerous countries, and the law enforcement agencies in some other industrialized countries (e.g., England) are also using stored tissue samples for forensic purposes. Likewise, the debate about the appropriate uses of stored tissue samples is taking place in other parts of the world. As in the United States, informed, concerned individuals and professional organizations in other countries are discussing the implications of stored specimens. This concern is being translated into policy statements for genetics societies, statements of principles for genetic research (e.g., by the Human Genome Organization or HUGO), governmental policies regarding DNA banking, and transnational statements regarding human rights in the era of molecular genetics (e.g., by the Council of Europe, by the International Bioethics Committee of the United Nations Education, Social, and Cultural Organization or UNESCO).

Given the common practices of storing tissue specimens for multiple purposes, a growing number of individuals in philosophy, biomedical ethics, law, medicine, biomedical research, hospital administration, politics, sociology, and other professional fields are increasingly raising questions about the ethical, legal, and policy implications of these practices. Are individuals who provide blood samples or other tissue samples in *clinical* settings adequately informed that the samples may later be used for research purposes? Are participants in *research* studies given information about the scientific purpose(s) for which their stored tissue sample(s) may be used? Are they told that their tissue sample may be kept frozen for years, perhaps stripped of personal identifiers, or possibly transformed into a cell line that will last forever? Are they given laboratory-specific information regarding procedures that will be followed to protect the confidentiality and privacy of any personal information derived from the tissue sample? Do they have any ownership or control of the tissue sample once it has been turned over to biomedical investigators? Can they expect to have future access (in consultation with an informed physician or genetic counselor) to any personal information derived from the banked samples that may be of clinical relevance to them? Will they be told how the investigators plan to handle future third-party access (e.g., by relatives, personal physicians, or insurance companies) to the stored DNA sample? Will they be informed of the possibility of secondary use, namely, that their DNA sample may later be transferred in some form (e.g., a cell line) to other scientists to be used for scientific purposes that differ from the original scientific study?

In other situations, are the parents of a newborn baby given information about the medical and epidemiological reasons for which a blood sample was taken from the baby? Are they told that the dried blood spots will be stored for years and possibly be used in future scientific studies? Will participants in future CDC projects be informed if plans exist to store their tissue samples for subsequent research studies? Will the FBI and state departments of forensic science adequately protect stored DNA samples from unauthorized use? Will men and women enlisting in the armed services be adequately informed about their right to request the destruction of their DNA samples and any related personal information in the DoD's DNA Registry?

A multidisciplinary research seminar was held at the University of Iowa in June 1996 to address some of these questions, to come up with answers for some of them, and to raise other questions about current practices pertaining to stored tissue samples. Entitled "Ethical and Legal Implications of Stored Tissue Samples," the 1996 Obermann Faculty Research Seminar was part of a series of annual faculty research seminars jointly funded by the Obermann Center for Advanced Studies and the UI Vice President for Research. The seminars are advertised nationally, applications are received from academicians throughout the country, and experts on particular topics are invited to address the group of academic researchers from multiple disciplines.

This seminar on stored tissue samples was co-directed by two professors in the UI College of Medicine: Jeffrey Murray, M.D., the director of the genome center, and Robert Weir, Ph.D., the director of a program in biomedical ethics. Having frequently discussed some of the ethical issues involved in genetics research, we had also talked about some of the ethical problems connected with the DNA banking practices common to genetics laboratories. With this background, we decided to propose leading a multidisciplinary faculty seminar that would discuss DNA banking practices, but move beyond DNA banking by geneticists to include an investigation of the ethical and legal implications of stored tissue samples in multiple settings: pathology laboratories, blood banks, newborn screening programs, bone and tissue banks, genetics laboratories, technologically assisted reproduction programs, the CDC, forensic science settings, the military, and the international Human Genome Diversity Project (HGDP). We selected twelve persons to join us from the field of seminar applicants, and we invited eight experts to give us presentations about the use of stored tissue samples in a variety of clinical and research settings, the CDC, the FBI and state departments of forensic sciences, and the armed forces.

We especially wanted the invited presentations and the seminar discussions to address some of the recent focal points for controversy in the ongoing debate about the appropriate use of stored specimens. In particular, we planned the seminar so that some of the specific presentations and discussion sessions focused on (1) the controversy in recent years over how the requirements of informed consent apply to retrospective and prospective scientific studies of stored samples; (2) the disagreements that have appeared in the debate about informed consent among geneticists and pathologists, especially regarding the appropriate role of informed consent for research done with anonymous or anonymized tissue samples; and (3) the controversy that has taken place in many countries and among many population groups regarding the research use of stored samples in the international arena, especially the projected plans of the HGDP to gather and store numerous tissue samples worldwide for the purpose of creating a reference library of the genetic diversity of the whole human species.

All of the selected participants produced research papers for discussion and critique at the seminar. Some of the essays address the ethical, legal, and/or policy implications of storing particular types of human tissue samples, ranging from whole bodies and body parts (Susan Lawrence) to newborn blood spots (Therese Lysaught, Jeffrey Murray, and others) to umbilical cord blood (Dorothy Vawter) to the particularly controversial storage of cryopreserved human embryos (Amy Sparks). Other essays explore the implications of stored tissues, with blood samples being used by most authors as the prototypical example, from the perspectives of epidemiology, bioethics, law, philosophy, particular population groups, the forensic sciences, the military, and the international community. The papers were revised in the months following the seminar, and most of them are included in this volume. In addition, several of the invited experts provided essays for this book. All of the essays, with one exception, are original to this volume. They are organized in three thematic parts.

Part I, Stored Tissue Samples in Specific Clinical and Research Settings, contains five essays that suggest both the variety of tissue samples that are being stored and the various purposes for which they are stored. The first three essays focus on the practices and implications of using stored samples in specific clinical settings, while the last two address some of the implications of using stored samples for particular types of nonclinical research. Therese Lysaught, an ethicist in religious studies, joins Jeffrey Murray and other co-authors in describing a pilot program at UI that uses anonymized newborn screening cards to gather statewide information about several significant medical conditions; the authors then analyze the implications of informed consent in the context of newborn screening. Dorothy Vawter, a philosopher, discusses current practices regarding the storage of umbilical cord blood and presents a comprehensive proposal for improving these practices. Amy Sparks, a research scientist in reproductive endocrinology, describes the procedures used in human embryo cryopreservation and discusses some of the benefits and problems connected with the long-term freezing of human preembryos in assisted reproduction programs. As to the nonclinical research use of stored samples, Karen Steinberg and her co-authors at the CDC describe the importance of being able to use stored DNA samples and cell lines for genetic research in epidemiologic studies. Henry Greely, a law professor and board member of the HGDP, indicates how the leaders of the not-yet-funded HGDP in the United States and elsewhere plan to protect the moral and legal rights of persons (and groups) who provide blood samples for this controversial international project.

Part II has eight essays that provide multidisciplinary perspectives on stored tissue samples. Susan Lawrence, a medical historian, provides a very helpful historical introduction to the practice of storing body parts and dead bodies for the purposes of medical education and research. Mary Ann Cutter, a philosopher, describes how some biomedical scientists, philosophers, attorneys, insurance representatives, and other citizens in the state of Colorado worked together to draft a legislative bill to protect the privacy of genetic information and limit third-party access to that information; the text of the state law is included at the end of her essay. Curtis Naser, another philosopher, analyzes the moral obligations that biomedical investigators have toward the individuals who provide them with tissue samples, with particular attention to the question of what kinds of obligations, if any, researchers have to report research results to these individuals and families. Karen Gottlieb, an attorney, explores several legal models pertaining to property rights and suggests that the model of the trust may provide the best legal framework for handling the competing interests involved in the practice of storing tissue samples.

The other essays in this section contain model documents that have been developed by the authors for the purpose of dealing with the ethical, legal, and policy implications of stored samples in practical ways and, in particular, in ways that may be protective of the interests of individuals (and groups) who provide tissue samples to biomedical investigators. The model documents are included at the end of the essays. Jon Merz, an attorney, and Pamela Sankar, a research scientist, provide a model consent form for genetic studies and analyze the results of a pilot study using the consent form with a small group of volunteers. Bartha Knoppers, a law professor in Montreal, presents another model consent form for genetic studies and describes some of the current views about stored tissue samples in Canada. Robert Weir suggests that the development and use of a new type of advance directive in hospitals and clinics may enable individuals to express a choice regarding the purposes for which their stored tissue samples may be used. William Freeman, a physician, emphasizes the importance of community values among Native Americans and how these values influence decisions about stored tissue samples.

Part III, Special Issues in the Use of Stored Tissue Samples in Forensic and Military Settings, contains four essays. John Hicks, formerly with the FBI and now working in a state department of forensic sciences, describes the development of the CODIS system and other DNA databanks currently being used in law enforcement. Jean McEwen, a law professor, offers a careful analysis of the policy considerations in using stored DNA samples to solve crimes. Kenneth Kipnis, a philosopher, provides an ethical analysis of the Hawaii case that served as a catalyst for some of these changes made by the DoD to provide greater protection for the privacy and other long-term interests of enlisted military personnel. Victor Weedn, the chief administrator of the DoD DNA Registry, describes the development of this registry, its achievements and promises, and the recent revisions in policies.

The ethical, legal, and public policy implications of stored tissue samples are numerous and quite complex. For that reason, the essays in this collection do not attempt to address all of the important questions that will need, in time, to be answered about this relatively new subject. Neither do the authors try to make policy recommendations that might apply to all stored tissue samples in all sorts of clinical, research, forensic, and military settings. The practices connected with stored samples are too variable, the competing interests are too important, the stakes are too high, and the implications of the practices are seemingly without end. Therefore we have attempted merely to provide an overview of some of the practices, analyze a number of the implications, and provide some recommendations and model documents that others may find useful. It is our collective hope that in the midst of the frequently heated debate about stored tissue samples, this book may provide some light.

PART I
Stored Tissue Samples in Specific Clinical and Research Settings

A Pilot Test of DNA-based Analysis Using Anonymized Newborn Screening Cards in Iowa

M. Therese Lysaught, Lisa Milhollin, Ryan Peirce, Jane Getchell, William Rhead, Jan Susanin, Jeannette Anderson, and Jeffrey C. Murray

Since the early 1960s, newborn screening programs for inborn errors of metabolism have served as a standard component in routine neonatal health care in the United States and have played an important role in fostering child health.[1-3] Currently, roughly 4 million newborns are screened each year in the United States. From the beginning, these programs have evolved within and been conducted under the jurisdiction of the individual states.[4] Since these programs have been developed on a state-by-state basis, screening policies vary widely, both with regard to diseases screened for (anywhere from three to eleven conditions, including biotinidase deficiency, branched chain keto-acidemia, congenital adrenal hyperplasia, congenital hypothyroidism, cystic fibrosis, galactosemia, homocystinuria, phenylketonuria, hemoglobinopathies, toxoplasmosis, and tyrosinemia) and with regard to regulatory policies.[5-6]

The Iowa Neonatal Metabolic Screening Program (INMSP) is located with the agency of the University of Iowa Hygienic Laboratory (the Hygienic Lab), the state of Iowa's primary agency of public health analysis and information. The INMSP obtains blood samples in the form of blood-spotted filter-paper cards from each of the 37,000 – 40,000 babies born in Iowa each year and uses these to screen for five metabolic disorders: hypothyroidism, phenylketonuria (PKU), galactosemia, congenital adrenal hyperplasia (CAH), and hemoglobinopathies. Until recently, a sixth disorder, branched chain ketoacidemia, also known as "maple syrup urine disease" (MSUD), was also assayed, but MSUD screening was discontinued due to lack of cost effectiveness. Using different microbiological, biochemical, and radio-immuno assays, the INMSP detects roughly three dozen total cases of these disorders per year. In these cases, early detection and diagnosis leads to dietary and other interventions which, if followed carefully, can reduce or forestall the often catastrophic effects of these diseases, such as severe mental retardation or early death.

We obtained newborn screening filter cards from the INMSP for a pilot project using DNA-based analysis. The purpose of this study was twofold.

3

First, we wanted to determine the suitability of using DNA-based techniques on these samples on a large scale as alternatives to the INMSP's microbiological, biochemical, and radio-immuno assays. The above disorders can be detected through various types of metabolic assays, since the immediate and severe effects of the disease are directly related to abnormally high levels of specific metabolic products. The etiologic cause of four of the five conditions, excepting hypothyroidism, are, however, genetic. Because of mutations in relevant genes, these individuals fail to produce a protein necessary for normal metabolism or produce a defective form of a protein. Consequently, these conditions seem likely candidates for detection and diagnosis through DNA-based analysis. Moreover, other disorders stemming from genetic mutations do not result in the types of metabolic changes that can be assayed through these techniques, but recent advances in human genetics have made direct detection of disease-causing DNA mutations possible.[7] In some instances, again, early detection and treatment may improve outcome. However, one consideration for any newborn screening program or comprehensive population screening study is the ability efficiently and accurately to process large numbers of samples in a reasonably short period (quickly enough to initiate an efficacious therapeutic intervention). To move from metabolic assays to strictly DNA-based techniques would require that DNA-based assays could be performed under these constraints.

As a second purpose of this study, we wished to ascertain the efficacy of using these samples and DNA-based techniques for measuring various types of genetic variation in the Iowa population, where "genetic variation" encompasses both carrier frequencies for disease-related mutations and normal trait variation. As mentioned, the specimens for the INMSP are collected, transported, and analyzed via "Guthrie" or filter-paper cards. These Guthrie cards in general, when not discarded by states after the newborn screening assays are complete, have been described as "inchoate 'DNA banks.'"[8-9] Along these lines, it was recognized that these samples could provide a sort of genetic databank for the Iowa population, which, after the development of an efficient technique for extracting DNA from the filter cards, could serve as a useful reference or control database for comparison in other genetic research or could provide important public health information.

As with most developments in biomedicine and genetics, these projects — though technical and data-oriented on their face — cannot be separated from the ethical issues that surround them. In particular, two sets of issues are raised. First, how would the introduction of DNA-based techniques alter the practice of newborn screening? What additional concerns or issues might these techniques introduce? What lacunae in current newborn screening practices does the specter of these techniques illuminate? A second issue is that of "DNA databanking." Specifically, for our purposes, what issues arise when samples obtained from patients for one purpose (e.g., newborn screening) are then used for secondary purposes unrelated to the original intent (e.g., research, forensic, diagnostic, or commercial purposes)? What different issues are presented by the uses of "anonymized" samples versus samples that retain identity linkages to the original patient? These questions are addressed in our discussion.

First we describe our pilot test of DNA-based analysis using anonymized newborn screening cards in Iowa. After testing several methods for extracting DNA samples from the blood spots on the filter-paper cards, we carried out an analysis for three different disease-producing mutations: the cystic fibrosis (CF) $\Delta F508$ mutation, variations in exon 12 of the phenylalanine hydroxylase gene (mutations in which contribute to PKU), and variations in the gene responsible for MCADD (Medium Chain Acyl-CoA Dehydrogenase Deficiency). These genes represent three different classes of conditions relative to newborn screening programs: (1) PKU screening is currently conducted in all fifty states using traditional methods; (2) CF is screened for in two states using metabolic assays, with pilot programs for the addition of a DNA-based confirmation assay being tested in Wisconsin and internationally[5, 10–14]; and (3) MCADD is not currently screened for in any state in the United States.

Methods

In 1989 the Hygienic Lab began participating in a study sponsored by the Centers for Disease Control (CDC) which sought to determine the prevalence of human immunodeficiency virus (HIV) infection in newborns.[15–16] For this study, the Hygienic Lab utilized the newborn screening filter cards from the INMSP to determine HIV seroprevalence for the state of Iowa. Prior to being entered into the HIV study, the filter cards were rendered anonymous: name identifiers were removed, and each card was assigned a random number. Although random, this number remained correlated with the INMSP database of demographic and clinical information created from the original sample. (For each sample tested, the INMSP enters into its database the sample number, the test results, and a set of demographic characteristics of the newborn.) Consequently, for each anonymous sample, important information has been preserved, but it is impossible to trace a particular sample back to a particular newborn.

While in a number of states newborns' screening cards are retained for different lengths of time and policies regarding their testing and subsequent usage vary,[4, 8] in Iowa, once these samples were analyzed by both the INMSP and the Hygienic Lab/CDC HIV study, they would be destroyed. Prior to our study, this was done. Following review by both the Iowa State Board of Health and the Birth Defects Institute, we were able to obtain these samples for the purpose of this study. From July 1994 through May 1995, 31,249 newborn screening filter cards were obtained from the INMSP via the Hygienic Lab.

DNA was extracted from 8,920 samples in 96-well microtiter plates. Using a ⅛" punch, a ⅛" blood-spot sample was punched from each newborn screening card directly into one well of the plate. (Spaces were left for positive and negative controls.) After autoclaving, extraction solution was added to the sample, the sample was processed, and the resulting supernatant was transferred, using a multichannel micropipet, to a fresh 96-well microtiter plate in which the samples were frozen and stored. These plates also then served as templates for PCR analysis. We are in the process of developing an optimal method for long-term storage of the blood-spot filter-paper cards.[8]

A PCR-based protocol was developed, and we assayed 7,194 samples for the presence of the ΔF508 mutation in the cystic fibrosis transmembrane conductance regulator gene (CFTR), the common mutation accounting for approximately 70 percent of the incidence of cystic fibrosis. Cystic fibrosis is the most common severe autosomal recessive disorder affecting Caucasians of European descent, with an incidence of approximately 1 in 2,500 births. The CFTR ΔF508 mutation is a three base-pair deletion which is easily detected on 6 percent polyacrylamide gels. Control DNA was provided by Coriell.

In addition, we developed a polymerase chain reaction (PCR)–based assay to detect mutations in exon 12 of the phenylalanine hydroxylase (PAH) gene and tested 1,070 samples. Different mutations in this gene when present in recessive fashion contribute to the disease phenylketonuria (PKU), which occurs in approximately 1 in 12,000 births. Individuals with PKU lack the enzyme which metabolizes the amino acid phenylalanine; the resulting elevated phenylalanine levels can result in severe brain damage. Early intervention and a diet low in phenylalanine can prevent mental impairment.

This assay detected three known mutations, R408W, Y414C, and IVS12nt1, as well as two other variants. These variants all resulted from nucleotide substitutions rather than deletions or insertions and were therefore not detectable by polyacrylamide sequencing gels. Instead, these samples were analyzed using mutation detection electrophoresis (MDE) gel solution in a single strand conformational polymorphism (SSCP) protocol. To determine which signals corresponded with which variants, anonymous specimens from individuals known to have PKU were extracted, amplified through PCR, and analyzed on

MDE gels. The samples showing variations under the gel conditions were excised and sequenced. The sequence data enabled identification of the particular mutation. These samples then served as controls.

We are now in the initial phases of testing for a mutation in the gene responsible for MCADD, an autosomal recessive disorder that has been associated with Sudden Infant Death Syndrome in a small percentage of SIDS cases. MCADD can also cause a disorder associated with mental retardation. Again, since presymptomatic diagnosis and dietary intervention can minimize symptoms and forestall life-threatening episodes, and there appears to be one common point mutation in Caucasian populations, MCADD is a natural candidate for this approach. A single mutation, T1067C, comprises about 85 percent of known cases of MCADD, and we designed primers to amplify a 188-bp segment of DNA that includes this region. Fortuitously, it also flanks a A985G change that causes MCADD in a small group of cases.

Results

As noted above, DNA samples were prepared from 8,920 blood-spot filter-paper cards. Of the 7,194 samples assayed for the CFTR ΔF508 mutation, 6,659 individuals did not carry the mutation, 177 individuals were heterozygous for the mutation, and 1 individual was homozygous; 357 samples did not produce an interpretable result (through failure to amplify or defects in the gels).

The CF screening on neonatal cards from August 1994 to August 1995 yielded the following results:

No. tested	7,194
No. failures	375 (5.6%)
Carrier rate	1/38
Allele frequency	0.013
Heterozygotes (carriers) detected	177
Homozygotes detected	1

The MCADD pilot DNA screening on neonatal cards (May 20, 1996) had the following results:

No. tested successfully	857
No. of mutations	13
A985G	11
T1067C	2
Carrier rate	1/67
Predicted homozygotes in Iowa per year (40,000 births)	2

The results of the PKU screening on neonatal cards (July 9, 1995) were as follows:

No. tested	1,070
No. of failures	252 (23.5%)
No. of variants	73 (6.8%)

This results in a carrier frequency of 1:38 for the CFTR ΔF508 mutation in the Iowa population, which is similar to that reported in a study of the Wisconsin population [10,11] as well as in other Caucasian populations. Although the overall sample failure rate for the CF portion of the pilot study was 5 percent, the rate improved over the course of the study as the protocol was optimized; for the last 2,460 samples, the rate dropped considerably, to 1.4 percent (35 out of 2,460). We hope that, with additional modifications of our current protocols, the current sample failure rate will fall even further.

Of the 1,070 samples assayed for the variants in exon 12 of the phenylalanine hydroxylase gene, 997 did not show evidence of a detectable mutation and 73 individuals with variants were found. While these 73 variants comprise a large number of PKU mutations, the variability of our SSCP results makes it likely that most of these will be sequence polymorphisms and not etiologic mutations.

An SSCP assay was used to screen 857 newborn screening samples for the MCADD mutations. Eleven individuals were heterozygous for T1067C and two for A985G. Thus, 1.5 percent of Iowa newborns are heterozygotes for MCADD, and we would predict 1 in 17,000 newborns (about 2 per year) to be homozygous affected. This assay could readily be carried out by a screening facility.

While the first aim of this study was to develop and conduct DNA-based analyses on dried blood spots on a large scale, a second aim was to develop a databank of anonymous samples for control purposes and other genetic research. As mentioned above, at the conclusion of this study, a sample bank of 31,249 blood-spot filter-paper cards had been obtained; 8,920 of these were prepared as DNA samples with a volume of approximately 150 microliters. These DNA samples are frozen and stored in capped 96-well microtiter plates, providing for relatively easy storage, maintenance, and utilization. At the same time, the original source of each sample is maintained on the filter-paper cards, making verification or re-extraction relatively easy and ensuring that samples will remain available for subsequent research. This pool will provide an important resource for conducting comprehensive surveys of genetic variation in the Iowa population.

Discussion

Through this study, we have developed a relatively efficient procedure for extracting DNA from large numbers of samples. As the protocol was optimized, we were consistently able to extract DNA from over 98 percent of the samples. With all steps of the protocol — extraction, PCR, storage — conducted in 96-well microtiter plates, we were able to process large numbers of samples relatively efficiently. Much of this process could be automated, increasing efficiency.

But even under manual conditions the efficiency of the DNA-based assay is comparable to that required for a newborn screening program. For example, with a birth rate for the state of Iowa of approximately 37,000–40,000 annually and 20 percent repeat specimen (see below), the INMSP processes an average of 900 samples per week, conducting six different metabolic assays on each specimen with a staff of six. In the DNA-based protocol we developed, it was relatively easy for one person to extract and PCR 1,600 samples per week. For the cystic fibrosis protocol, using the 6 percent polyacrylamide gels made the analysis relatively straightforward; because each gel could be loaded five or six times, it is feasible for one person to analyze the same 1,600 samples within the same time frame. The SSCP/MDE protocol for the PKU assay presented more challenges. Since it was not amenable to double-loading and the results of the SSCP procedure seemed more variable, it was not as efficient. Moreover, our results demonstrate that, to date, we have been able to assess accurately the frequency of the cystic fibrosis mutation in the state of Iowa, and we find that the frequency is similar to that identified in other predominantly Caucasian populations. Finally, although the results are preliminary, we did not observe evidence of contamination from filter-card to filter-card or evidence of cross-contamination between extracted and stored samples within the plates when handled carefully, even though the samples were processed in close proximity.

If DNA-based techniques came to be used in place of traditional microbiological or biochemical assays, would it be a zero-sum exchange? Would it simply mean the substitution of one technical approach for another? Decidedly not. Because of the nature of genetic information and the current social and cultural context into which DNA-based newborn screening would be introduced, additional issues must be considered carefully to determine whether DNA-based techniques are appropriate for programs such as newborn screening, and, if so, under what conditions or parameters. These issues include advantages, cost, precision or diagnostic efficacy, scope of application, collateral information, and informed consent.

Advantages: Solution to Problem of Early Discharge
and Mutation Identification

DNA-based techniques would provide one primary advantage over current traditional methods. If technically feasible, DNA-based assays would offer a solution to what has become a significant problem for many state newborn screening programs, namely, the current practice of early discharge of infants. In an effort to reduce health care costs, many insurance providers and HMOs either encourage or require that healthy infants be discharged twenty-four hours after birth; some infants are being discharged as early as twelve hours. This has presented a problem for newborn screening programs insofar as many newborn screening tests rely on time-dependent changes in the concentration of an analyte in the blood for diagnosis.[5] If a sample is taken too early, the true concentration of these compounds in the infant's blood may be masked by maternal analytes, rendering false negative results. Until technological advances enable age-independent analyses, the INMSP will continue to request a second specimen on roughly 17 percent (or 7,800) of all babies tested annually. This results not only in increased costs; clearly, some of these babies will be missed.

A second possible advantage of DNA-based techniques is that, in making the diagnosis, they not only would indicate that an infant suffered from a particular disease, but would often be able to specifically identify the mutation or mutations responsible for the disease-state. As genetic medicine becomes more sophisticated, this may render information relevant to diagnosis and treatment (e.g., some mutations may cause more severe symptoms than others). However, it may be more efficient to reserve DNA-based assays for confirmatory tests on the small subsample of newborns who are determined to be "presumptive positives" through metabolic assays. This approach is being tested in Wisconsin and elsewhere for cystic fibrosis.[10-14]

Cost and Diagnostic Efficacy

While DNA-based techniques could resolve the problem of false negatives due to early discharge and offer enhanced diagnostic precision in some cases, they would not necessarily result in reduced costs or reduced numbers of false negatives. Currently, the metabolic screening assays used to detect PKU, galactosemia, MSUD, CAH, hypothyroidism, and hemoglobinopathies are relatively inexpensive and efficient.[5] The INMSP currently charges $25.00 for the battery of five tests. The costs of a genetic assay are comparable, in the range of approximately $2.00 per assay, when one takes into consideration the costs of supplies and labor.

But while the direct costs of the genetic assays are comparable to those for the metabolic assays, a difficulty arises in the area of precision or diagnostic accuracy due to the genetic nature of these diseases. Each condition can be caused by any number of mutations, each of which may require a different DNA-based assay. For example, over 100 disease-related mutations have been reported in the PAH gene. Our protocol assayed for a number of mutations in exon 12, a region of the gene which seems to be particularly susceptible to mutations and which is the location of some of the more frequent mutations. And while we detected variants in seventy-three individuals, the individual listed in the INMSP database as a "presumptive positive" for PKU based on the metabolic assay performed by the INMSP appeared as "normal" in our assay. Thus, to design an efficient protocol which would not give false-negative results would be quite difficult under the current technological conditions. A condition such as CF would be more amenable, since such a large proportion of the mutations occur at one locus; but again, although the ΔF508 mutation accounts for approximately 70 percent of the cases of cystic fibrosis, approximately 400 other disease-causing mutations in the CFTR gene have also been identified. Likewise, while in MCADD 85 percent have a single mutation, other mutations can contribute to disease.

But while a particular gene may be susceptible to a large number of mutations (the PAH gene, for example) the metabolic disease-producing effects of different mutations are, in general, similar (elevated levels of the amino acid phenylalanine, which can be measured through a single assay which measures gene expression). Consequently, the current consensus holds that DNA-based assays are not yet sufficiently "cost-effective" and are susceptible to false negative results. The American Society of Human Genetics and others [17–18] have argued on this basis that CF screening on a population-wide basis is premature at this time. Likewise, although a large number of PKU mutations have been identified through this protocol, at the present time we conclude that current methodologies are more appropriate and cost-effective for carrying out this analysis.

Scope of Application and Collateral Information
The possibility of large-scale genetic screening next raises the question of the scope of conditions to which it could be applied. At issue in this question

is whether genetic information, obtained through DNA-based techniques, is different in kind from the sort of medical information obtained through traditional metabolic assays.[19] Current metabolic techniques assay for single, well-defined conditions that result in active disease states. DNA-based assays would yield not only this information but what we could call "collateral information" as well.

Two types of collateral information can become available through genetic assays. A first type is information predictive of the infant's possible medical future. DNA-based assays could detect conditions of late onset presymptomatically, possible predispositions to certain conditions, "behavioral" traits, or diseases for which no therapy exists. A second kind of collateral information is heterozygosity or carrier status. These types of information are materially relevant not only to the individual newborn; both categories divulge information about parents, siblings, and other relatives as well: that they may also be carriers or bearers of latent illness. Thus, not only is the information detected through DNA-based assays different in kind; it is different in scope as well.

Clearly, in the context of newborn screening programs, testing for these sorts of conditions differs little from the genetic testing of children in other contexts. Although far from resolved, the contentious debate surrounding the propriety of the genetic testing of children has recently begun moving toward a tentative resolution. The particulars of this debate as well as the outlines of the emerging consensus can be found in the joint statement of the American Society of Human Genetics/American College of Medical Genetics[20] and an analysis by D. C. Wertz et al.[21]

Genetic tests for children can be separated into two basic categories: (1) tests that provide an immediate or timely medical benefit and (2) those that do not but might prove medically useful at a later time or might provide some sort of psychosocial benefit. Agreement is unanimous regarding the first category: testing that may detect conditions for which treatment or preventive measures are available is similar to other medical diagnostic evaluations and is not only ethically sound but mandated.[20–21]

With regard to the second category of genetic tests on children — those that offer no immediate medical benefit — there is less unanimity, precisely because of the collateral information that is divulged by these tests and the risks of harm that it presents to both individual children and their families. Certainly, these sorts of tests provide certain benefits, as noted by the ASHG/ACMG: either increased or reduced medical surveillance (as appropriate); early intervention; preventive measures, including lifestyle changes; clarification of diagnosis; reduction of anxiety and uncertainty; opportunity for psychological adjustment; ability to make realistic plans for education, employment, insurance, and personal relationships; alerting other relatives to genetic risk; and avoiding or preparing for the birth of a child with genetic disease.[20]

However, the current consensus holds that these sorts of benefits, when calculated in the context of individual testing, are greatly outweighed by the risks of harm presented by collateral information. These risks include alteration of self-image (latent feelings of unworthiness, "survivor guilt," pessimism about the future, blaming oneself for the illness and the burdens it places on the family); distortion of parents' perception of the child (manifested possibly in the overindulging "vulnerable child syndrome," stigmatization, or scapegoating and rejecting); lowered expectations by self, parents, and others for education, employment, and personal relationships; and alerting relatives to reproductive or health risks.[22–23] In addition, this sort of information may generate rather than reduce anxiety. N. A. Holtzman notes that anxiety generated by false positive results from neonatal assays is, at times, difficult to dispel, even with follow-up testing.[24] Finally, as has been discussed at length elsewhere,[25–30] this sort of information presents the additional risk of illegitimate access, in this era of increasing computerized and electronic datakeeping, by third parties (i.e., insurers, employers, educational institutions) with the attendant possibilities for discrimination. These types of discrimination can exacerbate and reinforce the social stigmatization and marginalization that often accompany chronic illness and "difference."

Based on the scope of these risks, many persons find it difficult to justify subjecting children to genetic tests that provide no immediate medical benefit. The ASHG/ACMG recommends that "if the medical or psychosocial benefits of a genetic test will not accrue until adulthood, as in the case of carrier status or adult-onset diseases, genetic testing should generally be deferred."[20] Exceptions are made to take into account the emerging identity, cognitive ability, and self-determination of children, especially as they move through adolescence. Consequently, the recommendations almost categorically oppose testing children under the age of seven (understood as the age where children are beginning to be capable of "assent"); they allow for more flexibility and contextual decisionmaking as the age, maturity, and ability of the child to participate in the decision to be tested increase.

Thus, when located in the context of the genetic testing of children, the issues of the scope of application of DNA-based assays in newborn screening and the management of collateral information seem relatively straightforward. Current newborn screening programs exemplify the first category mentioned above. Newborn screening programs have been developed within a framework of preventive therapeutic medicine guided by the two ethical principles of preventing harm and providing benefit: the goal of these programs has been to identify affected infants prior to imminent development of symptoms where treatment is available in order to prevent serious morbidity or death.[22] Harvey Levy has identified four traditional criteria that have governed newborn screening programs: (1) that there be a disease, not simply a laboratory variation; (2) that the disease should cause significant problems; (3) that the problems caused by the disease be amenable to treatment directed at preventing symptoms; and (4) that a marker for the disease be identifiable in the newborn prior to the appearance of symptoms and irreversible damage.[23] The use of well-defined DNA-based assays in newborn screening, guided by these criteria, would likely meet with widespread support.

Likewise, it would probably be difficult to justify the implementation of DNA-based assays in a newborn screening context for diseases for which the benefit of early intervention is uncertain or no therapy exists, for presymptomatic or susceptibility testing, or for carrier testing. While one could conceivably extrapolate the benefits listed earlier to a public health context (e.g., presymptomatic testing could identify, far in advance of their symptoms, individuals who will develop specific disorders; this information could direct prevention, surveillance, and early-intervention efforts toward those who need them most), the risks would likewise be extrapolated and, in a public health context, would be magnified exponentially.

Current newborn screening programs have, of course, already wandered into some of this territory. For some conditions, DNA-based or traditional assays are relatively straightforward, but early medical or psychosocial intervention is not known to affect outcome. Consensus has not been reached on this issue, for example, with regard to neonatal testing for cystic fibrosis, using either metabolic assays or a two-tiered (metabolic/DNA-based) approach.[23–24, 31] Moreover, carrier status information already emerges from newborn screening technologies: identification of an affected child identifies both parents as carriers. The move toward DNA-based assays, however, would exacerbate this already difficult problem by introducing a new variable into the outcome of newborn screening tests: DNA-based tests would, like current tests for hemoglobinopathies, detect not just disease incidence but heterozygosity as well. If the stated and enacted purpose of newborn screening programs is the diagnosis and treatment of early-onset disease, how might information on heterozygosity be handled? If heterozygosity for a recessive condition is detected in an infant, it might seem prudent — and guided by the same preventive therapeutic goals as newborn screening — to counsel the parents for both to be tested, to determine the disease risk for future offspring. This has, in fact, come to be understood by some as a secondary goal of newborn screening programs.[22-23] Is there an obligation to make carrier status for a particular disease (e.g., PKU) available to identified infants, either as part of their medical record or when they reach reproductive age?

The Committee on Assessing Genetic Risks of the Institute of Medicine, in its 1994 report *Assessing Genetic Risks*, addressed both of these issues. First, with regard to the scope of application, it articulated three principles that should guide the development of newborn screening programs, namely, that there is: (1) clear benefit to the newborn; (2) a system in place to confirm the diagnosis; and (3) treatment and follow-up available for affected newborns regardless of families' ability to pay.[32] This would disqualify presymptomatic or susceptibility screening; the Council of Regional Networks of Genetic Services (CORN) concurs.[33] The committee further recommends that the development of new population-based newborn screening programs be viewed as research protocols and be conducted under established guidelines for human subjects research, requiring informed consent and well-designed and peer-reviewed pilot studies that demonstrate safety, effectiveness, and clear benefit to the newborn prior to implementation. Finally, they counsel that carrier status information (and by analogy, other sorts of collateral information) on newborns should be withheld from either or both parents in the absence of a specific request for the information. This accords with the findings of the ASHG/ACMG and others. We affirm these guidelines and recommend that the development of newborn screening programs be limited to those with demonstrable clinical outcomes. This conclusion derives both from a sense of the purpose and practice of medicine, of which genetics is a part, and from a sense of stewardship of community resources.

Informed Consent in Newborn Screening

The ability of parents to request possible carrier status findings requires that they be informed in advance that such information will be available; this requires that they know that a sample has been obtained from their child and that such a test is going to be performed, which is not often the case. This brings us to the role of informed consent in newborn screening. Like many other facets of newborn screening, the role of informed consent has evolved in an ad hoc manner, and policies vary widely from state to state. Currently, forty-eight states and the District of Columbia have statutes regulating newborn screening. Delaware and Vermont conduct screening on a voluntary basis but have not regulated these programs by statute. In three jurisdictions (District of Columbia, Maryland, and North Carolina) screening is entirely voluntary, while in five (Arkansas, Iowa, Michigan, Montana, and West Virginia) it is mandatory; the rest legally permit parents to "opt-out."[4]

The extent to which parents are informed of this option, however, is unclear. Lori Andrews' 1985 study of state newborn screening programs found that only thirteen states require or specify that parents be informed that neonatal screening tests are even going to be performed; only four of these states require that parents be given an opportunity to object. In thirty-two additional states, Andrews found there to be no requirement for informing parents that the tests are to be conducted, for obtaining their consent, or for apprising them of their right to refuse (although most states permit parents this right, specifically on religious grounds).[4] A recent statement of CORN, however, maintains that "most state screening programs use informed refusal."[34]

In Iowa the statutes governing newborn screening provide for what could be called "informed screening" but not for informed consent. The statute states: "Parents or guardians shall be informed of the type of specimen, how it is obtained, the nature of the diseases being screened, and the consequences of treatment and nontreatment. Should a parent refuse the test, said refusal shall be documented in writing and will become a part of the medical record."[34] The main strength of the Iowa statute is that the parents are to be informed that a sample is to be taken and that the tests are to be conducted. But while the statute requires written documentation of parental refusal (the grounds for which are not specified), it does not specifically require consent or written documentation of consent. Furthermore, while the content of the information provided to parents is relatively comprehensive (including the consequences of treatment and nontreatment), the language of the statute addresses issues related to metabolic screens. The law clearly does not understand this information according to the paradigm of "genetic" information; it does not apprise the parents of the types of collateral information that might be obtained from a genetic test or therefore of the risks and benefits of the test itself.

Although controversy still exists, consensus is shifting toward agreement that newborn screening ought to be understood under a model of genetic information and that, at the least, it ought to be governed by standard canons of informed consent. The Committee on Assessing Genetic Risks of the Institute of Medicine recommended that "informed consent should also be an integral part of newborn screening, including disclosure of the benefits and risks of the tests and treatments."[32] Likewise, the proposed Genetic Privacy Act (see below) would require written parental authorization before obtaining a sample for testing.[35] Some persons believe, however, that the costs of obtaining (in terms of the time of the practitioner) and of documenting such consent would be prohibitive.[36] Additionally, such information, even if properly communicated to parents, might discourage them from consenting. States would have to weigh the value of the practice of parental consent against the low risk that the child will suffer from one of the diseases tested for. Nevertheless, given the changing nature of the information being obtained through newborn screening and the evolution in current understandings of informed consent in medicine, it will be increasingly difficult to justify conducting newborn screening in the absence of informed consent. The content of such consent is a separate matter and is addressed below.

NEWBORN SCREENING FILTER CARDS AS DNA DATABANKS: ETHICAL CONCERNS SURROUNDING SECONDARY USES

Until technological advances are made, many of the issues surrounding the use of DNA-based assays in newborn screening programs will remain hypothetical; it is prudent, however, to think them through carefully and shape provisional policies in advance of exigency. A second set of issues is, however, upon us: issues related to DNA databanking and secondary use of newborn screening samples. Recently, the general issue of DNA databanking and secondary use of biological samples has received significant attention. A review of this discussion is necessary to set the context for consideration of the ethical issues surrounding newborn screening filter cards as DNA databanks.

DNA Databanking: An Overview

The American Society of Human Genetics (ASHG) outlined points to consider regarding DNA banking and analysis as early as 1987.[37] Philip Reilly initiated discussion of newborn screening filter cards as a form of DNA databanking in 1992.[9, 8] In 1995 DNA databanking was addressed in four separate settings: the American College of Medical Genetics (ACMG),[38] a workshop held under the aegis of the National Center for Human Genome Research (NCHGR),[39] a working group under the aegis of the National Institutes of Health/ethical, legal, and social implications (of genome research) (NIH/ELSI) program that drafted the Genetic Privacy and Nondiscrimination Act,[19] and a study of informed consent in genetic research conducted by Robert Weir and Jay Horton at the University of Iowa.[40]

DNA databanks can be comprised of samples gathered in different contexts. Reilly identifies at least six: (1) academically based repositories of scientists who are studying one or more genetic disorders; (2) commercially based repositories that offer DNA banking as a service to researchers and individuals who may have some reason to store their DNA; (3) state-based DNA forensic banks; (4) DNA banking by the military to assist in the identification of human remains; (5) specimens obtained for clinical diagnosis and then retained; and (6) newborn screening cards.[9, 8, 28]

The extent to which newborn screening programs have become de facto or "inchoate" DNA databanks is unclear. McEwen and Reilly, in a study published in 1994, noted that currently forty (or 75 percent) of the newborn screening programs in the United States retain the blood-spot filter cards from one year to indefinitely.[8] CORN, however, maintains that only eighteen states retain their cards for more than one year, stating that "most newborn screening programs destroy all residual DBS samples within a year after the newborn screening analytical process has been completed."[33] McEwen and Reilly further note that most who retain these cards have begun doing so recently and that there is a trend nationally toward retaining them and toward retaining them for longer periods as their value as a databank is increasingly recognized. CORN concurs with this latter point.

Samples collected in newborn screening labs, as well in other repositories, can be used for four types of secondary purposes: forensics, diagnostics, research, or the development of commercial products. They can be used for these secondary purposes in two forms, either retaining identifying linkages to the original source or in an "anonymized" fashion. Finally, a distinction is generally made between biologic samples that have already been collected (i.e., existing repositories) and the collection of samples in the future.

Consideration of issues surrounding secondary uses of newborn screening samples returns us to the issue of informed consent raised earlier. The recommendations of the ACMG mentioned earlier, the NCHGR Workshop on Genetic Research on Stored Tissue Samples, the Genetic Privacy Act, and the Weir/Horton study pertain almost exclusively to issues of informed consent. While a detailed account of these recommendations is beyond the scope of this essay, a brief summary will provide a context for thinking through issues of consent for newborn screening.

In specifying the content of the information that ideally ought to be communicated to patients/research participants who become the source of the genetic material collected in these databanks, the four sets of guidelines and recommendations recognize the importance of the traditional, central element of informed consent: in order to protect the research participant's autonomy and to minimize harm, participants must be apprised of the nature of the project and the possible risks and benefits that might accrue to them through participation; they can authentically choose to undertake certain courses of action if they value the end sufficiently to deem the risks worth taking. In addition, these four proposals expand on this traditional understanding to encompass a more substantive understanding of the relationship between the patient/participant and the investigator. They attend seriously to the participants' contribution to the research endeavor, almost locating participants as equal partners with investigators.

Generally, these four sets of recommendations treat the use of identifiable or linkable samples and anonymized samples separately. Given their slightly different foci, not all of these four documents highlight the same concerns. However, broad areas of agreement can be identified. With regard to *identifiable or linkable samples* to be collected in the future, these findings recommend that fully informed consent, governed by well-established canons for both the practice of medicine and research involving human subjects, should be obtained. They recommend that patients/research participants should receive standard information regarding (1) the original purpose, risks, and benefits of the clinical test or research project; (2) retention of the sample, including location and conditions under which it will be retained; (3) possible secondary uses of the sample; and (4) possible ramifications for the individual of secondary uses. The patients/participants ought then be accorded the rights to consent and determination corresponding to these areas.

These recommendations also take up the issue of how to treat identifiable samples that have already been collected, already reposing in databanks, for which the sources may not have been thoroughly informed when they gave their original consent. How ought one then proceed? For research proposing to use these in an identifiable manner, three options have been presented. First, if possible, the source of the identifiable sample should simply be recontacted and give consent for the further use. Objections were raised, particularly in the NCHGR document, that this would be impracticable and would prove prohibitive to investigators.[39] Consequently, a second course of action proposed that the investigator and the IRB should revisit the consent document of the person who provided the sample to determine whether, in that context, he or she had agreed to the use of the sample for genetic research. The workshop concluded that, while it would probably be difficult to infer consent from most informed consent documents (given their general inadequacy), this would be a valid course of action; if it was successful, further consent would not be necessary. Finally, following federal regulations, if the research involves no more than minimal risk, and the investigator can *demonstrate* that reconsenting the participants would be prohibitively burdensome, members of the workshop agreed that consent might be limited or waived in some circumstances.[40]

Finally, in general, these four sets of recommendations say very little about the use of *anonymous or anonymized samples* (the NCHGR statement provides the most extensive discussion); for the most part, they simply presume the propriety of the use of anonymized samples for secondary purposes. This accords with the recommendations of both the NIH Office of Protection from Research Risks (OPRR) and the Committee on Assessing Genetic Risks of the Institute of Medicine, who endorsed the use of anonymous stored samples for genetic research.[32, 41] This is also in keeping with the federal regulations which exempt from the requirements for protection of human participants the use of existing specimens "if the information is recorded by the investigator in such a manner that subjects cannot be identified, directly, or through identifiers linked to the subjects."[42, 39]

This high degree of consensus, however, does not mean that the issue of the use of anonymized samples is settled. Some members of the NCHGR Workshop suggested, for example, that anonymizing an existing identifiable sample without seeking consent for the specific secondary research project or other use is problematic, insofar as the researchers had an opportunity to obtain consent but did not pursue it.[39] Others question whether biological samples can truly be anonymized, especially given the increasing power of computers to store data, network, and search multiple databases.[43] Members of the NCHGR Workshop defined a sample as anonymous "if and only if it is impossible under any circumstances to identify the original source." They concluded that this is more possible with data sets involving large population groups (even when certain demographic or clinical information is retained), but questioned whether this was truly possible for a small group of samples (e.g., from the laboratory of an individual researcher).[39] Ellen Wright Clayton further suggests that even the process outlined in the Genetic Privacy Act (GPA) for ensuring unlinkability is inadequate.[44]

But even if one could guarantee that the sample could not be linked back to its source, Clayton further argues that using anonymized samples is not simply nonproblematic.[44] Arguments for the use of anonymized samples are premised primarily on the concept of benefit versus harm. Through the use of anonymized samples, advocates argue, benefits can accrue to the public good through the acquisition of knowledge and the development of useful therapies. At the same time, since the samples are anonymous, no harm can come, via the research, to the individuals who donated the samples. Clayton maintains, however, that the use of anonymous samples without the participants' consents (which would pertain to the use of samples in existing repositories) or the open-ended blanket consent for the use of anonymized samples could harm participants in two ways. First, broadening the more traditional notion of informed consent (as mentioned above), Clayton suggests that samples that are anonymized could be used for research that could stigmatize or harm the particular demographic group to which the individual belongs (e.g., women, African Americans); harm could thereby come to the individual. Second, taking a more substantive view of the participants' involvement in the research endeavor, Clayton argues that the use of anonymized samples could harm the participants' interests by potentially involving them in research that they would find objectionable (e.g., certain sorts of behavioral research) even if it did not harm them directly; such research would make them collaborators in a project that they would find offensive or antithetical to their values, commitments, and understanding of the common good.

To address this issue, Clayton recommends that research protocols using anonymized samples *not* be exempt from IRB review and that in their risk/benefit calculations IRBs consider not only harm to the individual participant but the larger possibility of harm to society or to particular groups within society. She also concurs with the recommendations outlined in these various documents that patients/participants be given the ability, as part of the consent process, to determine whether their samples will be retained in an identifiable or anonymized fashion and be apprised that their samples might possibly be used for research. Philip Reilly, on the contrary, strongly objects to the suggestion that individuals might be permitted to prohibit anonymous use of their samples. Arguing that this would alter a long-standing practice in medical research, he believes it would be unnecessary "and possibly socially harmful," by prohibitively increasing the expense of valuable research in order to "only abstractly protect individual autonomy." [36]

Council of Regional Networks for Genetic Services' "Guidelines"

In 1996 CORN issued a statement entitled "Guidelines for the Retention, Storage, and Use of Residual Dried Blood Spot Samples after Newborn Screening Analysis." [33] They report that currently most states have few or no procedures for retaining, storing, or retrieving and most programs have no laws or regulations governing the use of what they term "residual DBSs (dried blood spots)." CORN strongly recommends that each newborn screening program begin by developing a sound justification for either saving or discarding DBSs after analysis is complete; this justification ought to be based on anticipated secondary uses of DBSs, the public health goals of the newborn screening program, and sound scientific data about long-term storage and analyte stability. If a program decides to retain its DBSs, it should develop duration parameters, storage guidelines, and retrieval procedures (including extensive documentation systems) consistent with the uses articulated in its justification. Finally, they recommend that each organization establish a review process, a method for prioritizing and agreeing to requests, and a written policy to govern release of DBSs.

The guidelines articulate the importance of informed consent, noting that with current consent practices issues of ownership and secondary use remain unresolved and need to be clarified. In general, though, they say little about what information that consent ought to contain, with one exception: "The collection form and educational material for parents could indicate that the sample becomes the property of the state and that, unless the parents object in writing, the sample may be used without personal identifiers in studies related to preventing birth defects and disorders of the newborn or for protecting public health."[33] They are, however, explicit about the parameters which should govern release. First, as noted above, each request for release of DBSs should be subject to a review process within the agency. In addition, for all proposals (except for internal anonymous research uses), whether the samples are identifiable or anonymized, they recommend review and approval by "a Human Subjects Review process." They articulate one primary criterion that should guide the internal review, namely, that secondary uses of DBSs should contribute to the primary goals of newborn screening — public health or family health. CORN seems equally open to the use of anonymized and identifiable samples. The guidelines note that anonymized samples negate the need for parental consent, although they do recognize Clayton's concerns. The release of identifiable samples, however, or of identifying information, requires a signed parental consent, and they state that a protocol for obtaining parental consent needs to be developed. If implemented, these guidelines would result in elaborate documentation and retrieval systems aimed at ensuring privacy and confidentiality.

NEWBORN SCREENING BLOOD-SPOT FILTER CARDS
AS DNA DATABANKS

Given these findings concerning DNA databanks in general and the retention, storage, and use of newborn screening samples, what factors ought to guide newborn screening programs as they consider whether or not their facilities will retain samples and indeed establish a DNA databank and as they evaluate individual requests for secondary release of these samples? Three factors are primary: informed consent, goal of the secondary use, and review process. A framework based on these factors should be helpful in addressing the different issues presented by research, legal/forensic, diagnostic, and commercial requests for these samples.

Before considering issues particular to different secondary uses, serious attention needs to be given to the process and content of informed consent in the current practice of newborn screening. This reflects in part the evolving understanding of informed consent within the scientific, legal, and ethical community. But more importantly, the trend toward seeing newborn screening labs as DNA databanks which can provide samples for secondary purposes has fundamentally altered the nature or status of the blood-spot filter card. Previously, one could have argued that newborn screening was simply one of a series of diagnostic assays performed under the umbrella of general parental consent to actions promoting neonatal health. But now the blood-spot filter card has become a commodity, an item with "value," to be used for purposes unrelated to the health of the individual newborn. In this new context, it will be increasingly difficult to justify conducting newborn screening in the absence of informed consent.

What information ought to be included in this informed consent process? We find that most of the items specified by the ACMG, the NCHGR, the GPA, and Weir/Horton regarding informed consent for DNA banking in general are strongly supported with regard to newborn screening. Clearly, the information about the primary purpose, risks, and benefits of the tests themselves is required and should be explained thoroughly to parents. Furthermore, states would have to offer compelling justifications for not including information on retention, possible secondary uses, and access to subsequent information. Once state newborn screening programs develop protocols governing retention, storage, and use of residual DBSs, this information should be easy to convey to parents.

Until issues of ownership are clarified, some areas will remain contentious. As noted above, the CORN guidelines suggest, without discussion and contrary to others' recommendations,[19, 40] that newborn screening samples should become the property of the state. If so, at what point would these ownership rights be established? How would this affect parents' abilities to make initial specifications about the disposition of their child's sample? Would parents be able to specify that the sample should be destroyed rather than retained? Would they be able to do so at a later date? Would they be able to specify which secondary uses they would permit and which they find objectionable? Would they be able to specify whether the sample ought to be anonymized or remain identifiable? Would they be able to specify which investigator or institution may have access to their child's sample? Are there analogies for such transfer of ownership to the state, in total, in the areas of public health and medicine, and, if so, what are the limits of these analogies with regard to newborn screening?

Much more work needs to be done with regard to these issues of ownership. In the meantime, restrictions of parental authority in these areas would make secondary uses of newborn screening samples much more difficult to justify. We suggest that, in thinking through this relationship between parent, child, and state, it might be more fruitful to use a different model for understanding newborn screening cards (or samples retained in most DNA databanks), seeing them not as commodities to be "owned" but rather as material held in "trust" by the state and the newborn screening laboratory for purposes of public health and for the interests of the individual contributor. This suggests a fiduciary rather than a proprietary role for the state and the newborn screening laboratory. Insofar as the cards contain information about individuals which can affect them materially, individuals should be able to retain some interests in and rights *vis-à-vis* the samples. They should be able to decide whether their cards are to be retained or not, whether they can be used for secondary purposes, and, if so, what those purposes might be. At the same time, this model would suggest that newborn screening programs be understood as foundations or trusts, managing a finite public resource with implications for the common good. Examining the issues of ownership/stewardship as modeled by trusts and foundations in the United States context might provide a useful, although imperfect, analogy.

One distinctive characteristic of foundations or trusts is that they are generally circumscribed by specific goals which delimit the deployment of their resources. So likewise, we would like to suggest, are newborn screening programs. These programs, as mentioned above, have been established to promote two related goals: individual/family health and public health. Newborn screening programs exist, first, to protect and promote the health and well-being of the individual newborn; this original purpose ought never be contravened. Thus, uses that could bring risk to the individual newborns or their families, even if balanced by greater social goods, ought to be disallowed. The second goal, as noted by CORN, is the promotion of the goals of newborn screening and public health. Secondary uses that contribute to these goals, without compromising the well-being of the individual sources, ought to be permissible.

How is it to be determined whether a particular request falls within the parameters circumscribed by these goals? Especially at this early juncture, each request should be evaluated on a case-by-case basis through a thorough, goal-oriented review process. First, as CORN suggests, each newborn screening program should identify and articulate (in written form) what it understands to be its goals. Based on these, as CORN also recommends, each newborn screening program should develop a written protocol for the review of requests for secondary release. This process should include review and approval by both the newborn screening lab and/or state oversight body and the investigator's local IRB.

In conducting this review, the reviewers ought to look at three issues. The first consideration would be whether proposed investigation directly fosters the purposes of newborn screening and public health, as discussed above. A second and related consideration would be the impact of the use of the samples and the research project's potential for harm to society as a whole or to a particular social group (the point raised early by Clayton). Insofar as newborn screening programs are guided by public health considerations, newborn screening programs must necessarily broaden the concept of "harm" from a narrowly individualized application; this broader vision makes consideration of the impact of research on certain social groups an integral part of the evaluation process. Third, this review process ought to evaluate requests based on scientific and allocation criteria. The NCHGR, for example, suggests that, for both previously anonymized samples and samples which are to be anonymized, IRB review is appropriate and ought to consider five factors: (1) can the information be obtained any other way; (2) is the proposed investigation scientifically sound; (3) how difficult would it be to recontact subjects and obtain consent; (4) if the samples are finite, what impact will this have on the clinical needs of the patient and family; and (5) will the pursuit of anonymous research preclude the sources from obtaining effective medical interventions?[39] Thus, newborn screening cards ought not be used simply because they are available and expedient. Two issues must be taken into account regarding the use of these cards as a public resource. First, is the proposed use scientifically sound and is it reasonable to presume that useful information will be forthcoming? In other words, some clear "benefit" should be justifiably anticipated. Second, since the newborn screening databank is a public resource, one request should not deplete a particular sample or sample set. The newborn screening laboratory should only release part of the original sample (which CORN recommends) or should require that the secondary user make samples available to others.

Given the relative novelty of the use of newborn screening cards for secondary purposes, the concerns that surround them, the dubious consent conditions under which many currently retained samples were obtained, and the dearth of protocols within newborn screening laboratories concerning their use, it would be reasonable to recommend that for a certain defined period all proposals utilizing newborn screening cards (both identifiable and anonymized) be thoroughly reviewed by institutional IRBs as well as the appropriate state agencies responsible for newborn screening. At the end of this period, these protocols could be retrospectively reviewed, problems identified, concerns allayed, and guidelines established. We suggest that this would be a cautious yet constructive way to proceed.

This framework, then, should be able to provide guidance for the spectrum of secondary uses for which newborn screening cards might be requested: research, legal (or forensic), diagnostic, or commercial. First, research conducted utilizing newborn screening cards could contribute to the goals of newborn screening and public health. At this juncture, it is difficult to imagine research scenarios which would *require* identifiable samples. Thus, we suggest that only anonymized samples be released for research, unless a compelling case can be made by the investigator and specific consent is obtained from the parents and/or source. This accords with the recommendations of the Committee on Assessing Genetic Risks.[32] Implementation of a review process, such as that outlined above, should ameliorate concerns about the use of previously obtained anonymized samples. Samples obtained in the future should carry with them permission to be enrolled in research in an anonymized fashion. If samples are to be released with identifying information attached, parents should be recontacted for consent. This step would also partially ameliorate concerns regarding the lack of original consent with previously stored samples. To reiterate CORN's recommendations, each agency needs to develop very carefully justified and written procedures for retention, storage, use, and processing of newborn screening cards and once armed with these procedures should still proceed very cautiously. In developing these procedures, great care will need to be taken with regard to the protections of confidentiality and privacy, given the public nature of the databank.

Second, release of newborn screening cards for legal or forensic purposes would be justifiable only on a more limited basis. Clearly, these samples would need to be released in an identifiable form; the use of large quantities of anonymized newborn screening samples to gather data on genetic variations within a population would not, for example, be justified given that this particular application does not fall under the aegis of the goals of newborn screening or public health. With regard to individual situations, the CORN guidelines maintain (although they do not discuss) that samples should be released in legal cases only "after careful consideration" and consultation with legal counsel. CORN does provide examples of compelling circumstances in which such use might be appropriate, primarily for determination of a previously unknown cause of death of the newborn from which the sample was obtained. Beyond issues of benefit to an individual or family of an individual source, or the determination of issues of negligence against a laboratory, it would be difficult to justify legal uses of newborn screening samples within a public health framework.

Ought newborn screening samples be used for secondary diagnostic purposes? Again, the range of justifiable situations in which this might be appropriate is more limited. For if, for example, the source of the individual sample is alive, diagnostic tests could be conducted on fresh samples taken within explicitly medical settings, where proper informed consent and counseling could be provided. This would be more appropriate. The use of these samples for diagnosis of later-onset conditions, should new diagnostic tests be developed, would not, per our discussion above, be appropriate within a newborn screening context. Again, in the case of a deceased child, retained newborn screening samples might be able to provide useful information to families regarding diagnosis of siblings, linkage studies, or subsequent decisions about pregnancies. Release for diagnostic use in these settings could be justified under a broad understanding of "benefit to the newborn," if one perceives a child and his or her interests as being intimately connected with those within the family network. Release in these circumstances would require parental consent, and issues of confidentiality and privacy would need to be well protected.

Finally, ought newborn screening cards be released to commercial entities for the purpose of developing proprietary products or services? This is an area which has received the least attention with regard to DNA databanking overall and newborn screening in particular. The CORN guidelines allude briefly to the possibility of commercial requests, noting only that "reimbursement should also be considered for provision of DBSs to commercial manufacturers for research applications." The premise of this position is that commercial ventures can help offset the costs associated with the storage and retrieval of the newborn screening cards. Within the framework that we have developed, release for commercial use could be justified only in the context of an investigation explicitly designed to benefit public health, particularly the goals of newborn screening (i.e., diagnosis of conditions for which treatment is available and for which immediate intervention will make a difference). Beyond this, it is difficult to imagine plausible scenarios. In addition, the possibility of commercial release again raises issues of ownership and profit-sharing. Clearly, it is not unreasonable to suggest that ownership rights in the samples ought not be transferred to commercial interests and that a percentage of the profits from a commercial venture should devolve to the newborn screening program for the benefit of public interests (cognitive of the issue of conflict-of-interest that this might raise).

If such release is approved, ought the samples be released in an identifiable or anonymized form? Straightforward anonymizing of the samples provides the strongest safeguards on privacy and confidentiality but eliminates the possibility of profit-sharing with the individual sources. An alternative might be to reobtain the consent of those whose samples are to be used and then to release them in an anonymized fashion, a percentage of the profits then devolving equally to all who participated in the study. Clearly, this issue needs further study.

Conclusion

This study illustrates a relatively easy and efficient method for conducting DNA-based analyses on large numbers of samples derived from blood-spot filter cards. This method, when used on samples from the INMSP, could be used to determine allele- or carrier-frequencies within the Iowa population. This would provide a means of identifying additional types of genetic disorders that affect Iowa newborns and could thereby provide useful data to inform legislative or other public decisionmaking regarding public health policy and expenditures.

With further refinements, this approach could feasibly be used to develop DNA-based analyses for newborn screening programs. Such an application is not recommended at this time. Although technical issues concerning diagnostic efficacy could be resolved, and although DNA-based analyses would resolve certain problems like early discharge of newborns, DNA-based assays also introduce the issue of collateral information, and they pose real risks to newborns and their families. Until guidelines or legislation are implemented that will minimize those risks, current methodologies will remain more appropriate and cost-effective. We further hold that if DNA-based assays are introduced into newborn screening, the scope of application should be limited to the diagnosis of diseases in newborns for which treatment is available and for which immediate intervention makes a difference in morbidity or mortality. Testing for presymptomatic conditions, susceptibility, or carrier status is not appropriate within the parameters of newborn screening.

Finally, we recommend that well-established standards for obtaining informed consent from parents for newborn screening be implemented wherever newborn screening is conducted, especially in light of the developing trend toward seeing repositories of newborn screening samples stored in state facilities as DNA databanks amenable to secondary uses. With regard to secondary use of newborn screening samples, appropriate informed consent ought to be obtained for these uses. We recommend that prior to the release of newborn screening samples for secondary purposes state newborn screening labs, in conjunction with CORN, develop thorough written guidelines and procedures to govern retention, storage, and release, and institute substantive review processes to determine which instances of secondary use correspond with the goals and responsibilities of newborn screening programs. In light of this, we suggest that both identifiable and anonymized samples can be used in the context of research, with appropriate protections. Further study needs to be done regarding legal and commercial applications. Overall, it remains a question of how to balance legitimate interests and goals of research that contributes to the common good while protecting the well-being and interests of those newborns who contribute to the research endeavor.

Notes

1. M. R. Seashore, "Genetic Testing and Screening: III. Newborn Screening," in W. T. Reich, ed., *Encyclopedia of Bioethics*, revised edition (New York: Macmillan, 1995), pp. 991–993.

2. M. R. Seashore, "Neonatal Screening for Inborn Errors of Metabolism: Update," *Seminars in Perinatology* 14 (1990): 431–438.

3. K. L. Acuff and R. R. Faden, "A History of Prenatal and Newborn Screening Programs: Lessons for the Future," in R. R. Faden, G. Geller, and M. Powers, eds., *AIDS, Women, and the Next Generation* (New York: Oxford, 1991), pp. 59–93.

4. L. B. Andrews, *State Laws and Regulations Governing Newborn Screening* (Chicago: American Bar Association, 1985).

5. Committee on Genetics, Newborn Screening Fact Sheets, *Pediatrics* 98 (1996): 473–501.

6. "Newborn Screening," *American Family Physician* 50 (1994): 354–358.

7. F. S. Collins, "Positional Cloning: Let's Not Call It Reverse Anymore," *Nature Genetics* 1 (1992): 3–6.

8. J. E. McEwen and P. R. Reilly, "Stored Guthrie Cards as DNA 'Banks,'" *American Journal of Human Genetics* 55 (1994): 196–200.

9. P. R. Reilly, "DNA Banking [letter]," *American Journal of Human Genetics* 51 (1992): 1169–1170.

10. P. M. Farrell, R. A. Aronson, G. Hoffman, and R. H. Laessig, "Newborn Screening for Cystic Fibrosis in Wisconsin: First Application of Population-based Molecular Genetics Testing," *Wisconsin Medical Journal* 93 (1994): 415–421.

11. R. G. Gregg, B. S. Wilfond, P. M. Farrell, A. Laxova, D. Hassemer, and E. H. Mischler, "Application of DNA Analysis in a Population-screening Program for Neonatal Diagnosis of Cystic Fibrosis (CF): Comparison of Screening Protocols," *American Journal of Human Genetics* 52 (1993): 616–626.

12. K. B. Hammond, S. H. Abman, R. J. Sokol, and F. J. Accurso, "Efficacy of Statewide [Colorado] Neonatal Screening for Cystic Fibrosis by Assay of Trypsinogen Concentrations," *New England Journal of Medicine* 325 (1991): 769–774.

13. B. Wilcken, V. Wiley, G. Sherry, and U. Bayliss, "Neonatal Screening for Cystic Fibrosis: A Comparison of Two Strategies for Case Detection in 1.2 Million Babies," *Journal of Pediatrics* (Australia) 127 (1995): 965–970.

14. E. Ranieri, B. D. Lewis, R. L. Gerace, R. G. Ryall, C. P. Morris, P. V. Nelson,

W. F. Carey, and E. F. Robertson, "Neonatal Screening for Cystic Fibrosis Using Immunoreactive Trypsinogen and Direct Gene Analysis: Four Years' Experience," *British Medical Journal* 308 (1994): 1469–1472.

15. M. Pappaioanou, J. R. George, W. H. Hannon, M. Gwinn, T. J. Dondero, G. F. Grady et al., "HIV Seroprevalence Surveys of Childbearing Women — Objectives, Methods, and Uses of Data," *Public Health Report* 105 (1990): 147–152.

16. M. Gwinn et al., "Prevalence of HIV Infection in Childbearing Women in the United States: Surveillance Using Newborn Blood Samples," *JAMA* 265 (1991): 1704–1708.

17. C. T. Caskey, M. M. Kaback, and A. L. Beaudet, "The American Society of Human Genetics Statement on Cystic Fibrosis Screening," *American Journal of Human Genetics* 46 (1990): 393.

18. S. Elias, G. J. Annas, and J. L. Simpson, "Carrier Screening for Cystic Fibrosis: A Case Study in Setting Standards of Medical Practice," in G. J. Annas and S. Elias, eds., *Gene Mapping: Using Law and Ethics as Guides* (New York: Oxford University Press, 1992).

19. G. J. Annas, L. H. Glantz, and P. A. Roche, "Drafting the Genetic Privacy Act: Science, Policy, and Practical Considerations," *Journal of Law, Medicine, and Ethics* 23 (1995): 360–366.

20. American Society of Human Genetics, Board of Directors, and American Society of Medical Genetics, Board of Directors, ASHG/ACMG Report, "Points to Consider: Ethical, Legal, and Psychosocial Implications of Genetic Testing in Children and Adolescents," *American Journal of Human Genetics* 57 (1995): 1233–1241.

21. D. C. Wertz, J. H. Fanos, and P. R. Reilly, "Genetic Testing for Children and Adolescents: Who Decides?" *JAMA* 272 (1991): 875–881.

22. M. R. Seashore and C. Walsh-Vockley, "Introduction: New Technologies for Genetic and Newborn Screening," *Yale Journal of Biology and Medicine* 64 (1991): 3–7.

23. H. Levy, "Newborn Screening Perspective," *Yale Journal of Biology and Medicine* 64 (1991): 17–18.

24. N. A. Holtzman, "What Drives Neonatal Screening Programs?" *New England Journal of Medicine* 325 (1991): 802–804.

25. P. Billings, M. A. Kohn, M. de Cuevas, J. Beckwith, and J. S. Alper, "Discrimination as a Consequence of Genetic Testing," *American Journal of Human Genetics* 50 (1992): 476–482.

26. The Ad Hoc Committee on Genetic Testing/Insurance Issues, "Genetic Testing and Insurance," *American Journal of Human Genetics* 56 (1995): 327–331.

27. Council on Ethical and Judicial Affairs, American Medical Association, "Use of Genetic Testing by Employers," *JAMA* 266 (1991): 1827–1830.

28. J. E. McEwen and P. R. Reilly, "Genetic Testing and Screening: VI. Legal Issues," in W. T. Reich, ed., *Encyclopedia of Bioethics*, revised edition (New York: Macmillan, 1995), pp. 1000–1005.

29. T. H. Murray and J. R. Botkin, "Genetic Testing and Screening: VII. Ethical Issues," in W. T. Reich, ed., *Encyclopedia of Bioethics*, revised edition (New York: Macmillan, 1995), pp. 1005–1011.

30. P. M. McCarrick, "Scope Note 22: Genetic Testing and Genetic Screening," *Kennedy Institute of Ethics Journal* 3 (1993): 333–354.

31. B. S. Wilfond, "Screening Policy for Cystic Fibrosis: The Role of Evidence," *Hastings Center Report* 25 (1995): S21–S23.

32. L. B. Andrews, J. E. Fullarton, N. A. Holtzman, and A. G. Motulsky, eds., *Assessing Genetic Risks: Implications for Health and Social Policy* (Washington, D.C.: National Academy Press, 1994).

33. B. L. Therrell, W. H. Hannon, K. A. Pass, F. Lorey, C. Brokopp, J. Eckman, M. Glass, R. Heidenreich, S. Kinney, S. Kling, G. Landenburger, F. J. Meaney, E. R. B. McCabe, S. Panny, M. Schwartz, and E. Shapira, "Guidelines for the Retention, Storage, and Use of Residual Dried Blood Spot Samples after Newborn Screening Analysis: Statement of the Council of Regional Networks for Genetic Services," *Biochemical and Molecular Medicine* 57 (1996): 116–124.

34. Iowa Admin. Code section 470-4.1 (136A) (1987).

35. Genetic Privacy and Nondiscrimination Act of 1995, S. 1416, 104th Congress, 1st Session (1995).

36. P. R. Reilly, "Panel Comment: The Impact of the Genetic Privacy Act on Medicine," *Journal of Law, Medicine, and Ethics* 23 (1995): 378–381.

37. Ad Hoc Committee on DNA Technology, American Society of Human Genetics, "DNA Banking and DNA Analysis: Points to Consider," *American Journal of Human Genetics* 42 (1988): 781–783.

38. American College of Medical Genetics, Storage of Genetics Materials Committee, "Statement on Storage and Use of Genetic Materials," *American Journal of Human Genetics* 57 (1995): 1499–1500.

39. E. W. Clayton, K. K. Steinberg, M. J. Khoury, E. Thompson, L. Andrews, M. J. E. Kahn, L. M. Kopelman, and J. O. Weiss, "Informed Consent for Genetic Research on Stored Tissue Samples," *JAMA* 274 (1995): 1786–1792.

40. R. F. Weir and J. R. Horton, "DNA Banking and Informed Consent — Part One," *IRB* 17 (1995): 1–4; and "DNA Banking and Informed Consent — Part Two," *IRB* 17 (1995): 1–8.

41. Office for Protection from Research Risks, *Protecting Human Research Subjects: Institutional Review Board Guidebook* (Washington, D.C.: U.S. Government Printing Office, 1993).

42. 45 CFR sec. 46.101(b)(4) (1994).

43. L. O. Gostin, "Genetic Privacy," *Journal of Law, Medicine, and Ethics* 23 (1995): 320–330.

44. E. W. Clayton, "Panel Comment: Why the Use of Anonymous Samples for Research Matters," *Journal of Law, Medicine, and Ethics* 23 (1995): 375–377.

An Ethical and Policy Framework for the Collection of Umbilical Cord Blood Stem Cells

Dorothy E. Vawter

The ethical assumptions and commitments implicit in umbilical cord blood collection policies and practices are reviewed in this essay. In addition, a framework is proposed for understanding the meaning and importance of respecting cord blood donors and for assessing the adequacy of alternative cord blood policies.

First, some introductory comments are in order. Cord blood donation should not be treated simply as a type of risk-free donation of blood or hematopoeitic stem cells, nor simply as a type of risk-free use of an abandoned surgical tissue. Cord blood collection and quality control practices can pose a range of risks to the infant and its parents that they would not otherwise be exposed to, if not for their involvement in the donation of cord blood. In this respect, cord blood donation usually involves multiple live tissue donors, each requiring policy provisions to adequately respect and protect them.

It is a mistake to focus on the risks to the donors associated with collecting the cord blood and to overlook and/or discount other risks, such as those associated with establishing the quality of the cord blood. It is also a mistake to claim that donation poses no risk, as sometimes is done, rather than to claim that the risks of donating cord blood are minimal or reasonable. These mistakes, together with continuing confusion about whose consent to donation is necessary, and why, are resulting in inadequate disclosure and consent practices for those involved in the donation of cord blood.

I argue that cord blood donation, properly understood, is a unique, complex type of live tissue donation, exposing multiple persons, including an infant without decisionmaking capacity, to risks to their health, privacy, and well-being. Cord blood donation is more properly considered a unique type of family tissue donation than a routine blood donation or surgical waste donation by a single donor.

An adequate framework of ethical and policy objectives for the collection of cord blood presupposes clarity regarding current practices regarding the collection, donation, testing, storage, and use of umbilical cord blood; the risks that cord blood practices can pose to the health, privacy, and/or well-being of the infant and its closest relatives; and the respect and protection owed cord blood donors and their closest relatives as live tissue donors.

Background

Hematopoietic stem cell transplants are used to treat patients who have abnormal bone marrow stem cells or who have lost their bone marrow to high dose chemotherapy or radiation treatments for cancer. Hematopoietic stem cells are responsible for producing the full range of blood cells necessary for such crucial functions as transporting oxygen, responding to infection, and clotting. These stem cells are present to varying degrees in several different tissues, including bone marrow, peripheral blood, fetal blood, fetal liver, and placental and umbilical cord blood (cord blood).

Collecting blood from the umbilical cord is not new. As an alternative to drawing blood directly from the newborn, for instance, small amounts of cord blood are routinely collected for the purpose of establishing the health of the infant. Cord blood is also collected for the purpose of autologous blood transfusion in premature or ill newborns.[1] Procuring and storing cord blood for the purpose of hematopoietic stem cell transplants, however, is new. The first report of a cord blood transplant was in 1972, the first report of a successful cord blood transplant was in 1989, and the first community and private cord blood banks were established in 1992 and 1993.[2] The cord blood of approximately 10,000 infants has been banked for private and community use, and approximately 500 cord blood transplants have been performed as of spring 1997.[3]

Cord blood that is stored for private use is reserved for related allogeneic or autologous transplants, although cord blood has yet to be used for autologous stem cell transplant.[4] Private storage increases the chances that a family member in need of a stem cell transplant will have access to suitably matched stem cells. Siblings with the same genetic parents have a 25 percent chance of having suitably matched bone marrow, but have a 50 percent chance of suitably matched cord blood.[5] Moreover, related cord blood transplants appear to offer better outcomes for recipients than unrelated cord blood transplants.[6]

Cord blood donated to a community bank is used primarily for research and unrelated allogeneic transplantation. When someone who donated cord blood to a community bank, or a close genetic relative, develops a need for a stem cell transplant, should the cord blood unit still be available, it may be used for autologous or related allogeneic transplant as well.

Early results suggest that cord blood stem cell transplantation is very promising. However, it remains an unproven and investigational procedure. The International Cord Blood Transplant Registry has reported on 44 children receiving related cord blood transplants for a wide variety of illnesses, by 26 different transplant teams using diverse protocols.[7] More recently, the

Eurocord Transplant Group and the European Blood and Marrow Transplant Group reported the results of a larger retrospective review: 143 cord blood transplants (related and unrelated) in children and adults performed at 45 transplant centers.[8] The results of two important Phase I studies have been published: one included 25 subjects and the other 18 subjects.[9] A five-year, $30 million, multisite study is currently being supported by the National Heart, Lung and Blood Institute (NHLBI) of the National Institutes of Health (NIH) to assess the adequacy of unrelated cord blood transplants from community cord blood banks for the treatment of a variety of cancers and genetic diseases in children and adults. Researchers are studying, among other things, the feasibility of conducting repeat infectious disease tests in infant cord blood donors and the effect of cell dose and HLA disparities on the success of transplants. In the meantime case reports of single cord blood recipients remain common in the medical literature.[10]

Most cord blood transplants, to date, have been performed in children with serious, life-threatening conditions. The list of conditions in which cord blood stem cell transplants have engrafted, with few adverse affects, is growing quickly and already includes several types of hematopoietic malignancies (e.g., acute lymphocytic leukemia, acute myelocytic leukemia, chronic myelocytic leukemia, juvenile chronic myelogenous leukemia), autoimmune diseases, metabolic storage disorders and other genetic diseases (e.g., b-thalassemia, sickle cell disease, Fanconi's anemia, Gunther's disease, Hunter's syndrome, Lesch-Nyhan syndrome, severe aplastic anemia, severe combined immune deficiencies [SCIDs], and Wiskott-Aldrich syndrome).

Preliminary reports of transplants in approximately twenty adults suggest that the number of stem cells found in some cord blood collections may also be sufficient to treat adults.[11] The value of transplants in treating conditions such as HIV, metastatic breast cancer, and accidental high dose irradiation is being studied as well.[12]

ADVANTAGES OF CORD BLOOD STEM CELLS

For the estimated 8,000 to 10,000 patients who die each year for lack of a suitable stem cell transplant, cord blood provides a promising alternative source of such cells. In fact, cord blood stem cells appear to have several important advantages over other possible sources of stem cells for transplant. Umbilical cords and placentas are widely available, and procuring cord blood is less invasive, less risky, and less costly than procuring bone marrow or procuring stem cells from peripheral blood. Cord blood banks may also offer the easiest way to increase the availability of stem cell transplants for members of ethnic and racial minorities who have human lymphocyte antigens (HLA) profiles not commonly found in bone marrow registries. The increased availability of matched stem cells for members of ethnic and racial minorities in cord blood banks, together with lower costs, promises to eliminate many of the inequities in the current supply and distribution of stem cell transplants.

Community cord blood banks can make stem cells available for transplant more quickly than can other sources of unrelated stem cells. These banks, though they still have less than optimal numbers of stored units, already routinely provide patients with cord blood for transplant with less delay than large bone marrow registries.

Moreover, cord blood stem cell transplants may present lower risks to recipients than other stem cell transplants. Infectious agents such as cytomegalovirus (CMV), hepatitis B, HIV, and Epstein-Barr virus are less common in cord blood than in mature bone marrow. Preliminary studies suggest that cord blood may pose lower risks of serious graft versus host disease (GVHD) than bone marrow and may allow for greater HLA mismatches between donor and recipient. Gene therapy using cord blood stem cells is especially promising since these stem cells have an increased capacity to proliferate.

Current Practice and Policy

CORD BLOOD BANKS AND STORAGE FACILITIES

Several different types of cord blood banks and storage facilities are under development in the United States, Europe, and Japan (see figure 1). There are private storage facilities for families who wish to store cord blood for their own personal use, as well as community banks to which families may donate cord blood, thereby making it available to anyone who meets the bank's requirements (e.g., ability to pay, "first come, first served," greatest need, most likely to benefit, and so forth). Some banks are located within full service blood centers, others are not (e.g., they are sometimes located within facilities cryopreserving a wide range of human tissues). Since cord blood banks need not be licensed or accredited in most states, there is concern that the safety and quality of the services provided may not be uniformly high. Financial support for private and community banks may come from public funds, private funds, or a combination of both.

Private Cord Blood Storage Facilities

In the United States private for-profit storage facilities, such as Cord Blood Registry, Cryo-Cell, United States Cryobanks of Florida, and ViaCord, offer parents, usually for a fee, the option of storing their infant's cord blood for

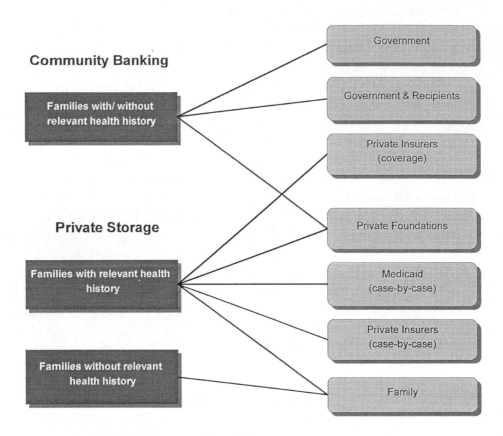

Payer

Community Banking

Government

Families with/ without relevant health history

Government & Recipients

Private Insurers (coverage)

Private Storage

Private Foundations

Families with relevant health history

Medicaid (case-by-case)

Private Insurers (case-by-case)

Families without relevant health history

Family

FIG. 1. *Cord blood storage and banking arrangements.*

possible autologous or related allogeneic transplant. In Canada Lifebank offers families private storage of cord blood. Fees for private storage range from approximately $250 to $1,400 for initial processing and $50 to $95 for annual storage costs. The fees charged families over the first eighteen years of storage, assuming no change in the annual fee, total between $1,125 and $3,115, or between $5 and $15 per month. The large variation in the processing fees reflects, at least in part, differences in the quality control and tissue typing services provided by each of the facilities. For example, whereas some perform a wide range of tests before storing the cord blood, others simply store the cord blood and leave it to the family to arrange for testing, should a need for the cord blood arise.

Numerous hospital and university blood banks agree, upon request, to collect and store cord blood for a family member. For example, in a study of 45 transplant centers that performed 143 cord blood transplants (78 of which were from related donors), 65 of the cord blood units came not from major community cord blood banks, but from "the vicinity of the [transplant] center." [13]

Private storage for families with a relevant health history is widely supported, especially when access to private storage does not depend on the family's ability to pay. Public and private payers for health care services are increasingly agreeing to pay for the collection, processing, and storage of cord blood for enrollees with a history of certain diseases, either on a case-by-case basis or as part of their standard benefits package.[14] Some foundation and grant monies are being made available for such families as well.[15] The Cord Blood Registry, through its Designated Transplant Program, offers storage free of charge to families who have a medical history suggesting a high likelihood of someone within the family needing a stem cell transplant. Access to this type of private storage is based on family need, rather than on the family's ability to pay and aversion to risk.[16]

The most controversial types of banks are private for-profit storage facilities that actively promote cord blood storage for families without health histories suggesting a realistic need for a stem cell transplant. Many persons worry that unlicensed and unaccredited private storage facilities may be unscrupulously exploiting the fears, vulnerabilities, and ignorance of expectant parents, selling them services of questionable quality that they do not need, to further the interests of the storage facility's stockholders rather than the interests of the families or individuals who are ill and having difficulty finding a suitable stem cell transplant. Concerns have also been voiced that encouraging healthy, risk-averse, financially secure families to store cord blood privately may undermine the success of more important community banks.

At the present time private storage facilities are probably the most common source of information for parents regarding cord blood donation. Insofar as their materials are designed to recruit expectant parents to engage in an activity that supports the bank's profit motive, their primary intent is not necessarily to inform. Private cord blood storage facilities routinely send glossy advertisements to expectant parents promising "peace of mind," "a spare immune system for life," and "a form of biological insurance for their infant and other family members," should they agree, and be able, to pay for the processing and storage fees. One brochure claims that cord blood will be available for the duration of the child's lifetime and that transplants boast a 90 percent success rate.[17] There is no accompanying definition of "success," no reporting of the bank's statistics concerning "successful" transplants, no mention that stored cord blood has yet to be used for autologous transplant, nor any clear statement that cord blood storage and transplantation are investigational procedures. At least one private storage company offers investors stock over the counter and reserves the right to sell components of the cord blood that it removes prior to cryopreservation.[18]

Community Cord Blood Banks

Community cord blood banks have been started in England, France, Germany, Japan, Italy, Spain, and the United States. In the United States there are several publicly funded community banks and one privately funded bank. The optimal number and distribution of community cord blood banks remains unclear.

The New York Blood Center was the first to receive federal funding from the NHLBI at the NIH to study the feasibility of developing a community cord blood bank. It began collecting cord blood in 1993 and has provided stem cells for 367 transplants as of May 1997.[19] It provides cord blood for approximately twenty transplants per month and currently is the largest community bank in the United States. Other NHLBI-funded community cord blood banks under development in the United States are located at Children's Hospital of Orange County, Duke University, and the University of California at Los Angeles. As of June 1996, the New York Blood Center began charging $15,300 for the cord blood units it releases for transplantation, making it a privately, as well as a publicly, funded community cord blood bank.

The Cord Blood Stem Cell Bank at the University of Arizona funds a community bank with private funds from the International Cord Blood Foundation. Fees from families that select private storage with the Cord Blood Registry help fund free cord blood donations to the community bank.[20] More than 800 cord blood samples have been accepted by the International Cord Blood Foundation's community bank.[21]

Several universities report that they are establishing community cord blood banks, including St. Louis University, the University of Chicago, the University of Colorado Health Sciences Center, the University of Massachusetts Medical Center, the University of Minnesota, and the University of Texas Southwestern Children's Medical Center.[22]

Parents who donate to community banks relinquish all rights to the donated unit. Community banks, unlike private storage facilities, support research and may release cord blood for use in clinical or nonclinical research as well as for therapeutic purposes. Should the infant or another family member later need a stem cell transplant, and should the donated unit still be in the community bank, it is possible that the family may receive the unit it donated for community use. A study of 143 cord blood transplants, in which

78 cord blood units were from community banks in New York, Milan, Paris, and Düsseldorf and another 65 were from other sources, suggests that at least some of the 78 recipients who received cord blood from a related donor received the unit from a community bank.[23]

Community cord blood banks that allocate cord blood in ways that conflict with the purpose of a community bank and/or with the spirit in which parents donated the cord blood are ethically troublesome. For instance, allocating cord blood based on (a child's) ability to pay conflicts with the ethical and policy objective of eliminating inequities in access to stem cell transplants, a central purpose of community banks. Such policies may raise serious questions of justice and threaten public trust in cord blood donation, and transplantation medicine generally.

COLLECTION AND CONSENT PROCEDURES

When procuring cord blood for purposes of hematopoietic stem cell transplant, the goal is to procure as large a quantity as possible. The size of the placenta, the length and condition of the umbilical cord remaining attached to the placenta after clamping, the training and motivation of the procurers, the collaboration of the delivery team (and parents), and the timing of cord clamping all affect the amount of cord blood collected. Abnormalities of the placenta or umbilical cord interfere with cord blood collection in approximately one out of ten deliveries.[24]

Several different procedures currently are being used to collect cord blood. A standard procedure has yet to be established. To begin with, there is disagreement concerning the most appropriate time to clamp the cord. Cord blood procurers interested in maximizing cord blood collection have called for clamping the cord as soon and as short as possible.[25] The obstetrical literature on cord clamping ranges from suggesting that the cord be clamped immediately to suggesting that one should wait until the cord stops pulsating, until the infant starts breathing, or until thirty to sixty seconds after delivery.[26] The lack of professional consensus has been used to support recommendations to clamp the cord immediately for purposes of cord blood collection. Some physicians have expressed concern, however, that early cord clamping may pose possible risks to the infant since it entails the infant receiving less blood. Several cord blood guidelines and protocols now insist that the delivery procedures not be changed in the interests of cord blood collection.[27] Some in the cord blood field have called for studies of the effects of early cord clamping, to determine both the effects on the quantity of blood collected and the effects on the infants' health.[28]

Regardless of the timing of the cord clamping, some persons collect cord blood only while the placenta is in utero,[29] some collect only from a delivered placenta,[30] some collect from a delivered placenta when collection from the placenta in utero failed,[31] or collect both before and after the delivery of the placenta.[32]

Cord blood procurement before delivery of the placenta, using syringes to withdraw blood from the umbilical vein, usually takes two to five minutes.[33] Since the period between delivery of the newborn and delivery of the placenta averages between five and ten minutes, in utero procurement will not always be possible or successful.[34]

Banks that collect cord blood ex utero use specially trained, dedicated staff to procure cord blood with blood transfusion sets. This technique is reported to take approximately five to ten minutes and to yield amounts of cord blood comparable to techniques used when the placenta is in utero.[35] In light of the need for specially trained, dedicated staff, cord blood collected by this method is available only at designated institutions.

With the exception of the New York State Department of Health, guidelines for cord blood donation and the cord blood literature generally say remarkably little about what information should be disclosed to potential donors.[36] It is, therefore, left to individual banks to decide that it is important to provide prospective donors with clear descriptions of such issues as procedures associated with procurement, testing, banking, and use of cord blood; risks to the infant's and any other family member's health and privacy; benefits; alternatives (e.g., private storage and community banking, procurement after delivery of the placenta rather than before); procedures that are investigational in nature; the chances that cord blood may not be safely or successfully procured;[37] and the chances that cord blood stored for autologous, related, or unrelated use will ever be used.[38]

Despite the great variation in collection and consent procedures possible, two important models of cord blood collection can be distinguished and compared (see figure 2). Advocates of the *In Utero Collection Model* maintain that it is the easiest, most reliable method for health care professionals not specifically trained in cord blood procurement to collect sufficient quantities of uncontaminated blood. They maintain that collection prior to the delivery of the placenta poses no risks to donors and does not interfere with the delivery process. Collection costs are low, making private storage a practical option for families — regardless of their geographic location. It permits donation by the most diverse set of donors and, although used most often for private storage, can be used for community banking as well.[39] Finally, it is respectful of the parents and infants involved and preserves trust in organ and tissue donation.

IN UTERO COLLECTION MODEL

Collected from placenta while in utero
Woman consents before labor and collection
Bank responsible for ensuring consent is valid
Screening (and testing) of mother/family for infectious and genetic disease before collecting
Collected by staff without special training
Collected from families delivering anywhere in the U.S.
Parents assigned primary responsibility for equipment, handling, and shipping

Pros

Respectful of parents and infant
Preserves trust in organ and tissue donation
Easiest, most reliable collection method; doesn't require special training
Increases access to storage/donation, few geographic limitations
Low cost
Increases diversity of cord blood collected
Suitable for both community donation and private storage

Cons

Consent process tends to be weak, not face to face
Increased chance of lower volumes
Increased risks to infant/mother due to OB staff being distracted during collection
Increased risk of accidental loss of unit
Alters physician-patient relationship

FIG. 2. *Cord blood collection models.*

EX UTERO COLLECTION MODEL

Collected from placenta ex utero
Woman's consent sought after collection
Specially trained procurers responsible for consent
Screening and testing of woman/family for infectious and genetic disease after collecting
Collected by specially trained dedicated staff
Collected only from families delivering in designated institutions

Pros

Lower risk to woman and infant due to less distraction of the OB staff
Expands availability of stem cells in community banks
Consent process is face-to-face by trained individuals
Collections of consistently high quality and volume
Supports research

Cons

Disrespectful of parents and infant
Women's consent may not be voluntary
Restricts access to storage/donation
Inefficient, collects many ineligible cord blood units
Costly
Undermines trust in organ and tissue donation
Diversity of cord blood collected depends on the range of participating institutions and the communities they serve
Not suitable for parents desiring private storage

The advantages of the *Ex Utero Collection Model*, which uses a specially trained and dedicated staff, include the standardization of the volumes collected, reduced contamination, and fewer missed samples.[40] The advantage of procuring cord blood only after delivery of the placenta is that it is more respectful and protective of donors to separate collection procedures from delivery procedures.[41] Ex utero procurement also avoids losses of cord blood units in the case of a sudden delivery of the placenta or having to attend to the woman or infant.

The Ex Utero Collection Model seeks the woman's consent after cord blood has been procured. The dedicated cord blood collectors inform the women whose placentas "have been successfully bled" that cord blood has been procured for donation to a community bank.[42] Before the women leave the hospital, their consent is sought for an interview, for access to their own and their infant's hospital charts, for a blood sample, and for a swab of the infant's cheek. They are informed that they may direct that the cord blood be discarded.

The justification for delaying attempts to secure the woman's consent until after collection is based on the fact that many of the women who deliver in the hospitals cooperating with community banks receive their prenatal care, if any, outside of the hospital. This makes it difficult to obtain health histories and consent prior to the woman being admitted for labor and delivery. Since it is widely considered to be too disrespectful to approach a woman during labor with a decision about donating cord blood, and since procurement must occur within a short period after delivery, supporters of the Ex Utero Collection Model believe it is appropriate to delay consent and screening until after cord blood collection.

The Ex Utero Collection Model disregards the objections some parents will have based on deep personal beliefs and attitudes toward delivery practices and the disposition of the placenta. It substitutes a policy of presumed consent for a policy of explicit informed consent. Presumed consent in a non-emergency setting, for a nontherapeutic activity that poses risks to the health and privacy of the patient and her newborn in the interests of a possible stranger, is an *unjustifiably disrespectful consent policy*. Seeking parental consent in advance of cord blood procurement is not impossible; it simply presents some logistical challenges. The ethical and policy commitments implicit in this set of practices entail ranking respect for donors low compared with commitments to efficiency and increasing the number of cord blood units available for transplant.

This disrespect for donors is thought by supporters of the Ex Utero Collection Model to be offset by the commitment to protect donors. The model aims to protect both the women who are delivering and their newborns from the risks associated with procuring cord blood while the placenta is in utero, such as delayed recognition of, and attention to, health problems in the infant or mother while the obstetrician's or the midwife's attention is directed at collection.[43]

Another important drawback to the Ex Utero Collection Model is that it tends to be suitable only for cord blood donation to community banks. Many families desiring private storage will not be able to arrange to deliver in designated institutions at times when collection staff are available.[44]

Banks using In Utero Collection Model for cord blood collection typically screen potential donors and obtain consent to donation two to three months prior to delivery. These banks prefer to screen potential donors and establish their eligibility prior to delivery and cord blood collection so as to reduce the number of ineligible collections. The consent process usually consists of the bank sending the expectant mother written materials, including invitations to call the bank if she has any questions. She is usually asked to answer one or more health-related questionnaires and sign several separate consent documents.[45]

The consent process in the In Utero Collection Model shifts the responsibility for consent disclosures from health care professionals who are directly responsible for the health and well-being of the mother and infant or directly engaged in procurement-related activities to *strangers in distant locations* who store and bank the blood. Face-to-face verbal disclosures are replaced by written materials from the storage facility. The rationale for assigning the storage facility responsibility for informing the woman about donation and obtaining her consent stems from a concern that the consent process would be inconsistent and inadequate if left to each individual obstetrician or midwife who agrees to collect cord blood. Aside from the difficulty of educating all obstetricians and midwives about cord blood banking, this consent procedure is designed to avoid imposing substantial time commitments and introducing a major barrier to their willingness and ability to support the procurement of cord blood. It also supports equitable access to cord blood storage, donation, and transplantation, at least by those who can read and understand English or other languages into which the consent material is translated. However, it makes it difficult, if not impossible, for those responsible for securing consent to assess donor comprehension and voluntariness.

The In Utero Collection Model is respectful of families who wish to store or bank cord blood, but who would not otherwise be able to, because they choose not to or cannot deliver in a facility that has been specifically approved for collection. Collection during the third stage of labor, however, poses some risks to the infant and parents that might be avoided if methods could be developed for procuring cord blood after delivery of the placenta. While an easy, reliable, and practical procurement technique that does not require special training has been developed for procuring cord blood while the placenta remains in utero, it appears unlikely that a similar procedure can be developed for procuring cord blood from delivered placentas. Implicit in the In Utero Collection Model is the view that expanding the availability of stem cell donation, and ultimately transplants, to all in our community is important enough to justify consent and procurement procedures that are less than maximally respectful and protective of the parents and infants from whom cord blood is procured.

REGULATIONS, STANDARDS, AND GUIDELINES
FOR UMBILICAL CORD BLOOD

Most cord blood guidelines are directed at collecting cord blood for community banks, but some include provisions or identify exceptions pertaining to the collection of cord blood for private storage and related allogeneic or autologous transplant. A review of existing policies and guidelines provides a window into the depth of confusion and disagreement regarding the ethical and policy objectives that should inform cord blood guidelines and procedures.

Federal Guidelines

The Food and Drug Administration (FDA) has noted that cord blood raises special concerns regarding the protection of potential recipients since less information is available about the health history of newborn donors than about adult blood donors. It also has expressed special concern for families who may be asked to consider storing cord blood for their own private use. The rise of several for-profit cord blood storage facilities heightened the FDA's interest in regulating the safety, potency, and purity of cord blood used for clinical purposes and in overseeing staff qualifications and advertising activities. Until it enacts regulations specific to cord blood donation and banking, the FDA advises cord blood banks to consult the blood regulations 21 CFR 606, 640.

The FDA proposed regulations in 1995 that would have regulated cord blood as a biologic.[46] As a biologic it would have fallen within the definition of a drug and become subject to product licensure as well as establishment licensure. Many persons within the cord blood community opposed the proposed regulations, arguing that they were not only unnecessary, but harmful to potential recipients. The regulations, they predicted, would restrict the availability of cord blood transplants for years to come to those patients meeting strict eligibility requirements and narrow research objectives. As it takes years, using FDA standards, to definitively establish the efficacy of interventions for very rare conditions, regulating cord blood as a biologic, they argued, would adversely affect the health and lives of patients whose access to this potentially life-saving intervention is in the meantime restricted.

In February 1997 the FDA invited public comment on a proposed new approach to regulating cellular and tissue-based products. Instead of requiring cord blood and cord blood facilities to be licensed, it proposed that facilities be required to register with the FDA, list the products at their facility, screen and test donors for a specific list of communicable diseases, label their products clearly and accurately, and promote their products in balanced and non-misleading ways.[47] The policy focus of the FDA's 1997 proposal is to protect potential recipients from health risks.

State Guidelines

The New York State Department of Health's *Guidelines for Collection, Processing and Storage of Cord Blood Stem Cells* are the only comprehensive state guidelines developed to date on cord blood.[48] Cord blood banks licensed to operate in New York are required to comply with the guidelines. The guidelines are unusual in that they acknowledge that the donation of cord blood may pose risks to the infant and mother and include provisions aimed at respecting and protecting infant donors and their parents.

> Collection of cord blood for the express purpose of harvesting stem cells should be performed in a manner which would not alter the delivery of the infant; would not increase the likelihood of any adverse reaction in the infant or mother; and/or would not preclude appropriate medical management of the infant or mother, including collection of cord blood diagnostic specimens. . . . *In utero* collection is an invasive procedure and should be performed by the obstetrician or allied health care professional responsible for delivery of the infant, with full consideration of possible adverse effects on the mother and child.[49]

Several provisions are concerned with the respect and protection owed infant donors and their parents. The guidelines address, for instance, such matters as minimum qualifications for persons seeking consent, disclosure requirements, when consent should be sought, and from whom. Consent should be sought "by an individual appropriately trained in the informed consent process, and with sufficient knowledge of all aspects of cord blood collection, processing and storage, as well as relevant applications of the stem cell product."[50] The consent process should include disclosure of all options, the financial ramifications of the collection and storage procedure, and the limitations to any implied guarantees or warranties. When cord blood is collected from the placenta in utero, consent must be obtained before collection; when it is collected ex utero, consent should, whenever possible, be obtained prior to the onset of labor, but must be obtained before storing the stem cells. Ideally consent is obtained from both parents, according to the guidelines, yet it is sufficient to obtain the consent of one parent or legal guardian. Since the guidelines require the woman to provide a health history and one or more blood samples for infectious disease testing, it appears that in practice the consent of one parent may be sufficient only when that one parent is the mother.

In the interests of protecting potential recipients, the guidelines require a personal and family medical history of the biologic mother in all cases and the biologic father, if available. The woman's blood must be tested for infectious diseases at least once within thirty days prior to, or seventy-two hours after, delivery. The cord blood should be tested for bacterial and fungal contamination. Cord blood that is donated to a community bank should undergo Class I and maybe Class II HLA typing shortly after collection; cord blood to be stored for private use can postpone HLA typing. Cord blood or a sample of the infant's blood possibly should be tested for infectious diseases. And, according to the New York guidelines, cord blood banks may consider retaining samples of the cord blood and the woman's blood for future testing.

Professional Guidelines

The *Standards for Blood Banks and Transfusion Services*, developed by the American Association of Blood Banks (AABB) in 1995, include provisions concerning cord blood donation. The standards require a personal and family medical history of both the biologic mother and biologic father (if known), infectious disease testing of a sample of the mother's blood, and consent by the "mother of the cord blood donor," in accord with applicable law concerning consent on behalf of minors.[51] A sample from the cord blood or the infant's blood should be typed for ABO group, and a sample of the mother's blood, the cord blood, or the infant's blood should be tested for unexpected red cell antibodies. The singular policy objective of these standards is to protect potential recipients of cord blood.

The AABB and the North American Task Force for Development of Standards for Hematopoietic Cell Transplantation include cord blood in their proposed standards for hematopoietic progenitor cells.[52] The draft standards are similar to the existing AABB standards and require obtaining personal and family health histories from both the biologic mother and father and collecting a blood sample from the mother for infectious disease testing. In contrast to its treatment of bone marrow and peripheral blood progenitor cell donation, the draft takes no position on whether consent for cord blood donation is required at all, on whose consent to cord blood donation is necessary, or on what information must be disclosed to potential donors. Instead, the draft simply states, "Informed consent for cord blood donation must be obtained in accordance with all applicable laws and regulations."[53] The draft standards prohibit using cord blood for allogeneic transplant if the mother, father, or sibling of the infant donor has a genetic disorder that may affect graft survival in the recipient. These draft provisions primarily are committed to protecting potential recipients and include little attention to other ethical or policy objectives.

The Foundation for the Accreditation of Hematopoietic Cell Therapy (FAHCT) published its first edition of *Standards for Hematopoietic Progenitor Cell Collection, Processing and Transplantation* in September 1996.[54] These standards are intended to be minimum guidelines. While they focus on protecting potential recipients, they direct some attention to respecting and protecting donors.

Provisions directed at protecting recipients include requiring personal and family medical histories of the genetic mother and father, and the gestational mother when she is not the genetic mother; prohibiting unrelated donor transplantation if the mother, father, or sibling of the infant donor has a genetic disorder that may affect the recipient; requiring infectious disease testing of the "prospective maternal donor"; requiring the recipient to give explicit consent to receive cord blood when the woman has positive infectious disease tests; saving aliquots of cord blood for later testing as necessary; and permitting blood tests on the infants directly rather than limiting blood tests to samples of cord blood.

Provisions directed at respecting and protecting donors include assessing the risks to the donor from the collection procedure; reporting any abnormal finding to the prospective donor and documenting recommendations for follow-up care; protecting all records and communications as privileged and confidential; and requiring consent from the gestational mother either prior to delivery of the child or within seven days after delivery of the infant. It is left unclear, however, to what the woman is asked to consent. The only thing she must specifically consent to, according to the FAHCT guidelines, is the use of cord blood for transplantation when she has a positive infectious disease test. In addition, cord blood facilities must have a transfusion facility or a twenty-four-hour blood bank, an intensive care unit, and emergency services. This last set of provisions suggests that cord blood donation poses risk of serious physical harm to donors, harm that cannot simply be avoided or minimized by restricting cord blood collection practices, but which requires cord blood facilities to have the capacity to respond with life-saving medical interventions.

The AMA Council on Ethical and Judicial Affairs issued a Current Opinion on fetal umbilical cord blood in 1994, which it updated in 1996.[55] The council's recommendations focus on respecting and protecting infant donors. The council recommends requiring that (1) the umbilical cord be clamped according to "normal" protocol rather than early or in some other way that might endanger the infant, (2) infants known to be at risk for a condition that might be treatable with a cord blood transplant have their cord blood placed in private storage, rather than donated to a community bank, (3) both the infant's parents be informed of the risks of donation and provide their written informed consent, and (4) infants whose cord blood was donated to a community bank be given priority should they ever need a cord blood transplant.

This review of existing guidelines indicates a lack of agreement on several important points:

when consent should, or may, be obtained (e.g., before labor, before delivery, or a week after cord blood collection);

from whom (e.g., mother, both parents, both genetic parents and the gestational mother, either the mother or the father, or a guardian);

why (e.g., because the mother serves as the infant donor's surrogate, because the mother is the maternal donor);

for what (e.g., collection and public donation, the terms of the storage agreement, maternal HIV blood tests);

what information should be disclosed (e.g., all storage and banking options, details regarding private storage agreements, only information required by law); and

by whom (e.g., persons specially trained in informed consent and the collection and use of cord blood).

There are also important differences in the assessment of the types and severity of risks, if any, that collection poses to donors (e.g., none, severe physical harm requiring life-saving interventions, invasions of privacy) and the level of risk cord blood collectors and banks should be permitted to impose on infant donors in the interest of protecting potential recipients (e.g., blood draws for quality control testing for anonymous recipients, labeling of cord blood so it may be traced to the donor, saving aliquots of cord blood for tests that may be developed in the future, and requiring additional examination and testing of the infant donor months or years after cord blood was collected). Sufficient attention has yet to be directed at the full range of ethical and policy objectives concerning cord blood collection.

Risks Associated with Cord Blood Donation

Information provided to cord blood donors on the topic of risks tends to focus on risks to recipients. Mothers, for instance, are usually informed of their responsibility to protect recipients from potential harm. In the interest of protecting potential recipients, some community banks require women to consent to return three to six months after donation for further blood tests and examinations of their infant, or at least to consent to provide follow-up information about the health of their infant within a year of cord blood donation as well as to report any new serious illness within the family.[56]

Cord blood consent forms and educational materials tend to assure women that collection and donation pose no risk to themselves or their infant. This is not entirely surprising since many persons in the cord blood community apparently share this view. Easily the most frequently repeated claim about cord blood is that donation poses no risk to donors.[57] Yet this is clearly an overstatement, as indicated by simultaneous statements that occasionally appear in consent materials hinting at possible contraindications to donation based on the health interests of the mother and infant or risks to the woman's and infant's privacy.

Cord blood donors and their parents are at risk of several types of possible harm. Parents of infant cord blood donors are at risk of unauthorized contact by persons seeking a matched stem cell transplant and recontact by the recipient. They may be pressured to authorize a follow-up donation of their child's bone marrow.[58] Without Certificates of Confidentiality to protect donor information from subpoena, banks cannot assure parents that they will not be subjected to unauthorized contact or violations of their or their child's privacy.[59] Follow-up donation of bone marrow places infant cord blood donors at risk of significant discomfort as well as physical harm. Blood draws and cheek swabs may be performed in the infant solely to establish the quality of the donated cord blood. Infant donors may also be at risk of harm, should the delivery be manipulated so as to increase the collection of cord blood.[60] Both the infant and the woman are exposed to at least some risk when cord blood is procured from the placenta in utero, if the obstetrician or midwife should become distracted from the needs of the woman and/or infant while collecting the cord blood. Cord blood collection entails the health care professionals' agreement to attend to the hypothetical health interests of the infant, a close genetic relative of the infant, or even a complete stranger. Clearly this introduces an external consideration, if not an important modification, into the traditional duties that health care professionals owe their patients.

Procedures aimed at reducing risks of physical harm to potential recipients associated with the relatively unknown health histories of infant cord blood donors pose special risks to the privacy of the infant donor and its closest relatives. Access to the woman's and the infant's medical records may be requested by persons not directly involved in their health care. Sensitive social and family health histories may be collected regarding family members (e.g., parents, grandparents, siblings), often without their explicit knowledge or consent. Genetic testing of cord blood, and storing DNA samples from the infant and mother (or both parents) for possible future testing for as yet unidentified conditions, may be requested to protect against unwittingly transmitting a genetic disease to a transplant recipient. Cord blood donation therefore poses risks to the donating family as a whole, including possible identification of genetic disease(s), identification of mistaken paternity, and breaches of other confidential information concerning the health and social history of all family members about whom information is collected in the interests of protecting potential recipients.

Respect and Protection Owed Cord Blood Donors

RESPECTING CORD BLOOD DONORS

At first glance cord blood donors might seem to be owed no greater respect and protection than a routine blood donor.[61] Important differences, however, render the provisions designed to respect and protect those involved in routine blood donation inadequate for those involved in cord blood donation. As discussed earlier, cord blood donation poses important risks to infant donors and their families, risks greater than those associated with routine blood donation.

Greater confusion exists concerning who needs to be involved in cord blood donation than in routine cord blood donation, and the consent process is more complex. One of the donors, the infant, lacks decisionmaking capacity and requires a surrogate decisionmaker. The decision as to whether to store the cord blood for the infant's or a relative's use or whether to donate it to the community is a weightier decision than in the case of the routine blood donor.

Unlike blood donation that involves only a single adult donor, cord blood donation involves more than one donor and should be understood to be a type of family donation.

Cord blood donation differs from routine blood donation in that cord blood donors can only donate a limited, nonrenewable quantity of the desired cells. Donating cord blood is a one-time opportunity, with the window of opportunity being limited to approximately the fifteen-minute period immediately after the clamping of the umbilical cord. Given the limited number of cells that individual cord blood donors can provide, generally a cord blood donor can only assist a single recipient, at best.[62] Cord blood recipients are at risk of receiving an insufficient number of stem cells and are extremely dependent on the donor for additional cells, should the transplant fail.

The respect owed live organ and tissue donors has yet to be explicated in terms as clear and precise as those in the Uniform Anatomical Gift Act detailing the respect owed to cadaver organ and tissue donors. The following is a proposed articulation of what it means to treat live tissue donors, and live cord blood donors most specifically, with respect:

No one should be used for the educational, research, or therapeutic
   objectives of others without their, or their surrogate's, prior knowledge
   and consent, regardless of the risks involved.
Respect and protect everyone exposed to risks to their health, privacy, or
   well-being that they would not otherwise be exposed to, if not for their
   involvement in the donation of cord blood.
Eliminate unnecessary risks to the health, privacy, and well-being of cord
   blood donors.
Ensure that procedures for collecting, testing, and banking cord blood
   expose infant donors to no more than minimal risk, in the interests of
   anonymous recipients.
Ensure that procedures for procuring, testing, and privately storing
   cord blood expose infant donors to risks that either are no more than
   a minor increase over minimal risk or are reasonable relative to the
   benefits to the infant or to a close family member of the infant.
Permit parents with decisionmaking capacity to accept reasonable risks to
   themselves in the interests of assisting others (e.g., potential cord blood
   recipients).
Do not procure cord blood without disclosing all information that
   reasonable persons would wish to know in advance and obtaining
   valid informed consent from all involved (i.e., donors, surrogate
   decisionmakers, close family members with personal or cultural

objections, and individuals directly affected by contractual obligations with cord blood facilities).

Develop consent procedures and documents that reflect a full understanding of whose consent to the various activities related to cord blood donation is necessary and why.

Ensure that consent is informed and voluntary.

WHOSE CONSENT TO CORD BLOOD DONATION IS NECESSARY AND WHY?

Current consent guidelines and practices for donating cord blood usually require the mother's consent, without elucidating why the woman's consent is necessary, why it is sufficient, and what information must be disclosed during the consent process. A close reading suggests several possibilities: only the infant is a donor (and the mother, as the infant's guardian, may consent on behalf of the infant); both the infant and the mother are donors; the infant and the parents are donors. Cord blood bank documents waver between suggesting that the mother is consenting on behalf of the child only, consenting on behalf of herself and her child, and consenting on behalf of herself, her child, and her family.

Most authors on cord blood donation do not address the involvement of fathers in either the donation or the consent process, but some explicitly assert that the father's consent is unnecessary.[63] The AMA Council on Ethical and Judicial Affairs and Jeremy Sugarman and his colleagues provide important exceptions.[64] They suggest that the consent of both parents should be sought.

The question of whose consent to organ or tissue donation is required is an important one. Family members, for example, are asked to consent to cadaver donation, not because they are themselves considered donors, but rather because it is considered important to respect family members' feelings regarding cadaver donation. And family members are asked to consent to live organ or tissue donation by minors, again not because the family members are donors, but because the family members serve as the child's surrogate decisionmakers.

There are four reasons why the ethical and policy objectives of respect for, and protection of, the infant cord blood donor and its parents require the consent of both the mother and the father.

Consent of Parents in Their Role as Surrogate Decisionmakers for the Infant
Cord blood is part of the infant's blood supply until the umbilical cord is clamped. As indicated above, procuring cord blood poses risks to the infant's health and privacy. Respect for, and protection of, the infant requires a sur-

rogate consent by the parents to cord blood procurement, testing, and donation. The mother and the father share the obligations and privileges to make decisions that are protective and respectful of their child (e.g., the consent of both parents is necessary for enrolling a child in risky nontherapeutic research). Since both parents have the right and responsibility to represent the interests of their children and to make surrogate decisions on their behalf, cord blood must not be procured without the parents' or guardians' knowledge and surrogate consent. Assuming that both parents are reasonably available, on grounds of their status as surrogate decisionmakers alone, both the mother's and the father's consent to cord blood donation should be required.

Consent of Parents Out of Respect for Their Feelings as Close Relatives of the Infant Cord Blood Donor

Seeking the consent of parents should be required based on respect for their feelings as close relatives of the infant donor regarding cord blood collection. This is especially important since it is widely understood that some parents have deep personal and/or cultural attitudes toward the birthing experience, including the handling and disposition of the placenta. Moreover, insofar as birthing experiences are understood to belong to the family, and not simply to the mother and her delivery team, decisions about whether to permit cord blood collection during the third stage of labor — before the delivery of the placenta — may rightfully be decisions that fathers should be invited to participate in, as well as mothers.

Consent of Parents as Parties to Contractual Agreements and Waivers

The consent of both parents is important to protect each of them as well as their infant and other family members in significant financial and other contractual arrangements required by storage facilities and community banks. For example, parents may be required to agree to such things as waiving their family's interest in any cord blood they donate to a community bank, paying for private storage, and rules governing who may request the release of privately stored stem cells and under what conditions and who will have dispositional authority in the case of divorce, separation, or inability or unwillingness to pay private storage fees.

Consent of Parents as Donors of Cord Blood

While most types of tissue donation have historically been understood to involve only one donor, some of the new approaches to quality control testing, as well as new types of tissue donation, are changing this view. Requiring blood samples from multiple family members for genetic studies and routinely collecting other private and sensitive information about the health and social behavior of multiple members of the focal donor's family change the donation from one by a single donor to a donation by multiple donors. All people exposed to risks to their health, privacy, or well-being that they would not be exposed to if not for their involvement in the donation of cord blood should be considered cord blood donors and treated with the respect and protection owed to this type of live donor. Respect for, and protection of, parent donors of cord blood requires that they be informed about cord blood procurement, its related activities, and risks to themselves and that cord blood be procured only with their voluntary informed consent.

In the case of cord blood donation to a community bank and most cases of private storage, the mother clearly should be considered a donor for many of the same reasons that a woman who donates fetal tissue for purposes of transplantation is considered a donor.[65] The mother is asked to provide information about her health and social history, release her medical records for open-ended "fishing expeditions" in search of pertinent infectious disease and genetic information, permit the cord blood to be labeled with an identifier that links the blood to her, and provide a blood (or DNA) sample, which may be stored with the cord blood, to assist with quality control testing in the future. In addition, she may be asked to agree to changes in delivery procedures and changes in her and her infant's relationship with the delivery team, agree to provide follow-up information about her infant's and her family's health, agree to be recontacted for additional information in the future, and/ or agree to receive and consider possible requests for additional stem cell donations by her child. Although they are not always acknowledged, these procedures and practices pose risks (as well as inconveniences and burdens) to the woman's health, privacy, and well-being that she would not otherwise be exposed to if not for her involvement in the donation of cord blood.

Requiring the mother to consent to provide a blood sample, not only for infectious disease testing, but also for genetic testing, including possible genetic tests that may become available in the future, is particularly problematic. As genetic testing develops, it is anticipated that banks will need to conduct additional genetic tests on the banked samples. Genetic testing of cord blood and accompanying blood samples significantly increases the risks of harm to the privacy and well-being of donor families.

There is considerable controversy about how to handle this issue with the storage of blood and tissues generally. Sugarman and his colleagues maintain that parents "need to be informed about how such testing is anticipated to be performed. . . . when testing will be performed, whether specific informed consent for look-back testing will be obtained, who will be notified of the results (e.g., the donor, the parents, or others), and how the information will be communicated to them."[66]

There is currently no acknowledgment in cord blood circles that activities to establish the quality of donated cord blood pose any risks to the father. However, health and social information about the father is clearly relevant to establishing the safety of the cord blood. It is not that banks do not seek this information, but that they usually ask the mothers to provide it. Since mistaken paternal data can complicate or mislead HLA typing and other quality assessments of the placental blood, information is better obtained from fathers directly.[67] While the benefits of infectious disease testing of blood drawn from fathers may not justify its cost, genetic testing to confirm paternity and assist with HLA or other evaluations may become more common in the future.

Making information about identified fathers available to cord blood banks, regardless of how the information is obtained or who provides it, poses risks to a father's privacy and well-being. Respect for, and protection of, fathers involved in cord blood donation requires that they be informed and have the opportunity to consent or refuse to provide the private and sensitive information being sought about them and the opportunity to consent or refuse to risk their privacy and well-being.

Only in the unlikely event that all three of the following conditions exist might the mother and father not be a donor of cord blood: (1) there are no quality-control procedures posing risks to either the mother's or father's health, privacy, or well-being (e.g., when cord blood is procured for autologous transplantation only); (2) there are no changes in the delivery procedures in anticipation of cord blood procurement; and (3) cord blood is procured only after delivery of the placenta. While under these rare circumstances the consent of the mother and father as *donors* might not be necessary, their consent is still necessary insofar as they are the surrogate decisionmakers for the infant, insofar as it is important to respect their feelings as close relatives of the cord blood donor, and insofar as they are entering important contractual agreements with the storage facility or community bank.

A Proposed Ethical and Policy Framework for Cord Blood Collection

An ethical framework specifically for cord blood donation is needed to guide the development and assessment of cord blood policies and procedures. It is important to be explicit about the ethical and policy objectives at stake and to agree on their relative priority. In the absence of a clear and agreed-upon ethical framework, cord blood organizations and guidelines are directing disproportionate attention to some ethical and policy objectives to the exclusion of or even at the expense of others. The proposed framework identifies and prioritizes the major ethical and policy objectives. For instance, it assigns top priority to respect for infant donors and requires that each of the other objectives be constrained by and consistent with this objective.

The proposed framework for cord blood donation consists of the following seven fundamental ethical and policy objectives, in order of priority:

1. Respect infant cord blood donors.
2. Protect infant cord blood donors.
3. Respect and protect the closest relatives of infant cord blood donors.
4. Maintain and/or enhance public trust in organ and tissue donation generally.
5. Protect and benefit cord blood recipients.
6. Increase fair access to hematopoietic stem cell transplants.
7. Increase the number and diversity of banked units of cord blood.

Policies and procedures directed at any one of these objectives should be constrained by, and consistent with, the requirements of all higher objectives.

Ideally, a cord blood policy would fully realize each of the fundamental ethical and policy objectives. Since this is highly unlikely, prioritizing the objectives and trading one off in favor of another will be necessary at times. Ethical and policy frameworks for cord blood donation that focus on a single fundamental objective (e.g., protection of recipients) to the exclusion of the others invariably not simply neglect, but actually undermine one or more of the other ethical and policy objectives. The challenge is to develop a set of provisions governing cord blood collection that reflects a justifiable weighting of the fundamental ethical and policy objectives.

Respect for prospective donors is arguably the most important ethical and policy objective in any adequate framework for live tissue donation, and cord blood donation more specifically. This means that policies and practices that fail adequately to inform potential donors and/or their surrogates of the full range of information relevant to cord blood donation, fail adequately to ensure comprehension and voluntariness, or fail to obtain consent in advance of procurement are disrespectful of donors and can rarely, if ever, be justified.

Obligations to protect donors and recipients, especially donors and research subjects who lack decisionmaking capacity and require surrogate consent, are also very important. The balance of risks and benefits in cord blood collection is most favorable in the case of an infant known to have a condition that can be successfully treated with an autologous transplant. It is easier to justify the risks to an infant associated with cord blood procurement when the cord blood is to be used for the infant or an immediate family member than when cord blood is to be collected for the possible benefit of an anonymous recipient. Parents, however, are permitted in our society to consent on behalf of their child to the child's participation in research if it poses minimal risk or a minor increase over minimal risk, even when the research offers no prospect of direct benefit to the child.[68] Similar reasoning may be used to justify permitting infants to donate cord blood to community banks, if cord blood collection poses no more than minimal risk to the infant.

Obligations to protect competent adults from risks of harm are less stringent than obligations to protect infants and others who cannot assess the risks for themselves. Certain thresholds of safety are required as a means of providing protection (e.g., the risks must be reasonable in light of expected benefits), but it is not required that everything possible be done to protect donors and recipients. Informing donors, surrogates, and recipients, in terms they can understand, of the risks and of the limits on the protections that can be promised is itself an important form of protection. When balancing protection of donors against protection of recipients, it is necessary to consider the probability and severity of the harms to each party. It should not simply be assumed that protection of the recipient from risks of physical harm should always outweigh concern for protecting donors from harms of other sorts, such as risks to privacy or to social or psychological well-being. While sacrificing respect for live tissue donors should not be permitted, some degree of risk to both donors and recipients is permissible, and more risk is permissible for persons with decisionmaking capacity than for persons without, and more risk is permissible in the case of therapeutic benefits for the individual or a close family member than for strangers.

Efforts to encourage donation and increase the number of cord blood units available for transplant should be consistent with, rather than damaging to, the more important ethical and policy objectives of respect for and protection of donors and recipients. Before developing policies to encourage donation, it is appropriate first to eliminate barriers and disincentives to donation. Currently there are financial barriers to private storage of cord blood and geographical and language barriers to community donation. The development of policies that remove these barriers is respectful and protective of prospective infant donors and their parents. Nevertheless, encouragement is disrespectful when it is based on incomplete, misleading, or irrelevant information and when it exploits the fears of parents.

The extent to which it is appropriate at this time actively to encourage either cord blood storage or donation depends on the answers to several important questions: Is cord blood collection, banking, and transplant safe and effective, proven, or investigational? How long can stem cells safely be stored? What are the risks to the donors' health and privacy? What are the probabilities that a person with no relevant family health history will need a stem cell transplant? What are the chances of someone finding well-matched unrelated stem cells in a community bank? And what are the advantages of having an autologous or related allogeneic stem cell transplant versus an unrelated one?

As many of these questions are still under investigation, it would appear to be premature, especially in the case of donation to a community bank, to implement policies of "routine inquiry" (i.e., to require that women be asked whether they have made plans to donate cord blood) or "required request" (i.e., to require that women be asked, "Do you wish to donate cord blood?").

Conclusion

Based on frameworks developed for other types of organ and tissue donation, this essay proposes a framework of ethical and policy objectives to guide the assessment and development of cord blood policies and procedures. This framework suggests that guidelines proposed by professional organizations and current practices reported in academic journals and in cord blood bank materials do not, in general, give sufficient priority to respecting or protecting donors. They tend instead to give disproportionate attention to protecting recipients and/or increasing the number and diversity of cryopreserved cord blood units. There are probably many reasons for this, including a tendency to focus too narrowly on the lack of physical risk associated with collecting cord blood relative to other methods of collecting stem cells and overlooking or discounting the full range of risks that donating and banking cord blood pose to the health, privacy, and well-being of the infant, the mother, and the father.

It is important to understand the full range of ethical and policy objectives that should inform cord blood collection practices and the relative priority that should be assigned to each. Understanding what respect and protection is owed to cord blood donors requires understanding cord blood practices, the risks these practices pose, and the meaning and importance of respect for live tissue donors. Respect for cord blood donors requires developing consent procedures that are based on a clear understanding of whose consent to cord blood collection is necessary, for what, and why. Far from being a risk-free form of blood or waste tissue donation, cord blood donation is a unique and complex type of family tissue donation.

Acknowledgments

I wish to acknowledge the fellowship support provided by the Obermann Center for Advanced Studies at the University of Iowa and the contributions of the participants in the Obermann Center's 1996 Faculty Research Seminar on Ethical and Legal Implications of Stored Tissue Samples.

Notes

1. Ami Ballin, "Autologous Umbilical Cord Blood Transfusion," *Archives of Disease in Childhood* 73 (1995): F181–F183; Ellen M. Biafono et al., "Collection and 28-Day Storage of Human Placental Blood," *Pediatric Research* 36(1) (1994): 90–94; Sanford Anderson et al., "Retrieval of Placental Blood from the Umbilical Vein to Determine Volume, Sterility, and Presence of Clot Formation," *American Journal of Diseases of Children* 146 (1992): 36–39; and American Association of Blood Banks, *Standards for Blood Banks and Transfusion Services*, 15th ed. (Bethesda, Md.: American Association of Blood Banks, 1993), p. 4.

2. Milton Ende and Norman Ende, "Hematopoietic Transplantation by Means of Fetal (Cord) Blood: A New Method," *Virginia Medical Monthly* 99 (1972): 276–280; Eliane Gluckman et al., "Hematopoietic Reconstitution in a Patient with Fanconi's Anemia by Means of Umbilical-cord Blood for an HLA-identical Sibling," *New England Journal of Medicine* 321(17) (1989): 1174–1178; David T. Harris, "Experience in Autologous and Allogeneic Cord Blood Banking," *Journal of Hematotherapy* 5 (1996): 124; and Pablo Rubenstein et al., "Unrelated Placental Blood for Bone Marrow Reconstitution: Organization of the Placental Blood Program," *Blood Cells* 20 (1994): 587–600.

3. Mary Horowitz, International Symposium and Workshop on Cord Blood Transplantation, Indiana University School of Medicine, March 9, 1997.

4. John E. Wagner, "Regulation of Placental and Umbilical Cord Blood Stem Cells," *Journal of Hematotherapy* 6 (1997): 2; see also Joseph Wiley and Jeffrey A. Kuller, "Storage of Newborn Stem Cells for Future Use," *Obstetrics and Gynecology* 89(2) (1997): 300–303.

5. Judith Randal, "Cord Blood Offers Patients New Blood Cell Source," *Journal of the National Cancer Institute* 87(3) (1995): 164–166.

6. Eliane Gluckman et al., "Outcome of Cord-blood Transplantation from Related and Unrelated Donors," *New England Journal of Medicine* 337(6) (1997): 373–381; see also John E. Wagner et al., "Allogeneic Sibling Umbilical-cord-blood Transplantation in Children with Malignant and Non-malignant Disease," *Lancet* 346 (1995): 214–219.

7. Wagner et al., "Allogeneic Sibling Umbilical-cord-blood Transplantion in Children," pp. 214–219; see also Eliane Gluckman et al., "Cord Blood Banking for Hematopoietic Cell Transplantation: An International Cord Blood Transplant Registry," *Bone Marrow Transplantation* 11 (1993): 199–200.

8. Gluckman et al., "Outcome of Cord-blood Transplantation," pp. 373–381.

9. Joanne Kurtzberg et al., "Placental Blood as a Source of Hematopoietic Stem

Cells for Transplantation into Unrelated Recipients," *New England Journal of Medicine* 335(3) (1996): 157–166; John E. Wagner et al., "Successful Transplantation of HLA-matched and HLA-mismatched Umbilical Cord Blood from Unrelated Donors: Analysis of Engraftment and Acute Graft-versus-Host Disease," *Blood* 88(3) (1996): 795–802.

10. Gluckman et al., "Hematopoietic Reconstitution in a Patient with Fanconi's Anemia," pp. 1174–1178; G. Lambertenghi Deliliers et al., "Case Report: Unrelated Mismatched Cord Blood Transplantation in an Adult with Secondary AML," *Bone Marrow Transplantation* 18 (1996): 469–472; M. N. Fernandez et al., "Case Report: HLA Haploidentical Cord Blood Cell Transplant in a 15-year-old, 50 kg Weight Patient: Successful Treatment for Chronic Myeloid Leukemia after Myeloid Blastic Transformation," *Bone Marrow Transplantation* 17 (1996): 1175–1178; I. Zix-Kieffer et al., "Case Report: Successful Cord Blood Stem Cell Transplantation for Congenital Erythropoietic Porphyria (Gunther's Disease)," *Bone Marrow Transplantation* 18 (1996): 217–220; Jean-Philippe Laporte et al., "Cord Blood Transplantation from an Unrelated Donor in an Adult with Chronic Mylogenous Leukemia," *New England Journal of Medicine* 335(3) (1996): 167–170; S. Issaragrisil et al., "Brief Report: Transplantation of Cord-blood Stem Cells into a Patient with Severe Thalassemia," *New England Journal of Medicine* 332(6) (1995): 367–369; R. Pahwa et al., "Successful Hematopoietic Reconstitution with Transplantation of Erythrocyte-depleted Allogenic Human Umbilical Cord Blood Cells in a Child with Leukemia," *Proceedings of the National Academy of Sciences* 91 (1994): 4485–4488; and Mudra Kohli-Kumar et al., "Haemopoietic Stem/Progenitor Cell Transplant in Fanconi Anaemia Using HLA-matched Sibling Umbilical Cord Blood Cells," *British Journal of Haematology* 85 (1993): 419–422.

11. Pablo Rubenstein, "The New York Blood Center Experience," presentation at the Third International Cord Blood Stem Cells: Banking, Expansion, and Transplants, Martha's Vineyard, Mass., May 20–22, 1996; Jean-Philippe Laporte et al., "Cord Blood Transplantation from an Unrelated Donor in an Adult with Chronic Mylogenous Leukemia," *New England Journal of Medicine* 335(3) (1996): 167–170; John E. Wagner et al., "Successful Transplantation of HLA-matched and HLA-mismatched Umbilical Cord Blood from Unrelated Donors: Analysis of Engraftment and Acute Graft-versus-Host Disease," *Blood* 88(3) (1996): 795–802.

12. Norman Ende et al., "Potential Effectiveness of Stored Cord Blood (Non-frozen) for Emergency Use," *Journal of Emergency Medicine* 14(6) (1996): 673–677.

13. Gluckman et al., "Outcome of Cord-blood Transplantation," p. 374.

14. See Cord Blood Registry, "Managed Care of America Brings Cord Blood Banking to Its Member Health Plans," *Cord Blood News* 2(1) (1997): 6; and ViaCord, "Insurance Coverage for Private Cord Blood Banking," *ViaCord Journal* 2 (1997): 8.

15. ViaCord, "The Bone Marrow Foundation," *ViaCord Journal* 2 (1997): 2; Cord Blood Registry, "Family Assistance Program Leads to Transplant," *Cord Blood News* 2(1) (1997): 1; see also Cord Blood Registry, "New Patient Billing Program Implemented," *Cord Blood News* 2(1) (1997): 3.

16. Cord Blood Registry, "CBR Provides Free Cord Blood Banking for Families at Risk," *Cord Blood News*, 2 (2) (1997): 6.

17. United States Center for Cord Blood, "Cord Blood Storage Program [brochure]" (Altamonte Springs, Fla.: United States Center for Cord Blood, 1996).

18. CRYO-CELL, "Lifespan Informed Consent and Stem Cell Storage Agreement," (1996): 4; CRYO-CELL, "CRYO-CELL International, Inc. Approved for NASDAQ Listing" (January 13, 1996).

19. Pablo Rubenstein, "Cord Blood Banking," International Symposium and Workshop on Cord Blood Transplantation, Indiana University School of Medicine, March 9, 1997.

20. David T. Harris, "Experience in Autologous and Allogeneic Cord Blood Banking," *Journal of Hematotherapy* 5 (1996): 123–128; and Paul Billings, "Stop Cord Waste" (San Mateo, Calif.: International Cord Blood Foundation, no date).

21. David T. Harris, "Experience in Autologous and Allogeneic Cord Blood Banking," pp. 123–128.

22. Geralyn M. Meny, "Issues in the Development of a Local Cord Blood Bank," *Journal of Hematotherapy* 5 (1996): 145–148; and Jeffrey McCullough, "Establishing and Operating a Placental Cord Stem Cell Bank," presentation at Third International Conference, Cord Blood Stem Cells: Banking, Expansion and Transplants, Martha's Vineyard, Mass., May 20–22, 1996.

23. Gluckman et al., "Outcome of Cord-blood Transplantation," pp. 373–381.

24. Pablo Rubenstein, "The New York Blood Center Experience," presentation at the Third International Cord Blood Stem Cells, Martha's Vineyard, May 20–22, 1996; and David T. Harris, "Experience in Autologous and Allogeneic Cord Blood Banking," *Journal of Hematotherapy* 5 (1996): 127.

25. John E. Wagner et al., "Transplantation of Umbilical Cord after Myeloablative Therapy: Analysis of Engraftment," *Blood* 79 (1992): 1879; John Wagner et al., "Response," *Blood* 80(6) (1992): 1624; Eliane Gluckman, "European Organization for Cord Blood Banking," *Blood Cells* 20 (1994): 601–608; Eliane Gluckman et al., "Clinical Applications of Stem Cell Transfusion from Cord Blood and Rationale for Cord Blood Banking," *Bone Marrow Transplantation* Supplement 9 (1992): 114–117; Pablo Rubinstein et al., "Unrelated Placental Blood for Bone Marrow Reconstitution: Organization of the Placental Blood Program," *Blood Cells* 20 (1994): 599; Denis English et al., "Collection and Processing of Cord Blood for Preservation and Hematopoietic Transplantation," in Ellen M. Areman, H. Joachim Deeg, and Ronald A. Sacher, eds., *Bone Marrow and Stem Cell Processing: A Manual of Current Techniques*, (Philadelphia: F. A. Davis Company, 1992), p. 383; Francesco Bertolini et al., "Placental Blood Collection: Effects on Newborns [letter]," *Blood* 85 (11) (1995): 3361–3362; Edward A. Boyse et al., "Preservation of Fetal and Neonatal Hematopoietic Stem and Progenitor Cells of the Blood," U.S. Patent number 5,004,681 (April 2, 1991), p. 15; Eliane Gluckman, "Discussion," *Blood Cells* 20 (1994): 599; and Cord Blood Registry, "Steps for the Collection of Cord Blood with the Cbr™ Collection Kit" (San Mateo, Calif.: Cord Blood Registry, no date).

26. John E. Wagner and Hal E. Broxmeyer, "Response," *Blood* 80(6) (1992): 1624; Norman Ende, "Collection of Umbilical Cord Blood for Transplantation [letter]," *Blood* 80(6) (1992): 1623; William S. Grizzard et al., "Collection of Umbilical Cord Blood for Transplantation [letter]," *Blood* 80 (6) (1992): 1623; Norman Ende, "Use of Human Umbilical Cord Blood for Stem-cell Transplantation (HLA-matched, Unmatched; Clinical, Ethical, and Legal Aspects)," in Daniel Levitt and Roland Mertelsmann, eds., *Hematopoietic Stem Cells: Biology and Therapeutic Applications* (New York:

Marcel Dekker, 1995), p. 335; see F. Gary Cunningham et al., *Williams Obstetrics*, 18th ed. (Norwalk, Connecticut: Appleton and Lange, 1989), pp. 318–319; G. J. Hofmeyr et al., "Hasty Clamping of the Umbilical Cord May Initiate Neonatal Intraventricular Hemorrhage," *Medical Hypotheses* 29 (1989): 5–6; G. J. Hofmeyr et al., "Periventricular/Intraventricular Haemorrhage and Umbilical Cord Clamping," *South African Medical Journal* 73 (1988): 104–106; Peter Dunn, "Banking Umbilical Cord Blood," *Lancet* 340 (1992): 309; Arthur J. Moss and Michelle Monset-Couchard, "Placental Transfusion: Early versus Late Clamping of the Umbilical Cord," *Pediatrics* 40 (1) (1967): 109–126; and Otwin Linderkamp, "Placental Transfusion: Determinants and Effects," *Clinics in Perinatology* 9 (3) (1982): 559–592.

27. For example, New York State Council on Human Blood and Transfusion Services, *Guidelines for Collection, Processing and Storage of Cord Blood Stem Cells* (Albany: New York State Department of Health, 1997).

28. Paul R. McGurdy, "The National Heart, Lung and Blood Institute and Cord Blood Stem Cell Transplantation," presentation at Second International, Cord Blood Stem Cells: Banking, Expansion and Transplants: An Alternative to Bone Marrow, San Francisco, Calif., October 16–18, 1995; see Moss and Monset-Couchard, "Placental Transfusion: Early versus Late Clamping of the Umbilical Cord," pp. 109–126; and Otwin Linderkamp, "Placental Transfusion: Determinants and Effects," *Clinics in Perinatology* 9 (3) (1982): 559–592.

29. Gesine Kogler, "The Düsseldorf Methodology," presentation at Third International, Cord Blood Stem Cells: Banking, Expansion and Transplants, Martha's Vineyard, Mass., May 20–22, 1996; Eliane Gluckman, "European Organization for Cord Blood Banking," *Blood Cells* 20 (1994): 601–608; Eliane Gluckman et al., "Clinical Applications of Stem Cell Transfusion from Cord Blood and Rationale for Cord Blood Banking," *Bone Marrow Transplantation Supplement* 9 (1992): 114–117; and Edward A. Boyse et al., "Preservation of Fetal and Neonatal Hematopoietic Stem and Progenitor Cells of the Blood," U.S. Patent number 5,004,681 (April 2, 1991).

30. Pablo Rubenstein et al., "Unrelated Placental Blood for Bone Marrow Reconstitution: Organization of the Placental Blood Program," *Blood Cells* 20 (1994): 587–600; Pablo Rubenstein et al., "Stored Placental Blood for Unrelated Bone Marrow Reconstitution," *Blood* 81 (7) (1993): 1679–1690; Geralyn M. Meny, "Challenges in the Development of a Local Cord Blood Bank," presentation at Second International, Cord Blood Stem Cells: Banking, Expansion and Transplants: An Alternative to Bone Marrow, San Francisco, Calif., October 16–18, 1995; and C. W. Turner et al., "A Modified Harvest Technique for Cord Blood Hematopoietic Stem Cells," *Bone Marrow Transplantation* 10 (1992): 89–91.

31. Cord Blood Registry, "Steps for the Collection of Cord Blood with the Cbr ™ Collection Kit"; and Edward A. Boyse et al., "Preservation of Fetal and Neonatal Hematopoietic Stem and Progenitor Cells of the Blood," U.S. Patent Number 5,004,681 (April 2, 1991), pp. 15–16.

32. John E. Wagner et al, "Umbilical Cord and Placental Blood Hematopoietic Stem Cells: Collection, Cryopreservation, and Storage," *Journal of Hematotherapy* 1 (1992): 167–173; Cord Blood Registry, "Steps for the Collection of Cord Blood with the Cbr ™ Collection Kit"; Keiichi Isoyama et al., "Study of the Collection and Separation of Umbilical Cord Blood for Use in Hematopoietic Progenitor Cell Transplantation,"

International Journal of Hematology 63 (1996): 95–102; and Jill Hows et al., "Human Cord Blood: A Source of Transplantable Stem Cells?" Bone Marrow Transplantation 9, Supplement (1992): 105–108.

33. Cord Blood Registry, "Cord Blood: Making An Informed Decision [brochure]" (San Mateo, Calif.: Cord Blood Registry, 1996).

34. Helen Varney, Nurse-Mid-wifery, 2nd ed. (Boston: Blackwell Scientific Publications, 1987), p. 363.

35. Rubenstein et al., "Unrelated Placental Blood for Bone Marrow Reconstitution," p. 589.

36. New York State Council on Human Blood and Transfusion Services, Guidelines for Collection, Processing and Storage of Cord Blood Stem Cells.

37. Robert A. Dracker, "Cord Blood Stem Cells: How to Get Them and What to Do with Them," Journal of Hematotherapy 5 (1996): 145–148.

38. Joseph M. Wiley and Jeffrey A. Kuller, "Storage of Newborn Stem Cells for Future Use," Obstetrics and Gynecology 89 (2) (1997): 300–303; and Joanne Kurtzberg, "Umbilical Cord Blood: A Novel Alternative Source of Hematopoietic Stem Cells for Bone Marrow Transplantation," Journal of Hematotherapy 5 (1996): 95–96.

39. David T. Harris, "Experience in Autologous and Allogeneic Cord Blood Banking," Journal of Hematotherapy 5 (1996): 123–128; St. Louis Cord Blood Bank at Cardinal Glennon Children's Hospital is a community bank that uses a variation of the In Utero Collection Model.

40. Jeffrey McCullough et al., "Proposed Policies and Procedures for the Establishment of a Cord Blood Bank," Blood Cells 20 (1994): 615; and Pablo Rubenstein et al., "Stored Placental Blood for Unrelated Bone Marrow Reconstitution," Blood 81 (7) (1993): 1679–1690.

41. Rubenstein et al., "Stored Placental Blood for Unrelated Bone Marrow Reconstitution," pp. 1679–1690.

42. Rubinstein et al., "Unrelated Placental Blood for Bone Marrow Reconstitution," p. 587–600; see also Geralyn M. Meny, "Issues in the Development of a Local Cord Blood Bank," Journal of Hematotherapy 5 (1996): 145–148.

43. Rubinstein et al., "Unrelated Placental Blood for Bone Marrow Reconstitution," p. 588.

44. Jeffrey McCullough, "Issues of Establishing and Operating a Cord Blood Bank," International Symposium and Workshop on Cord Blood Transplantation, Indiana University School of Medicine, March 10, 1997.

45. The Cord Blood Registry, for example, asks the expectant mother to sign a general consent form for the donation; an "attestation of truthfulness" regarding the responses she supplied to questions concerning her own, and the biological father's, family health histories, at risk behaviors, and ethnic backgrounds; a "recontact statement" promising to provide additional health information about the infant within the first year of life and about serious future illness within the family, as well as agreeing to be recontacted by the bank; a consent form for maternal blood storage; authorization to release medical records; and a form releasing the physician or midwife from liability.

46. Food and Drug Administration, "Draft Document concerning the Regulation of Placental/Umbilical Cord Blood Stem Cell Products Intended for Trans-

plantation or Further Manufacture into Injectable Products," Docket No. 96N-0002 (December 1995); see also Food and Drug Administration, "Proposed Approach to Regulation of Cellular and Tissue-based Products," Docket No. 97N-0068 (February 1997).

47. Food and Drug Administration, "Proposed Approach to Regulation of Cellular and Tissue-based Products."

48. New York State Council on Human Blood and Transfusion Services, *Guidelines for Collection, Processing and Storage of Cord Blood Stem Cells.*

49. New York State Council, *Guidelines*, pp. 1–5.

50. New York State Council, *Guidelines*, pp. 1–5.

51. American Association of Blood Banks, *Standards for Blood Banks and Transfusion Services*, 17th ed. (Bethesda, Md.: American Association of Tissue Banks, 1995) pp. 8, 58.

52. American Association of Blood Banks, "Proposed Hematopoietic Progenitor Cell Standards," *News Briefs* 18 (5) (1996): 9–16.

53. American Association of Blood Banks, "Proposed Hematopoietic Progenitor Cell Standards," p. 10.

54. Foundation for the Accreditation of Hematopoietic Cell Therapy (FAHCT), *Standards for Hematopoietic Progenitor Cell Collection, Processing and Transplantation* (Omaha: FAHCT, 1996).

55. AMA, Council on Ethical and Judicial Affairs, "2.165 Fetal Umbilical Cord Blood," *Code of Medical Ethics: Current Opinions with Annotations*, 1996–97 ed. (Chicago, Ill.: American Medical Association, 1997).

56. G. Kogler, "The Düsseldorf Methodology," presentation at Third International, Cord Blood Stem Cells: Banking, Expansion and Transplants, Martha's Vineyard, Mass., May 20–22, 1996.

57. Stuart E. Lind, "Ethical Considerations Related to the Collection and Distribution of Cord Blood Stem Cells for Transplantation to Reconstitute Hematopoietic Function," *Transfusion* 34 (1994): 828; David T. Harris et al., "Collection, Separation and Cryopreservation of Umbilical Cord Blood for Use in Transplantation," *Bone Marrow Transplantation* 13 (1994): 141; Rubenstein et al., "Stored Placental Blood for Unrelated Bone Marrow Reconstitution," p. 1679; John E. Wagner et al., "Umbilical Cord and Placental Blood Hematopoietic Stem Cells: Collection, Cryopreservation, and Storage," *Journal of Hematotherapy* 1 (1992): 172; and Cord Blood Registry, "Cord Blood: Making An Informed Choice [brochure]" (San Mateo, Calif.: Cord Blood Registry, 1996).

58. See Mudra Kohli-Kumar et al., "Haemapoietic Stem/Progenitor Cell Transplant in Fanconi Anaemia Using HLA-matched Sibling Umbilical Cord Blood Cells," *British Journal of Haematology* 85 (1993): 419–422. There are anecdotal reports of at least three patients receiving bone marrow transplants from two- and three-year-old children who had previously donated cord blood; International Symposium and Workshop on Cord Blood Transplantation, Indiana University School of Medicine, March 9, 1997; see also Eliane Gluckman et al., "Outcome of Cord-blood Transplantation from Related and Unrelated Donors," *New England Journal of Medicine* 337 (6) (1997): 375–376.

59. One bank suggests that one of the benefits of cord blood storage is that it provides "a registered genetic identification source in cases of children who are lost, kid-

napped, or runaway." This alleged benefit itself suggests possible risks to the child's privacy, should the bank be unable, or unwilling, to limit the use of the stored cord blood and related blood samples for the purpose for which it was stored. Privacy risks are especially high if others, such as law enforcement officials, are permitted access to any of the donors' genetic information for purposes unrelated to the donation.

60. Arthur J. Ammann, "Placental-blood Transplantation [letter]," *New England Journal of Medicine* 336 (1) (1997): 68.

61. For a discussion of the respect owed blood donors, see M. H. Sayers, "Duties to Donors," *Transfusion* 32 (5) (1992): 465–466.

62. There is an anecdotal report that the parents of two children with Fanconi's anemia requested that the cord blood of a sibling, which was 4 HLA matched to both affected children, be split and provided to both; International Symposium and Workshop on Cord Blood Transplantation, Indiana University School of Medicine, March 9, 1997

63. Jeffrey McCullough et al., "Proposed Policies and Procedures for the Establishment of a Cord Blood Bank," *Blood Cells* 20 (1994): 610.

64. Jeremy Sugarman et al., "Ethical Aspects of Banking Placental Blood for Transplantation," *Journal of the American Medical Association* 274 (22) (1995): 1785.

65. See Dorothy E. Vawter et al., "Ethical and Policy Issues in Human Fetal Tissue Transplants," *Cell Transplantation* 4 (5) (1995): 479–482.

66. Sugarman et al., "Ethical Aspects of Banking Placental Blood for Transplantation," p. 1784.

67. See Sugarman et al., "Ethical Aspects of Banking Placental Blood for Transplantation," p. 1784.

68. Department of Health and Human Services, Code of Federal Regulations, Title 45, Part 46, Subpart D (revised June 18, 1991).

Human Embryo Cryopreservation:
Benefits and Adverse Consequences

Amy E. T. Sparks

The first report of a pregnancy from a cryopreserved human embryo sparked many ongoing ethical and legal debates regarding the practice of human embryo cryopreservation, cryopreserved embryos' rights, and embryo "ownership."[1] Development of technology that allows fertilization of oocytes in vitro, cryopreservation of the embryo either before or after completion of the fertilization process, and long-term storage of the cryopreserved embryos has introduced new methods of treating infertility, novel means of family formation such as embryo donation and gestational surrogacy, and a potential to preserve a woman's ability to reproduce. As with many medical technologies, the benefits of in vitro fertilization and embryo cryopreservation are balanced with adverse consequences and unanticipated problems. In this instance, some of the problems specifically pertain to the long-term storage of tissue samples that might, if implanted into women's bodies, develop into individual human beings like the rest of us.

This essay focuses on these types of stored tissue samples by discussing the practical aspects of embryo cryopreservation, the moral status of embryos as related to the biology of the cell at the time of cryopreservation, and the issues that have emerged since the introduction of embryo cryopreservation in human in vitro fertilization laboratories. The recommendations made here are based on positions taken by the ethics committee of the American Society for Reproductive Medicine, as well as policies developed by the Center for Advanced Reproductive Care at the University of Iowa.

Embryo Cryopreservation during Infertility Treatment

The use of cryopreservation technology for preservation of early human embryos has been shown to enhance the efficiency and cost effectiveness of establishing pregnancy through in vitro fertilization.[2-4] Improved controlled ovarian hyperstimulation protocols allow production and collection of large numbers of oocytes and subsequent production of numerous embryos during a single infertility treatment cycle. Transfer of good-quality multiple embryos does increase the clinical pregnancy rate per treatment cycle. However, it also increases the risk of a multiple pregnancy.[5-6] Embryo cryopreservation provides patients and physicians with the option to transfer a limited number of embryos to reduce their risk of a multiple pregnancy[7-8] and the ability to suspend excess embryos in time for transfer at a later date.[7]

For example, a retrospective analysis of 610 patients who had undergone 1,000 oocyte retrievals at the University of Iowa revealed that 56 percent ($n =$ 561) of the cycles had embryos in excess of the number desired for transfer cryopreserved.[2] Transfer of "fresh" embryos after the 1,000 oocyte retrievals led to 294 (29.4 percent) deliveries. There have been an additional 66 deliveries following 373 transfers of the cryopreserved embryos, with 56 of the pregnancies occurring in women who did not conceive during the "fresh" cycle. The delivery rate per oocyte retrieval was improved by 6.6 percent after cryopreservation and subsequent transfer of excess embryos. The actual contribution of the cryopreserved excess embryos to the delivery rate per oocyte retrieval is likely to continue to increase due to the fact that an additional 1,890 embryos for 295 patients remained in storage at the time of analysis.

For some patients, the cryopreservation of "potential babies" is unthinkable. Yet for many patients, the opportunity to have embryo transfers is appealing because this can be done without additional cycles of ovarian hyperstimulation by daily injections of hormones and without several trips to the infertility clinic for blood samples, ultrasounds, and oocyte retrieval. Additionally, B. J. Van Voorhis et al.[2] determined that cryopreservation of excess embryos is a cost-effective method of increasing the delivery rate per cycle of ovarian hyperstimulation (see table 1). If embryo cryopreservation is an acceptable option for patients, it is important that each patient be made aware of the biology of the cells and the risks and benefits associated with embryo cryopreservation prior to initial infertility treatment.

TABLE 1. *Cost Effectiveness of Assisted Reproduction Procedures*

Procedure	Initiated Cycles[a]	Embryo Transfers	Deliveries	Infants Born	Total Cost[b]	Cost per Delivery
Fresh Cycle	237	199	58	76	2,101,977	36,241
Frozen Cycle	97	89	18	24	197,158	10,953
Total	334	288	76	100	2,299,135	30,252

[a] Initiated cycles include all women who started ovarian hyperstimulation for oocyte retrieval or hormone replacement for cryopreserved embryo transfer.
[b] Costs were determined for procedures performed at the University of Iowa in 1992.

Use of Embryo Cryopreservation for Oocyte Preservation

The widespread use of embryo cryopreservation in the United States and Canada is quite evident in the American Society for Reproductive Medicine/ Society for Assisted Reproductive Technologies 1993 Registry Report.[9] In 1993 a total of 234 of the 267 assisted reproduction programs voluntarily reporting their results performed 6,672 embryo thawing procedures. Some (478 procedures or 7 percent) of the embryo thaws had no viable embryos for transfer. The delivery rate per cryopreserved embryo transfer was 12.8 percent (791/ 6,194) for programs reporting to the registry in 1993.

There are some situations when embryo transfer after controlled ovarian hyperstimulation is undesirable. Transfer of cryopreserved embryos during a non-gonadotropin-stimulated cycle has been shown to be an effective alternative to fresh embryo transfer during a gonadotropin-stimulated cycle when patients are at risk of severe hyperstimulation or have a thin endometrial lining which may not provide an optimal environment for embryonic implantation into the uterus.[10]

Embryo cryopreservation also may be used as a tool to preserve oocytes. Unlike the routine use of cryopreservation to preserve sperm, oocyte cryopreservation is currently only used experimentally. Poor oocyte survival and fertilization rates postthaw and a high incidence of polyploidic fertilization force embryologists to fertilize the oocytes prior to cryopreservation in order to form a stable cell that is more likely to survive cryopreservation than the unfertilized oocyte. Currently, women at risk of loss of ovarian function[11-12] or those who wish to quarantine donor oocytes[13] must have the oocytes inseminated, and only fertilized oocytes may currently be cryopreserved.

Research in animals has demonstrated that oocytes and ovarian function can be preserved by cryopreservation and subsequent transfer of ovarian tissue.[14-16] This approach to oocyte and ovarian function preservation in humans may be possible, but only after a significant amount of highly scrutinized research. A recent report of normal fertilization and subsequent development of mature human oocytes that had been cryopreserved and thawed prior to insemination by intracytoplasmic sperm injection offers hope that someday we will be able to cryopreserve unfertilized oocytes.[17]

Fertilization and Early Embryonic Development

Human embryos may be cryopreserved at the pronuclear, two- to eight-cell, or blastocyst stages of development. The stage that leads to the best embryo survival and/or pregnancy rate is difficult to determine due to the variety of embryo cryopreservation and thawing protocols,[18] whether or not embryos are selected for cryopreservation based on progression of development and embryo quality grades (pronuclear vs. cleavage stage embryos),[19-20] and the location to which the embryos are transferred (uterus vs. fallopian tube).[21] The stage of development that is ethically acceptable to suspend in time and perhaps later dispose of the cell(s) will undoubtedly remain a contested issue. Decisions regarding the cryopreserved embryo's ultimate disposition may involve assessment of the cryopreserved tissue's moral status as related to its biology at the time of cryopreservation.

PRONUCLEAR STAGE CRYOPRESERVATION

Fertilization is a process that starts with penetration of a sperm through the zona pellucida and concludes at syngamy when the male and female chromosomes intermingle before the first cell division. The pronuclear stage, sometimes termed the prezygote stage,[22] is recognized as one of the few readily observed markers of the fertilization process. Pronuclei may be observed approximately twelve to twenty hours after oocyte insemination. Each pronuclear envelope contains haploid genetic material from the sperm and oocyte. The pronuclear stage concludes when the membranes disappear and the twenty-three chromatids from each pronucleus assemble and form a spindle. At no time during the one-cell stage do the chromosomes from the two gametes coexist within a nuclear envelope.

Programs that cryopreserve embryos at the pronuclear stage typically cryopreserve all but the two to four embryos to be transferred one to forty-eight hours later. Embryo selection for transfer at the pronuclear stage is random since the morphology of pronuclear stage embryos is unrelated to the embryo's ability to develop and subsequently implant. Postthaw survival of embryos cryopreserved at the pronuclear stage is easily diagnosed by observation of passage through syngamy to the first cleavage. Our experience at the University of Iowa has been that over 85 percent of pronuclear stage embryos survive cryopreservation and thawing.

For persons who are opposed to cryopreservation of cleavage-stage embryos based on religious beliefs or moral views, prezygote or pronuclear stage cryopreservation may be an acceptable method of preserving oocytes and sperm undergoing the process of fertilization. As an example of this approach, the German Embryo Protection Law forbids production of more embryos than can be transferred at one time, with a maximum of three embryos. Since only oocytes that have completed syngamy are recognized as embryos, supernumerary pronuclear stage oocytes or prezygotes may therefore be cryopreserved in order to avoid generation of more than three embryos as defined by the law.[23]

Approximately thirty hours after insemination, the first cell division occurs. The two-cell stage represents the first time that the two sets of genetic material are combined within a nuclear membrane. Some scientists and philosophers have regarded the two-cell stage as the true end of fertilization.[24] Human embryo development is supported by the maternal genome through the second cell division (four-cell stage). Transcriptional activation of the embryonic genome is believed to be associated with significant changes in protein synthesis between the four- and eight-cell stage.[25]

Cryopreservation of early cleavage stage embryos allows laboratory personnel to culture the embryos for twenty-four to forty-eight hours postinsemination prior to cryopreservation. Morphology of cleaved embryos can be assessed, and those with exceptional quality may be preserved for the fresh transfer. The remaining embryos that have demonstrated a normal rate of development and are of good to fair quality may be cryopreserved. Disadvantages associated with cryopreservation of cleavage-stage embryos include a lower postthaw survival rate than with embryos cryopreserved at the pronuclear stage, and postthaw survival is often difficult to determine because living and dying or dead blastomeres may coexist within the zona pellucida.

BLASTOCYST STAGE CRYOPRESERVATION

The blastocyst stage is typically reached six to seven days after oocyte insemination. This stage is characterized by the presence of a single layer of trophoblast cells, a fluid-filled cavity, and an inner cell mass. Researchers have suggested that transfer and cryopreservation of embryos at the later stages of development may lead to higher pregnancy rates than those achieved with earlier stage embryo transfers.[26–27] Beneficial aspects of blastocyst transfers and cryopreservation may include the selection of high quality embryos that have demonstrated good development ability ($<$ 60 percent of all pronuclear stage embryos reach the blastocyst stage), improved synchronization between embryo development and the uterine lining at the time of transfer, and the enhanced implantation rate per blastocyst transferred, which may allow for transfers of one or two embryos, which may reduce the risk of multiple pregnancies.

Moral Status of the Cryopreserved Embryo

Three positions on the moral status of the human embryo arose from discussions of the American Fertility Society's Ethics Committee (the organization is now the American Society for Reproductive Medicine).[28-29] The positions included recognition of the embryo as having the same moral status as any human being, denial of any moral status to the embryo, and a third position which served as an intermediate between the two extremes. The view that cleavage-stage human embryos should be recognized as human beings is based on the following: (1) a unique genotype is established at the conclusion of fertilization regardless of whether the end of fertilization is defined as completion of syngamy or completion of the first cell division; (2) the unique genome is functional (i.e., transcription is taking place) between the four- and eight-cell stage of development; and (3) when provided the appropriate environment, the zygote or cleavage-stage embryo has the potential to develop into a full-term fetus. In contrast, the view that the early human embryo does not have the moral status of a human being can be supported with the following points: (1) embryonic development is supported almost exclusively by the maternal genome through the second cell division; (2) the blastomeres remain totipotent (undifferentiated) through the third cell division;[30] (3) the product of fertilization may not lead to development of an individual due to the fact that only 30–40 percent of early embryos produced in vivo result in live births;[31] and (4) twinning, or the formation of a chimera (fusion of multiple embryos), may occur at any time prior to primitive streak formation (day 14), meaning that the individuality of the embryo is ultimately determined when the primitive streak is formed.

The ethics committee of the American Society for Reproductive Medicine,[28, 29, 32] adopted an intermediate stance on the moral status of prezygotes and early human embryos. The committee grants the prezygote and early human embryo some moral status based on genetic individuality and development potential. Basically, the prezygote or early embryo deserves more respect than somatic or germ cells, but not the respect owed to an individual human being since it may never realize its developmental potential. This view of intermediate moral status, shared by many regulatory agencies and advisory boards, has permitted the practice of in vitro fertilization and human embryo cryopreservation worldwide.

Cryopreserved Embryo Disposition

Once the decision to cryopreserve embryos has been made, patients and infertility treatment programs need to address issues regarding the storage and future use of the embryos. In response to a recent article on posthumous use of sperm and embryos,[33] A. Trounson and K. Dawson stated, "Couples and individuals who use gamete and embryo freezing services must be made fully aware of their rights and responsibilities to issue clear instructions, especially with respect to disposal of frozen embryos and gametes."[34] It is critical that the patients be made aware of their rights and responsibilities prior to initiating treatment in an infertility program. Patients are advised to review all consents prior to enrollment in a treatment program.

Some countries have chosen to manage embryo cryopreservation issues through legislation and/or regulatory commissions.[35] By contrast, assisted reproduction programs in the United States continue to function without federal regulation.[36] Most programs in the United States have based their practices on guidelines provided by the ethics committee of the American Society for Reproductive Medicine,[28, 29, 32] in-house ethics committees and institutional review boards, the values of the communities they serve, and the values of the personnel performing the procedures. The ethics committee of the American Society for Reproductive Medicine suggests that the gamete providers (or those to whom they transfer their gametes) should have primary decisional authority, within the limits set by institutional policies and applicable law.[32] It is assumed that programs tailor their consents to fit the guidelines and/or committees mentioned above, as well as accommodating extraordinary situations that they either anticipate or have previously encountered.

Patients who had their embryos cryopreserved during the early years of many in vitro fertilization programs typically did not have to commit to deciding the ultimate fate of their cryopreserved embryos prior to cryopreservation. This oversight has led to ethical and legal dilemmas for many in vitro fertilization laboratories and patients. Today patients are asked to provide written consent for both embryo cryopreservation and embryo disposition or grant dispositional authority in the event of a variety of situations. Cryopreserved embryo disposition options may or may not include the following: (1) continued storage for mutual benefit of the potential parents; (2) anonymous embryo donation to another infertile couple; (3) donation of the embryos for research approved by an institutional review board; or (4) embryo disposal. If the disposition option(s) offered and designation of dispositional authority are not acceptable to the patients, the patients need to reassess whether or not they wish to proceed with embryo cryopreservation.

Decisions about embryo disposition need to be made prior to embryo cryopreservation. H. W. Jones, Jr., et al.[37] suggest that embryo cryopreservation or cryopreserved embryo storage consent documents address embryo disposition or dispositional authority in the event of any of the following situations: death or disability of one or both of the prospective parents, legal separation or divorce of the prospective parents, limited storage time for these human tissues, the abandonment of the embryos, transfer of custody of the embryos, or mandated decisions about embryo disposition.

DEATH OR DISABILITY OF ONE OR BOTH
OF THE PROSPECTIVE PARENTS

Awareness of the need to address embryo dispositional authority in the event of death of the prospective parents was heightened after the 1983 death of a couple who had cryopreserved embryos in storage.[38] The Rioses died in a plane crash without instructions regarding disposition of the cryopreserved embryos in the event of their death. The situation was further complicated by lack of an heir, absence of a will, a substantial estate, and the fact that the Los Angeles couple had their IVF performed in Australia.

Embryo cryopreservation consent forms usually either grant dispositional authority to the infertility program in the event of death of prospective parents or require the patients to determine the posthumous fate of the embryos prior to cryopreservation. If dispositional authority is assumed by the infertility program, patients should be fully informed of the potential posthumous uses of the embyros, including disposal, research, or donation to an infertile couple. If there is a potential for posthumous transfer of the embryos to any female other than the woman from whom the oocytes were retrieved, all screening required of embryo donors should be completed prior to embryo cryopreservation.

LEGAL SEPARATION OR DIVORCE OF THE PROSPECTIVE PARENTS

Failure to establish dispositional authority in the event of divorce led to the widely publicized embryo custody battle in the divorce case of *Davis v. Davis*.[39] As with posthumous embryo disposition, the ultimate fate of the cryopreserved embryo(s) in the event of divorce should be addressed in the cryopreservation consent document. Programs should use every mechanism possible to confirm that both partners agree to the thawing and transfer of the embryos. Requiring the presence of both partners at the time of cryopreserved embryo transfer or requiring witnessed signatures of both partners on embryo thaw/transfer consent documents is generally recommended.

Dispositional authority in the event of legal separation or divorce may be granted to either the couple or the infertility program. If the couple has dispositional authority, it is recommended that the option for embryo disposition be chosen prior to cryopreservation. If the couple is granted dispositional authority and a disposition option is not chosen prior to embryo cryopreservation, the program should include a statement regarding resolution in the event that the couple fails to agree on the disposition issue. For example, the University of Iowa Embryo Cryopreservation consent document states:

> In the event of divorce during the embryo cryopreservation storage period, the written authorization of both husband and wife is required for disposition and/or transfer of cryopreserved embryos. Specifically, both husband and wife must agree to the transfer, anonymous donation, or early discarding of frozen embryos. Otherwise, in the absence of subsequent mutual agreement cryopreserved embryos will be discarded at the end of the stated storage period [of two years] according to this agreement.[40]

LIMITED CRYOPRESERVED EMBRYO STORAGE TIME

It is important to appreciate the length of time a cryopreserved embryo may be stored without adversely affecting embryo viability. Cryopreserved embryos are typically stored in liquid nitrogen ($-196°C$). Cells stored in temperatures below $-130°C$ lack metabolic activity that could reduce cell viability. Storage below $-130°C$ prevents heat-dependent reactions due to the crystalline state of intra- and intercellular water. As long as the cells are maintained at $-196°C$, the only known potential for embryo damage is degradation of deoxyribonucleic acid (DNA) caused by background radiation. Based on normal background radiation of 0.1 rads/year, it has been predicted that the very sensitive mouse oocyte should maintain its genetic integrity for over 200 years when maintained at $-196°C$.[38]

Situations that could arise if the cryopreserved embryo storage period is not limited include the following: (1) an accumulation of large banks of abandoned embryos; (2) the transfer of embryos to women who are far beyond "normal" reproductive age; and (3) the transfer of embryos from one generation to another. Storage period limitations may refer to the number of years following cryopreservation, the number of years since the patient's most recent transfer, or the age of the prospective mother.

A set number of years addresses the storage facility's need to control the size of its cryopreserved embryo inventory, but it may not best serve the needs of the patient. For example, a storage period of five years may initially seem rather generous, yet our data suggest that some patients may want an even longer period, if given that option. With a 1993 national delivery rate of 20 percent per oocyte retrieval (6,665/33,202), it is reasonable to assume that most couples will have their cryopreserved embryos transferred within two years of cryopreservation.[9] At the University of Iowa 111 patients cryopreserved a total of 739 embryos while undergoing infertility treatment in 1993. Of these, 22 patients who cryopreserved excess embryos in 1993 conceived and delivered babies following transfer of fresh embryos. As of January 1, 1996, 57 of the 111 patients who had cryopreserved embryos in 1993 had thawed 377 of the 739 embryos, which means that almost half of the patients from 1993 had cryopreserved embryos remaining in storage after two years.

If a patient who was fortunate enough to conceive and deliver following her 1993 fresh embryo transfer had sixteen embryos cryopreserved, she still has the potential for up to four additional embryo transfers. While her chances of conceiving after each cryopreserved embryo transfer are low, she may prove to be a rare patient who conceives and delivers after each transfer. A set number of years of storage may not allow a young couple who stored a large number of embryos to realize fully the benefits of a good ovarian stimulation and high embryo quality. If the infertility program has established a storage period based on a limited number of years following cryopreservation (e.g., less than ten), the infertility program may attempt to avoid cryopreservation and storage of large numbers of embryos by limiting the ovarian stimulation and subsequent number of oocytes produced. Alternatively, if the program simply does not wish to store embryos for a long time, it may allow the embryos to be transferred to another storage facility.

The American Society for Reproductive Medicine suggests limiting storage of these tissue samples to "the normal reproductive span of the oocyte donor or only as long as the original objective of the storage procedure is in force."[32] Storage may be limited by either the woman's age or her reproductive capacity. J. A. Robertson[41] argues that a time limit based on women's reproductive capacity may discriminate against a woman who is incapable of gestation and wishes to have the embryos transferred to a gestational surrogate. The same may be said for a storage policy based on a woman's age.

Our program has chosen to limit the storage period to the fiftieth birthday of the embryo recipient. The embryo cryopreservation fee includes two years of storage. At the end of the two years, patients are contacted by certified mail and given embryo disposition options, which include continued storage for a fee. Should the couple fail to respond to reasonable efforts to contact them at the end of the initial two-year storage period, the embryo cryopreservation consent document states that the embryos will be discarded.

EMBRYO ABANDONMENT

Despite the emotional, physical, and financial investment required of couples that have cryopreserved embryos, some couples fail to maintain contact with the embryo storage facility and abandon their embryos. Several programs are now finding that cryopreserved embryos are frequently abandoned by their parents, who simply lose touch with the infertility clinic. For example,

D. M. Saunders et al.[42] attempted to contact 438 couples that had embryos stored at their laboratory in Australia. Many couples (167 couples or 38 percent of them) did not respond. An additional 42 couples (9.6 percent) could not be located, with the result that their embryos were abandoned. As another example, clinicians at the prestigious Bourne Hall Clinic in Cambridge indicate that over 30 percent of the patients who have cryopreserved embryos in their laboratory have completely lost contact with the clinic.[43]

Although the number of patients who fail to maintain contact with the embryo storage facility is small, failure on the part of the fertility program to cover embryo disposition choices or authority in situations of embryo abandonment or unpaid storage fees can lead to significant problems. Robertson states that "no program should discard embryos as abandoned until diligent efforts to locate the depositing couple have been made."[44] How does one define the limits of diligence? The specific routes of attempted contact should be stated in the embryo cryopreservation agreement. Furthermore, if a fee is to be assessed for embryo storage, the extent to which a program will go to collect storage fees prior to the program's assumption of dispositional authority should be stated in either the embryo cryopreservation consent or storage agreement.

TRANSFER OF EMBRYO CUSTODY

For a variety of reasons, some couples may desire that their embryos be sent to another infertility treatment program or storage facility. This practice is widely accepted by some programs and prohibited by others. The University of Iowa Embryo Cryopreservation consent document states:

> Each embryo resulting from the fertilization of the wife's (or donor's) ovum with the husband's or requested donor sperm will be owned by University Hospitals for the mutual benefit of the husband and wife. Cryopreserved embryos will be utilized at this facility and will not be shipped to another facility except [in the event the program closes].[40]

The statement regarding ownership or custody of the embryos was established due to our program's desire to limit transport of embryos in order to avoid the risks associated with transport and the liability risk of shipping the embryos to an unqualified program.

Nevertheless, ethical and legal problems can develop regarding the transfer of embryos. For example, the Jones Institute in Norfolk had intended that all embryos cryopreserved at its facility would also be thawed and transferred there. The Yorks had undergone infertility therapy at the Jones Institute and, upon relocation, requested that their embryos be shipped to a program nearer to their new home. The Jones Institute denied the Yorks' request, and in 1989 the Yorks sued the Jones Institute in federal district court for custody of their embryos and won.[45] The custody was awarded on the grounds that restriction of the embryos to the Jones Institute was not explicitly stated in the consents that the patients signed prior to treatment.

Programs that prohibit transfer of cryopreserved embryos to another facility must clearly state this position in their consent form(s) and also must confirm that the patients are fully aware of this policy prior to embryo cryopreservation. However, programs that generally prohibit cryopreserved embryo transfer to other programs out of concern over the questionable competence of the receiving program may, in some cases, consider laboratory accreditation certificates and infertility registry data to be sufficient evidence that the receiving program is capable of optimizing the patient's chance of conceiving following thawing and transfer of the cryopreserved embryos.

REQUESTED DECISIONS ABOUT EMBRYO
DISPOSITION AFTER TREATMENT

Patients who have not transferred all of their cryopreserved embryos within a specific storage period or have opted to discontinue their efforts at achieving pregnancy through assisted reproductive technologies usually have the authority to determine embryo disposition. Some patients struggle with the decision, while others arrive at their decision prior to embryo cryopreservation. Our program attempted to contact 200 couples by registered mail. These couples had a total of 1,317 cryopreserved embryos that had been cryopreserved prior to January 1, 1994.[46] The couples were asked to commit to one of four embryo disposition options: (1) discard the stored embryos, (2) donate the embryos for research, (3) permit anonymous embryo donation to another couple, or (4) continue storage of the embryos for a fee. The letter stated that failure to return the embryo disposition form would result in embryo discard. A significant number of couples (49 couples or 24.5 percent) received notification, but did not return the embryo disposition form, and 7 couples (3.5 percent) could not be located. Of the remaining couples, 10 couples (5 percent) could not commit to a decision and asked for an extension, 18 couples (9 percent) donated their embryos for research, 26 couples (13 percent) chose anonymous embryo donation to another infertile couple, 36 couples (18 percent) chose to discard, and 54 couples (27 percent) opted to continue storage for future transfers.

We evaluated patient response in relation to the outcome of their treatment cycles: 71 percent of the 200 patients we attempted to contact had a live birth following a previous fresh or frozen embryo transfer. We found that embryo disposition selection was not significantly affected by patient age, number of embryos in storage, length of embryo storage, outcome of the cycle from which the embryos were cryopreserved or other treatment cycles, religion, or source of gametes.

Although it is not statistically significant, it is interesting to note that the patients who specifically chose to discard the stored embryos had experienced a pregnancy rate of 40 percent (10/25 transfers), in comparison with a 100 percent (3/3) clinical pregnancy rate for the couples who donated the embryos for research, a 7 percent (1/15) rate for those who opted for anonymous embryo donation to another couple, a 39 percent (29/75) rate for those who wanted to pay for continued storage, and a 20 percent (9/44) rate for those who chose not to respond. As already stated, the failure of these couples to respond was tantamount to a decision to discard the embryos.

It has been our experience that very few couples seeking in vitro fertilization services question whether or not excess embryos should be cryopreserved. Unfortunately, the emotional, physical, and financial stresses of a cycle of in vitro fertilization usually overshadow thoughts regarding the moral status of the material that is to be cryopreserved or how its disposition will be handled in the future. Nevertheless, all patients having the option of cryopreserving embryos should be counseled by their health care providers before decisions regarding embryo cryopreservation and, if embryos are to be cryopreserved, the disposition of the embryos. Aside from the need to establish embryo disposition plans, couples also need to be aware of the risks associated with the technical aspects of embryo cryopreservation. The more the embryos are handled, the higher the risk of embryo loss due to negligence. Patients also should be fully aware of risks associated with equipment failure, breakage of the straws or vials in which the embryos were cryopreserved, and embryo damage during the cryopreservation and thawing procedures.

Many couples view embryo cryopreservation as a way to maximize their reproductive potential from one cycle of controlled ovarian hyperstimulation. However, family planning, religion, fear of damage to the embryos, and personal values lead some patients to chose to forgo embryo cryopreservation. The individuals who counsel patients on the issue of embryo cryopreservation must be appreciative of all patients' wishes and the values that have led them to their decision.

In summary, developments in assisted reproduction technologies have provided clinicians with many valuable tools for the treatment of infertility. The practice of human in vitro fertilization and embryo cryopreservation is now widespread, representing one particular type of storage of human tissues that differs in kind from all the other types of stored tissue discussed in this volume. While embryo cryopreservation is recognized as one of the giant leaps forward, the large numbers of banked embryos present us with an adverse consequence of our technology. There is no doubt that other problems will arise as programs continue to grow and new technologies are introduced.

Notes

1. A. Trounson and L. Mohr, "Human Pregnancy Following Cryopreservation, Thawing, and Transfer of an 8 Cell Embryo" *Nature* 305 (1983): 707–709.

2. B. J. Van Voorhis, C. H. Syrop, B. D. Allen, A. E. T. Sparks, and D. W. Stovall, "The Efficacy and Cost Effectiveness of Embryo Cryopreservation Compared with Other Assisted Reproductive Techniques," *Fertility and Sterility* 64 (1995): 647–650.

3. X. J. Wang, W. Ledger, D. Payne, R. Jeffrey, and C. D. Matthews, "The Contribution of Embryo Cryopreservation to In-vitro Fertilization/Gamete Intra-fallopian Transfer: 8 Years Experience," *Human Reproduction* 9 (1994): 103–109.

4. J. A. Kahn, V. von Dring, A. Sunde, T. Sørdal, and K. Molne, "The Efficacy and Efficiency of an In-vitro Fertilization Programme Including Embryo Cryopreservation: A Cohort Study," *Human Reproduction* 8 (1993): 247–252.

5. F. Azem, Y. Barak, Y. Yaron, M. R. Peyser, A. Amit, M. P. David, I. Yovel, and J. B. Lessing, "Transfer of Six or More Embryos Improves Success Rates in Patients with Repeated In Vitro Fertilization Failures," *Fertility and Sterility* 63 (1995): 1043–1046.

6. French National IVF Registry (FIVNAT), "Analysis of 1986 to 1990 Data," *Fertility and Sterility* 59 (1993): 587–595.

7. Y. Englert, F. Devreker, E. Bertrand, M. Hannes, C. Rodesch, and M. van den Bergh, "Double Instead of Triple Embryo Transfer as a Prevention of Multiple Pregnancies, in IVF Clinical Results," *Human Reproduction* 8 (Suppl. 1; 1993), abstract 18.

8. M. Nijs, L. Geerts, E. van Roosendaal, G. Segal-Bertin, P. Vanderzwalmen, and R. Schoysman, "Prevention of Multiple Pregnancies in an In Vitro Fertilization Program," *Fertility and Sterility* 59 (1993): 1245–1250.

9. "Assisted Reproductive Technology in the United States and Canada: 1993 Results Generated from the American Society for Reproductive Medicine/Society for Assisted Reproductive Technology Registry," *Fertility and Sterility* 64 (1995): 13–21.

10. J. L. Frederick, T. Ord, L. M. Kettle, S. C. Stone, J. P. Balmeceda, R. H. Asch, "Successful Pregnancy Outcome after Cryopreservation of All Fresh Embryos with Subsequent Transfer into an Unstimulated Cycle," *Fertility and Sterility* 64 (1995): 987–990.

11. C. A. Winkel and G. T. Fossum, "Current Reproductive Technology: Considerations for the Oncologist," *Oncology* 7 (1993): 40–51.

12. J. R. Brown, E. Modell, M. Obasaju, and Y. K. King, "Natural Cycle In-vitro Fertilization with Embryo Cryopreservation Prior to Chemotherapy for Carcinoma of the Breast," *Human Reproduction* 11 (1996): 197–199.

13. F. C. Hamer, G. Horne, E. H. E. Pease, P. L. Matson, and B. A. Lieberman, "The Quarantine of Fertilized Donated Oocytes," *Human Reproduction* 10 (1995): 1194–1196.

14. C. J. Candy, M. J. Wood, and D. G. Whittingham, "Follicular Development in

Cryopreserved Marmoset Ovarian Tissue after Transplantation," *Human Reproduction* 10 (1995): 2334–2338.

15. R. G. Gosden, D. T. Baird, J. C. Wade, and R. Webb, "Restoration of Fertility to Oophorectomized Sheep by Ovarian Autographs Stored at −196°C," *Human Reproduction* 9 (1994): 597–603.

16. R. G. Gosden, M. I. Boulton, K. Grant, and R. Webb, "Follicular Development from Ovarian Xenografts in SCID Mice," *Journal of Reproduction and Fertility* 101 (1994): 619–623.

17. D. A. Gook, M. C. Schiewe, S. M. Osborn, R. H. Asch, R. P. S. Jansen, and W. I. H. Johnston, "Intracytoplasmic Sperm Injection and Embryo Development of Human Oocytes Cryopreserved Using 1,2-Propanediol," *Human Reproduction* 10 (1995): 2637–2641.

18. J. Testart, B. Lassalle, R. Forman, A. Gazengel, J. Belaish-Alart, A. Hazout, J. D. Rainkorn, and R. Frydman, "Factors Influencing the Success of Human Embryo Freezing in an In Vitro Fertilization Program," *Fertility and Sterility* 48 (1987): 107–112.

19. J. Cohen, G. W. DeVane, C. W. Elsner, C. B. Fehilly, H. I. Kort, J. B. Massey, and T. G. Turner, Jr., "Cryopreservation of Zygotes and Early Cleaved Human Embryos," *Fertility and Sterility* 49 (1988): 283–289.

20. C. B. Fehilly, J. Cohen, R. F. Simons, S. B. Fishel, and R. G. Edwards, "Cryopreservation of Cleaving Embryos and Expanded Blastocysts in the Human: A Comparative Study," *Fertility and Sterility* 44 (1985): 638.

21. B. J. Van Voorhis, C. H. Syrop, R. D. Vincent, D. H. Chestnut, A. E. T. Sparks, and F. K. Chapler, "Tubal versus Uterine Transfer of Cryopreserved Embryos: A Prospective Randomized Trail," *Fertility and Sterility* 63 (1995): 578–583.

22. H. W. Jones and C. S. Schrader, "The Process of Human Fertilization: Implications for Moral Status," *Fertility and Sterility* 48 (1987): 189–192.

23. S. Al-Hasani and E. Siebzehnubel, "Frozen Pronuclear Oocytes: Advantages for the Patients," *Human Reproduction* 10 (1995): 3084–3085.

24. H. W. Jones and C. S. Schrader, "And Just What Is a Pre-embryo?" *Fertility and Sterility* 52 (1989): 189–191.

25. P. Braude, V. Bolton, and S. Moore, "Human Gene Expression First Occurs between the Four- and Eight-cell Stages of Preimplantation Development," *Nature* 332 (1988): 459–461.

26. F. Olivennes, A. Hazout, C. Lelaidier, S. Freitas, R. Fanchin, D. de Ziegler, and R. Frydman, "Four Indications for Embryo Transfer at the Blastocyst Stage," *Human Reproduction* 9 (1994): 2367–2373.

27. K. E. Wiemer, B. Dale, Y. Hu, N. Steuerwald, W. S. Maxson, and D. I. Hoffman, "Blastocyst Development in Co-culture: Development and Morphological Aspects," *Human Reproduction* 10 (1995): 3226–3232.

28. Ethics Committee of the American Fertility Society, "Ethical Considerations of the New Reproductive Technologies in Light of Instruction on Respect for Human Life in Its Origin and the Dignity of Procreation Issued by the Congregation for the Doctrine of the Faith," *Fertility and Sterility* 49 (Suppl. 1; 1988): 1S-7S.

29. Ethics Committee of the American Fertility Society, "Ethical Considerations of the New Reproductive Technologies," *Fertility and Sterility* 53 (Suppl. 2; 1990): 31S-36S.

30. J. L. Hall, D. Engel, P. R. Gindoff, G. L. Mottla, and R. J. Stillman, "Experimen-

tal Cloning of Human Polyploid Embryos Using an Artificial Zona Pellucida," *Fertility and Sterility* 60 (Suppl. 1; 1993): 1s.

31. C. J. Roberts and C. R. Lowe, "Where Have All the Conceptions Gone?" *Lancet* 1 (1975): 498.

32. Ethics Committee of the American Fertility Society, "Ethical Considerations of Assisted Reproductive Technology," *Fertility and Sterility* 62 (Suppl. 2; 1994): 29S–34S.

33. E. Corrigan, S. E. Mumford, and M. G. R. Hull, "Posthumous Storage and Use of Sperm and Embryos: Survey of Opinion of Treatment Centers," *British Medical Journal* 313 (1996): 24.

34. A. Trounson and K. Dawson, "Storage and Disposal of Embryos and Gametes," *British Medical Journal* 313 (1996): 1–2.

35. "International Overview of IVF Regulations," in Jennifer Gunning and Veronica English, eds., *Human In Vitro Fertilization* (Vermont: Dartmouth Publishing Company, 1993), pp. 143–179.

36. H. W. Jones, Jr., "The Time Has Come," *Fertility and Sterility* 65 (1996): 1090–1092.

37. H. W. Jones, Jr., "Cryopreservation and Its Problems," *Fertility and Sterility* 53 (1990): 780–784.

38. C. Wood, B. Downing, A. Trounson, and P. Rogers, "Clinical Implications of Developments in In Vitro Fertilization," *British Journal of Medicine* 289 (1984): 978–980.

39. *Davis v. Davis*, 842 S.W.2d 588 (Tenn. 1992).

40. Center for Advanced Reproductive Care, University of Iowa, "Embryo Cryopreservation Consent Document," originally approved for use in April 1987.

41. J. A. Robertson, "Ethical and Legal Issues in Cryopreservation of Human Embryos," *Fertility and Sterility* 47 (1987): 371–381.

42. D. M. Saunders, M. C. Bowman, A. Grierson, and F. Garner, "Frozen Embryos: Too Cold to Touch?" *Human Reproduction* 10 (1995): 3081–3082.

43. P. R. Brindsden, S. M. Avery, S. Marcus, and M. C. MacNamee, "Frozen Embryos: Decision Time in the UK," *Human Reproduction* 10 (1995): 3083–3084.

44. J. A. Robertson, "Legal Troublespots in Assisted Reproduction," *Fertility and Sterility* 65 (1996): 11–12.

45. *York v. Jones*, 717 F. Supp. 421 (E.D. Va 1989).

46. C. H. Syrop, A. E. T. Sparks, B. J. Van Voorhis, S. J. Hahn, J. R. Kantamneni, and D. W. Stovall, "Embryo Adoption and Embryo Research: Will Patients Donate Their Embryos?" *Fertility and Sterility* 64 (1995): 208s.

Use of Stored Tissue Samples for Genetic Research in Epidemiologic Studies

Karen K. Steinberg, Eric J. Sampson,
Geraldine M. McQuillan, and Muin J. Khoury

Advances in genetic technology, such as the polymerase chain reaction (PCR)[1] and the work of the Human Genome Project to map and sequence the human genome,[2-4] are expediting our understanding of the genetic determinants of common disease. For example, better understanding of genetic factors is important in determining susceptibility to infectious agents such as HIV,[5] and in identifying populations who are at risk for cancer because of exposure to environmental hazards such as cigarette smoke and aniline dyes.[6-9]

DNA is now being used in epidemiologic investigations to study genetic risk factors.[10] Genetic risk factors include rare gene mutations such as the BRCA1 mutation, which confers high risk for breast or ovarian cancer,[11-12] as well as genetic polymorphisms, such as the polymorphic genes that code for carcinogen-metabolizing enzymes that affect the way people process carcinogens, thereby increasing or decreasing their risk for sporadic forms of cancer.[13]

Because of PCR and other new technologies that have become a part of routine molecular methods in the last decade, specimens other than fresh, whole blood can be used for DNA analysis, in many cases allowing researchers, for the first time, to analyze specimens collected in the field.[14] In fact, all nucleated cells, including blood cells and cells from hair follicles, buccal swabs, and urine specimens, are suitable specimens for DNA analysis.[15-22] This ease of accessibility for the study of DNA and advances in DNA technology give genetic risk factors the potential to increase the precision of risk assessment in public health investigations.

As often occurs with technologic advances, however, DNA technology has developed faster than our understanding of all the attendant risks or our ability to protect the public from these risks. The Public Health Service has a special responsibility to be vigilant and cautious in the use of this technology when collecting specimens from people as part of public health practice. In this essay we discuss the specific experience of the Centers for Disease Control and Prevention (CDC) with the Third National Health and Nutrition Examination Survey (NHANES III) DNA Bank to illustrate the ethical and social issues that can arise during the creation of DNA banks and how the CDC, with others, addressed these issues.

NHANES is a family of surveys that the National Center for Health Statistics began conducting in 1966. The NHANES program has four main objectives: (1) to estimate the prevalence of common diseases and risk factors for those diseases in the U.S. population; (2) to detect trends for diseases and risk factors; (3) to help explain the causes and natural history of diseases; and (4) to provide normal values for the U.S. population.[23-27]

NHANES III serves as an example of a large survey in which specimens were stored for later use to test new hypotheses about pathophysiology and risk factors for disease. The NHANES DNA Bank, which was established as part of NHANES III, includes uncultured mononuclear cells stored in liquid nitrogen from 19,553 study participants and immortalized lymphoblastoid cell lines from 8,532 participants.

Though an extensive consent form signed by participants in the survey included a statement telling them that a portion of their blood would be frozen and used for future research, specific mention of genetic testing was not included. Even though the NHANES III consent document conformed to federal regulations[28] and was standard for the time that it was written, the CDC decided to review the consent form in light of the potential for using stored specimens for genetic research.

To address issues relating to informed consent and genetic testing, the CDC drew on the resources of the National Center for Human Genome Research (NCHGR; renamed the National Human Genome Research Institute or NHGRI in 1997) through its Ethical, Legal, and Social Implications (ELSI) Branch. In July 1994 the CDC and the NCHGR sponsored a workshop addressing issues of informed consent for genetic research on stored tissue samples at which handling of the NHANES III DNA specimens was specifically discussed. In a subsequent article based on the dialogue that occurred during and after the workshop,[29] some of the workshop participants formulated these recommendations: (1) informed consent is required for all genetic research using linkable samples unless conditions of the federal regulations for limitation or waiver of this requirement[30] are met; (2) informed consent should not be required for genetic research using anonymous samples but may be considered appropriate if identifiers are to be removed from currently identifiable samples; and (3) institutional review boards (IRBs) could usefully review all protocols that propose to use tissue samples for genetic research.

With regard to NHANES III, the consent document did not discuss genetic testing, and conditions for waiver of informed consent were not met. According to recommendation 1, linked testing could be done only if research participants were recontacted and gave their informed consent. Given the number of participants involved and the geographic distribution, recontacting them would be a complex, expensive, and time-consuming task. In the interim, according to recommendation 2, "anonymized" testing could be considered in the current NHANES III situation. The American Society of Human Genetics distinguishes anonymous from "anonymized" specimens.[31] Anonymous specimens are biological materials originally collected without identifiers and are impossible to link to their sources. Anonymized specimens are biologic materials that were initially identified but have subsequently been irreversibly stripped of all identifiers and are impossible to link to their sources.

Participants in the CDC/NCHGR workshop noted that testing of "anonymized" specimens is permissible under federal regulations, but recommended that IRBs consider the following points during their assessment of proposals to anonymize samples: (1) whether the information can be obtained in a manner that allows individuals to consent, (2) whether the proposed research is scientifically sound, (3) how difficult it would be to recontact research participants, (4) whether the samples are finite, and (5) how the availability of effective medical interventions affects the appropriateness of pursuing anonymous research.

After carefully considering the recommendations of the workshop and the concept of anonymizing NHANES III tissue samples, the NHANES IRB concluded that it was appropriate to anonymize the samples.

Much of the difficulty involved in the general issue of informed consent for genetic testing relates to the basic philosophical issue of whether DNA testing is different from other forms of testing. G. J. Annas [32] cited three characteristics supposedly unique to DNA testing: DNA testing (1) provides a future diary of the patient's health, (2) gives information on other family members, and (3) has a history of misuse. Although these three characteristics are usually valid with regard to testing for highly penetrant mutations associated with serious diseases, examples can be given of other forms of testing that have the same characteristics.

Furthermore, for DNA testing that does not identify high-risk, high-penetrance mutations, the relevance of these distinguishing characteristics is even less clear. For example, many genes are present in two or more alternate forms in populations. Variation may be benign, such as the variation that produces differences in eye color, or variation may influence risk for disease, such as the differences that carcinogen-metabolizing enzymes have on cancer susceptibility. These characteristics are less of a factor in studies of genetic variations that increase the risk for disease only slightly. The altered risk for disease is similar to that associated with well-characterized risk factors, such as cholesterol.

Clearly, no generalizations can accurately characterize all DNA tests, and each situation must be considered carefully. Testing of identifiable specimens for relatively benign polymorphisms that have a small impact on risk for disease (with risk depending on other genes as well as environmental factors) should entail less risk for loss of insurance, psychological distress, or social stigmatization than testing for the genetic mutations that will almost ensure that a person will develop a serious disease. Therefore, the requirements for pretest and posttest counseling, as well as for other safeguards, should be greater for tests for these more risk-laden mutations.

Since the recommendations of the CDC/NCHGR workshop were published, at least two professional groups have written guidelines for genetic testing of stored tissue samples,[31, 33] and a first step toward insurance reform has been taken.[34]

Because many issues surrounding informed consent for genetic testing remain unresolved, the NHANES III DNA specimens will only be provided for anonymized research at this time. By using this approach, genetic material from this representative sample of the U.S. population will be made available to the research community for important research into the role of genes in health and disease.

The goal of public health practice is to take necessary actions to improve the health of populations. However, because of a lack of effective interventions for genetic disorders, classical medical genetics has had almost no role in public health practice. A further barrier to the use of genetics in public health settings has been the abuse associated with past use of eugenics and the concept of reducing the carrier rate of genetic disorders as a means to improving the health of populations. There is also a keen awareness that the measures needed to provide protection from insurance and job discrimination have not kept pace with the rapid advances in genetic technology. But as interventions become available, methods for detecting genetic disorders *are* being used increasingly in public health settings. Population screening of newborns for disorders such as phenylketonuria (PKU) is considered by many professionals to be an example of the use of genetics in a successful public health intervention. As more interventions for preventing the adverse outcomes associated with genetic disorders become available, the pressure will grow to incorporate what is known about genetic risk factors into public health investigations and disease prevention efforts.

Human genetics is not a new discipline in the public health arena. Numerous CDC programs have a significant genetic component. For example, in the area of public health assessment, the CDC has programs for hemophilia surveillance and birth defects monitoring. In the area of genetic epidemiology, the CDC collaborates with outside institutions to study the genetic bases for birth defects and chronic and infectious diseases, including neural tube defects, osteoporosis, and acquired immunodeficiency syndrome (AIDS). As already indicated, the CDC has also established a unique, nationally representative resource, the NHANES III DNA Bank, to study genetic determinants of common diseases. In the area of quality assurance, the CDC, in partnership with the Health Resources and Services Administration (HRSA), conducts the National Newborn Screening Quality Assurance Program. With regard to health interventions, the CDC supports the National Program to Prevent Iron Overload and evaluates the reduction of morbidity following newborn screening for sickle cell disease. In the area of communication and information dissemination, the CDC is developing a CD-ROM to educate health care professionals about the genetic basis of cancer and has published statements on HLA-H and hemochromatosis. Perhaps most importantly, the CDC is playing a leadership role in national discussions on the ethical use of genetics in public health, for example, by co-sponsoring the conference discussed earlier.

In light of CDC's programs that use genetic information to prevent morbidity and mortality, the technologic progress in molecular genetics, and the uncertainties about the ethical use of genetic information, CDC director Dr. David Satcher mandated in the fall of 1996 that the CDC-wide Task Force on Genetics in Disease Prevention create a strategic plan to determine the appropriate and ethical role for genetics in disease prevention at the CDC. After receiving the input of internal and external constituents including scientists, public health professionals, ethicists, lawyers, consumers of genetic and public health services, and representatives from industry and academia, the task force presented the draft strategic plan in the spring of 1997. The plan, a conceptual framework for a public health program in genetics that emphasizes the ethical and safe use of genetic technology, includes public health assessment, evaluation of genetic testing, and communication. With this plan in place, the CDC looks forward to playing a leadership role in the evolving use of genetic risk factors, which includes genetic testing of stored tissue samples, to increase the precision of risk assessment in public health research.

Notes

1. R. K. Saiki, T. L. Bugawan, G. T. Horn, K. B. Mullis, and H. A. Erlich, "Analysis of Enzymatically Amplified β-globin and HLA-DQ α DNA with Allele-specific Oligonucleotide Probes," *Nature* 324 (1986): 163–165.

2. V. A. McKusick, "Mapping and Sequencing the Human Genome," *New England Journal of Medicine* 320 (1989): 910–915.

3. J. D. Watson, "The Human Genome Project: Past, Present and Future," *Science* 248 (1990): 44–49.

4. D. L. Ellsworth, D. M. Hallman, and E. Boerwinkle, "Impact of the Human Genome Project on Epidemiologic Research," *Epidemiologic Reviews* 19 (1997), in press.

5. J. J. Just, "Genetic Predisposition to HIV-1 Infection and Acquired Immune Deficiency Virus Syndrome: A Review of the Literature Examining Associations with HLA," *Human Immunology* 44 (1995): 156–169.

6. I. Stucker, J. Cosme, P. Laurent, S. Cenee, P. Beaune, J. Bignon, A. Depierre, B. Milleron, and D. Hemon, "CYP2D6 Genotype and Lung Cancer Risk according to Histologic Type and Tobacco Exposure," *Carcinogenesis* 16 (1995): 2759–2764.

7. D. A. Bell, C. L. Thompson, J. Taylor, R. Miller, F. Perera, L. L. Hsieh, and G. W. Lucier, "Genetic Monitoring of Human Polymorphic Cancer Susceptibility Genes by Polymerase Chain Reaction: Application to Glutathione Transferase Mu," *Environmental Health Perspectives* 98 (1992): 113–117.

8. F. F. Kadlubar and A. F. Badawi, "Genetic Susceptibility and Carcinogen-DNA Adduct Formation in Human Urinary Bladder Carcinogenesis," *Toxicology Letter* 82–83 (1995): 627–632.

9. C. B. Ambrosone, J. L. Freudenheim, S. Graham, J. R. Marshall, J. E. Vena, J. R. Brasure, A. M. Michalek, R. Laughlin, T. Nemoto, K. A. Gillenwater, A. M. Harrington, and P. G. Shields, "Cigarette Smoking, N-acetyltransferase 2 Genetic Polymorphisms, and Breast Cancer Risk," *JAMA* 276 (1996): 1494–1501.

10. National Center for Health Statistics, "Plan and Operation of the Third National Health and Nutrition Examination Survey, 1988–94," *Vital and Health Statistics*, series 1 (1994).

11. Y. Miki, J. Swensen, D. Shattuck-Eidens, P. A. Futreal, K. Harshman, S. Tavtigian, Q. Liu, C. Cochran, L. M. Bennett, and W. Ding et al., "A Strong Candidate for the Breast and Ovarian Cancer Susceptibility Gene BRCA1," *Science* 266 (1994): 66–71.

12. B. Newman, R. D. Millikan, and M. C. King, "Genetic Epidemiology of Breast and Ovarian Cancers," *Epidemiologic Reviews* 19 (1997), in press.

13. D. W. Nebert, R. A. McKinnon, and A. Puga, "Human Drug-metabolizing Enzyme Polymorphisms: Effects on Risk of Toxicity and Cancer," *DNA Cell Biology* 15 (1996): 273–280.

14. M. A. Austin, J. M. Ordovas, J. H. Eckfeldt, R. Tracy, E. Boerwinkle, J.-M. Lalouel, and M. Printz, "Guidelines of the National Heart, Lung, and Blood Institute Working Group on Blood Drawing, Processing, and Storage for Genetic Studies," *American Journal of Epidemiology* 144 (1996): 437–441.

15. R. Decorte and J. J. Cassiman, "Detection of Amplified VNTR Alleles by Direct Chemiluminescence: Application to the Genetic Identification of Biological Samples in Forensic Cases," *EXS* 58 (1991): 371–390.

16. R. Higuchi, C. H. von Beroldingen, G. F. Sensabaugh, and H. A. Erlich, "DNA Typing from Single Hairs," *Nature* 332 (1988): 543–546.

17. C. R. Newton, C. Summers, L. E. Heptinstall, J. R. Lynch, R. S. Finniear, D. Ogilvie, J. C. Smith, and A. F. Markham, "Genetic Analysis in Cystic Fibrosis Using the Amplification Refractory Mutation Systems (ARMS): the J3.11 MMPI Polymorphism," *Journal of Medical Genetics* 28 (1991): 248–251.

18. D. M. Thomson, N. N. Brown, and A. E. Clague, "Routine Use of Hair Root

or Buccal Swab Specimens for PCR Analysis: Advantages over Using Blood," *Clinica Chimica Acta* 207 (1992): 169–174.

19. B. Richards, J. Skolestsky, A. P. Shuber, R. Balfour, R. C. Stern, H. L. Dorkin, R. B. Parad, D. Witt, and K. W. Klinger, "Multiplex PCR Amplification from the CRTR Gene Using DNA Prepared from Buccal Brushes Swabs," *Human Molecular Genetics* 2 (1993): 159–163.

20. M. S. Hayney, G. A. Poland, and J. J. Lipsky, "A Noninvasive 'Swish and Spit' Method for Collecting Nucleated Cells for HLA Typing by PCR in Population Studies," *Human Heredity* 46 (1996): 108–111.

21. E. R. B. McCabe, S. Z. Huang, W. K. Seltzer, and M. L. Law, "DNA Microextraction from Dried Blood Spots on Filter Paper Blotters: Potential Applications to Newborn Screening," *Human Genetics* 75 (1987): 213–216.

22. D. C. Jinks, M. Minter, D. A. Tarver, M. Vanderford, J. F. Hejtmancik, and E. R. B. McCabe, "Molecular Genetic Diagnosis of Sickle Cell Disease Using Dried Blood Specimens on Blotters Used for Newborn Screening," *Human Genetics* 81 (1989): 363–366.

23. National Center for Health Statistics, "Plan and Initial Program of the Health Examination Survey," *Vital and Health Statistics*, series 1 (4) (1965).

24. H. W. Miller, National Center for Health Statistics, "Plan and Operation of the National Health and Nutrition Examination Survey, United States, 1971–73," *Vital and Health Statistics*, series 1, 10a and 10b (1973).

25. A. Engel, R. S. Murphy, K. Maurer, and E. Collins, National Center for Health Statistics, "Plan and Operation of the HANES I Augmentation Survey of Adults 25–74 Years, United States, 1974–75," *Vital and Health Statistics* series 1, 14 (1978).

26. K. Mauer, National Center for Health Statistics, "Plan and Operation of the Hispanic Health and Nutrition Examination Survey, 1982–83," *Vital and Health Statistics*, series 1, 19 (1985).

27. National Center for Health Statistics, "Plan and Operation of the Third National Health and Nutrition Examination Survey, 1988–94," *Vital and Health Statistics*, series 1, 32 (1994).

28. L. B. Andrews, J. E. Fullarton, N. A. Holtzman, and A. Motulsky, eds., *Assessing Genetic Risk: Implications for Health and Social Policy* (Washington, D.C.: Washington National Academic Press, 1996), pp. 116–145.

29. E. W. Clayton, K. K. Steinberg, M. J. Khoury, E. Thomson, L. Andrews, M. J. Kahn, L. M. Kopelman, and J. O. Weiss, "Informed Consent for Genetic Research on Stored Tissue Samples," *JAMA* 274 (1995): 1786–1792.

30. 45 CFR §46 (1994).

31. ASGH Report, "Statement on Informed Consent for Genetic Research," *American Journal of Human Genetics* 59 (1996): 471–474.

32. G. J. Annas, "Privacy Rules for DNA Databanks: Protecting Coded 'Future Diaries,'" *JAMA* 270 (1993): 2346–2350.

33. Storage of Genetics Materials Committee, American College of Medical Genetics, "ACMG Statement on Storage and Use of Genetics Materials," *American Journal of Human Genetics* 57 (1995): 1499–1500.

34. U.S. Public Law 104: Health Insurance Reform Act of 1995.

Informed Consent, Stored Tissue Samples, and the Human Genome Diversity Project: Protecting the Rights of Research Participants

Henry T. Greely

The proposed Human Genome Diversity Project (HGDP) is an ambitious effort to create a reference library of the genetic diversity of the whole human species. One important aspect of that reference library will be stored samples of human tissue that can be the subjects of DNA analysis. In that respect, the HGDP, which has already seen more than its share of controversy,[1] may become entangled in the ongoing dispute over informed consent for the use of stored tissue samples.[2]

It should not. Although the HGDP does hope to have a large, generally accessible repository of human DNA samples, the ethical guidelines for informed consent proposed by some parts of the HGDP are a sensitive effort to protect the rights of participants in its research, as individuals and as populations. The draft Model Ethical Protocol for Collecting DNA Samples[3] proposes both substantive and procedural safeguards for research participants and their tissue samples. Those safeguards, if implemented, should eliminate most concerns about informed consent for stored tissues samples collected for the HGDP. Difficult questions do remain, however, concerning access of the HGDP to samples collected earlier.

This essay describes the proposed HGDP, discussing the ethical concerns the project has raised and its responses to them. It also describes the specific role of stored tissue samples in the HGDP and analyzes the appropriateness of the project's use of stored tissue samples, both newly collected and previously saved, given the ethical guidelines it has proposed. Six years after it was first proposed, nothing is certain about the still-unfunded HGDP, but its use of newly collected stored tissue samples should not be problematic.

The Human Genome Diversity Project

The Human Genome Project plans to map and sequence the 3 billion nucleotide pairs of the DNA forming "the" human genome. But humans vary genetically, with an average difference between any two individuals on the order of one in every thousand nucleotide pairs of DNA (0.1 percent) out of

3 billion pairs. As a result, all people are different genetically, and there exist over 5 billion human genomes, not just one. This vast diversity, both the result and the cause of human evolution, will *not* be studied by the Human Genome Project, but is the *raison d'être* of an independent project, complementary to it — the HGDP. This section briefly explores the reasons for the HGDP, its planned activities, its history, and its current organization and status.

The study of human genetic variation is not new; it has been going on for almost eighty years and has generated a considerable volume of data.[4] In recent years, the analytic techniques of molecular genetics have made it possible to analyze DNA directly, rather than its products. In addition, geneticists and mathematicians have combined to produce a rigorous mathematical theory of evolution. This combination of new ways to analyze genetic material and a theoretical model to apply to that material can provide new information about human population genetics of unprecedented width, depth, and accuracy — *if* DNA is available from an appropriate sample of the world's population.

Improved information about human population genetics can be important for at least four reasons. First, thus far the vast majority of detailed research into human genetics has been done with Europeans or North Americans of European descent and so has omitted the 80 percent of the world's population that is not of European ancestry. It is fundamentally unfair to the majority of humanity to describe "the" human genome without including a representative sample of all humans. Second, studying human genetic diversity will help us to understand better the workings of evolution in humans, including the ways in which culture influences evolution. Third, greater knowledge of human genetic diversity will improve medicine, both because it will advance the study of those genetic diseases found largely in non-European populations and because genetic variation is basic to better understanding of a host of diseases found in all peoples. Finally, studying human diversity will help us uncover our shared human history. Genetic results, when interpreted along with evidence from anthropology, archaeology, history, linguistics, and other fields, will help map human migrations and expansions in prehistoric times.

The HGDP will collect DNA samples from participating donors all over the world and store them in both physical and digital repositories. The samples and data will be generally accessible to scientists and scholars. There will be three major phases for the implementation of the HGDP: sampling DNA, storing the samples, and analyzing them. The three phases can and should overlap, because the information gained in each phase can influence the way in which the project is continued.

The HGDP wants to collect a *representative* sample of human genetic variation. In initial discussions of the project, two approaches were debated: a purely geographic sampling of individuals and a sampling of populations. In reality, great flexibility in sampling will also be needed in order to economize on effort and cost. Some samples will be acquired randomly within a particular geographical area; some will be samples collected to answer specific medical, historical, genetic, or anthropological questions; and some will be collected from particular human populations. All sampling, of course, will depend crucially on the willingness of groups and individuals to participate in the project.

The project plans to store two types of DNA samples from participating individuals or groups, on whatever basis they are selected. Some participants from each sample would be asked to give a small amount of blood, 5 to 20 ml per person, to be preserved as cell lines obtained from B lymphoblasts. This has the advantage of providing a potentially unlimited amount of DNA for future study; it has the disadvantage of being expensive. Most of the physical samples would not be transformed into cell lines. Instead, DNA directly extracted from blood, saliva, mouth scrapings, or hair roots would be stored and used directly or amplified by methods under study. The project would like ultimately to have DNA from cell lines for at least 10,000 people and DNA from other sources for at least 100,000 people. This would provide a cell line from about one person out of every 500,000 and a DNA sample from one person out of every 50,000 in the world.

HGDP samples will be stored in facilities that can preserve them carefully, generally through freezing with liquid nitrogen, and that will make them available to researchers, while protecting the donors' identities. Central facilities will be very useful, but some of the storage will also be done in repositories where the samples are collected. Stored samples will be available for analysis by researchers anywhere in the world. For homogeneity and efficiency, it is essential that practically all samples collected be tested for a large, standard, and uniformly assayed battery of DNA polymorphisms. This first-level analysis should be done as part of the project, with the results to be generally available quickly through a computerized database. Individual researchers could then test samples for different polymorphisms, depending on the questions they are interested in. Their results should also be entered in the database.

The HGDP was first suggested in print in 1991,[5] and shortly thereafter the Human Genome Organization (HUGO) appointed a committee to study the idea. After several planning workshops funded by the United States National Science Foundation (NSF), National Institutes of Health (NIH), and Department of Energy, the project was formally organized at an international meeting at Alghero, Sardinia, in September 1993. In January 1994 it was formally adopted by HUGO.

Currently, the HGDP consists entirely of an international executive committee and regional committees for Europe, China, and North America, with other committees being formed. The regional committees, made up of researchers from the geographical regions who work within those regions, are to be the project's operating units; the international executive committee is to provide coordination, guidance, and some overall standards for how the work should proceed. Both the regional and the international committees are, at this point, engaged largely in seeking funding and planning the implementation of the project. No DNA collection is going on now as a formal part of the HGDP, although related projects have started in Europe, with European Union funding, and in China. Both of those projects may eventually become associated with the HGDP.

Moving the project from planning to implementation has proven more difficult than expected. Part of the problem has been financial; budgets for science have not been overflowing in the past few years and new projects of any sort have faced particularly high hurdles. Another part, however, has been an unexpected degree of political opposition to the project from organizations purporting to speak for indigenous peoples. Several such organizations have attacked the project, arguing that it is yet another form of oppression and exploitation by the dominant culture against indigenous peoples.[6] Over the past few years, the project has defined its aims and methods more clearly in an effort to exclude such exploitation, in part as a salutory result of this opposition. Those changes have not mollified its most vocal opponents.[7] Nevertheless, the project continues to search for funding.

The project has estimated that it could collect, preserve, and analyze about 500 different human populations around the world for about $25 to $35 million over five to seven years — about 1 percent of the total amount spent on the Human Genome Project. The U.S. government, as the world's largest single funding source for science, is an obvious source of funding, but, although the HGDP has been mentioned specifically in the administration's budget proposals for the NSF for the last three fiscal years, no substantive funding followed. In the spring of 1997 the NSF did award grants totally about $600,000 for pilot studies in human genetic diversity. Those grants went to projects that explored either the technical problems of preserving DNA samples or the ethical and legal issues raised by the project.[8]

Perhaps more importantly, the National Research Council (NRC), with funding from NSF and NIH, appointed a committee to study the HGDP. The NRC Committee, chaired by Dr. Jack Schull, began meeting in April 1996; its report was due in the summer of 1997. Members of the project expect a favorable report, which they hope will lead to significant federal support. A negative report may well end the HGDP, at least as a global project.

Ethical Issues Raised by the HGDP and Its Responses

The ethical, legal, and social issues raised by the HGDP were first addressed in a planning workshop held in Bethesda, Maryland, at the NIH on February 17, 1993. That workshop, which I organized, identified three main classes of issues: informed consent, property, and racism. That classification remains accurate.

The informed consent issues have focused largely on two points. First, there has been some question whether research participants, particularly those from populations far removed from modern science, could understand the project sufficiently to give truly informed consent. Second, some persons have questioned whether consent should be sought from the individual, the group, or both.

The property issues revolve around the tissue samples that HGDP will collect. Some of the concerns have focused on the patenting of cell lines or sequences derived from the project; others have concerned the commercial uses of such material, whether patented or not.

Any examination of the genetics of populations raises the specter of racism. It has proven all too easy for scientists and laypersons to slip from the existence of statistical differences in the genetic variation of populations to the idea that some populations — almost always their own — are genetically "superior." Some have feared that the project, by even looking at differences in the genetic variation of populations, would reinforce the idea that there are meaningful genetic differences between human populations.

These ethical issues have been addressed by three bodies involved with the HGDP: the full HGDP itself at its organizational meeting in September 1993; the Ethical, Legal, and Social Implications (ELSI) Committee of HUGO in early 1996; and the North American Regional Committee of the HGDP. The guidelines set out by each of those bodies are discussed below.[9]

The HGDP addressed some of these issues at its organizational meeting at Alghero, Sardinia, in 1993.[10] By consensus, the assembled group agreed that informed consent was absolutely critical to participation in the project. It stressed that the project would take appropriate action to protect the privacy of those who participated, would seek no commercial benefit from the materials it collected, and would do everything it could to ensure that, should those materials have financial value, a fair share of that value would return to the participating populations.

HUGO has an international committee on the ethical, legal, and social implications of genetics. In late 1995 this ELSI Committee proposed a set of guidelines for genetics research,[11] which the HUGO Council adopted as its policy in March 1996.[12] HUGO intends this statement to guide the HGDP, the Human Genome Project, and other work in human genetics. According to the statement, the HUGO-ELSI Committee bases its recommendations on the following four principles:

recognition that the human genome is part of the common heritage of humanity;
adherence to international norms of human rights;
respect for the values, traditions, culture, and integrity of participants; and
acceptance and upholding of human dignity and freedom.

The statement lays out ten "commandments" for genomic researchers, built around the following concepts:

1. scientific competence;
2. accurate and understandable communication between researchers and research participants;
3. consultation with potential participants before research starts;
4. informed decisions to consent to participate;
5. respect for any choices made by participants with regard to storage or other uses of materials or information taken or derived from them;
6. confidentiality of genetic information;
7. the importance of continued cooperation and collaboration between and among participating individuals, populations, and researchers;
8. disclosure and avoidance of actual or potential conflicts of interest;
9. prohibition of undue inducements to participate; and
10. continual review, oversight, and monitoring of research.

The Alghero principles and the HUGO statement provide a useful general framework for the ethical implementation of the HGDP, but the actual guidelines concerning the collection and use of HGDP materials necessarily must be much more detailed. Before the project is implemented, the HGDP's International Executive Committee will have to adopt a minimum level of detailed ethical guidelines for all regions participating in the project, but it has not yet acted. Its North American Regional Committee, however, has written a proposed Model Ethical Protocol, as previously mentioned.[13]

The Model Protocol sets out the current thinking of the North American Regional Committee on the ethical issues raised by the process of collecting DNA samples. Among other topics, it discusses how to approach populations that might participate in the research, the process of seeking both individual and collective informed consent, the provision of benefits (including possibly medical services) to the participating populations, protecting individual and group privacy and confidentiality, combating racism, and providing the population with control over the uses of the tissue samples and information it shares with the project. The overall aim of the protocol is to encourage researchers and participating populations to act as partners in uncovering information about both the population and our entire human species.[14]

The provisions of the Model Protocol that are most relevant to the issues of stored tissue samples are discussed below, but it may be useful to highlight the two most important innovations it proposes. First, the Model Protocol requires that, where research is being done with communities having a strong cultural identity and an internal structure of authority, researchers obtain not only the informed consent of individual participants, but also the informed consent of populations.[15] Those communities might include linguistic, ethnic, or even religious groups. They certainly would encompass most Native American populations, at least in the United States and Canada, where tribes and their governments usually have official status.

This group consent would be sought from whatever legal or social authorities were appropriate in an individual population's culture. Although this kind of collective consent has long been, as a practical matter, a de facto requirement for many kinds of anthropological or epidemiological studies, the Model Protocol is the first document to hold that it can be an ethical requirement. Of course, even in North America much HGDP research will not involve collections from such culturally defined populations, but will involve broad, diffuse populations where group consent is neither feasible nor important to the group. But where it does involve culturally defined populations, the group should be treated as a research subject just like the individual group members whose DNA is analyzed.

The second innovation in the Model Protocol relates to the first — the participating population would not only have to consent to its participation in the project, but could control how its materials and information were used.[16] During the process of group informed consent, the population would be given the opportunity to limit or condition the uses made of the tissue samples or cell lines it contributed and information derived from them. The population might choose to allow the patenting of "inventions" derived from its materials or forbid it; it might allow commercial use of its materials or information obtained from them, ban such use, or require compensation for such use.

The population's choices would be documented as part of the informed consent process. Then samples or data from the HGDP repositories would only be released to researchers who have bound themselves by contract, "through materials transfer agreements" or "database access agreements," to abide by the limitations set by each participating population with respect to each sample. These contracts could be enforced by the populations or by the HGDP on their behalf; at the very least, they would "cloud the title" to any product derived from HGDP work enough to force any company to negotiate with the population.

Stored Tissue Samples in the HGDP

The HGDP anticipates creating one or more repositories of tissue samples, as well as one or more databases containing information derived from those tissue samples. This section spells out the HGDP's plans for those resources in more detail, discussing the nature of the physical repositories for HGDP samples, the database to be associated with the repositories, protections for the confidentiality of research participants, and the extent of access to the samples and data.

As indicated earlier, the project expects to collect and preserve two kinds of samples from participating populations. Some blood from each population will be transformed into cell lines to provide potentially unlimited quantities of DNA. Far more samples will be taken and not transformed, but kept as limited quantities of DNA. These samples may include DNA derived from blood, cheek scrapings, hair roots, or other tissues or may just be the sampled tissues themselves, without the preparation of DNA from them.

The number of repositories for HGDP materials remains unsettled. There are some advantages to having a single storage facility. Having one facility would make it easier to control how the samples were processed and stored, as well as ensuring uniformity in how the samples were provided to interested researchers. On the other hand, distributed regional storage facilities have several advantages. They place samples physically closer to many researchers. If located in developing countries, they may provide an impetus for technology transfer and training for scientists in the host region. They may also assuage some political concerns about the "export" of tissue samples.[17] Combinations of centralized and decentralized strategies are possible — the project might use several repositories with complete collections spread across the world, one or a few complete repositories with several regional subcollections, or a set of regional subcollections. None of these issues has been determined; much will hinge on the levels of funding available for both central and regional repositories.

Where possible, the project plans to make use of existing tissue repositories to preserve the cell lines and tissue samples. The project has had some talks with the tissue collection facilities of the Coriel Institute. This private, nonprofit facility, located in Camden, New Jersey, already contains substantial collections of tissue samples and cell lines. The project could well contract with it for storage of samples from North America or from the entire world.[18]

The project's samples, however, will not be kept solely in physical form. The existence of samples and information about them will be kept in a computer database, which should be readily accessible from the Internet. New samples will be logged into the database as they become available for researchers. The project itself intends to analyze at least all the cell lines for a standard set of markers. The results of that analysis will also be entered into the database. In addition, when other researchers use samples from the project's repositories, they will be required to add the results of their analyses to the database, whether those analyses consist of additional markers or DNA sequences.

In this respect, the database would be similar to other databases that exist for genetic information and samples from humans or other species. The IMAGE Consortium — which stands for an Integrated Molecular Analysis of Genomes and their Expression — is administered by the Lawrence Livermore National Laboratory.[19] The IMAGE Consortium includes clones of complementary DNA (cDNA) that were created, and partially analyzed, by any of several participating institutions. Information about the clones, including whatever sequence data are known, the length of the inserted cDNA, the nature of the vectors used, and so on, is generally available on the World Wide Web. Specific clones can then be ordered from commercial vendors over the Internet. All IMAGE cDNA clones are accompanied by an agreement that provides, among other things, that "you will place all sequencing, mapping, and expression data arising from your use of the arrayed clones into public databases that provide data at no charge or at nominal cost (e.g., Genome Data Base for mapping data, GenBank for sequence data, or other public databases as appropriate for the type of data) promptly after the date on which such information is in a form suitable for submission to such databases and, at your option, steps reasonably necessary to protect your proprietary rights to such data have been taken."[20]

Since its founding meeting in Sardinia, the project has resolved to protect the confidentiality of the donors of its samples and the data derived from them.[21] The samples collected by the HGDP will be accompanied by substantial amounts of contextual information.[22] This information will include the identity of the participant and his or her answers to a standard questionnaire. The questionnaire seeks ethnographic information for each individual participant and his or her parents and spouse (or spouses). The information sought includes places of birth, native languages, ethnic self-identifications, and memberships in culturally significant subgroups such as clans or castes.

The project intends to limit general access to identifying information about either groups or individuals. The identity of the group cannot, obviously, be disguised too heavily or the data will not be useful for answering questions about the group. But those questions will rarely require knowledge of the individual village or community sampled. The exact location of the collection site can be provided only approximately, in a manner that obscures the exact community studied. For example, a set of samples might be identified as coming from people who identify themselves as Navajo (or Dine), located in a settlement in the northwestern quadrant of the Navajo Reservation. This kind of intentional fuzziness has been widely used in recent years by cultural anthropologists to protect the specific people with whom they have worked.

Individual identifying information would also not normally be available. Researchers could, if they wished, obtain most of the ethnographic information and information about familial relationships between the donors of different samples. But the individual participants' identities would not be accessible.

Thus far, however, the project has not concluded that it should "anonymize" its data by making it impossible for anyone ever to link a sample with a specific identifiable group or person. The North American Regional Committee, the only group within the project to have considered this issue in detail, believes that there may be some valid scientific reasons for researchers to learn these specific identities. It has proposed, in the Model Protocol, to allow researchers to request access to such information in some circumstances and with certain conditions: "If particular researchers can demonstrate that they need further detail for scientific work and can guarantee appropriate protection of individual confidentiality in their actions, such data could be revealed to them. If they could show a very strong need to contact an individual donor, that might be allowed, acting through a culturally sophisticated and appropriate intermediary."[23] The Model Protocol proposes that such identifying information be released only if the researchers can make such a showing to the HGDP, perhaps acting through its regional ethics subcommittee. If the populations or individuals can feasibly be contacted, their views on disclosure should also be sought.

The HGDP intends to make the samples it collects, and the data derived from them, available to all qualified researchers,[24] subject to certain conditions. Individuals anywhere in the world who met those conditions could have access to the database through the Internet, probably through a password-based security system. Such researchers could request copies of HGDP samples from the repositories, which would provide them at cost.

In order to have access to either the samples or the database, however, researchers would have to agree to be bound by the terms of contracts with the

HGDP. These contracts, which would take the form of a materials transfer agreement for the samples and a database access agreement for the data, would perform several functions. One such function has already been noted: the agreements would commit the researchers to contribute information they derived from the samples or data back to the database. Other functions are more in the nature of legal "boilerplate." They would require reference to the HGDP in publications involving the samples or data. They would describe (or, more likely, disclaim) any warranties connected with the samples or data. They would require the user to indemnify the HGDP and the repository for any claims concerning the researcher's use of the samples or data. But their most important function would be to define and protect the rights of participating populations to control the uses of the materials and information they provided.

The Model Protocol foresees these arrangements as embodying the agreements reached with the populations in the process of group consent. Those agreements would have to include decisions on whether inventions derived from the samples could be patented or used commercially. The agreements themselves will bind the recipient to use the samples or data only in ways consistent with the expressed wishes of the populations that provided them. The samples and data themselves will have to include a specification of the terms imposed by each population. The agreements will further provide that the populations, as well as the HGDP or the repository, have standing to enforce the agreements and that the recipient may distribute the samples or data to others only if those others also agree to be bound by the agreements.

Ethical and Legal Issues in the HGDP's Use of Stored Tissue Samples

In July 1994 the NIH and the Centers for Disease Control and Prevention (CDC) convened a workshop to recommend appropriate informed consent procedures for the use of newly obtained or existing tissue samples in genetic research. In December 1995 eight participants in that workshop published an account of the consensus they had reached.[25] Although their recommendations have no legal force and have not been adopted as the official policy of NIH or CDC, they offer the analysis of the issues that is both most complete and most protective of research participants. Hence, the Clayton group's recommendations are a useful starting point for considering the effects of these issues on the HGDP.

The Clayton group's recommendations distinguish between samples to be collected in the future and samples that have already been collected. This distinction is also useful for discussing the use of stored tissue samples by the HGDP. This section first discusses the HGDP's plans for collection and use of new samples, which it concludes should not raise serious issues. It then discusses the more troubling question of the HGDP's possible incorporation of previously collected samples.

The Clayton group made strong and specific recommendations concerning newly collected samples, beginning with the injunction that "people should have the opportunity to decide whether their samples will be used for research. This option should be presented when samples are collected for whatever reason if it is likely that the samples will also be used for research." [26]

It then urged that people who agreed to allow their tissue samples to be used for research be given the options of having their samples used in research where the individual donors were potentially identifiable or only in research where the donors cannot be linked to their samples. In either case, the Clayton group argued that the people deciding whether to participate in the research should be given information about the researchers' motivations and about the subjects' share, if any, in any profits from products developed using their samples. People considering participating in potentially identifiable research should also be told about the realistic chances of confidentiality, the circumstances under which they might be contacted again by the researchers, and their rights to withdraw themselves — and their samples — from the research. The group then stated that "because of the complexity of the issues that individuals must consider in deciding whether to participate in such research, the workshop participants believe that it is not desirable to ask sources to sign statements in which they agree to the use of their identifiable samples for research without being informed about the scope and potential consequences of the projects." [27]

The recommendations noted the views taken by some persons at the workshop that potential research participants must be given still further choices. These additional choices included control over whether the samples would be shared with other researchers and, if so, whether they would be shared with commercial researchers. If the samples were to be shared with other researchers, they should only be shared after all identifiers had been stripped from them. Furthermore, these workshop participants believed that subjects should be given the choice of picking specific research topics either as the sole permissible uses for the samples or as purposes for which the samples were *not* to be used.

The procedures to be used by the HGDP, as set out in the draft Model

Protocol, are largely consistent with these recommendations. All new samples would be obtained only after receiving the informed consent of the participating individual and, often, the individual's group. Participating groups and individuals would be told that the HGDP intended to create a generally accessible resource for studying human genetic diversity. The sample they gave could be used by any researchers, for any kind of research, but the participant's group would be able to limit any commercial use or patenting of products derived from the samples. Individual donors would not be able to choose, therefore, whether or not the samples should be shared or whether or not commercial use could be made of them, but, after learning of the project's plans and of the arrangements concerning control of the samples obtained from their group, they could intelligently choose whether or not they personally wanted to participate.[28]

The core recommendation of the Clayton group requires thorough informed consent for newly collected stored tissue samples, as does the Alghero Report of the HGDP and, in considerably more detail, the draft Model Protocol of its North American Regional Committee. This consistency on the main point coexists with potential conflicts between the group's recommendations and the project's plans in two respects: the specificity of the informed consent and the anonymity of shared samples.

For people considering participating in research where their identities could potentially be linked to the samples, the Clayton group thought it was "not desirable" that they agree to participate without "being informed about the scope and potential consequences of the projects." The HGDP currently plans to keep its data in a way in which they can potentially be linked with participant identities, although only through a controlled process. Given the HGDP's planned nature as a kind of lasting "reference library" of human genetic diversity, it is impossible to tell potential participants what research projects their samples might be used for, let alone the scope and potential consequences of those projects. The samples could be used over decades by researchers interested in human history, cultural anthropology, medicine, or other sorts of questions. Potential participants can and should be informed of the breadth of possible uses, but specificity, no matter how desirable, will be, by the nature of the project, impossible.

Second, some members of the Clayton group concluded that, even with the consent of the participants, samples should only be shared between researchers if all the identifiers were stripped from them. In the context of the Clayton paper, this appears to mean not only that the researcher receiving the information be unable to identify individuals, but that the researchers sending the material no longer be able to make those identifications. This requirement also runs counter to the planned nature of the HGDP resources and the project's current intention to keep identity potentially linked to samples.

The project's view on linkage may not be completely fixed. The matter has been little discussed within the project, and it is not clear that there are strong feelings about it. In general, though, the planners of the project have preferred to keep open the option to know the identity of the individual research participants. In some cases, that identity might be useful to resolve questions in analyzing the data, as when a similarity between two samples can be understood as a result of a familial relationship between their donors. In other cases, it would allow recontact with the individual if something of particular interest were found as a result of analysis of her or his sample. Finally, if, for example, a genetically linked disease were discovered for which an effective treatment was found, many in the project would feel a strong compulsion to pass that information back to research participants who were known to be at risk.

None of these reasons for maintaining the possibility of linkage is compelling; on the other hand, neither are the reasons for avoiding linkage. The HGDP intends to keep the samples, and the data derived from them, generally unlinked. Identities will not be automatically or easily available to the public or to researchers. Researchers would have to demonstrate a good reason for needing individual identities before the HGDP would release them. And this plan for controlled linkage, like the rest of the HGDP process, would be part of the informed consent process with both the individual participants and, where appropriate, their groups. HGDP samples could, if necessary, be made anonymous without harming the fundamental goals of the project; that step currently seems neither necessary nor advantageous.

The possible use of previously collected samples by the HGDP, on the other hand, raises more serious conflicts with the Clayton group's recommendations. The Clayton group notes that when samples are already anonymous, under the strict definition that requires that no one have information linking the samples to particular individuals, further research does not require informed consent under federal regulations.[29] It suggests, however, that institutional review boards (IRBs) should still review research proposals "to determine whether they are scientifically sound (particularly for protocols that have not already been subjected to peer review), whether they propose to address a significant problem, and whether the desired information could be obtained in a protocol that allows individuals to consent."[30] When, however, the samples are still linked to identifying information at the time the research is proposed and the researchers intend to preserve the linkage, the group argues that full informed consent is normally necessary.[31] That consent might be inferred from the consent when the samples were initially collected or might require recontact.

The most interesting discussion concerns neither of those two cases, but situations where the tissue samples are currently linked to identifiable individuals, but new researchers wish to "anonymize" the samples before beginning their work. The Clayton group urges that IRBs review the protocols for such research in light of the five following factors:

1. whether the information the researcher seeks can be obtained in a manner that allows individuals to consent (this includes the possibility of using tissue samples for which people had previously given permission for use in research);
2. whether the proposed investigation is scientifically sound and fulfills important needs;
3. how difficult it would be to recontact subjects (it is not necessary, however, to prove impracticability);
4. whether the samples are finite and, if used for research, may no longer be available for the clinical care of the source or his or her family (for example, use of tumor samples may be more problematic than use of transformed permanent cell lines); and
5. how the availability of effective medical interventions affects the appropriateness of pursuing anonymous research.[32]

Whether or how to make previously collected samples part of the HGDP's resource has not yet been discussed in detail within the HGDP. The draft Model Protocol, by its own terms, provides guidance for *new* collections, not the use of old ones. But there are previously collected samples that could well become part of the HGDP. Those samples fall into two general classes: samples collected for research into population genetics and other samples. Each class raises different issues.

The samples that have been collected for the purposes of population genetics research are less troubling. They exist in the laboratories of scientists working on these issues, many of whom are associated with the proposed HGDP. They were collected for the purpose of studying the population genetics of human groups; adding them to the DNA collection of the HGDP would merely enable a broader set of researchers to use them for that purpose. Hence, the extension of the samples to the HGDP might be viewed as within the initial informed consent, if such consent had been obtained. Proof that informed consent had been obtained for the collection of the samples and evidence of the contours of that consent would, of course, be crucial to permissibility of using the samples in the HGDP. If such informed consent had occurred, under the Clayton group's recommendations, such samples might therefore be usable in linked form.

Yet even with the prior consent, the addition of the samples to the HGDP would go beyond what the participants had agreed to by making the samples available to researchers with whom the participants had no contact and in whom they had reposed no trust. As a result, I believe it would be appropriate for the project to accept those samples only after they had been anonymized. The extension of the original understanding of the participants to the samples' use by the general research community would be, in large part, counterbalanced by the absolute assurance of personal confidentiality provided by this anonymity.

Whether such anonymizing of samples that were given with inferable consent to the research use falls within the Clayton group's recommendations concerning "anonymizing" past samples is unclear. In any event, the recommendations provide valuable guidance. For many of these samples, distance and time will make recontact for the purpose of obtaining informed consent quite difficult and, assuming appropriate initial informed consent, will argue strongly for the use of the samples. Research participants from the forests of central Africa who provided blood samples in the late 1960s cannot easily be recontacted. On the other hand, if the samples were collected from a site reasonably convenient to the researcher within the past few years, it might be appropriate to require recontact.

Of course, many existing samples that were *not* collected for the HGDP would be useful for it. In many parts of the world, blood banks could quite quickly provide geographically defined samples that could be enormously valuable for research. They would not be as useful as samples collected specifically for the HGDP, in large part because they would lack the ethnographic background information on participants that the HGDP will provide. They would be extremely easy and cheap to collect, however.

Whether such samples should be used by the HGDP seems quite questionable to me. They would have been given with absolutely no idea that they would ultimately be used for research into population genetics, human history, anthropology, or medical science. At the same time, if the samples were anonymized, the potential harms to the individuals would be minimal. Yet potential harms to the donors' groups would still exist, as these samples could not be anonymized as to group without stripping them of all value for the HGDP.

In this context, the five factors proposed by the Clayton group seem quite useful. Use of these kinds of previously collected samples goes well beyond the use of samples previously collected for population genetics research. Even when the Clayton group's recommendations are met, the HGDP might well be wise to avoid using samples that had been previously collected for purposes unconnected to population genetics research.

Conclusion

The HGDP raises many interesting, important, and complex ethical, legal, and social issues. For the most part, its use of stored tissue samples is not one of them. It will be based largely on newly collected samples, which are planned to be collected with informed consent that should eliminate most concerns. The major potential sticking point — the use of "controlled" anonymity by the project instead of complete and total delinking — is not of great importance to the HGDP and could be changed if necessary. To the limited extent that the project uses previously collected samples, there should not be much concern with its use of "anonymized" samples that were previously collected, with proper informed consent, for population genetics research. Whether or how it should use samples not collected for population genetics research, even when anonymized, remains unclear.

Acknowledgments

I would like to acknowledge the help of my research assistant, Joshua Wagner. In addition, much of the description of the HGDP is taken from work done jointly with Professor Luca Cavalli-Sforza, whose assistance is also gratefully acknowledged. I have been involved in the HGDP since February 1993. I am a member of the North American Regional Committee of the Human Genome Diversity Project and chair that committee's Ethics Subcommittee. Since early 1997 I have been a member of the International Executive Committee of the project. The views expressed in this essay are mine, except where noted, and cannot be assumed to be the views of the Human Genome Diversity Project or its North American Regional Committee.

Notes

1. See, e.g., Paul Salopek, "Genes Offer Sampling of Hope and Fear," *Chicago Tribune* (April 28, 1997), p. 1; Colin Macilwain, "Tribal Groups Attack Ethics of Genome

Diversity Project," *Nature* 383 (September 19, 1996): 288; John Maddox, "The Human Genome Diversity Project Needs Better Planning and a Pilot Project," *Nature* 377 (October 5, 1995): 372; Declan Butler, "Genetic Diversity Project Fails to Impress International Ethics Panel," *Nature* 377 (October 5, 1995): 373; Bette-Jane Crigger, "The Vampire Project," *Hastings Center Report* 25 (January 1995): 2; Patricia Kahn, "Genetic Diversity Project Tries Again," *Science* 266 (November 4, 1994): 720. For a look at some of the more extreme attacks on the HGDP, see the World Wide Web page of the Rural Advancement Foundation International (RAFI), probably the project's most vociferous opponent, at http://www.rafi.ca.

2. See Ellen Wright Clayton, Karen K. Steinberg, Muin J. Khoury, Elizabeth Thomson, Lori Andrews, Mary Jo Ellis Kahn, Loretta M. Kopelman, and Joan O. Weiss, "Informed Consent for Genetic Research on Stored Tissue Samples," *JAMA* 274 (December 13, 1995): 1786 (hereafter Clayton); American College of Medical Genetics, "Statement on Storage and Use of Genetic Materials," *American Journal of Human Genetics* 57 (1995): 1499; Eliot Marshall, "Policy on DNA Research Troubles Tissue Bankers," *Science* 271 (January 26, 1996): 440.

3. North American Regional Committee, Human Genome Diversity Project, "Proposed Model Ethical Protocol for Collecting DNA Samples," *Houston Law Review* 33 (1997): 1431–1473 (hereafter the Model Protocol). The history of the HGDP's ethics activities is recounted in Henry T. Greely, "The Proposed North American Model Ethical Protocol: An Experiment in the Ethics of Genetics Research," in *DNA Sampling: Human Genetic Research — Ethical, Legal, and Policy Aspects,* ed. B. M. Knoppers (forthcoming). Some broader possible implications of the HGDP's ethics work are discussed in Henry T. Greely, "The Control of Genetic Research: Involving the Groups Between," *Houston Law Review* 33 (1997): 1397–1430.

4. One recent book, written by three members of the HGDP's International Executive Committee, contains information on the geographic distribution of 110 genes, derived from over 86,000 records found in the scientific literature published before 1987. L. L. Cavalli-Sforza, P. Menozzi, and A. Piazza, *The History and Geography of Human Genes* (Princeton: Princeton University Press, 1994).

5. L. L. Cavalli-Sforza et al., "Call for a Worldwide Survey of Human Genetic Diversity: A Vanishing Opportunity for the Human Genome Project," *Genomics* 11 (1991): 490–491; Leslie Roberts, "Scientific Split over Sampling Strategy," *Science* 252 (1991): 1615.

6. The project has been opposed by, among others, the Foundation on Economic Trends, Petition of the Foundation on Economic Trends to the National Institutes of Health, June 30, 1994; the "Declaration of Indigenous Peoples of the Western Hemisphere Regarding the Human Genome Diversity Project" (often called the "Phoenix Declaration") adopted by seventeen groups on February 19, 1995, and reprinted in *Cultural Survival Quarterly* 20 (Summer, 1996): 63; and the "Mataatua Declaration on Cultural and Intellectual Property Rights of Indigenous Peoples," *Cultural Survival Quarterly* 20 (Summer, 1996): 52–53.

7. In one of its recent communiqués, RAFI has even stated that "the HGDP should be investigated by the U.N. Human Rights Commission, its files and membership should be fully disclosed, and HGDP should place itself under U.N. supervision":

RAFI communiqué, New Questions about Management and Exchange of Human Tissues at NIH (September/October 1995), available at http://www.rafi.ca.

8. I am the principal investigator on one of those grants, which will explore three issues in depth: contractual provisions for giving sample donors some control over the use of the samples, the use of previously collected tissue samples (an extension and deepening of this paper), and policies and laws of other countries that would affect the HGDP.

9. Ethical issues in the project have also been considered by a subcommittee of the International Bioethics Committee of the United Nations Education, Social, and Cultural Organization (UNESCO). This subcommittee report was discussed at the October 1995 meeting of the UNESCO International Bioethics Committee. The report discusses ethical issues in all of human population genetics, including the HGDP, without making detailed recommendations for resolving those issues; UNESCO International Bioethics Committee Subcommittee on Bioethics and Population Genetics, "Bioethics and Human Population Genetics Research" (1995), available at http://www.biol.tsukuba.ac.jp/~macer/PG.html.

10. "HGDP Summary Document" (the Alghero Report; 1995), available at http://www.leland.stanford.edu/group/morrinst/HGDP.html.

11. HUGO Committee on Ethical, Legal, and Social Implications, "Statement on the Principled Conduct of Genetics Research," *Genome Digest* (March 1996): 2 (Bartha Maria Knoppers, principal author). See also Bartha Maria Knoppers et al., "Ethical Issues in International Collaborative Research on the Human Genome: The HGP and the HGDP," *Genomics* 34 (1996): 34.

12. David Dickson, "HUGO Approves Ethics Code for Genomics," *Nature* 380 (March 28, 1996): 279.

13. Model Protocol; see *supra* note 3 above.

14. See Model Protocol, pp. 1438, 1469–1472.

15. Model Protocol, pp. 1443–1447.

16. Model Protocol, pp. 1465–1469.

17. In India, for example, a proposal for an Indian human genome diversity project included the requirement that "research is done by Indian scientists in Indian laboratories, and that no samples are sent out of the country": K. S. Jayaraman, "India Approves Genetic Diversity Study," *Nature* 384 (December 5, 1996): 394.

18. The project has also recently had talks with the CEPH (the Centre d'Etudes des Polymorphismes Humaines) in France. Although some critics of the project have claimed that its samples would be stored at the American Tissue Type Collection in Maryland, the project's sponsors have had no serious discussions with that organization.

19. G. Lennon, C. Auffray, M. Polymeropoulos, and M. B. Soares, "The I.M.A.G.E. Consortium: An Integrated Molecular Analysis of Genomes and Their Expression," *Genomics* 33 (1996): 151. See the IMAGE Consortium Web page, http://www.bio.llnl.gov/bbrp/image/image.html.

20. The "Agreement in Good Faith concerning Use and Distribution of Arrayed cDNA Clones," IMAGE Consortium (Lawrence Livermore National Laboratory), available at http://www.atcc.org/hilights/tasc2.html#img.

21. Alghero Report; see note 10 above. These issues of confidentiality are discussed in more detail in Model Protocol, pp. 1461–1464.

22. As discussed below, this information would necessarily include the terms and conditions under which the population allows the materials or data to be used.

23. Model Protocol, p. 1463.

24. The idea of a "qualified researcher" has not been fully worked out. Out of respect for the concerns of participating populations, the project does not want the samples, in particular, or perhaps the data, to be available to anyone curious about them. They are intended as tools for research and the project would like to limit their use to legitimate researchers. At the same time, the project has no desire to act as a censor, allowing some researchers access while denying it to others, based on their credentials or their politics. The eventual resolution may be to provide access only to those who can demonstrate, by virtue of their employment or their training, that they are presumptively able to pursue scholarly or intellectual questions with these materials.

25. Clayton, p. 1786.

26. Clayton, p. 1791.

27. Clayton, p. 1791.

28. Of course, the potential exists for a group decision to influence strongly the individual's decision and even to deter an individual from deciding not to participate. Researchers collecting samples for the HGDP will have to be sensitive to this possibility and must take care to protect the realistic ability of individuals to say "no" when their group says "yes." Privacy in the collection process should help keep that choice real.

29. Clayton, p. 1787.

30. Clayton, p. 1791.

31. Clayton, p. 1791. The article does recognize exceptions for public health emergencies or when the regulatory requirements for a waiver from informed consent are met under 45 CFR Sections 46.116(d) (1994).

32. Clayton, p. 1791

PART II
Multidisciplinary Perspectives: History, Biomedical Research, Ethics, and Law

Beyond the Grave — The Use and Meaning of Human Body Parts: A Historical Introduction

Susan C. Lawrence

In a recent essay on the use of body parts from newly dead human beings for organ transplants and medical research, Ruth Chadwick concludes that "*rational* ethical arguments have failed to hold sway in thinking about the dead [as exploitable objects] because of possible strong *intuitions* about the respect due to the corpse. It has been accepted, however, that the corpse has importance as a symbol, and that foetal remains and particular parts of the body have especially strong symbolism which cannot be ignored."[1] Chadwick appeals, throughout her article, to vague references from the past to support her point that corpses were "symbols" of the living human being and that this "symbolic" presence explains the common "intuition" that the dead — like the living — deserve respect. She assumes, like many other contemporary writers, that she need not justify that the living deserve respect, nor that more might be said about just what it is — and was — that corpses and their parts symbolize. While Chadwick's philosophical reflections primarily concern organs, and not entire bodies or small tissue samples, her approach to the meaning of human body parts is typical in that it rests upon a set of relatively recent values primarily expressed in secular Western cultures. Certainly Chadwick is quite right to stress that symbolic meanings must be understood in order to ground an ethical position on the appropriate use of human materials; what is not clear from her comment, however, is just how much those symbolic meanings have varied over time and place and how much they still vary among people from diverse political, economic, intellectual, and religious backgrounds within Western societies.

In this essay I outline the wide range of ways that human beings have used body parts in the past, primarily within Anglo-American cultural frameworks and experiences. I concentrate on practices much more than on the formation of theories (e.g., development of abstract legal perspectives or philosophical analyses of the "body") or the expression of particular ethical principles (e.g., should body parts be used? should medical researchers be allowed to use tissue samples stored from days before informed consent?). A focus on historical actions, including suggestive comments on how these actions made sense at particular times and places, offers us a way to look at the harmonies and tensions between expressed values and cultural practices.[2] At a time when taking, storing, and using human tissues for a variety of purposes seems to have become a common practice in Western biomedicine with little advance discussion about their status in law or contemporary ethics, a historical perspective can sharply remind us that practices always express cultural values (whether overt or hidden) and that cultural values vary considerably among different populations, even within a single overarching group defined by religious or political boundaries, be they medieval Europeans or twentieth-century Americans. To create useful, fair, and sensitive ethical guidelines for future use of human materials requires that we take the diversity of beliefs and practices of a pluralistic society into account.

Because this essay offers a very broad historical survey, I do no more than raise significant connections between beliefs and practice, introduce a few general themes, and refine the way that we ask questions about the "ownership" and "use" of human parts (skeletons, organs, blood, or tissues). I have two overarching points to make. First, beliefs about the location of humanness and personal identity — in the body, the brain, the soul, or combinations of these "places" — shape the meaning and value that humans ascribe to body parts. Hearts, blood, brains, and eyes, for instance, have long seemed more powerful, more central to personhood, or more attuned to spiritual connections than hair, saliva, leg muscles, or kidneys. Hence generalizations about "human parts" whether in historical research or in ethical guidelines will founder unless we recognize that different religious and cultural groups ascribe different hierarchies of values to body parts *and* that these change over time. In the same vein, I claim that the ways in which humans have used body parts at any particular time and place depended directly on the meaning (status, power, value, etc.) attached to the human being from whom they came. The corpses of saints and the corpses of criminals in the medieval period had widely differing meanings, despite their apparent similarity as dead human beings. These meanings — whether taken literally or understood as symbolic of "higher" ideas — allowed pieces of the former to be venerated and pieces of the later to be reviled and "punished."

Second, I emphasize that the principles of "autonomy" and "informed consent," which have emerged specifically in twentieth-century Western cultures shaped by beliefs in democratic government, a service-capitalism economy, and secularly defined law and moral codes, have started to transform practices previously imbued with religious beliefs about life after death and/or specific social rituals that demonstrated "respect" for dead bodies and their parts. Performing specific rituals over the dead, be these for "proper" burial, entombment, or cremation, has long been held, indeed, to be one of the central characteristics distinguishing the "truly human" from the animal.[3] Disposing of the corpses of other people as if they were unwanted animal carcasses has been a ubiquitous way of identifying certain individuals or entire peoples as unworthy of respect, from the suicide hung at the crossroads in early modern Europe to the mass graves of attempted genocides. From this perspective, I suggest that part of the ongoing revulsion, or at least ambivalence, that many people feel about using parts of human bodies (if not other people's, at least their own)[4] for medical or scientific purposes comes from deep cultural beliefs that proper disposal of the dead means laying the body to "rest" — literally in burial, symbolically in cremation — with all the deceased's parts and organs together. Putting the values of autonomy and informed consent into practice, of course, demands that kin, ministers, physicians, and hospital administrators (among many others) all respect the decisions of an individual about what happens to his or her cells, tissues, organs, and entire body during life and after death. Understanding and respecting why people refuse to donate parts of themselves for others to use is just as important (although "irrational" to some) as accepting why other people do so willingly. Until all of the living believe that use of their own and their loved ones' body parts in therapeutics, teaching, and research actually demonstrates appropriate "respect" for the individual dead person, the tension between those who want parts for these purposes and those who refuse to give them will persist.

These points clearly make sense for human materials (entire corpses, significant organs) that obviously embody a sense of human identity and personhood, parts that individuals should be able to have disposed of in ways that are meaningful to them. Tissue samples (bits of organs taken for biopsy, a few vials of blood, small sections stored in pathology labs for histological examination), in contrast, appear too small to matter. Like the hair, saliva, and skin cells that we shed every day, it seems almost absurd to worry about a "proper," respectful laying to rest of such scraps. Yet, as other essays in this volume emphasize in several different ways, even tiny pieces of individual people have taken on new meanings and new values over the past decade. The abstract knowledge that nearly all of our cells contain our own unique versions of DNA now has concrete implications for personal identity. Laboratory techniques can produce individualized DNA profiles in a matter of hours from either fresh or stored tissue samples. Serious issues of privacy for the living and the dead and of profit for genetic researchers are but two of the areas where the recent developments in science will quite literally reshape human attitude toward their own cells. Just as Western societies have witnessed transformations in beliefs about the use and meaning of entire corpses and the use of the viable organs of the newly dead, so too will we experience a cultural shift — and cultural conflicts — in attitudes toward minute parts. Whether these will be resolved by procedures for informed consent and adherence to the values of personal autonomy remains to be seen.

In this essay, I range over many centuries and touch on a wide variety of "uses" for human body parts. I do so in order to juxtapose practices and debates that I have not yet seen considered together. It has seemed as though the uses of body parts in religious worship, in criminal law, in medical treatments, in medical education, and in anthropological research have all been primarily considered within each discrete and isolated field. Each area of life or thought defines the "body" in different ways; these ways in turn justify the exemption of parts from burial (or reburial) and allow pieces to be put in storage or on display. Because such attitudes can diverge widely from each other and yet somehow co-exist in the same legal and moral universe, even as that universe changes over time, their comparison offers us possible insights into current areas of conflict and compromise.

I organize my discussion around the basic areas of human experience that have dominated beliefs about human body parts and the uses to which they have been put. While the discussion is roughly in chronological order, I must stress that all of these areas are at work at all times, either implicitly or explicitly. These are religion, political/legal, and medical. I close with my view of the specific ways in which a historical perspective contributes to the meaning and treatment of stored tissue samples.

Religion: The Sacred and the Profane

I begin with religion because so much of the literature concerning dead human bodies emphasizes the very basic social practice of the proper disposal of the dead for religious reasons. These reasons have sometimes been explicitly theological: correct burial, entombment, or cremation of the dead body is necessary for the existence and happiness of the person in the next life, either right after death or at some point in the future. Whether involving a literal concept of bodily resurrection (as in certain strands within Christianity) or a symbolic one sensitive to a "natural" integrity of the decaying corpse, such religious beliefs create strong and important rituals around the disposal of the dead body. These rituals, moreover, often serve to protect the living from the anger or revenge of the newly dead and hence incorporate the power of fear of the corpse as well as love and respect for the dead person.

Even when religious dogma places less emphasis on the intact presence of the corpse for a period after death (as with cremation), social rituals developed through both religious and more broadly cultural beliefs have almost universally stressed that certain acts display appropriate respect for the dead.[5] The nearly ubiquitous notion of the importance of showing "respect" for the human corpse has its roots deep in religious traditions, no matter how secularized this "respect" became in nineteenth- and twentieth-century Western societies.[6] In turn, mutilation of the dead body, delayed burial, disinterment, and inept treatment of the corpse during embalming, the funeral service, and burial have all been interpreted as marks of "disrespect" that nineteenth- and twentieth-century Anglo-American courts have judged to be liable as torts in common law. Close relatives who suffer emotional distress from such acts have thus won damages, whether or not they explicitly appealed to violations of religious beliefs.

Within the Judeo-Christian tradition, the dead body and its disposal acquired intense religious meaning. The ancient Hebrews, in practices that continue in orthodox Judaism, insisted upon the immediate burial of their dead and a ritualized period of mourning for the family and community. The continuing concerns about the "uncleanliness" of the corpse and desecration of the body by cutting into it — "mutilation" — have shaped a long tradition of resistance to autopsies and the dissection of Jews for teaching purposes.[7] Christianity, in its emergence from Judaism in the context of Greco-Roman culture, developed a much more complex theological relationship to the dead. In part, the rejection of Jewish laws and customs helped early Christians to distinguish themselves from the older religion, and denying the innate "uncleanliness" of the corpse was part of this larger trend. That Roman law similarly held the corpse to be offensive, requiring burial outside the city, for instance, and absolutely forbidding the violation of buried or entombed remains, similarly demarcated Christianity from the dominant pagan culture.[8]

Yet the crucial significance of the physical and spiritual resurrection of Christ meant that Christians also needed to deal more particularly with the meaning of the dead body both at the time of death and for its resurrection at the Last Judgment. Caroline Walker Bynum has explored, in sophisticated detail, the conflicting perspectives among Christians from the church fathers of the third century to the theologians at the start of the fourteenth century on just how resurrection was supposed to occur. Much of the theological and liturgical discussion among church elites centered on the importance of the material resurrection of the body as vital for the continuance of the individual. Even with a separate soul constituting a distinctly immaterial spiritual self, the full self, these men argued, emerged with the individual personhood of lived experience in particular flesh. Thus, the debates on the self in the afterlife (did a person continue to have a gender? an age? physical evidence of valued martyrdom?), even when "perfect" (which meant?) with God, constantly dealt with the problem of the apparent physical decay of the corpse and its eventual role in defining the self after death. Some sort of bodily resurrection, in short, was profoundly necessary for medieval thinkers, at the same time that it raised considerable anxiety about the burial of the whole body. It was a considerable comfort for some, for example, to believe that a person would be reunited with an amputated limb when made perfect at Judgment, just as other damaged parts would be made whole and well again for eternal happiness.[9]

Such arguments for the material resurrection of the body as it was in life (not, of course, as a decayed corpse),[10] however, had a tense relationship with another practice developed within medieval Christianity: the importance and power of saints' relics.[11] Holy relics included pieces of the true cross and objects, like clothing, that saints had used in life; they also included body parts, primarily bones, blood, and hair, but also sometimes organs and completely mummified corpses. One argument made at the time, of course, was that such pieces — particularly necessary parts like bones and organs — would be reunited with the saint at Judgment, but that in the meantime the saint had a perfect body in heaven. At the same time, however, relics of bone and flesh were quite literally part of the saint and still invested with her or his spiritual power. They were not mere symbols, then, but active spiritual material, existing, as Christ had, in at least two places at once. Relics, moreover, could be further divided over time and thus distribute a particular saint's presence and benefits to more people.[12]

The crucial difference between the ostensibly horrifying practice of cutting up the bodies of holy people soon after death, or the at least unsavory willingness to disinter bodies and distribute what was left of the remains (usually bones, but sometime mummified flesh), and such acts on the body of a common sinner rested in the purpose of the dismemberment and the subsequent veneration of the parts.[13] Laid in appropriate reliquaries, some of which were complex works of art, the saint's body parts in some sense were more than respected: they were venerated and adored.[14] Of course, Catholic priests and theologians were extremely careful not to permit idol worship. The remains themselves were not literally divine. Instead, the presence of part of the saint's body allowed the worshiper to concentrate on the lessons of the saint's life — even if just holiness in general — and to find a path to the saint, who was alive in heaven, for intercession with God. The presence of relics was clearly not necessary for miracles to occur, yet their proximity acted rather like a catalyst. By simply existing they encouraged people to take pilgrimages to visit them, to fear them if not properly revered, and to credit their presence with healing powers.[15]

As sacred and powerful objects, relics became important adjuncts to the founding of new churches and monasteries during the European expansion of Catholicism in the fourth to fourteenth centuries. They also became items of exchange, pieces "gifted" for favors, for prestige, and for political and religious influence, as well as more crudely marketed commodities.[16] Indeed, the proliferation of relics, especially the increasing number of forged ones, raised the ire of Catholic reformers throughout the later Middle Ages.[17] Sixteenth-century Protestant reformers, in turn, not only criticized the undoubted reverence for false relics, but quickly denied the canonization of saints and abolished the veneration of human remains as outright idolatry. The concern over the authenticity of holy parts and objects led, during the Counter-Reformation, to the pope's creation of the "Sacred Congregation for Indulgences and Relics."[18] True relics continue to have an important place within twentieth-century Catholicism, although it is far more difficult to have new ones accepted by the church. The use and treatment of relics are closely regulated by canon law, which states, for example, that selling relics is simony and hence forbidden.[19] If there is still a cash market for relics, it is either underground or based upon the material, artistic, or historic value of the reliquary, not upon its spiritual power. Stories told about pious priests and monks casting out the bones of ordinary people when they were discovered to be forgeries, Protestants destroying previously saintly relics, and French revolutionaries smashing the Catholics' sacred remains, moreover, attest to the ways in which lack of respect for these human fragments had potent religious and political meaning.[20]

Law: Property and Torts

Just as parts of the saintly body were long venerated in Western culture, so were the bodies, and parts of bodies, of dying heretics and criminals burnt, dismembered, hung to rot, or crudely buried outside of consecrated ground in order to continue their punishments into the next life. All of these marks of excommunication and infamy, moreover, served secular powers (for the church technically could not execute people) throughout the medieval and early modern periods as ways to terrorize potential wrongdoers.[21] While all Protestant denominations rejected the adoration of saints' relics, most Protestant sects and Protestant rulers continued to include public execution and public humiliation of the corpse as important elements of punishment for the most heinous criminals, especially murderers, until the eighteenth or, in some instances, the nineteenth centuries. "Respect" and "decent" burial, in short, were only for "respectable" and "decent" people.

The association of mutilation of the corpse with postmortem penalties for murderers offered the earliest rationale for the official use of dead bodies in medicine for nontherapeutic purposes. From at least the early fourteenth century, evidence exists that academic physicians had begun to supervise public dissections of human cadavers. Starting in Italy, at the University of Bologna, it appears that secular rulers granted a few corpses of executed criminals to be cut up to demonstrate the parts of the body in association with readings from standard texts. Elite physicians, assisted by local surgeons, held these "anatomies" perhaps two or three times a year.[22] By the early modern period, it is clear that in some cities the "anatomies" were open to nonmedical people who found edification in seeing the inside of a human being accompanied by a learned account of God's handiwork.[23] Such audiences also felt satisfaction in observing the last visible rendering of justice upon the criminal.[24] Whether or not people believed in the literal resurrection of the body, the murderer — who was already excommunicate in Catholic jurisdictions — suffered symbolically. Secular rulers also intended that the final indignity of dissection, and then burial (if at all) in unconsecrated ground, would deter would-be felons from the crime. By the mid-eighteenth century in England, the state further linked the penalty for premeditated murder with anatomical dissection by surgeons for the pedagogic benefit of practitioners and apprentices. The 1752 Murder Act replaced the judge's discretion to add dissection to the sentence of death with the requirement that the corpses of murderers in London were to be cut up at Surgeons' Hall.[25]

The official connection between dissection and punishment for murder carried significant political and cultural meaning in the following decades. Between the 1740s and 1800 medical education expanded in London, as it did in other major cities, and getting a good medical training increasingly required that all students actually dissect a human body with their own hands instead of simply watching a dissection with a large crowd of pupils. Surgeons' apprentices and other students soon found that the official anatomies of murderers were insufficient and turned to corpses "resurrected" from graveyards for needed material. By the late eighteenth century "professional" body-snatchers — who were not medical students or anatomists — had begun a profitable business supplying dissecting rooms with material. It is highly likely that such body-snatching had gone on discreetly for centuries; but by the early nineteenth century the demand for cadavers had increased to the point where laypeople could no longer tolerate the violation of cemeteries and the commodification of the dead. Disgust at the practice intensified, as Ruth Richardson amply describes, because body-snatchers took the dead from respectable graves instead of just "using" the bodies of the very poor. This shift led, after convoluted political turns, to the Anatomy Act of 1832.[26] This act became the standard model for anatomy acts passed in Canada, Australia, and other British territories, as well as in various states in America from the mid-1830s to the 1920s.

The provisions of the Anatomy Act of 1832, to which I return below, stemmed not only from a major shift in ideas about appropriate medical training, but also from the status of the corpse in law and contemporary regulation of burials. Laws governing appropriate burial, including, for instance, the requirement to provide a reasonable interment for any stranger dying in one's house when no relatives could be found, had emerged in both church law and common law by the early modern period. An equally complex body of law developed around the proper disposal of corpses during times of famine and epidemics, when the secular powers of city, parish, or state needed to ensure burial, and sometimes even cremation, for those whose relatives could not manage it. Such provisions led, in turn, to laws regulating burial for reasons of "public health," a discipline that with hindsight may be seen developing in medieval cities, but which is clearly articulated only early in the nineteenth century.[27]

A central question in Anglo-American law, and of considerable import for the political implications of the use of parts of dead human bodies, is the extent to which a property relationship can exist between the living and the corpse. The hallowed traditions of English common law state that there can be, in fact, no ownership of a dead human body at all. What has evolved, instead, are definitions of "legal possession" of the body. Those who own the property where a person dies have proper "possession" until someone with a greater claim arrives to take possession of the corpse for burial. Such a claim, in turn, rests upon the responsibility of kin to ensure that the body is decently interred, and the order of duty follows degrees of relationship: from spouse, to adult children, to parents, and so on through near kin back to the owner of the property where the person died.[28]

The origins of the principle that "there can be no property in a dead corpse" are, as many English legal texts complain, quite obscure. Indeed, according to the best historical and legal analysis I have seen to date, this precept emerged from a series of errors in understanding early modern jurists and in interpreting fragments of reports of seventeenth-century cases. As Paul Matthews explains, however, once the principle (even if incorrectly based) became enshrined in common law, it became the common law and was so treated by judges from the eighteenth century on.[29] This point is extremely significant, for it means that in Britain the corpse itself *and its parts* have no standing under the law for damage, theft, exchange, or inheritance.[30] None of the ways in which property is defined, managed, or transferred in either criminal or civil law can apply directly to the dead body. Mutilation of a dead body, inappropriate disinterment, and the like must thus be handled under laws specifically about the corpse. Because it is not property, the body cannot be willed by its owner, although the kin can of course try to fulfill the deceased's (lawful) wishes. Before the Anatomy Act of 1832, therefore, a person could not be prosecuted for "stealing" a dead body, either before or after burial, because it was not theft; someone caught with a "resurrected" corpse could only be charged with the theft of the shroud or winding sheets or the coffin, if that was also taken too. These were the property of those who provided them or, failing that, of the next of kin. This interesting situation meant that those tried for body-snatching usually faced only a misdemeanor (due to the small value of winding sheets and shrouds), instead of a felony, which at this period was punishable by death.

In the United States, as writers on the law have discussed in detail, the corpse is usually considered "quasi-property." It is not true property, a point of view inherited from English common law, yet it has some of the elements of a property relationship with the living. In effect, "quasi-property" means that, just as in the case of right and duty of possession in England, kin (or legal alternates) have the privilege and responsibility to see that the dead relative is disposed of properly. As in English law, a hierarchy of relationship degrees lays out the order of precedence in making the funeral and burial decisions.[31] In both English and American law, moreover, the requirements of public health and the public interest in the apprehension of criminals give authority to various branches of government to interfere with the kin's plans for burial or cremation. Public health concerns might dictate further medical investigation or immediate cremation of a "dangerous" corpse; the police and the court system can order autopsies, and the storage of a dead person, to satisfy the needs of investigation and justice. Samples of the corpse's body fluids, organs, and tissues can then be kept after the dead body is released for burial for as long as needed by the prosecution and defense to run tests.

This body of law, in England and America, nicely deals with the death and final disposal of most people. When conflicts and complaints about the treatment of the corpse arise, many problems end up in civil, rather than criminal, courts. While a hospital, government agency, undertaker, or burial manager cannot be sued for damage to "property" if someone feels that the body of his or her relative has been abused, the offended kin may sue for wrongs done to the feelings, dignity, respect, or status of the surviving (and presumed loving) relations. Much case law in both nations exists on this process, and U.S. courts have heard claims for damages for the distress caused by, among other things, mutilation by unauthorized autopsy, mutilation by unauthorized dissection, negligence in gathering up the body parts of someone killed by a train, improper embalming, use of a too-small coffin, and fraud in returning ashes from a group cremation instead of from individual cremations, as the company promised. In all of these cases, the relatives had to convince the court that the mistreatment had severely disturbed them, occasioning emotional pain by the lack of proper respect shown for the remains of those close to them. While relatives can be distressed by such wrongs, moreover, the way that these actions work means that strangers cannot sue on the same grounds. The courts have decided, at least so far, that without a close relationship with the deceased during life a person, even the executor of the estate, cannot be distressed enough to bring a valid claim for damages.[32]

Combining the principle that there is "no property in a body" (or that the corpse is only "quasi-property") with the duty of the householder (or equivalent) to dispose of the body of an unclaimed person dying on his or her property and with the case law that denied "strangers" the grounds to sue for maltreatment of a corpse gives the underlying mind-set not only for the cultural and political formation of the British Anatomy Act of 1832, but also for subsequent Anglo-American legislation on unclaimed corpses. In brief, the act allowed the overseers of the poor, parish offices, masters of workhouses, hospital administrators, and magistrates to provide the bodies of those who died in their care (or who died on the street or in some other public place) to licensed anatomists working at licensed medical schools, *provided that* the individual had not explicitly stated that he or she did not want to be dissected or that the relatives of the deceased objected. In effect, the act meant that a poor person dying with no relatives at hand to object could be dissected if the official with "legal possession" of the body (i.e., those in positions listed above) so decided. At this point, hired undertakers moved the corpse to a medical school, where the anatomist took "legal possession" of the cadaver. In 1832 the act specified that the anatomist could have the body for eight weeks, at which time the law required that *all* the remains be buried "decently."[33]

As Ruth Richardson has stressed, this legislation embodies not only important elements of political maneuvering by the classes with power and wealth to protect their own graves, but also a continued association of dissection with punishment, in this case punishment for dying while dependent on the state or charity (via poor rates, workhouses, hospitals) for support.[34] The act did manage, however, at least to express upper-class sensibilities about the final disposal of even the very poor and abandoned in proper graves and their concern that bodies, even if in fragments, be interred with all of their parts. Under the powers invested in the newly created "Inspectorate of Anatomy," the government's officers supervised the act, which eventually supplied an adequate number of cadavers for medical schools' demands.

The Anatomy Act in Britain was modified slightly in 1872, and reworked in 1984, but the basic status of the corpse in law and the primary responsibility and rights of kin to dispose of the dead have not changed.[35] Similarly, when the commonwealth nations and states of the United States adopted the British Anatomy Act, each legislative body modified it to suit local conditions and jurisdictions, but kept the essential idea — the use of state-dependent, "unclaimed" bodies for anatomy teaching in medical schools — intact.[36] Until World War II — for reasons as yet not clearly understood — the part of the act allowing the explicit *donation* of one's own body after death for dissection was very rarely invoked; by 1951 voluntary bequests had only reached 40 percent of the annual supply for dissection, climbing to between 70 and 100 percent in the 1960s and the 1970s.[37] In most areas in the United Kingdom and the United States today, donations of bodies (many expressed well before death) to medical schools fill the educational demand; in the United Kingdom, however, the old law is still on the books and is occasionally applied to the bodies of the unclaimed dead.

In a very important sense, as this discussion has shown, the law actually has had very little to say about human body parts other than for anatomical dissection or proper burial before the development of organ transplants and complex biochemical and genetic studies. Legislation passed between the 1960s and 1980s in Britain and the United States (e.g., the 1968 Uniform Anatomical Gift Act) has more or less dealt with the issues and procedures involved in organ transplants, particularly in declaring that human body parts for transplantation cannot be knowingly exchanged "for valuable consideration."[38] Yet there was, and still is, a large shadowy area where medical practitioners and scientists take, keep, and use "worthless" bits of human bodies without questions of law, "respect," or responsibility crossing their minds. The various "anatomical" and "tissue" acts governing dissection and organ transplants have major loopholes, in fact, when it comes to the disposition of human material not for therapeutic purposes, but for medical and scientific research. The 1987 amended Uniform Anatomical Gift Act (which most states have adopted in some form or other), for example, prohibits the sale of organs and tissues for transplant, but *not* — by obvious omission — for use in teaching and research.[39] This is the case, I believe, in part because researchers have taken "useless" human material for centuries without the practice being seen as problematic by people or groups with both significant political power and moral objections. In the past twenty years, however, the constant expansion of clinical research requiring blood and tissue samples and the exponential growth in the amount of personal information that can be recovered from body parts mean that issues of lawful possession, respectful disposal, informed consent, and biological privacy have taken on new force and new urgency.[40]

Science and Medicine: Body Parts and Artifacts

The first use of human body parts for what we could reasonably call "medicine" in Western culture appears in therapeutics. Heinrich von Staden has observed (following Mary Douglas' important insights in her *Purity and Danger*) that the early Greeks, from whom we have a fairly large number of well-studied texts, used "impure," "polluted," "dirty," or similarly despised materials for therapeutic ends. The underlying rationale was simple: in certain diseases, conditions, or individual cases, the disorder-causing problem needed to be "drawn out" or (in a modern metaphor) neutralized, by the most potent of substances. The worst, most unsavory, "dangerous," and forbidden things had considerable power and hence, if applied carefully, could cure. Among the unsavory and forbidden substances were various kinds of animal feces, poisonous plants, and, in certain contexts, human blood, tissues, and bones. The use of human material was rare, but it persisted. Von Staden reports, for example, that a Greek physician, Artemon, prescribed drinking spring water "from a murdered person's skull" for epilepsy. Almost two thousand years later, seventeenth-century European pharmacopoeias contained remedies that required "mummy" — the dried remains of human bodies.[41]

Such beliefs might seem to be no more than odd stories from quasi-magical folk traditions, except that they reveal the way in which credible medical practitioners can essentially *redefine* certain body parts. Laying "therapeutic" over "offensive" or "disgusting" shifts the moral category of using human parts from intolerable to permissible. In Western societies, the continuation of the taboos against using parts of dead (and living) human beings as food or fertilizer fails to shift the moral category of this material from intolerable to permissible, despite logical arguments about the possible utility of such practices.[42] Similarly, using parts of dead bodies to make artistic works (outside of certain historical curiosities) has been taken as inappropriate, if not totally offensive.[43] Hence the therapeutic use of human substances, from blood transfusions to the implantation of fetal brain cells into people with Parkinson's disease, is and will continue to be controversial precisely because medicine's power to redefine the meaning of human parts requires much more than rational arguments about beneficial outcomes. It requires, I suggest, a certain coherence, or compatibility, between the kind of body part employed, the proposed purpose, and the broader, often emotional, value of the body part — or the dead body as a whole — to the living.

The appeal to therapeutic benefit, nevertheless, is currently the most convincing way to make the use of human substances acceptable. The appeal to "science" is much more fraught with ambiguities. An argument for educational necessity — as with the "need" for human cadavers for medical students — falls somewhere in the middle, as certain practices, such as dissection, have been justified by the presumed therapeutic benefit of well-trained practitioners. In the following discussion, I concentrate on the use of human body parts for "science," without explicit analysis of the development of reasons for use in teaching, primarily because the rhetoric of formal medical education and training has always included the necessity of educating neophytes in the medical "sciences," whatever those have been at different times and places.[44]

Anatomy was, of course, the first "science" that needed human body parts for study, although much of the early work that the Greeks, and then Greco-Romans, did on the structures of bodies was done on animals considered analogous to humans.[45] Physiology — knowledge of how the body functioned — depended in part on descriptions of body parts, but, until the eighteenth and nineteenth centuries, was shaped around what moderns tend to see as "merely" philosophical constructs, particularly the system of the four humors and three (or more) basic "souls" or well-springs of action, such as digestion/nutrition and the motions of muscles. As noted in the section on law above, the study of human gross anatomy changed in the fourteenth century, with the occasional demonstration of the interior parts of the body on the corpses of criminals. But it is important to stress here that until the "solids" (organs, etc.) were seen as significant locations of normal and pathological processes for which some therapy could be devised most practitioners considered that intensive attention to the details of human structure was nearly irrelevant to clinical practice. The academic study of anatomy for elite practitioners expanded in sixteenth-century Italy, as the notable example of Vesalius' monumental *On the Fabric of the Human Body* (1543) attests.[46]

Thus, during the centuries in which Europeans most actively gathered and partitioned the physical remains of holy people, medical practitioners actually had relatively little interest in dissecting, describing, and mapping human remains for the sake of "knowledge."[47] The former was sacred; the latter profane. At the same time, however, men of the law became interested in seeking the marks of crime — especially poison and dead wounds — within the bodies of those (usually important people) who died unexpectedly. The need to understand the evidence produced with forensic autopsies, in fact, may well have been one of the key reasons why demonstrative human dissection began at the University of Bologna, a major center for the study of law in the thirteenth and fourteenth centuries.[48] Medical men, for both legal and, increasingly, medically diagnostic reasons, performed postmortem investigations of the body's interior over the next centuries, but many of these were focused on answering specific questions about the cause(s) of death, and they were rarely open explorations into pathological anatomy before the eighteenth and nineteenth centuries. Autopsies were more acceptable to people than is generally assumed, primarily because the procedure could be restricted to certain areas of the body (e.g., excluding the head) and were always restricted in time. A postmortem physical examination might take a few hours, but after that the usual arrangements for the funeral and burial continued. The corpse, then, while disfigured by the operation, was (supposedly) interred with all of its parts and with appropriate "respect" and "decency." Certainly relatives and friends objected to autopsies, and usually had their way, until the later development (in the nineteenth century) of the "interests" of the state, superseding the interests of kin for evidence in criminal investigations.[49]

More significant than the increasing number of autopsies in the early modern period was, I believe, the start of museums that contained specimens of human body parts. The historical development of the "museum" itself, from private collections to state institutions, has recently received critical academic study. In one sense, medieval churches had "collections," as did the courts of monarchs and nobles who acquired, and sometimes displayed, various "interesting" objects. But it was not until the sixteenth and seventeenth centuries that collecting and display became a specific goal, with items set into dedicated spaces and attention spent on printing catalogs. As Paula Findlen details, the beginning of collections of items of "natural history" is particularly intriguing, as some collectors tried to gather together material that would present all the regularities and curiosities of the natural world.[50] Fascination with "odd" animals, plants, and rocks had, of course, existed since the Greeks wrote texts describing natural phenomena and the Roman author Pliny composed his encyclopedic account of all things familiar and strange. During the medieval and early modern period, however, nature's wonders primarily revealed the hand of God, discussed both in sophisticated theological treatises on God's creation and in the traditions of hermeneutic, magical, and symbolic lore. In both genres, human-produced "monsters" (malformed fetuses and newborns) embodied moral and spiritual messages, signaling God's general displeasure, the wages of sin, the foolish behavior of the pregnant woman, or warnings about future catastrophes.[51] It is not too surprising, then, that some of the first anatomical specimens of human parts preserved for display were abnormal fetuses, who hardly counted as "human" at all to their observers. They were kept, however, as objects to be studied, not simply as hideous displays to be feared and interpreted as portents. The early modern collections of natural materials, as Findlen argues, then helped to shift the interest in creatures, plants, and rocks from the magical and metaphysical to the natural and rationalistic.[52]

Just when anatomy professors at universities, and surgeons in their guilds, started to collect human parts for study and teaching is still obscure. Certainly there were articulated skeletons and separate human bones (perhaps prepared from dissected criminals) kept for examination by the sixteenth century. Bones, of course, as the longest-lasting parts of the human body, were available to be "found" in ways that other parts were not; bones, once dried, moreover, did not generally need to have anything else done to preserve them. In contrast, it was quite difficult to save any other part of the body unless it could be desiccated rapidly in a relatively sterile environment (as the Egyptians knew with their embalming methods, and Europeans knew with salting and drying). In general, however, keeping specimens of human parts in ways that would allow future examination of their structures was not done until a series of new techniques for anatomical study and preservation appeared between the 1660s and 1680s. Injections of mercury into arteries and veins revealed tiny vessel patterns. Injecting liquids that solidified, especially colored waxes, allowed the tissues to be removed after the liquid hardened, while preserving the shape and distributions of the arteries and veins. Even more significant was the discovery, in the early 1660s, that parts placed in "spirits" (high-proof alcohol) in a sealed glass container would not decompose. Both high-quality glass containers and spirits were quite expensive at the time, however, and so "potted" specimens did not become widespread until the nineteenth century, when improvements in glass and spirit manufacture made cheaper containers and preservatives possible.[53]

These new methods led to a passion for collecting anatomical materials. Anatomy collections in Amsterdam, Leyden, Paris, London, Bologna, and Padua all became well known by the mid-eighteenth century. In London nearly all the successful anatomy teachers created their own sets of materials for study and teaching, and these became valuable resources.[54] By the mid-eighteenth century most surgeon-anatomists deliberately tried to preserve specimens of pathological structures, as well as normal anatomy. In the first decades of the nineteenth century in the medical schools that developed around hospitals, examples of diseased organs and tissues were frequently linked to specific case records or autopsy-room log books.[55] With the shift to the anatomy of tissues — histology — from the 1840s on, gross anatomical specimens made room for collections of slides, which in turn prompted techniques for preserving slide samples for research and teaching. Anatomy museums also housed papier-mâché casts and models made of wood and wax, as well as diagrams and illustrations.[56]

As this sketch of the basic history of anatomical collections suggests, typical historical accounts are remarkably quiet about the source of the human materials for specimens. In part this stems from the way that the collectors recorded and labeled their materials. The "objects" were universalized into "the bones of the leg" or "a fetus of three months" or "a liver displaying cirrhotic change." Such abstractions of the particular nicely fulfilled the needs of teachers and students, for whom the specimens were supposed to represent "typical" human structures, whether "normal," "diseased," or "deformed."[57] Presumably some parts came from lawfully dissected criminals, without asking the executed person for "donations"; but it is very doubtful that these bodies accounted for many of the specimens. "Resurrected" corpses more than likely provided the bulk of the organs and sections preserved in eighteenth-century England and elsewhere. Specimens from snatched bodies had no provenance, perhaps not even names; "consent" to their donation was, by definition, a moot point. Under the Anatomy Act of 1832, moreover, the provision for complete burial of the dissected person literally meant that in Britain no organs or sections could be removed for preservation in anatomical collections, although enforcing this was problematic.[58]

"Interesting" parts from autopsies also ended up in museums, and perhaps postmortem inquiries furnished some apparently normal organs for study and preservation, especially after the Anatomy Act went into operation. It is nearly impossible to know if the relatives who permitted an autopsy also gave permission for specimens to leave the body. In a few instances in their accounts, medical writers noted that the relatives or attendants denied permission to remove organs. They offered such explanations to account for possible errors in descriptions that they gave from memory, from notes, and from on-the-spot sketches. In others, as suggested by a story that an early nineteenth century medical student at St. Thomas' Hospital told his family in a letter, determined practitioners performed autopsies even when they knew that permission had not been given. With such practices adding excitement to medical life, presumably removing a part, such as the heart or stomach, could be easily justified and then disguised by adding stuffing, closing the incision, and placing the corpse in a shroud.[59]

By the mid-eighteenth century common law principles in England held that no one had property in dead human bodies or parts of dead human bodies. But anatomists behaved otherwise. As I have already discussed, there were people who removed bodies from graveyards to sell to anatomists in the eighteenth century, although plenty of "amateurs" (i.e., medical students) did this work without payment. Such "trade" ostensibly went on in secret, although it is likely that quite a few people were aware of these practices but did not raise a fuss when only the bodies of the very poor or unknown were taken.[60] It is important, then, that a "trade" in preserved body parts went on quite openly in the eighteenth century and probably continued into the nineteenth and twentieth centuries. Several of the men who lectured on anatomy in London and who acquired their own teaching specimens retired or died with quite a bit of money tied up in their collections, and these were sometimes put up for sale. A few printed catalogs of the auctions for anatomical preparations survive and show beyond doubt that human pieces were sold and bought for cash.[61] After the 1832 Anatomy Act required the burial of all the parts of dissected bodies, the inspector of anatomy for London blithely told anatomy lecturers to purchase necessary anatomical specimens "from the Continent," ironically endorsing an international trade in human body parts because the law would not support a local one.[62]

In recent law review literature on the status of body parts as property, the only lawsuit regularly cited that specifically concerned anatomical specimens occurred in Australia in 1908. In *Doodeward v. Spence*, ultimately considered by the High Court of Australia, Mr. Doodeward was a showman who displayed "the preserved corpse of a stillborn child with two heads." Entrepreneurs had put on "freak shows" including deformed animals, living dwarves, and "fat ladies" at least since the seventeenth century in Europe, and such exhibits had become popular parts of traveling circuses in the nineteenth and early twentieth centuries.[63] Doodeward's stillborn fetus was nothing really new at this time, but it offended some local sensibilities, and he was prosecuted for "indecent exhibition of the corpse." The police removed the specimen, placing it in a university museum; when he demanded its return, they gave him only "the bottle and preserving fluid."

When the three judges of the High Court considered the claims, they divided over the application of the common law principle that human bodies are not property combined with the problem that "lawful possession" was usually given to those who wished to bury the body, not to keep it bottled in preserving fluid. Hence neither the police department nor the university had any claim to the fetus that was better than Doodeward's. The court eventually ruled, two to one, that the specimen be returned to Doodeward. One of the majority decided this on the grounds that the stillborn fetus was not a human corpse. The other, Justice Griffin, however, argued that

> when a person has by the lawful exercise of work or skill so dealt with a human body or part of a human body in his lawful possession that it has acquired some attributes differentiating it from a mere corpse awaiting burial, he acquires a right to retain possession of it, as least as against any person not entitled to have it delivered to him for the purpose of burial, but subject, of course, to any positive law which forbids its retention under the particular circumstances.[64]

Until further research uncovers lawsuits that involve treating other (non-fetal) anatomical specimens as property, the significance of the Doodeward case rests on Griffin's attempt to articulate a criterion that distinguishes anatomical specimens from other possible uses of parts of dead bodies. As Paul Matthews points out, however, this is a weak argument, considering that skilled work on other "natural" objects does not make them into the personal property of the worker.[65] For Matthews, the key argument here is that a person who possesses anatomical specimens can only be challenged by "a person with a better right to possession." Following this point to its logical conclusion, moreover, clearly suggests that a "better right" rests only in people with the first right of possession (i.e., the relatives) who intend to dispose of the body and its parts.[66]

Lastly, anatomical and pathological collections have housed body parts removed during surgery, which mostly meant amputations before the invention of anesthesia in the 1840s and the spread of sterile operating techniques in the 1870s to 1890s. Very little is known about the history of living patients' reactions to the storage and display of their parts. A few recent legal cases, however, show that some people have in fact attached considerable meaning to the final fate of their excised tissue. A case in Dallas in 1975, for example, centered on a patient who sued for his intense distress upon learning that his excised eye had been lost down a drain; here he claimed damages for negligence, as well as for emotional pain.[67] In *Browing v. Norton–Children's Hospital*, in Kentucky in 1974, a man sought financial solace after the hospital cremated his amputated leg because he had a lifelong intense fear of fire and was very upset when imagining his leg burning.[68] As Browing, and others, have discovered, however, surgical consent forms generally contain language that gives the hospital control over excised tissues for disposal, educational use, or research. Even without formal consent, it has been understood that patients in effect "abandon" such materials at the hospital, and so they can hardly ask for them back weeks, months, or years later. Since very few patients have *intended* to keep, or to destroy or bury personally, their postsurgical parts, no accommodation is made for those who do not express their wishes before the procedure.[69]

Concern about the status of excised tissues will only intensify as human cells and human genetic material acquire monetary value.[70] While the cash market for anatomical specimens for medical museums was (and is) rather circumscribed, the market for developed cell lines and genes promises a great deal more. The case of *Moore v. the Regents of the University of California* (1988–1990) has raised serious issues about who can profit when, in this case, the spleen removed from John Moore for treatment of his hairy cell leukemia ended up providing his doctors with the primary cells for "a cell line that they later patented" with considerable commercial value.[71] As discussed above, notions about having property in the body have been resisted in the case of "ownership" over one's body after death; that legal position has made "ownership" in detached parts of one's own living body — as in Moore's case — troublesome to define in law, to say the least. As with the dead body, individuals do not "own" their postmortem body parts, but in most jurisdictions they have the right to determine the disposition of these parts for burial, cremation, or use in transplantation, without "receiving any valuable consideration."[72] To date, this "gift relationship" has defined the voluntary collection of blood for transfusions (except for some "payment for service" fees) and organs for transplants in Western nations. In these transactions among the living, both the donor (or kin) and donee have agreed to the exchange of blood and organs as a service to the injured and the ill, knowing full well that the "material" is, in a very important sense, priceless.

In Moore's case, of course, he did not want possession of his excised tissue in order to dispose of it properly; but neither did he understand that he was "giving" it to his physician for potentially *profitable* research. However valuable previous research on postsurgical or postmortem tissues has likely been in the past, Moore's case highlights what seemed to be an explicit, direct connection between an individual's cells and the resultant salable product. In 1990 the Supreme Court of California overturned the appellate court's decision that Moore had a valid claim. The majority arguments basically decided that Moore in fact had no ownership or right of possession in his cells once they were removed — with his consent — in the hospital; that imposing such ownership on one's own postremoval cells would unduly hinder important medical and scientific research; that in Moore's case his cells were not unique, and hence use of them did not invade his privacy; and that the patented cell line was "both factually and legally distinct" from Moore's original cells.[73] The court did agree that Moore's physicians should have told him about their research interests from the start, and hence they had not fulfilled the spirit of fully informed consent when performing the surgery and following his case (taking further blood and other samples) over the next several years.[74]

In the Supreme Court of California's decision on Moore's suit, Justice Arabian expressed his deep repulsion that a person (i.e., Moore, not the scientists who patented the cell line) could consider "the human vessel — the single most venerated and protected subject in any civilized society — as equal with the basest commercial commodity."[75] That Arabian identified Moore's *cells* — or even his spleen — as so much a part of the whole "venerated and protected" person that turning them into a commodity was as morally objectionable as commodifying a living or dead human being ironically speaks volumes for a notion of personhood embedded, like a saint's grace, in every speck of tissue. Considering the possible biochemical and genetic (hence possibly commercial) "value" of the vast numbers of identifiable tissue samples from autopsies and operations saved in pathological and anatomical collections, Moore's case will not be the last on this problem. Indeed, if Arabian's comment is to be taken literally, it already marks the beginning of a major cultural transformation in Western attitudes toward heretofore "worthless" parts of the self and others.[76]

Justice Arabian's moral position on Moore's cells is doubly ironic, moreover, given the past, and ongoing, treatment of some groups of presumably "venerated and protected subject[s]," as I have already discussed in the use of unclaimed paupers' bodies for medical school dissection. When we turn from biomedicine to anthropology, and from pathology departments to natural history museum displays, human body parts take on yet another set of political and cultural meanings. As histories of anthropology, discussions of natural history museums, and law review articles on Native American, Aboriginal, and other "origin peoples'" burials and remains make abundantly clear, people of European descent have systematically dug up, collected, transferred, preserved, and exhibited the remains (usually bones, but also "exotic" shrunken heads, human scalps with hair, and mummified connective tissues, for instance) of indigenous humans without any regard for permission from those who could be affected.[77] Newly influential indigenous peoples are not only disturbed over existing collections, moreover, but are also angry about the *continuing* extraction of remains from burial sites (even though now much more closely regulated) and the resistance to returning remains to indigenous people for proper reburial (even though some have already been "repatriated"). Museum authorities and scientists claim that the bones (and other parts) need to be examined before they can pass out of the sight and touch of experts. Indigenous people claim that such appeals to "science" mask ongoing racism and ethnocentrism.[78]

Religious and cultural concerns about proper respect for ancestors are central to indigenous peoples' claims for repatriation. "Theft" and "desecration" (or, at the very least, disrespect) continue for as long as the remains stay unburied in collections, whether or not on display in natural history museums.[79] Native American activism, at least in the United States, has led to federal (and some state) statutes outlining ways to obtain human remains and artifacts from public collections. As John Winski discusses in detail, the National Museum of the American Indian Act (NMAI, 1980) and the Native American Graves Protection and Repatriation Act (NAGPR, 1988, 1990) are two of the most important pieces of recent legislation. From my perspective, it is significant that the NMAI requires that all of the remains held by the Smithsonian first be "identified and inventoried" (since many have not been studied since deposit). Only after that research, which may take decades, "if the tribal origin of such remains can be adequately determined, the affected tribe must be notified and given an opportunity to request their return."[80] This act seems to me to reflect the spirit of the original Anatomy Act of 1832: presumably if remains are unidentifiable, or if the tribe they belonged to no longer survives, the remains have no one to suffer over them and to need their burial. In subtle contrast, the NAGPR extended control over the remains discovered at grave sites "to the lineal descendants of the deceased," or, if none exist, "to the Indian tribe on whose land the items are found," or, if on nontribal land, to "the tribe with the closest cultural affiliation to such remains."[81] This act in effect legislated a very broad notion of the "kin" who have an opportunity to care about the remains, and so to bury them.

Conclusion

Several legal commentators have explained how the NMAI and the NAGPR take steps toward dealing with the perceived difference in the way that indigenous peoples' remains have been treated compared with those of identifiable white settlers, whose remains have regularly been reburied when discovered.[82] From this perspective, it is interesting that the apparent sensitivity shown to settlers' bones has not yet been extended to anatomical specimens in medical museums. The people from whom they came, even if now nameless, are quite likely linked by genetic, ethnic, and cultural heritage to the population(s) of the area where the specimen originated.[83] Instead of raising concern about ongoing disrespect toward European, African, and Asian ancestors, however, relatively anonymous anatomical and pathological preparations of body parts somehow express (at least so far) the collective needs of humankind for progress in medical and scientific research and teaching. Whether subliminally categorized as "sacrifices" or "gifts" (especially by people who never actually see any specimens), these pieces have served appropriate goals (knowledge, better health care) in increasingly secular Western societies over the last century.

As I have discussed in this essay, no one can yet claim to *own* an anatomical specimen as property, although he or she may possess it. Legal reasoning in Anglo-American culture has nonetheless upheld the right of "kin" to decide its final disposition, assuming, of course, that a still-living person did not "abandon" his or her tissue in a hairbrush or in an operating suite. Without kin to present "a better right" to possession, once again, the parts and tissues can stay in the institution currently holding them. But of course these parts and tissues have "kin," and genetic studies could find them, given enough time and resources to do so. While DNA analysis of relatively recent human museum specimens is not a current intent or interest, discoveries of kin-relationships will likely be an inadvertent side result of historical-genetic research, which is rapidly expanding.[84] If so, being able to give anatomical specimens a collective identity (tribal, ancestral, familial) could quite literally create people who just might care about the status, location, display, or disposal of these remains.

Ethicists, lawyers, genetic researchers, and medical practitioners are currently developing policies that will guide the future collection and storage of human tissue specimens. In these discussions, the principles of personal autonomy and informed consent loom large, reflecting their increasing significance in many areas of medical research and practice. With still unidentified materials from the past, however, the question of "informed consent," expressing the autonomous wishes of the source person, is irrelevant. We can only speculate vainly about that person's possible decision, trying hard not to project our own assumptions and preferences onto a ghost. These ethical principles, moreover, will not easily solve the problems of privacy, patents, and potential profits on "useful" cells and genetic material collected in the present and future, as other essays in this collection make clear. From my historian's perspective, only the firm denial of commodification can possibly accommodate the diverse definitions of "respect" for human beings in a pluralistic society. I urge that we seriously consider restricting research material to tissues and fluids that are the generous, unrestricted gifts of informed adults and their families. I would also urge that development of commercially viable products from these gifts be limited to corporations bound to stringent requirements to reinvest profits into new research, to make a proportion of products available to those who cannot pay for them, and to value medical ethics above business practices. The gift relationship has maintained a fragile social and moral balance between personal beliefs and medical needs in the donation of cadavers for dissections and in the gift of organs for transplantation; it could do so as well for tissue samples.

Making adherence to these cultural values — autonomy, consent, and the gift relationship — more important than economic gain or research agendas would, of course, be extremely difficult and controversial; nor could they all be fulfilled to the same extent. We are too genetically intertwined to really be autonomous individuals anymore. My decisions about studies of my genome, or those of my as yet unburied ancestors, can affect not only my living relatives, but those yet to be conceived. But such has always been the case: human lives are too socially, economically, emotionally, and physically intertwined for us ever to have been really autonomous individuals, secure in our privacy and informed in our "free" consent. Genetic information will undoubtedly add more risks and fears, as well as hopes and pleasures, to how we live our lives. A historical perspective, nevertheless, offers many reminders that new knowledge and needs inspire cultural adaptions whose very complexities — even internal contradictions — in turn express multiple, conflicting values. How many of those our descendants end up believing in will depend not only upon our seemingly high ethical ideals, but also upon the mistakes we will inevitably make in trying to put them into practice.

Acknowledgments

I am grateful to the members of the 1996 summer Obermann Seminar on The Ethical and Legal Implications of Stored Tissue Samples for their comments on an earlier draft of this essay. Any errors in this revised version, however, are entirely my responsibility.

Notes

1. Ruth F. Chadwick, "Corpses, Recycling and Therapeutic Purposes," in Robert Lee and Derek Morgan, eds., *Death Rites: Law and Ethics at the End of Life* (London and New York: Routledge: 1994), p. 70 (emphasis added).

2. I broadly follow the analytical categories offered by cultural anthropologists such as Clifford Geertz. See, in particular, his discussion in "Ritual and Social Change: A Javanese Example," chapter 6 of his *The Interpretation of Cultures* (New York: Basic Books, 1973), pp. 142–169.

3. Jared Diamond, *The Third Chimpanzee: The Evolution and Future of the Human Animal* (New York: Harper Perennial, 1992), p. 44; Mary D. Russell, "Mortuary Practices at the Krapina Neadertal Site," *American Journal of Physical Anthropology* 72 (1987): 381–397.

4. Uniform Anatomical Gift Act (1987), in *Handbook of the National Conference of Commissioners on Uniform State Laws* (Buffalo, N.Y.: William S. Hein and Co., 1992), p. 169.

5. For an example, see Bruce Craig, "Bones of Contention," *National Parks* (July/August 1990): 17.

6. For an extended discussion of this process, see Thomas A. Kselman, *Death and the Afterlife in Modern France* (Princeton: Princeton University Press, 1993).

7. Fred Rosner, "Autopsy in Jewish Law and the Israeli Autopsy Controversy," in Fred Rosner and J. David Bleich, eds., *Jewish Bioethics* (New York: Hebrew Publishing Company, 1979), pp. 331–348; Byron R. McCane, "Bones of Contention? Ossuaries and Reliquaries in Early Judaism and Christianity," *Second Century* 8 (1991): 235–246; for an Islamic perspective, see Wajid Hussain, "Post-Mortem Examination: the Qur'ánic View," *Hamdard Islamicus* 15 (1992): 85–92.

8. James Bentley, *Restless Bones: The Story of Relics* (London: Constable, 1985), pp. 35–36, 60, 92; McCane, "Bones of Contention?" 236, 244–246; Victor Saxer, *Morts, martyrs, reliques en Afrique chrétienne aux premiers siècles* (Paris: Editions Beauchesne, 1980), details the formation of Christian funerary and burial practices during the first four centuries.

9. Caroline Walker Bynum, *The Resurrection of the Body in Western Christianity, 200–1336* (New York: Columbia University Press, 1995).

10. Bentley, *Restless Bones*, pp. 27, 39, 55, 65.

11. Christianity is not the only major religion to have relics. See Kevin M. Trainor, "When Is a Theft Not a Theft? Relic Theft and the Cult of the Buddha's Relics in Sri Lanka," *Numen* 39 (1992): 1–26; Bernard Faure, "Substitute Bodies in Chan/Zen Buddhism," in Jane Marie Law, ed., *Religious Reflections on the Human Body* (Bloomington: Indiana University Press, 1995), pp. 211–229.

12. Bentley, *Restless Bones*, and Bynum, *Resurrection*, deal extensively with these points.

13. For evidence that holy bodies were cut up soon after death, see Bentley, *Restless Bones*, pp. 37, 41–42, 94, 110–111, 155, 223.

14. For illustrations of some of the elaborate reliquaries, see Bentley, *Restless Bones*.

15. Bentley, *Restless Bones*, pp. 46–48, 69, 80–81; Bynum, *Resurrection*, has a much more nuanced analysis of these points throughout her work.

16. Patrick Geary, "Sacred Commodities: The Circulation of Medieval Relics," in Arjun Appadurai, ed., *The Social Life of Things: Commodities in Cultural Perspective* (New York: Cambridge University Press, 1986), pp. 169–193.

17. Bentley, *Restless Bones*, pp. 89–116.

18. Bentley, *Restless Bones*, pp. 216–227, esp. p. 224.

19. Rt. Rev. Mgr. Gerard Sheehy et al., *The Canon Law: Letter and Spirit, A Practical Guide to the Code of Canon Law* (Toronto: Liturgical Press, 1995), book IV, title IV, "The Cult of Saints, of Sacred Images and of Relics," can. 1190, §1 and §2.

20. Bentley, *Restless Bones*, pp. 169–193.

21. Michael M. MacDonald and Terence R. Murphy, *Sleepless Souls: Suicide in Early Modern England* (Oxford: Clarendon Press, 1990), pp. 15–31; Ruth Richardson, *Death, Dissection and the Destitute* (London: Routledge, 1987), pp. 32–37, gives a good summary of the standard historical account.

22. Nancy Siraisi, *Medieval and Early Renaissance Medicine* (Chicago: University of Chicago Press, 1990), pp. 82, 86–91; Roger French, "The Anatomical Tradition," in W. T. Bynum and Roy Porter, eds., *Companion Encyclopedia of the History of Medicine*, 2 vols. (London: Routledge, 1993), 1:81–101. These are both excellent surveys of the history of anatomy for this period.

23. Giovanna Ferrari, "Public Anatomy Lessons and the Carnival: The Anatomy Theatre of Bologna," *Past and Present* 117 (1987): 50–106; Jan C. C. Rupp, "Matters of Life and Death: The Social and Cultural Conditions of the Rise of Anatomical Theatres, with Special Reference to Seventeenth Century Holland," *History of Science* 28 (1990): 263–287; Susan C. Lawrence, *Charitable Knowledge: Hospital Pupils and Practitioners in Eighteenth Century London* (New York: Cambridge University Press, 1996), pp. 176, 182–183.

24. For a detailed account of popular gratification in witnessing a dissection of a murderer in 1829, see William Roughead, ed., *Burke and Hare* (Toronto: Canada Law Book Co., 1921), pp. 272–275.

25. Richardson, *Death*, pp. 35–37.

26. Richardson, *Death*, passim. The account of the passing of the Anatomy Act of 1832 is the subject of Richardson's book.

27. The details of burial law vary considerably under different jurisdictions and cannot be discussed here. For a brief survey, see Percival Jackson, *The Law of Cadavers, and of Burial and Burial Places* (New York: Prentice-Hall, 1950), pp. 22–28 (early history), and passim (footnotes) for precedents; for the United Kingdom, current statutes covering public health are given in David A. Smale, *Davies' Law of Burial, Cremation and Exhumation*, 6th ed. (Crayford, U.K.: Shaw and Sons, 1993), e.g., pp. 10, 35, 103, 192–194; for an early survey of public health regulations on burials, see Earl of Halsbury, ed., *The Laws of England*, 12 vols. (London: Butterworth and Co., 1908): 3:549–553.

28. Jackson, *Law of Cadavers*, 125–133; Lord Simonds, ed., *The Laws of England*, 12 vols. (London: Butterworth and Co., 1953), 4:3–5.

29. Paul Matthews, "Whose Body? People as Property," *Current Legal Problems* 36 (1983): 197–200; Matthews' account is quite fine, from my perspective, because he did considerable historical research to tease out what can be known from surviving documents about this principle. Most other authors just take the "no property in a corpse" position as well-established common law.

30. P. D. G. Skegg, "Human Corpses, Medical Specimens and the Law of Property," *Anglo-American Law Review* 4 (1975): 418.

31. Jackson, *Law of Cadavers*, pp. 125–133.

32. Jackson, *Law of Cadavers*, pp. 134–182, has a thorough survey of U.S. cases that occurred before 1950; for some recent cases, see *Scarpaci v. Milwaukee County*, Wis., 292 N.W.2d 816; *Grad v. Kaasa*, 314 S.E.2d 755; *Kirker v. Orange County*, 519 So.2d 682; *Christensen v. Los Angeles County*, 230 Cal. App. 3d 798 [1990 Cal. App. LEXIS 678].

33. Richardson, *Death*, pp. 198–215. The text of the Anatomy Act can be found

in compilations of Parliamentary Acts under 2 & 3 Gul. c. 75, An Act for Regulating Schools of Anatomy.

34. Richardson, *Death*, pp. 219–281.

35. Smale, *Davies' Law of Burial*, pp. 50–52, gives the current provisions of the 1984 act.

36. For a detailed survey of U.S. state laws on anatomy before the Uniform Anatomical Gift Act of 1968, see George H. Weinman, *A Survey of the Law concerning Dead Human Bodies, Bulletin of the National Research Council* 73 (December 1929). Many of the statutes Weinmann covers were first passed in the nineteenth century. There is considerable variation among state policies, but all provide that unclaimed bodies go to anatomy schools. The only exceptions, in some states, were for the bodies of strangers passing through a town (unless they were "vagrants") and ex-servicemen. Most states passed laws in the 1960s and then again in the 1980s to conform to the provisions of the Uniform Anatomical Act suggested by the Commissioners on Uniform State Laws. See their *Handbook* for 1968 and 1987. It is important to note that the 1987 amended Uniform Anatomical Gift Act allows coroners to approve the donation of organs from a person whose kin cannot be found within a fairly short amount of time. This provision was designed to increase the organ supply. Most states do not go this far, and require positive knowledge that the person agreed to be an organ donor, either from an organ donation card or from relatives. One of the few states that followed the provisions of the Uniform Anatomical Gift Act was Ohio. See *Ohio Revised Statues* §2108.02 (B7); Erik S. Jaffe, "'She's Got Bette Davis['s] Eyes': Assessing the Nonconsensual Removal of Cadaver Organs under the Takings and Due Process Clauses," *Columbia Law Review* 90 (1990): 528–574; Harry J. Finke, "*Brotherton v. Cleveland*: The Creation of Property Rights by a Federal Court," *City of Toledo Law Review* 23 (1992): 205–218.

37. Vickie Walker, "The Anatomy Act," unpublished undergraduate paper (supervised by Roy Porter, Wellcome Institute, London; assisted by Susan Lawrence), 1995, contains some examination of the act's records from 1934 to 1953; Richardson, *Death*, pp. 258–260. Richardson has noted the apparent correlation between the rise of bequesting and cremation in Britain. Both, she argues, stem from changing beliefs about life after death: a final decline of belief in literal resurrection and a broad social shift toward agnosticism and atheism. These points remain to be researched, however.

38. "Uniform Anatomical Gift Act," in *Handbook* (1987), p. 182 [§10(a)]. The adoption of the Uniform Anatomical Gift Act by each state means that each state has its own version of this act, although generally in agreement with the provisions of the Commissioners on Uniform State Laws. The 1968 version of the Uniform Anatomical Gift Act, however, did *not* contain language forbidding the purchase or sale of organs; indeed, it gave the donee, who could be a physician, hospital, or needy person, "absolute ownership" over the material without specifying how it could be transferred to another, except by continuing to call the exchange a "gift" (*Handbook*, [1968], pp. 182–193). For a detailed argument in favor of making organs into monetary commodities, see Roger Blair and David Kaserman, "The Economics and Ethics of Alternative Cadaveric Organ Procurement Policies," *Yale Journal on Regulation* 8 (1991): 402–452, and the response sustaining the gift relation by Ronald Guttman, "The Meaning of 'The Economics and Ethics of Alternative Cadaveric Organ Procurement Policies,'"

Yale Journal on Regulation 8 (1991): 453–462. See also Roy Hardiman, "Toward the Right of Commerciality: Recognizing Property Rights in the Commercial Value of Human Tissue," *UCLA Law Review* 34 (1986): 207–264.

For a survey of the legislation covering human tissues in Australia, see Magnusson, "The Recognition of Proprietary Rights in Human Tissue in Common Law Jurisdictions," *Melbourne University Law Review* 18 (1992): 612–616. Australian law covers tissues used in research as well as organs used in transplants and, according to Magnusson, prohibits donors "from trading in their own tissue, including blood, in the absence of ministerial permission." On the other hand, "reputable suppliers are permitted to sell processed tissue for medical or scientific purposes, so long as the tissue is itself obtained without payment" (p. 615). In his review, Magnusson basically argues for recognizing property rights in human parts and tissues on the basis of existing practices.

39. Uniform Anatomical Gift Act (1987), pp. 180, 182. Compare §6(a)(1) with §10(a). The latter states that the donees and purposes of an anatomical gift are "a hospital, physician, surgeon, or procurement organization, for transplantation, therapy, medical or dental education, research, or advancement of medical or dental science." Subsection (2) allows educational institutions to receive such gifts for "education, research"; §10(a), in contrast, only prohibits buying or selling parts "for transplantation or therapy." Education, research, and the more general "advancement of . . . science" are clearly *not* covered under this provision or any other. States have adopted this exact wording and general intent. See, for example, *Ohio Revised Statues* §2108.11 and §2108.12.

40. Office of Technology Assessment, U.S. Congress, "Ownership of Human Tissues and Cells," *New Developments in Biotechnology* (1987); Hardiman, "Toward the Right of Commerciality," pp. 207–210.

41. Heinrich von Staden, "Women and Dirt," *Helios* 19 (1992): 16; see also Philippe Ariès, *The Hour of Our Death*, trans. Helen Weaver (New York: Vintage Books, 1982), pp. 357–359; Karen Gordon-Grube, "Anthropology in Post-Renaissance Europe: The Tradition of Medicinal Cannibalism," *American Anthropologist* 90 (1988): 405–409.

42. Roughead, *Burke and Hare*, p. 66. In 1829 the notorious William Burke was executed for murdering poor people in Edinburgh and selling their corpses to Dr. Knox, a private anatomy teacher. According to Roughead's compilation of original documents, Burke was publicly dissected at the University of Edinburgh and his parts stored for student use. At the same time, however, his skin was also "tanned" and sold as souvenirs of the event. Several sites in Europe, moreover, mostly dating from the late medieval and early modern period, are still extant where human bones have been arranged in "decorative" motifs, in charnel houses, crypts of churches, and catacombs. These sites have an ambiguous status in the modern world: as macabre art, as testaments to sacred places, and as tourist attractions.

43. Chadwick discusses a U.K. case in which an artist displayed a model human head wearing ten-year-old laboratory specimens of fetuses in a commercial gallery. The artist and gallery owner were charged with offending public decency. Chadwick, "Corpses," pp. 66–67; for the original case report, see *R. v. Gibson* and another, 1 All ER 439, [1991]. Fredrik Ruysch (1638–1731) is one figure, well known among historians

of anatomy, who created "sculptures" out of human bones and natural objects in the seventeenth century. These were quasi–memento mori (reflections on death) and quasi-lessons in anatomical design. See K. B. Roberts and J. D. W. Tomlinson, *The Fabric of the Body: European Traditions of Anatomical Illustration* (Oxford: Clarendon Press, 1992), pp. 290–300.

44. Susan C. Lawrence, "Medical Education," in W. F. Bynum and Roy Porter, eds., *Companion Encyclopedia of the History of Medicine*, 2 vols. (London and New York: Routledge Press, 1993), 2:115–179.

45. Heinrich von Staden, "The Discovery of the Body: Human Dissection and Its Cultural Contexts in Ancient Greece," *Yale Journal of Biology and Medicine* 65 (1992): 233–241.

46. Roberts and Tomlinson, *Fabric of the Body*, passim.

47. Siraisi, *Medieval*, p. 40, tells the story of a group of nuns who opened the body of one of their sisterhood immediately after she died to look for signs of the passion, which they reportedly found in the holy woman's heart. In this case the "autopsy" was for evidence of spiritual elevation.

48. Siraisi, *Medieval*, p. 82.

49. Lawrence, *Charitable Knowledge*, pp. 181, 306–310.

50. Paula Findlen, *Possessing Nature: Museums, Collecting and Scientific Culture in Early Modern Italy* (Berkeley: University of California Press, 1994); in 1509, as well, Lucas Cranach compiled a "catalogue of relics" based on the collection of the Emperor Frederick. See Bentley, *Restless Bones*, p. 179.

51. Katherine Park and Lorraine Daston, "Unnatural Conceptions: The Study of Monsters in Sixteenth and Seventeenth Century France and England," *Past and Present* 92 (1983): 22–23, 25–38.

52. Findlen, *Possessing Nature*.

53. F. J. Cole, *A History of Comparative Anatomy: From Aristotle to the Eighteenth Century* (New York: Dover Publications, 1975 [first edition 1949]), pp. 180, 274–276, 445–450. See also J. N. Gannal, *History of Embalming, and of Preparations in Anatomy, Pathology, and Natural History*, ed. and trans. R. Harlan (Philadelphia: Judah Dobson, 1840), for detailed accounts of older methods and beliefs surrounding the methods of the Egyptians in Europe.

54. See, for example, John Teacher, *Catalogue of the Anatomical Preparations of Dr. William Hunter* (Glasgow: University of Glasgow, 1970 [edited reprint of 1900 edition]). The first manuscript description of Hunter's collection dates from 1782.

55. Russell Maulitz, *The Anatomy of Pathology in the Early Nineteenth Century* (New York: Cambridge University Press, 1987), has numerous details on this process for France and England.

56. For a presentation of more recent exhibits using anatomical specimens and models, see Eben J. Carey, *Medical Science Exhibits: A Century of Progress* (© A Century of Progress, 1936), pp. 31–33, and passim for photographs of exhibits at the Chicago World's Fair, 1933–1934; Sidney H. Daukes, *The Medical Museum: Modern Developments, Organization and Technical Methods* (London: Wellcome Foundation, 1929).

57. See Teacher, *Catalogue*, for numerous examples. On the general significance of universalizing body parts taken from, or drawn from, individuals, see Susan C. Law-

rence and Kae Bendixen, "His and Hers: Depictions of Male and Female Anatomy in Anatomy Texts for Medical Students, 1890–1989," *Social Science and Medicine* 35 (1992): 925–934.

58. Somerville to Eddison, Inspectorate of Anatomy, Outletter Book (General), 1832–1835, Jan. 11, 1833, PRO MH 74/12; Alcock to Goodfellow, Inspectorate of Anatomy, Letterbook (Miscellaneous), 1842–1858, Jan. 29, 1844, PRO MH 74/15.

59. Lawrence, *Charitable Knowledge*, pp. 235, 309–310.

60. Susan C. Lawrence, "Anatomy and Address: Creating Medical Gentlemen in Eighteenth-century London," in Vivian Nutton and Roy Porter, eds., *The History of Medical Education in England* (Amsterdam: Rodopi, 1995), pp. 206–212.

61. For examples, see [John Douglas], *A List of the Anatomical Preparations of the Late Mr. John Douglas* (London, 1758); and [William Partridge], *A Catalogue of Anatomical Preparations* . . . (London, 1766); copies of these catalogs held in the library of the Royal College of Surgeons of England (London) contain handwritten notes on the prices of specimens put up for sale at these auctions.

62. Alcock to Goodfellow, Inspectorate of Anatomy, Letterbook (Miscellaneous), 1842–1858, Jan. 29, 1844, PRO MH 74/15.

63. Robert Bogdan, *Freak Show: Presenting Human Oddities for Amusement and Profit* (Chicago: Chicago University Press, 1988).

64. *Doodeward v. Spence*, 6 C. L. R. [Australia] 414. See discussions of this case in Matthews, "Whose Body?" pp. 212–214, and Magnusson, "Proprietary Rights," p. 606; Skegg, "Human Corpses," pp. 418–420.

65. Matthews, "Whose Body?" pp. 219–220.

66. Matthews, "Whose Body?" pp. 220; he supports this with case about a dispute over conjoined twins that ended with the father's "better right" to the corpse, presumably in order to bury it. Matthews goes on to comment, however, that "this view deals only with civil law rights. A person retaining a corpse unburied might still be liable under the criminal law." In the 1984 Anatomy Act in Britain, however, which revised the 1832 law, the provisions state that the secretary of state, who licenses places for anatomical dissection, also licenses persons to "have possession of anatomical specimens." Smale, *Davies' Law*, p. 52. Skegg, "Human Corpses," pp. 418–420, argues that the law in England should be changed to make parts removed from dead bodies into property and/or to specify that human body parts "prior to burial or cremation" are "the subject of property." This author is writing, in 1975, specifically about anatomical specimens, not organs for transplant or human tissues with potential economic value.

67. *Mokry v. University of Texas Health Science Center at Dallas*, 529 S.W. 2d 802. The appellate court in Mokry reversed the lower court's dismissal of this case and ordered a new trial.

68. *Browing v. Norton–Children's Hospital*, 504 S. W. 2d 713 (Ky. 1974).

69. In Browing's case, he only thought about the fate of his "abandoned" leg weeks after it had been cremated: 504 S. W. 2d 713 (Ky. 1974); Moore at 793 P.2d 488. A surgical consent form appears at 558 S.W.2d 136–137, for a case on a different issue. It contains the statement "consent to the pathological study and disposal by the hospital authorities of any removed tissues."

70. Jaffe, "Nonconsensual Removal," pp. 531–532.

71. Jaffe, "Nonconsensual Removal," p. 540, citing *Moore v. Regents of Univ. of Cal.*,

215 Cal. App. 3d 709, 728–729, 249 Cal. Rptr. 494, 506–507 (1988), aff'd in part, rev'd in part, 51 Cal. 3d 120, 793 P.2d 479, 271 Cal. Rptr. 146 (1990).

72. All states have adopted the provisions of the Uniform Anatomical Gift Act as outlined by the National Conference of Commissioners on Uniform State Laws (see their *Handbook* [1987], p. 182) prohibiting a person from purchasing or selling "a part for transplantation or therapy, if removal of the part is intended to occur after the death of the decedent." The National Organ Transplant Act also forbids a trade in organs for donation.

73. 793 P.2d, pp. 488–497.

74. 793 P.2d, p. 497.

75. Quotation from Justice Arabian, 793 P.2d 497; the justices did agree, however, that the doctors were wrong not to have told Moore all along what had been done with his spleen (or part of his spleen) and chastised them for failing to fulfill the spirit of informed consent.

76. Recent draft legislation for Congress addresses some of the issues surrounding stored tissue samples. The McDermott Medical Privacy in the Age of New Technologies Act (H.R. 3482, May 16, 1996), now before Congress, centers on the privacy of health information in general, which subsumes knowledge obtained from genetic testing. Because the bill concentrates on access to information, however, it does *not* address concerns about taking samples and making tests per se; rather it would take over once the data were collected. The proposed Genetic Privacy Act (draft with commentary dated Feb. 28, 1995) by George Annas (et al.), in contrast, places considerable restrictions on researchers. A person wanting to make *genetic* tests on tissues is responsible for seeing that quite specific informed consent has been given by the individual from whom it came. This act does not address any other forms of testing and, if read narrowly, would not exclude analysis of human RNA in tissues. The language of the draft, moreover, is quite unclear on whether it would apply retroactively to all stored tissue samples, even if now ostensibly anonymous.

77. Paul Turnbull, "'Ramsay's Regime': The Australian Museum and the Procurement of Aboriginal Bodies, c. 1874–1900," *Aboriginal History* 15 (1991): 108–121; George W. Stocking, "Essays on Museums and Material Culture," in George Stocking, ed., *Objects and Others, History of Anthropology* (Madison: University of Wisconsin Press, 1985), 3:11; Michael M. Ames, *Cannibal Tours and Glass Boxes: The Anthropology of Museums*, 2nd ed. (Vancouver: University of British Columbia Press, 1992).

78. John B. Winski, "There Are Skeletons in the Closet: The Repatriation of Native American Human Remains and Burial Objects," *Arizona Law Review* 34 (1992): 187–214; Larry J. Zimmerman, "'Tell Them about the Suicide': A Review of Recent Materials on the Reburial of Prehistoric Native American Skeletons," *American Indian Quarterly* 10 (1986): 333–343; Ronald L. Grimes, "Desecration of the Dead: An Interreligious Controversy," *American Indian Quarterly* 10 (1986): 305–318; Gerald Vizenor, "Bone Courts: The Rights and Narrative Representation of Tribal Bones," *American Indian Quarterly* 10 (1986): 319–331; "Symposium: The Native American Graves Protection and Repatriation Act of 1990 and State Repatriation-related Legislation," *Arizona State Law Journal* 24 (1992): entire volume. Not all indigenous people agree with repatriation; indeed some have found the scientific study of their origins to be an important part of understanding who they are. For this approach, see Colin Pardoe,

"Sharing the Past: Aboriginal Influence on Archaeological Practice, A Case Study from New South Wales," *Aboriginal History* 14 (1990): 208–220.

79. Winski, "Skeletons in the Closet," p. 189.

80. Winski, "Skeletons in the Closet," p. 197.

81. Winski, "Skeletons in the Closet," pp. 197–198.

82. Vizenor, "Bone Courts," p. 323; Winski, "Skeletons in the Closet," pp. 188, 200–202.

83. For information on collections of anatomical specimens more or less open to the public, see Martin R. Lipp, *Medical Landmarks USA: A Travel Guide to Historic Sites, Architectural Gems, Remarkable Museums and Libraries, and Other Places of Health-related Interest* (New York: McGraw-Hill, 1991), pp. 133, 214–216, 350, 478.

84. An "intent" to discover ancestral linkages is explicitly present in the projects to study human diversity through genetic studies of peoples worldwide and research on quite ancient human remains. See the paper by Henry T. Greely in this volume. Also see Erika Hagelberg, "Ancient DNA Studies," *Evolutionary Anthropology* 2 (1993/1994): 199–207; and M. B. Richards and B. C. Sykes, "Authenticating DNA Extracted from Ancient Skeletal Remains," *Journal of Archaeological Science* 22 (1995): 291–299.

Negotiating Diverse Values in a Pluralist Society: Limiting Access to Genetic Information

Mary Ann G. Cutter

This essay explores negotiating diverse values in a pluralist society. It employs a case study of the development of public policy in the state of Colorado to regulate access and use of genetic information by the insurance industry in order to illustrate challenges in bringing resolution to disputes involving diverse values. The analysis is brought to bear on current discussions regarding the storage, access, and use of human tissue samples. In this essay, I argue that any resolution to debates regarding the storage, access, and use of genetic information turns on the values at stake and the theories employed to resolve them. Since these values and theoretical orientations differ and at times compete, it is imperative in deciding how genetic information is managed that the various values of stakeholders be considered. This is the case because it will be impossible to arrive at a single rule or public policy that will answer all of our questions or solve all of our value conflicts. Without an overriding grand ethical narrative, we are left with coming together to discuss and negotiate the values at stake and how best to proceed in specific contexts.

The Role of the State in Limiting Access to Genetic Information by Insurers

Essentially advances in medical science are causing information from genetic tests to be more useful in the diagnosis and treatment of human disease and illness. An implication of this is that some people are discouraged from participating in genetic testing and other means of genetic diagnosis because of the potential that insurers would use that information to deny or reduce health insurance coverage. In response to this concern, between December 1992 and June 1994, Coloradans engaged in a debate regarding the extent to which the insurance industry ought to have access to genetic information. The debate resulted in legislation signed into law on June 4, 1994, five months after being introduced into the Colorado legislature.

The Colorado Statute, which is included at the end of this essay, defines genetic testing as a direct laboratory test of human DNA, RNA, or chromosomes used to identify the presence or absence of alterations in genetic material associated with illness or disease.[1] The statute applies to entities that provide health, group disability, and long-term care insurance and are within the Colorado Insurance Commission's jurisdiction. The covered entities are prohibited from seeking, using, or keeping genetic information for underwriting or nontherapeutic purposes. Violation of the act is an unfair insurance practice subject to Insurance Commission sanctions. The statute provides a private right of action for individuals injured by wrongful use of genetic information, with both legal and equitable remedies available. Additionally, the prevailing party may recover attorney fees. In short, there are five parts to the statute: (1) intent (Section 1), (2) definitions (Section 2), (3) prohibitions (Section 3), (4) exemptions (Sections 4–10), and (5) sanctions (Sections 11–13).

Prior to the passage of the Colorado statute, eleven states (Alabama,[2] Arizona,[3] California,[4] Florida,[5] Louisiana,[6] Maryland,[7] Montana,[8] North Carolina,[9] Ohio,[10] Tennessee,[11] and Wisconsin)[12] restricted the use of genetic information and testing for use by insurers. Most of the states' restrictions narrowly apply only to one or two conditions or to carriers of a genetic disorder who remain unaffected by it. Two states (Arizona and Montana) broaden restrictions to include all single gene and chromosomal conditions. Ten states (Alabama, Arizona, California, Florida, Louisiana, Maryland, Montana, North Carolina, Ohio, and Tennessee) allow insurers to use genetic information that can be supported by actuarial data or, in some cases, reasonably anticipated experience. In 1992 Wisconsin passed a law that prohibits health insurers from requiring or requesting individuals to take a DNA test, to reveal whether they have undergone a DNA test, or to disclose DNA test results. Wisconsin also prohibits insurers from using DNA test results to determine rates and other aspects of health insurance coverage. Ohio's law, passed in 1993, calls for a ten-year moratorium on the use of information from genetic tests. New Jersey's law,[13] passed by the New Jersey General Assembly in June 1996, bans health insurance companies from denying access or setting higher rates for individuals who are genetically predisposed to certain diseases. Unlike other state laws, the New Jersey law prevents insurance companies from using information about family history, regarding it as genetic information.

Since the 1970s, then, state governments have engaged in debates regarding access and use of genetic information by insurers, employers, and others.[14] One can ask whether there is a more efficient way to address concerns regarding the handling of genetic information by insurers. One response is offered by the Task Force on Genetic Information and Insurance, a NIH–Department of Energy (DOE) Working Group on Ethical, Legal, and Social Implications of Human Genome Research.[15] According to the task force, the U.S. health care system should ensure universal access to and participation by all in a

program of basic health services, which should treat genetic services compa-
rably to nongenetic services. Participation in and access to a program of basic
health services should not depend on employment or disclosure of past, present, and future health status, including genetic. Such reform would render
state legislation moot. But more importantly, such reform would provide a
fairer and more equitable way to regulate medical information. Nevertheless,
the task force recognizes, as many of us do, that federal health care reform is
practically and politically a challenge and we do well to develop alternative
means of reducing the risk of genetic discrimination [16] through (at least) mor-
atoriums on the use of genetic tests in underwriting (as in the case of Ohio).

Here we may wish to keep in mind the role of public policy, which differs
from that of science. Public policy serves to articulate shared goals among
members of particular communities. It responds effectively to problems in
need of solutions. In contrast, science serves to provide explanations for natural phenomena. It does this through rigorous methods guiding hypothesis formation, observation, gathering of evidence, and formulation of explanation.
Public policy and science are two distinct enterprises yet work together, as in
the case of formulating public policy governing storage, access, and use of
genetic information. It is important, for instance, for public policy makers to
understand genetics. On this note, the task force encourages educational efforts to improve knowledge about genetics and genetic testing procedures and
results.[17]

Values That Guide Us and Those That Separate Us

The development of the Colorado statute limiting the use of genetic information by insurers illustrates an attempt to sort out the values that guide us
from those that separate us with an eye toward achieving shared goals. Such is
an exercise in ethics. Ethics is the study of right and wrong, and good and bad,
as it applies to the actions and character of individuals, communities, institutions, and society.[18] Generally in ethics we apply the terms "right" and "good"
to those actions and qualities of character that foster interest (i.e., a share or
participation in) or a claim. Alternatively, we apply the terms "wrong" and
"bad" to those actions and qualities that impair the interests of individuals,
communities, institutions, and societies. In Colorado, for instance, the concern was the impairment of the interests of those who had been diagnosed or
were worried about being diagnosed with a genetic disorder and thus were
candidates for loss or reduction of insurance, many of whom were children
and families with children. Put another way, the goal was to foster the interests

of individuals by ensuring access to health care insurance coverage for those who were undergoing or had undergone genetic testing.

Judgments regarding promotion and impairment are evaluative. That is, they involve values. Values (L. *valere*, to be strong, to be worth) are signs of significance in a world that can be other. A value is what makes an object or event worthy. We value insurance, for example, not because it is insurance but because it promotes the values of security and freedom from financial burden (e.g., through cost sharing) and in turn sickness and disease. In addition, health insurance promotes the value of health, for health care is likely not to be affordable and therefore possible without health care insurance. To the extent that we think that the insurance industry undermines these values, we judge it to be ineffective or unjust. On this analysis, then, interests are general ways of talking about categories of considerations that involve specific value judgments by moral agents, by agents who can choose.

Today there are two prominent ways to talk about interests. Both have roots in Western thought that span two and a half millennia. One way to talk about interests is in terms of the *consequences* of actions. Discussion about consequences requires that individuals be able to give well-founded reasons to explain why moral agents should or should not pursue the consequences of an action. Consequences that advance interests are labeled "right" or "good," and moral agents should pursue such consequences. Obtaining genetic tests may be considered good because it promotes the interests of the patient and related parties, particularly if preventive, palliative, or curative treatment can be offered. Allowing insurers access to genetic information may be good insofar as the information is used to provide actuarial data on emerging clinical problems that need attention and therefore coverage by current and potential clients. Storing genetic information in databanks is for some good because it allows clinicians and researchers to keep records on and subsequently study and learn from those diagnosed with genetic disorders. Likewise, storage by police enforcement experts is good in order to track residual offenders, particularly sexual offenders, in order to maintain a peaceable society.

Alternatively, consequences that impair interests are labeled "wrong" or "bad," and moral agents should not pursue such consequences. Allowing anyone access to genetic databanks may be considered bad because it impairs the interests of the relevant party or parties. This is the case in part because of the nature of information in databanks. Genetic information carries significant implications for the family members of the individuals tested. Genetic tests can diagnose future medical conditions prior to the onset of symptoms, and this presents special challenges to family members' privacy. In fact, some people hold that genetic information reveals the essence of an individual's being.[19] Furthermore, eugenics movements and the Nazi Party have demonstrated possible abuses of genetic information. Moreover, no one is immune from genetic variation and genetic risks. And so interests are impaired when genetic information is used to decline offering someone health insurance coverage, especially because the relevant party is losing the very thing that is so needed following a troublesome diagnosis, namely, health insurance for health care.

Alternatively, not allowing insurers access to genetic information is bad because the impact of genetic information on insurance rates and availability may be exaggerated. More seriously, the impact of restrictions on the voluntary insurance market, and on the risk classification system that is one of its essential elements, is largely ignored. Arnold Dicke[20] reminds us that risk classification has a threefold purpose: (1) to promote fairness, (2) to permit economic incentives to operate and encourage widespread availability of coverage, and (3) to protect the soundness of the financial security system. On this view and as a basic principle, any sound risk classification system should reflect cost-of-insurance differences based on relevant risk characteristics.

As one can see, consequences may conflict. While patients may judge unlimited access to genetic information to be bad because individuals for the most part do not like sensitive information made widely available, an insurer may judge unlimited access to be good because insurers should have access to information that potential and current clients do in order to prevent adverse selection.[21] Alternatively, while patients may judge limited access, particularly by the insurance industry, to be good because insurers ought not to cherry-pick (i.e., choose the best or most healthy of clients), insurers may label the activity bad because it represents financially unsound business practices. Furthermore, proponents of regulatory restrictions may hold that the Colorado statute is primarily a proactive approach that would not adversely affect health insurance costs, either for the insurers or for those insured, since persons who would most likely be adversely affected by the failure to pass such a statute would probably already be covered by health insurance. Insurers may respond that any attempt to undermine underwriting practices is bad or harmful to a voluntary insurance market.

In addition, one may argue that, given that the moral mission of the insurance industry is to spread risks to members of a community,[22] restrictions on underwriting practices are good. Insurers may respond that, given that the industry has no such moral mission but instead a financial one for present and future clients and employees, it is bad for the state to restrict underwriting practices. Furthermore, one may hold that state regulatory restrictions are bad because what is really needed is federal regulation in health insurance reform.[23]

To allow states to regulate their own practices permits a patchwork of laws and ultimately confusion nationwide. To permit states to address the issue of genetic discrimination is to act irresponsibly, denying the more pressing problem of fair and equitable access to health care. Much depends on one's stake in the debates.

Another way to talk about interests is in terms of a *right* or rights. A right is a claim to be treated in a certain way regardless of the consequences of doing so. Respect for rights promotes interests because it allows individuals freely to pursue things that are individually and communally valued. Societies committed to freedom should protect rights. Some hold the view, for example, that government should protect a citizen's right of privacy over medical, including genetic, information and that this right is grounded in the liberty interests granted by the Fourteenth Amendment of the U.S. Constitution.[24] Denial of rights damages interests because denial does not allow individuals freely to pursue things that they value. Societies committed to freedom should prevent the denial of rights. Nevertheless, denial of some rights may be justified when rights are in conflict. A patient's right to decide how her genetic information will be used during its storage may conflict with an insurer's right to request information that is relevant in risk-classification practices. And, given that genetic information is family information, storage and use as determined by a particular family member may conflict with another family member's right to decide for what purposes the information may be used. Depending on one's stake in the debates, one may decide to favor one or the other right.

Interests may conflict in yet other ways. Rights may conflict with consequences. An individual's right to the privacy of genetic information may conflict with a researcher's need to be able to obtain any and all relevant information about the health status of a potential or current subject or with the police's need to obtain a DNA sample from an offender involved in a sexual assault. Or protecting a claimed right of genetic privacy may conflict with good consequences and may in the end be harmful. Insurance companies may not offer certain services that they might otherwise, given the lack of ability to generate actuarial data on emerging conditions.

Because tradeoffs among interests are complex, constantly changing, and sometimes uncertain, there often are competing, well-reasoned ways to judge what is right and wrong and good and bad in the case of complex matters such as banking genetic data and providing access to and use of such data. For instance, there is good reason to hold that individual self-determination always has priority over the consequences of promoting individual or societal welfare. This is the position taken by George Annas.[25] And this is the position forwarded by the Colorado statute protecting access and use of genetic information when it declares that "genetic information is the unique property of the individual to whom the information pertains"[26] and that "information derived from genetic testing shall be confidential and privileged. Any release, for purposes other than diagnosis, treatment, or therapy . . . requires specific written consent of the person tested."[27] Alternatively, there is good reason to hold that a particular account of individual or societal welfare provides a weightier consideration in ethical and public policy decisionmaking. This is the justification for exemptions in the Colorado statute.[28] The position is that there are good reasons for allowing certain authorities (e.g., peace officers, district attorney, assistant district attorney, courts, and state board of parole) unconsensual access to genetic information, thereby overriding any right of genetic privacy.

Then again, we may decide that neither consequence- nor rights-based approaches provide an appropriate framework for thinking through the ethical implications of stored genetic information. We may decide that the language of consequences and rights is unhelpful and we need rather to consider alternative language to discuss such issues. Perhaps we should talk not about privacy but about how we can better care for each other.[29] Perhaps the appropriate language is one of spirituality and addresses honoring the traditions of certain cultures.[30] Perhaps, as this essay suggests, the language should be one of respect. Regardless of one's particular position, ethical debates bring together the interests and values of particular stakeholders and illustrate the difficulty in managing moral disagreement. Difficulty arises because values and theoretical orientations to assess such values can differ. Unfortunately, it is impossible to achieve or maximize each and every value at stake in debates. We are simply but profoundly human.

One of the emerging themes in this analysis of the values at stake in debates regarding storage, access, and use of genetic information is that contemporary culture lacks a univocal theoretical or conceptual basis for its thoughts, decisions, and actions. The contemporary or postmodern world is characterized by a loss of faith in monistic metaphors.[31] The result is a plurality of epistemological and moral views: meaning is equivocal, not univocal. For some, this is confusion; for others, it is a chance to celebrate diversity. Either way, moral authority of content-full guidelines is brought into question, leading to the postmodern predicament — the situation of not being sure who is the authority, especially on questions involving controversy and requiring address. To quote Jean-François Lyotard: "In contemporary society and culture — postindustrial society, postmodern culture — the question of legitimation of knowledge is formulated in difference terms. The grand narrative has lost its credibility, regardless of what mode of unification it uses, regardless of whether it is a speculative narrative [e.g., Kant] or a narrative of emancipation [e.g., Marx]." [32] We are, in short, without singular answers to troublesome questions regarding how to assess, weigh, and resolve conflict between and among ethical values. Such is a mark of a pluralist society.

Respect, Negotiation, and Reaching Consensus

It does not follow from the prior analysis that "anything goes." Many of us, including Lyotard, struggle with what constitutes limits on the use of force and the boundaries of appropriate sanctions. Although we may lack a grand ethical narrative, relativism is not the only option. There are constraints, resistances, or limits. There are similarities. There are common grounds. One of those constraints or common grounds in a society committed to freedom is respect.

By respect, I do not mean a minimal recognition of the self-determination of another in the moral community. I do not mean respect for only rational agents. I mean something else that can justify protection of genetic information for the innocent (e.g., children), vulnerable (e.g., children, the compromised elderly), and groups of individuals (e.g., ethnic groups, tribes), among others who are worthy. Consider the account of respect offered by Baruch Brody.[33] To show respect for persons is to value persons by *refraining* from eliminating the necessary conditions of personhood, which include life, bodily integrity, freedom to make choices and to act upon them, and so on. In addition, it means *acting to promote* the presence of such conditions. Respect involves, then, a negative and positive duty to others. On this view, respect is not dependent on the consent or rights of another. The obligation to show respect for persons is not an obligation to the person in question. It is an obligation to act in certain ways toward that person or persons. And so, on this analysis, respect is owed to the innocent and vulnerable, to communities of persons, as well as to rational agents.

What concerns me in this essay is the role that respect plays in the development of public policy. Negotiation (L. *negotiatio*, from *negotiari*, to carry on business), as a procedural expression of respect, is often the only way to resolve disputes where there is disagreement about what is proper to do. In the law, to negotiate means to conduct communications or conferences with a view toward reaching a settlement or agreement. It is the *process* of making and arranging the terms of a contract.[34]

At least four elements of negotiation may be distinguished. First is *access*.

Interested participants must have the opportunity to enter into debates. In the case of developing legislation in Colorado, numerous groups participated in discussions about regulating access and use of genetic information by the insurance industry. These groups or voices included, among others, those from the State Department of Public Health and Environment, insurance industry,[35] health lawyers,[36] physicians,[37] patients,[38] those trained in genetics,[39] health policy experts,[40] philosophers and bioethicists,[41] theologians,[42] the media,[43] interest groups,[44] and Coloradan citizens from various walks of life. Monthly meetings were scheduled at times and places convenient for those wishing to participate.

Second is *information* (L. *informatio*, a representation, outline, from *informare*, to give form to, to represent), which entails making available sufficient knowledge, instruction, or counsel. The goal here is to increase the understanding of participants so that discussion may proceed. In the case of developing legislation in Colorado, meetings entailed overviews of issues related to genetics and insurance, open discussion, and dissemination of relevant literature. It became clear early in discussions that many participants were not prepared to evaluate critically the use of genetic information in insurance practices. To remedy this, numerous meetings functioned as educational forums as opposed to debates.[45]

Third is *noncoercion* (L. *coercere*, to surround; *co-*, together + *arcere*, to confine). The very fabric of morality and of moral public policy depends on mutual respect. Failure to provide relevant information, deception threats, and outright threats of violence count as coercive tactics and ought to be avoided, as they were in the case of developing legislation in Colorado. However, one will need to distinguish between acts of coercion and those of peaceful manipulation. If one understands coercive actions as those that place or threaten to place a person in a disadvantaged state without justification, and if one defines peaceful manipulation as those actions that place or offer to place a person in an advantaged state to which the person is not entitled, coercions will be forbidden and peaceful manipulations will be allowed. The first violates the morality of mutual respect, but the second does not. In fact, peaceful manipulations undergird the very process of negotiation through which individuals fashion agreements that are grounded on respect.[46] In the case of developing legislation, peaceful manipulation of the parties involved in the debates is clearly practiced.

Fourth is *compromise* (L. *compromissus*, pp. of *compromittere*, to make a mutual promise), which involves adjusting or settling differences by mutual agreement, with concessions on both sides. In the case of the Colorado legislation, supporters of the bill met privately on numerous occasions with members of the insurance industry to clarify and settle disagreements prior to the introduction of the bill to the Colorado legislature. Disagreements centered on (1) how to define genetic testing, (2) what entities to regulate, (3) what entities to exempt, and (4) what sanctions to mandate. What became clear during discussions is that, despite their significant differences, parties were able to establish a shared goal, namely, to reform health care insurance. While members of the insurance industry held that reform was needed in order to develop a level playing field, others wished to provide access to genetic testing without fear of losing health insurance coverage. This shared goal of reform or change allowed the possibility of continued discussions regarding not *whether* the state should regulate but rather *how* the state should regulate access to genetic information by the insurance industry. In reaching consensus on key points prior to the introduction of the bill to the Colorado legislature, the stage was set for the successful passage of the bill as well as opportunities to educate members of the legislature, the media, and the public on issues regarding storage, access, and use of genetic information.[47]

In short, negotiation involving matters of public policy entails providing interested participants an opportunity to access discussions, sufficient information in order to understand the matter under discussion, a noncoercive environment, and a willingness to compromise. Negotiation as a procedural expression of respect offers the possibility of resolving conflict in a pluralist society. Brody's account of respect undergirds this analysis of negotiation precisely because it is not reducible to individual consent, to who actually is at the table, or to who yells the loudest. It is grounded on a view of morality that provides through public policy a forum for the achievement of shared goals fashioned by members of particular communities. Shared goals include refraining from harming and acting to promote necessary conditions of personhood, including bodily and mental integrity, which is for many made possible through health care and in turn health care insurance coverage.

Reflections on Debates Regarding the Storage, Access, and Use of Human Tissue Samples

This analysis has implications for current discussions regarding the storage, access, and use of human tissue samples.[48] In these discussions, ethical quandaries abound: (1) Should human tissue samples be stored at all? If so, how should they be stored? Where should they be stored? For how long should they be stored? (2) Who owns stored tissue samples? (3) What constitutes permissible uses of human tissue samples? (4) What constitutes free and informed consent in tissue banking practices? in clinical procedures involving stored human tissues? in research involving stored human tissues? in banking practices for military and forensic purposes? (5) Who should have access to human tissue samples? (6) Who should have access to information about human tissue samples? (7) How should we deal with the changing and fallible nature of data on human tissue samples? (8) Are mandatory tissue banks morally permissible? If so, what are the justifications? (9) Who should regulate human tissue banks and what should such regulations be? (10) Is it morally permissible to buy or sell human biological materials and, if so, what are the implications for equity of distribution? (11) What constitutes morally appropriate compensation for researchers and businesses for products using human tissue samples?

These questions may be clustered in terms of the major stakeholders and their probable values in the debates. First, there are those whose tissues are stored or archived, whose values include ownership, privacy, and those assigned to the good consequences that can arise for the donor or for others from appropriate uses of samples, among others. Second, there are those who wish to archive samples for their own clinical, research, or identification purposes. These include clinicians, researchers, public health specialists, the military, and forensic experts, whose values include the pursuit of knowledge, benefiting others, preventing foreseen harms, and securing public welfare, among others. Third, there are those who wish access to and use of samples others have stored. These include, among others already mentioned, members of the insurance industry, employers, adoption agencies, and schools.[49] Values include sharing resources, benefiting themselves and others, and minimizing harms. Fourth, there are those concerned about the implications of storing human tissues. These include individuals from varying professions such as science, medicine, government, law, ethics, and theology, whose values include those framing their professional commitment to serve and protect others.

One notes here that some values conflict and others complement. In terms of conflict, while some hold the view that privacy is the value that is to be preserved at all costs, others point out that there is much good to gain from the use of stored tissue samples, even when consent has not been secured. In terms of a complement, restricting access and use of archival samples permits the shared goal of securing public trust that samples will be handled in a confidential and responsible manner during the period in which samples are stored for clinical, research, military, or forensic purposes.

Given this geography of values, it is possible to conceive of the resolution of some of the debates regarding the storage, access, and use of stored tissue samples in terms of how to achieve shared goals. But this is not simply a conceptual exercise; it is in important ways practical. Given the divergent issues and values at stake in the various debates, we can expect that a single rule or public policy addressing all of our concerns and goals will not be forthcoming. It is imperative in discussing the storage, access, and use of human tissue samples that numerous and varying positions are considered prior to deciding whether human tissue samples should be stored in particular contexts, under what circumstances they should be stored, where they should be stored, over what period they should be stored, who should have access to them, and for what purposes they should be used, among other issues. This entails providing stakeholders access into discussions, establishing a forum for sharing information in a noncoercive environment, and moving toward compromise and ultimately consensus.[50] This is the case because respect is a precondition of the moral community.

Conclusion

The development of the Colorado statute limiting access and use of genetic testing information illustrates the challenges of negotiating ethical conflict in a pluralist society. It is incumbent on those organizing and engaging in debates regarding these and related bioethical issues to develop a forum for stakeholders to negotiate. Negotiation offers the possibility of resolving conflict in a pluralist society without recourse to force and in a manner that is morally defensible.

Notes

1. CRS 10-3-1104.7. See Lynda M. Fox, "New Technologies, New Dilemmas: S.B. 94-058 Limits Use of Genetic Testing Information," *Colorado Lawyer* 24 (February 1995): 275–276. The Colorado Governor's Commission on Life and the Law, which was charged with making recommendations regarding policy and legislation on ethical, scientific, and legal issues by the governor of Colorado, assumed a major leadership role in organizing discussion around this statute. Members of the Sub-committee on Genetics and Insurance included Fredrick Abrams, Lynda M. Fox, Judy Hutchison, Walter H. Oppenheim, Bernard Poskus, Dean A. Woodward, and myself as chair.
2. Ala. Stat. 27-5-13 (1982)
3. Ariz. Rev. Stat. 20-448(D)–(F) (1989).
4. Cal. Health and Safety Code, 1374.7 (1977); Cal. Insurance 10143(a) (1977); Cal. Insurance Code, 11512.95 (1977); Cal. Insurance Code, 10123.3 (1977); Cal. Health and Safety Code, 150(f) (1990), Cal. Ins. Code 11512.95, 10143 (West 1993).
5. Fla. Rev. Stat. 626.9706, 626.9707 (1978); Fla. Rev. Stat. 448.075 (1978); Fla. Rev.

Stat. 448.076 (1978); Fla. Rev. Stat. 228.201 (1978); Fla. Rev. Stat. 63.043 (1978); and 1994 Fla. Sess. Laws Serv. 980 (West).

6. La. Rev. Stat. 22: 652.1(D) (1982); and La. Rev. Stat. 23: 1002 (1982).

7. Md. Ann. Code 13-102, et seq. (1986); and Md. Ann. Code Art. 48A, 223(a)(3); 223(b)(4)(1986).

8. Mont. Code Ann. 33-18-206 (1991).

9. N.C. Stat. 58-45; 58-25; 58-65-70 (1975); and N.C. Stat. 95-28.1 (1975).

10. Ohio Rev. Code Ann. 3901.49 (Page 1993).

11. Tenn. Code Ann. 56-7-207 (1989).

12. Wisc. Stat. Ann. 631.89 (West 1991).

13. Jennifer Preston, "Bill in New Jersey Would Limit Use of Genetic Tests by Insurers," *New York Times* (June 18, 1996): 3.

14. For overviews, see Jean E. McEwen and Philip R. Reilly, "State Legislative Efforts to Regulate Use and Potential Misuse of Genetic Information," *American Journal of Human Genetics* 51 (1992): 637–647; Kathy Hudson et al., "Genetic Discrimination and Health Insurance: An Urgent Need for Reform," *Science* 270 (1995): 391–393; Harry Ostrer et al., "Insurance and Genetic Testing: Where Are We Now?" *American Journal of Human Genetics* 52 (1993): 565–577; and Marvin Natowicz et al., "Genetic Discrimination and the Law," *American Journal of Human Genetics* 50 (1992): 465–475.

15. NIH-DOE Working Group on Ethical, Legal, and Social Implications of Human Genome Research, *Genetic Information and Health Insurance: Report of the Task Force on Genetic Information and Insurance* (Washington, D.C.: NIH Publication No. 93–3686, May 10, 1993), p. 2.

16. Here I use the term "genetic discrimination" in the negative sense to refer to judgments and acts against an individual's interest or against the interest of members of that individual's family solely because of real or perceived differences from the "normal" genome in the genetic constitution of that individual. Genetic discrimination is problematic because genetic variation is not taken into consideration, not all variations cause disease or disorder, and much is still unknown about the relation between genotype and phenotype. See Natowicz et al., "Genetic Discrimination," 446, and Paul Billings et al., "Discrimination as a Consequence of Genetic Testing," *American Journal of Human Genetics* 50 (1992): 476–482.

17. For an informative overview of the views and practices of medical directors in the insurance industry who influence how applicants are rated, see Jean E. McEwen et al., "A Survey of Medical Directors of Life Insurance Companies concerning Use of Genetic Information," *American Journal of Human Genetics* 53 (1993): 33–45.

18. Larry McCullough and I developed this analysis in Biological Science Curriculum Study, *Mapping and Sequencing the Human Genome: Science, Ethics, and Public Policy* (Colorado Springs: BSCS, 1991), pp. 18–21.

19. Perceptions do not always match with reality; nevertheless, they are important in debates.

20. Arnold Dicke, "Genetic Discrimination: Actuarial Aspects," *Science* 270 (1995): 1265.

21. Adverse selection occurs when individuals have more information about their risk of illness than do insurance companies and base their insurance-purchasing decisions on such information. The imbalance allows these individuals at higher risk to

buy more insurance yet pay no more than those at lower risk. This may jeopardize the economic well-being of the insurance company or require companies to raise all premiums, as protection against adverse selection. See Ad Hoc Committee on Genetic Testing/Insurance Issues, "Background Statement: Genetic Testing and Insurance," *American Journal of Human Genetics* 56 (1995): 327–331.

22. Thomas Murray, "Genetics and the Moral Mission of Health Insurance," *Hastings Center Report* 22 (November–December 1992): 12–17.

23. This is ultimately the position offered by the Task Force on Genetic Information and Insurance (see note 15 above).

24. George Annas, "Privacy Rules for DNA Databanks," *Journal of the American Medical Association* 270 (November 17, 1993): 2346–2350.

25. Annas, "Privacy Rules," esp. p. 2349.

26. CRS 10-3-1104.7 (1a).

27. CRS 10-3-1104.7 (3a)

28. CRS 10-3-1104.7 (4-10).

29. See Rosemary Tong, *Feminine and Feminist Ethics* (Belmont, Calif.: Wadsworth, 1993).

30. Much more is needed on this topic. See the essay by William L. Freeman in this volume.

31. Jean-François Lyotard, *The Postmodern Condition: A Report on Knowledge*, trans. G. Bennington and B. Massumi (Minnesota: University of Minnesota Press, 1989 [1979]).

32. Lyotard, *The Postmodern Condition*, p. 37.

33. Baruch Brody, *Life and Death Decision Making* (New York: Oxford University Press, 1988), pp. 32–35.

34. *Black's Law Dictionary*, p. 1036.

35. These included Blue Cross/Blue Shield of Colorado, State Farm Insurance, and Mutual of Omaha.

36. These included Lynda M. Fox, Bernard Poskus, Susan Fox Buchanan, Garth Grissom, Mark Rothstein, and Michael Yesley, among others.

37. These included Fredrick R. Abrams, Walter H. Oppenheim, David Manchester, Ellen Mangione, James Delaney, and Jeffrey C. Murray, among others.

38. All patients and family members have requested to remain unnamed.

39. These included Lynda M. Fox, David Manchester, Joyce Hooker, and Vincent Wilson, among others.

40. These included Dean Woodward, Lua Blankenship, Richard Lamm, and Merril Stern, among others.

41. These included Thomas Murray, Stuart F. Spicker, Laurence B. McCullough, and Mark Yarborough, among others.

42. These included those on the Governor's Commission on Life and the Law, which has representation from various faith traditions.

43. See Angela Dwire, "Genetic Testing's Darker Side Feared," *Gazette Telegraph* (February 21, 1994): A1, A3; and Danette Winchell, "Senate OKs Limiting Genetic Testing Data," *Capitol Reporter* (February 23, 1994): 4.

44. These included those from the insurance industry, genetics interest groups, police force, and research community.

45. Here, thanks are owed to the National Center for Human Genome Research, which supplied numerous copies of the report by the Task Force on Genetic Information and Insurance (see note 15 above) for distribution in Colorado.

46. This analysis is developed by H. Tristram Engelhardt, *The Foundations of Bioethics*, 2nd ed. (New York: Oxford University Press, 1996), pp. 308–309.

47. The educational consequences are worthy in themselves.

48. Here tissue samples include all samples that can serve as DNA sources, including solid tissue, blood, saliva, and any other tissue or body fluid containing nucleated cells. Since the late 1980s, a wealth of literature has emerged on this topic. See essays in this volume, with particular attention to the notes. See also U.S. Congress, Office of Technology Assessment, *New Developments in Biotechnology — 1: Ownership of Human Tissue and Cells* (Washington, D.C.: U.S. Government Printing Office, 1987).

49. Issues regarding storing tissue samples are primarily raised by clinical practice, medical research, military identification procedures, and forensics. It is unlikely at this point that insurance companies, employers, adoption agencies, and educational institutions will want access to stored human tissue samples. The insurance industry, for example, will have access to such materials and the information that results in other ways. And academic institutions appear to be uninterested in access. Nevertheless, in developing the Colorado legislation, it became clear that many in the lay public fear access by institutions who wish genetic information in order to single out some individuals from others, based on the institution's financial and professional goals.

50. As a model, see the consensus work by Ellen Wright Clayton et al., "Informed Consent for Genetic Research on Stored Tissue Samples," *JAMA* 274 (December 13, 1995): 1786–1792.

Appendix:
The Colorado Statute Limiting Access
to Genetic Information
(Source: Regulation of Insurance Companies,
Colorado Revised Statute 10-3-1104.7)

10-3-1104.7. GENETIC testing — declaration — definitions — limitations on disclosure of information — liability — legislative declaration.

(1) The general assembly hereby finds and determines that recent advances in genetic science have led to improvements in the diagnosis, treatment, and understanding of a significant number of human diseases. The general assembly further declares that:

   (a) Genetic information is the unique property of the individual to whom the information pertains;

(b) Any information concerning an individual obtained through the use of genetic techniques may be subject to abuses if disclosed to unauthorized third parties without the willing consent of the individual to whom the information pertains;

(c) To protect individual privacy and to preserve individual autonomy with regard to the individual's genetic information, it is appropriate to limit the use and availability of genetic information;

(d) The intent of this statute is to prevent information derived from genetic testing from being used to deny access to health insurance, group disability insurance, or long-term care insurance coverage.

(2) For the purposes of this section:

(a) "Entity" means any sickness and accident insurance company, health maintenance company, nonprofit hospital, medical-surgical and health service corporation, or other entity that provides health care insurance, group disability insurance, or long-term insurance coverage and is subject to the jurisdiction of the commissioner of insurance.

(b) "Genetic testing" means any laboratory test of human DNA, RNA, or chromosomes that is used to identify the presence or absence of alterations in genetic material which are associated with disease or illness. "Genetic testing" includes only such tests as are direct measures of such alterations rather than indirect manifestations thereof.

(3) (a) Information derived from genetic testing shall be confidential and privileged. Any release, for purposes other than diagnosis, treatment, or therapy, of genetic testing information that identifies the person tested with the test results released requires specific written consent by the person tested.

(b) Any entity that receives information derived from genetic testing may not seek, use, or keep the information for any nontherapeutic purpose or for any underwriting purpose connected with the provision of health care insurance, group disability insurance, or long-term care insurance coverage.

(4) Notwithstanding the provisions of subsection (3) of this section, in the course of a criminal investigation or a criminal prosecution, and to the extent allowed under the federal or state constitution, any peace officer, district attorney, or assistant attorney general, or a designee thereof, may obtain information derived from genetic testing regarding the identity of any individual who is the subject of the criminal investigation or prosecution for use exclusively in the criminal investigation or prosecution without the consent of the individual being tested.

(5) Notwithstanding the provisions of subsection (3) of this section, any research facility may use the information derived from genetic testing for scientific research purposes so long as the identity of any individual to whom the information pertains is not disclosed to any third party; except that the individual's identity may be disclosed to the individual's physician if the individual consents to such disclosure in writing.

(6) This section does not limit the authority of a court or any party to a parentage proceeding to use information obtained from genetic testing for purposes of determining parentage pursuant to section 13-25-126, C.R.S.

(7) This section does not limit the authority of a court or any party to a proceeding that is subject to the limitations of part 5 of article 64 of title 13, C.R.S., to use information obtained from genetic testing for purposes of determining the cause of damage or injury.

(8) This section does not limit the authority of the state board of parole to require any offender who is involved in a sexual assault to submit to blood tests and to retain the results of such tests on file as authorized under section 17-2-201 (5) (g), C.R.S.

(9) This section does not limit the authority granted the state department of public health and environment, the state board of health, or local departments of health pursuant to section 25-1-122, C.R.S.

(10) This section does not apply to the provision of life insurance or individual disability insurance.

(11) Any violation of this section is an "unfair practice," as defined in section 10-3-1104 (l), and is subject to the provisions of sections 10-3-1106 to 10-3-1113.

(12) Any individual who is injured by an entity's violation of this section may recover in a court of competent jurisdiction the following remedies:

(a) Equitable relief, which may include a retroactive order, directing the entity to provide health insurance, group disability insurance, or long-term care insurance coverage, whichever is appropriate, to the injured individual under the same terms and conditions as would have applied had the violation not occurred; and

(b) An amount equal to any actual damages suffered by the individual as a result of the violation.

(13) The prevailing party in an action under this section may recover costs and reasonable attorney fees.

Researcher Obligations to Tissue and DNA Sample Sources

Curtis R. Naser

The Department of Health and Human Services policy regarding the use of human subjects in biomedical and behavioral research exempts "research involving the collection or study of existing data, documents, records, pathological specimens, or diagnostic specimens, if these sources are publicly available or if the information is recorded by the investigator in such a manner that subjects cannot be identified, directly or through identifiers linked to the subject."[1] More recently the proposed Genetic Privacy Act would exempt for research purposes the genetic analysis of tissues "that cannot be linked to any individual identifier."[2] Presumably this exemption is based on the understanding that tissues or data or both that are not linked to identifiers of individual persons pose no risks to those individual sources.[3] The effect of this policy exemption is that informed consent is not required of sources of tissue specimens or those to whom biomedical data correspond, so long as the specimens or data are not linked back to those individuals. Thus, surgically extracted tissues which are stored in hospital pathology labs may be sent to various researchers or state tumor registries without the knowledge or consent of the patient. Likewise, blood samples collected at blood banks or in routine phlebotomy may be supplied to researchers, so long as the identifiers of these samples have been removed. Furthermore, research protocols involving the use of such specimens and data are not subject to approval by institutional review boards (IRBs), which are mandated in all institutions receiving federal funds. But the primary purpose of such boards and the federal regulations applying to biomedical research is the protection of human subjects, and since the specimens and data are not linked to individual human subjects, there is no need for protection. Their anonymity provides all the protection they require.

No doubt this practice has facilitated a great deal of basic and applied biomedical research.[4] A ready source of human tissue, easily obtained, often accompanied by medical and epidemiological data, has surely contributed to the growth and development of medical knowledge and advanced the cause of medicine in its fundamental purpose of treating and caring for sick and disabled people.

However, with the development of genetic technology, and in particular high speed genetic testing and sequencing technology,[5] it may no longer be possible to guarantee the anonymity of unlinked tissue specimens. As participants of the Obermann seminar observed, an anonymous DNA sample is rapidly becoming an oxymoron. As genetic testing and sequencing technology becomes cheaper and faster, it will not be long before extensive genetic information becomes a part of the medical record, "a standard part of many diagnostic workups"[6] the confidentiality of which, particularly when computerized, is increasingly difficult to safeguard.[7] In any event, such information may readily and legally be passed on to insurers, pharmaceutical benefits managers, pharmaceutical manufacturers, and data management firms such as Equifax and IMS America which market medical records to insurers, employers, and other parties.[8] Further, the medical record is open to the perusal of various governmental agencies and unspecified numbers of individuals with general authorization to access patient records. Though the day when a detailed genetic analysis routinely appears in the medical record has not yet arrived, it will, all too soon.

We must therefore reassess the relationship between researcher and tissue source. First of all, we must consider whether we can continue to maintain that anonymous tissue samples are in fact anonymous. Absent genetic testing technology, such samples could quite plausibly be regarded as genuinely anonymous. But as genetic testing becomes fully integrated with the clinical practice of medicine and the medical record, can we reasonably maintain that such specimens are truly anonymous and that no harm to the source could come as a result of the unscrupulous use of such specimens and data?[9] The possibility of such harm suggests that, at the very least, we need to reassess the Department of Health and Human Services (DHHS) policy that exempts such research from IRB oversight.

A more ethically vexing problem arises, however, if we consider situations where researchers develop information from anonymous tissue samples that they believe is of clinical relevance, perhaps even of urgent clinical relevance, to the tissue source. Many "anonymous" tissue and DNA samples are obtained from tissue banks and registries which maintain files linking the samples back to the source. These identifiers are removed when samples are provided to other researchers. They are thus "anonymized" samples for which relinkage is possible. Do researchers have an obligation to recontact anonymous tissue sources if relinkage is possible? As long as such samples are genuinely anonymous, there is no problem for the investigator, since she cannot link the specimen back to the source. But the possibility of relinkage, either through a tissue bank's own records or through matching genotypes by a search of computerized medical records, as will become possible in the future, creates an ethical dilemma for the researcher.

In addition to the conscientious investigator, public health officials may find relinkage of "anonymous" tissue samples useful in investigating infectious diseases. The possibility of relinkage could very well advance an investigation, but at some cost — though not necessarily unjustifiable — to the privacy and autonomy of the supposedly "anonymous" tissue source. In either scenario, the possibility that anonymous samples can be relinked to their sources should be explained carefully to these persons as they contemplate providing samples for research.

Many would argue that "clinically relevant information" is of benefit to a person, and from a medical point of view this is true. But benefits and harms are not defined solely from the medical point of view. What constitutes a benefit to an individual is a function of values and life plans.[10] Under normal clinical circumstances, a physician will have some understanding of the patient's values, and in any event the patient has presumably solicited the physician's help and thus has "asked for" whatever diagnostic information the physician can provide. I suspect that many individuals would want to know clinically relevant information, even if they had not solicited it by engaging their physician. But genetic knowledge is rarely clear cut. Even dominant disorders such as Huntington's disease exhibit a range of variability in age of onset and speed of progression,[11] and many polygenetic disorders exhibit a wide range of variability and penetrance. If many patients with a familial history of Huntington's have so far been reluctant to avail themselves of the opportunity of genetic testing for this disease project,[12] how is a researcher to know whether or not the sources of anonymous tissue or DNA samples would even want to know whether they are at risk for, or in fact have, some clinically significant genetic condition?

Other problematic questions arise in this context. On what grounds is a researcher to determine what is clinically relevant information, particularly if the information is the novel product of a research protocol? And who should bear the costs of relinking anonymously donated tissue back to the source and then contacting the source and offering counseling regarding the research findings? For instance, Manning Feinleib notes that "special routes of communication may be needed for transmitting sensitive or complex information" resulting from research, such as HIV results and, we should add, genetic information.[13] This may be a small problem if the research involves only a handful of specimens. But the costs of recontacting in studies involving hundreds and sometimes thousands of patients, as in the CDC's NHANES III study, would be enormous.[14] Who should bear those costs: the research budget? the source (who didn't even solicit the information in the first place)? the insurance company?

Let us examine a concrete situation in which a researcher/physician may feel the obligation to pursue the links to anonymous tissue samples. Dr. X is the principal investigator of a NIH-funded study to characterize genetic polymorphisms in the HIV virus. It is suspected that certain polymorphisms may confer anti-HIV drug resistance. Dr. X has received several hundred anonymized HIV positive blood samples from an HIV tissue registry in another state. The registry has freely provided these samples and has set no prior conditions on their use, other than that they be used for HIV research. In the process of examining the virus derived from these samples Dr. X is able to demonstrate in vitro that approximately 10 percent are resistant to one of the newly approved protease inhibitors. Since the tissue samples arrived from the registry with bar-coded labels, Dr. X suspects that the registry might have encoded the samples and thus would be able to break the code and recontact the individual sources from whom the blood was taken in the first place.

Dr. X is concerned that these individuals are at risk of engaging in a physically and financially demanding treatment regimen that to her best clinical judgment will be of no use. These patients, if they take the drug, will realize all the side effects but fail to realize any of the benefits. In short, they will be harmed by taking this drug. As a clinician, Dr. X feels a *duty* to inform these patients of her findings in order to protect these patients from this harm. Should Dr. X attempt to contact the registry, explain her findings, and ask that the registry recontact either the patients or their physician?

Similar questions arise for the registry in the event of being recontacted by Dr. X. The registry may or may not have any policy on recontact of sources. Their obligations will also depend upon the specifics of the consent process by which they gathered the infected blood samples. There may have been no consent involved in the first place, the samples having come already anonymized from various hospital labs which may or may not have maintained identification links. Or the consent was a general consent for the use of blood samples for the purposes of HIV research, with no mention (or anticipation) of recontact. The registry may even have had the foresight to have covered the problem of recontact, stating, for instance, that since the samples would only be sent out stripped of all identifiers there would be no direct benefit to the source from the research. This may let the registry off the legal hook, but the moral problem is not therefore resolved. Both the physician and the registry now have information that may be of clinical benefit to the source. If relinkage is possible, are they not at least morally obligated to make that information available?

If there is a duty to recontact sources of anonymous samples, then it surely follows that there is a duty to recontact *identified* sources with clinically relevant information. Of course, if the sources were informed in the consent process that they would receive reports from the investigators on any clinically significant findings, then the individual researcher's moral dilemma is solved. Some authors have insisted that all research subjects are owed such benefits by virtue of their participation in research protocols by giving samples of tissue and/or medical information. This raises other problems, however. Some research protocols simply could not afford the costs of keeping sources informed, particularly considering that in genetics, counseling plays a crucial and expensive role in the clinical process. Kenneth Rothman has lamented that the entire discipline of epidemiology is being strangled to death by consent requirements for the review of medical records in retrospective epidemiological studies.[15] Likewise Wayne Grody has warned that just the burdens of obtaining informed consent for the anonymous uses of stored tissues (such as those in surgical pathology labs) "would seriously impede, or completely block, a major proportion of molecular research on human disease, especially impacting those research questions that can be addressed in no other way than through retrospective study of large numbers of archival specimens."[16] Adding to the burdens of the consent process, the duty to maintain contacts with sources and inform each of clinically relevant findings would turn the enterprises of molecular biology and epidemiology into vast clinical outreach programs. Rothman, Grody, and others have pointed out that research that occurs on anonymized but unconsented tissue samples has produced unparalleled social good.

On the other hand, a number of commentators have argued that research subjects are owed a special consideration by virtue of their contribution to the general welfare. Vicki Hannig, Ellen Wright Clayton, and Kathryn Edwards go the furthest in this regard, noting that genetic "research requires the assistance of certain individuals because they or their relatives have a problem that is the object of study and where the research is directed toward the diagnosis or treatment of this condition, research assumes the mantle of health care. In that setting, the law should not hesitate to impose on the researchers some duties of care toward those subjects as well, at least in the absence of explicit agreements to the contrary."[17] George Annas insists that "mechanisms must be developed to notify and counsel those whose DNA samples are in storage when new information that can have a significant health impact on the individual is obtainable from their stored DNA sample." [18] Manning Feinleib argues not only that epidemiologists have a duty to inform subjects of findings of medical import but that "if the subject has no regular physician, it may be incumbent on the epidemiologist to arrange access to a qualified physician." [19]

It appears, then, that there is genuine disagreement on the duties and responsibilities that researchers owe to the sources of the tissues and the information that is necessary to their activities. This disagreement pits the medical benefits owed to individual sources against the competing benefits to society of the research. We also see that respect for individual autonomy as embodied in the concept of informed consent is at odds with the social benefits of research on anonymized samples (and medical information) obtained without the individual's consent.

The ethical terms of this debate — autonomy, beneficence, and nonmaleficence — are typically deployed according to a judgment on the part of the commentator. A typical constellation of these principles is evidenced by Philip Reilly's comment that "many researchers do not understand why anyone would object to truly anonymous use of a tissue sample. By definition, no person could correlate any information derived from studying it with the person from whom it was derived. . . . The cost of such research would be indirectly increased by the invocation of rules that, to me, only abstractly protect individual autonomy. So few people are likely to forbid their samples to be used for anonymous research that the expense attached to asking the question and tracking the few samples that are not available for study seems a poor use of resources." [20] We see here that a person's *autonomy* is balanced against *social benefit* and the absence of likely individual *harm*. On the other hand, advocates for consent argue that the *costs* or *burdens* of the consent process are manageable and, in any event, *social benefit* is best served by *respecting the autonomy* of individuals and that the risks of *harm* (usually psychosocial in this context) to the source require the corresponding *benefit* of research results.

I think this dilemma can be averted by a patient analysis of the relationships between clinical practice, research, and the social/political context in which these take place. We need to be clear about the goals of clinical practice and how they give rise to and relate to biomedical research and in turn how these enterprises are constrained and influenced by both the social good and political rights. I argue below that patient autonomy is a *negative* political right (as well as a moral obligation) that in general rises above and is incommensurate with considerations of social good or utility. On the other hand, clinical benefits to individual research subjects are not *positive* rights and may be balanced against competing social goods. Benefits to the research subject ought to be proportional to, and commensurate with, the clinical risks of participation.

When research is largely removed from the clinical practice of medicine, as is often (though not exclusively) the case in research involving stored tissue samples, clinical obligations to the sources should be minimized because (1) the clinical risks to the subject are minimal to nonexistent, (2) there are serious problems with recontacting individuals who may not have agreed to such recontact, and (3) such efforts to provide clinical benefits to sources draw resources, both financial and administrative, away from the research enterprise. In general, the common good to be realized through biomedical research outweighs particular benefits that individual research subjects might realize in the absence of corresponding clinical risks attendant to the research itself. In the near future it will no longer be possible to guarantee the anonymity of tissue samples, however, because of the detailed genetic information which will be entered in the medical record. Thus, while in general researchers on tissue samples should be free of clinical obligations to sources, the informed consent of all future tissue sources and full IRB review of tissue research should be a requirement before research proceeds.[21]

In order that we may rigorously distinguish between *negative* autonomy rights on the one hand and *positive* rights to research benefits on the other, we must analyze the relationship between research and the clinical practice of medicine. Let us begin this analysis by examining the roots of medical practice in the concept of *compassion*. The *American Heritage Dictionary* defines *compassion* as a "deep feeling of sharing the suffering of another in the inclination to give aid or support, or to show mercy." This meaning derives from the Latin *com* meaning "*with*" and *passio* meaning "*to suffer*," the root from which we also derive the words "*passive*" and "*patient*." To show compassion is to suffer *with* another person. What is important from the medical standpoint, however, is that the *suffering with* another entails an *activity* on the part of a physician — the inclination to give aid or support. Edmund Pellegrino observes that compassion "means to suffer with, to bear together, to share in another's distress, and to be moved by desire to relieve distress."[22] This active sense of compassion is reinforced by a related concept in medicine: *care*. Albert Jonsen notes that the English "*care*" means to be "troubled by another's trouble" and concludes that "the agreement to care . . . is itself a moral act, for it initiates a series of activities explicitly designed to affect another person as a response to that person's manifest need."[23]

The physician is therefore moved by the suffering of another person, moved by a feeling of sharing that other person's suffering, with an inclination to give aid and support. The physician is thus affected by the suffering of another and *acts* in a way to ameliorate that suffering by whatever means are at his or her disposal. The actions have as their goal the restoration of health, and if this is not fully possible, assistance in disability or, at the very least, palliation of pain.

Compassion and care, thus understood, are characteristics that most persons share to varying degrees. What makes the physician's response different from other compassionate responses is the particular body of knowledge that the physician possesses by virtue of training, education, and experience. This knowledge gives the physician a practical power to affect the body of the patient in very specific ways to restore health and ameliorate pain. Let us observe that this knowledge — the art of medicine — arises out of the need to help others in distress and thus serves the fundamentally moral purpose of *benefiting* other persons who have become disadvantaged and vulnerable as a result of sickness and disease.[24] The Hippocratic text *Precepts* locates the art of medicine within the context of moral virtue of *philanthropia*: "For where there is love of man [*philanthropia*] there is also love of art [*philotechnia*]."[25] The art of medicine serves the moral purpose of compassionately responding to those who suffer the ravages of sickness and disease by the beneficent use of medical knowledge and art.

Already at the time of Hippocrates it was well recognized that the knowledge of the medical art could easily work to the detriment of the patient if not carefully and methodically applied, not to mention the use of such knowledge for immoral and unjust ends. Although the common and popular phrase *primum non nocere* (above all, do no harm) is probably not Hippocratic,[26] the notion that physicians should refrain from harming their patients has been a part of the moral core of medicine at least since Hippocrates. The Hippocratic Oath itself contains the injunction not to harm patients: "I will apply dietetic measures for the benefit of the sick according to my ability and judgment; I will keep them from harm and injustice."[27] And the "Epidemics," book 1, contains the following injunction: "As to diseases, make a habit of two things — to help, or at least to do no harm."[28]

Because it was recognized that the medical art was incomplete and that patient benefits (and, concomitantly, avoidance of patient harm) depended upon good medical knowledge, the duty to expand the horizons of the medical art through systematic observation and reasoning was explicit in the Hippocratic tradition.[29] Although the history of medicine exemplifies a wide variety of individual opinions regarding the necessity of research and experimentation, it is clear that the duty to continuously improve medical knowledge and art is an imperative stretching back to the dawn of medicine and is conceptually embedded in the complementary duties of beneficence and nonmaleficence.[30] What has changed between contemporary medical science and traditional medicine is the method for generating medical knowledge. What was a process of systematic observation, experience, and reasoning on the part of the physician has become the scientific process of analysis and experimentation. The difference is important because with the new methods the relationship of the physician (as contributor to medical knowledge) to the patient has been transformed into that of researcher and participant in research. The scientific method brought a quantum leap in the quality and quantity of medical knowledge at the cost of introducing a conflict of interest between the production of this knowledge and the best interests of the patient.

It is a commonplace in the literature on research ethics to note that the purpose of research is generalizable knowledge and that therefore the *benefits* of research redound, not to the particular participants upon whose bodies research is carried out, but to future unknown patients, society in general, or the common good. On the other hand, the clinical relationship is constituted, as described above, by compassionate response of the physician to benefit the particular individual patient who is sick and suffers. The result of these divergent purposes is an apparent conflict of interest when the physician undertakes a research protocol with his or her patients (or is faced with the decision of referring patients to research protocols). It has been argued that the exacting conditions necessary to satisfy a clinical research investigation, including the use of randomization, placebo controls, and standardization of treatment, all attenuate the physician's ability to act in the best interests of the patient according to his or her best judgment.[31]

The recent history of research involving human experimentation has unfortunately demonstrated that both physicians and scientists are capable of ignoring the best interests of their patients or subjects in the name of generating generalizable knowledge. The codes that govern biomedical research on human subjects have grown out of this recognition and have been designed to protect both the autonomy and welfare of individual research participants through scrupulous peer review of research protocols, public oversight through the system of local IRBs, and the institution of informed consent requirements. Two foundational principles thus presently govern the protection of human subjects: (1) the principle of autonomy and (2) the principle of beneficence/nonmaleficence.

Not only the practices of Nazi physicians but also those of well-intentioned researchers at various points in our recent past have led to the development of the doctrine of informed consent in order to protect persons from unwittingly becoming subjects in research protocols. The principle of autonomy forms the moral basis of this doctrine asserting that rational persons are to be treated as ends-in-themselves, that is, as determining their own goals and actions.[32] Not to inform individuals and seek their consent for their participation in a research protocol is to use them solely as a means for ends to which they have not assented and therefore do not share (even if they might share in the goals of the research had they been informed).

Besides the moral principle of autonomy, we must also recognize a political right to autonomy. A primary function of the liberal state is to guarantee the personal freedom of self-determination. Using someone in a research protocol without consent is a violation of this freedom and may even be legally actionable as a battery. In both the moral and political domains, we therefore recognize a *negative* right of persons to be free to determine their own actions; in order to protect this fundamental right, society has imposed upon researchers increasingly stringent requirements of informed consent.

In addition to safeguarding persons' autonomy as they enter a research protocol, it has also been necessary to insist that researchers minimize risks of harm to patients. The judgments here are complex and depend upon the nature of the research itself as well as the relative value of the knowledge to be gained. In general, patients and research participants should not be harmed or subjected to the risk of harm without the possibility of commensurate benefit to themselves for the sake of producing generalizable knowledge that is of benefit to everyone. Let us recall that the imperative to research arises out of the need for better medical knowledge in order that individual patients may be benefited and the risk of harm reduced. To harm one individual for the sake of others is contrary to the fundamental moral purpose of medicine. As Claude Bernard remarked in 1865, experiments that "can only harm are forbidden."[33]

The injunction against harming a person in a research protocol is also rooted in the moral and political right to autonomy. Such fundamental rights are protections enjoyed by the individual against the competing claims of society at large: they are rights that protect the individual from being taken as a means to some social good, no matter how important that good might be. We should note here that, as for many other things, there are limits to our rights of self-determination. I mean here not so much the limits imposed upon us by the state for the purpose of guaranteeing others' rights to self-determination (for instance, property rights), but rather the limits we find when the very existence of the state is threatened. The typical example of this is national defense. When the state is threatened it reserves the right to revoke the rights it has granted to individuals (or that we have granted to ourselves) in order to protect itself. Thus individuals may be conscripted for military service. The state may likewise also exercise rights against individual self-determination in matters of public health, requiring quarantining, vaccination, and the like.

Biomedical research, however, is not a good that in itself is necessary to the continuation of the state or the maintenance of the orderly fabric of society. As Hans Jonas has pointed out, "medical progress is an optional goal, not an unconditional commitment."[34] Certainly individuals may die earlier and suffer the ravages of disease without medicine and its continued project of expanding its knowledge and capabilities, but the state and its society can subsist just fine in the absence of a biomedical research enterprise. This is not to say that biomedical research and the fruits of its labor are not genuine benefits to society. But as Jonas points out, they are not benefits which individuals can arguably claim as a right. While a cure for cancer would be a great benefit to a large number of people, it cannot be claimed as anyone's right that a cure be found.[35] However, public health investigations can arguably override individual freedoms and protections of privacy on the basis that infectious diseases threaten the health and welfare of the citizenry in general, and, for the same reason, vaccinations can be mandated by the state for the protection of the general population. Thus we are led to distinguish between, on the one hand, negative rights which protect individuals from harm and from violations of their autonomy and, on the other, the positive benefits of medical science and practice. We cannot, in the name of producing the latter, violate the former.

For this reason, arguments such as Philip Reilly's and Wayne Grody's that pit the social benefits of medical research against the seemingly insignificant harms to the few individuals who might not have consented to research on their tissues are inadequate. First, from the moral perspective, we must recognize that violations of individual autonomy are not per se *harms*, but rather are *wrongs*, as Alexander Capron has pointed out.[36] By superseding or otherwise failing to consult individuals regarding the uses and disposition of their tissues after removal from the body, we fail to respect the individuals as autonomous self-determining agents. In effect, we treat them as a means to other ends that they may or may not share. Even if the person does not know that a violation has occurred, for instance, in the unconsenting use of a tissue sample or medical record, a wrong has nevertheless been done because we have "bypass[ed] the normal decision-making capacities of the agent."[37]

Although individual autonomy as a *negative* right of self-determination is a political right to which the goals of the research enterprise must be subordinated except when a political decision is made to the contrary, it does not therefore follow that individuals are as a matter of default entitled to any particular medical benefits other than the current standard care. This is contrary to the position of some commentators. For instance, Robert Veatch, in arguing an irreducible conflict between medical research and Hippocratic medicine, which he interprets as a single-minded practice of acting in the best interests of the patient, suggests "changes in the protocol designed to increase the benefits to the subject even if it means compromising certain other benefits of the research." [38] Similarly, Hannig, Clayton, and Edwards would seek to formalize what many clinicians may already feel: that researchers incur clinical obligations to tissue sources. On the other hand, imposition of such clinical obligations would place an enormous financial and administrative burden upon the research enterprise. Some research may not be possible if researchers become clinically responsible to the sources of the materials they use.

Privileging the greater good of society would seem, then, to run roughshod over the obligation of the physician to act in the best medical interests of the patient/subject. But as we have seen, although medicine is rooted in the compassionate response to patient suffering, what distinguishes medicine from other forms of compassionate response is the particular body of knowledge it employs to respond to the suffering of patients. The obligation to develop and expand this body of knowledge is also clearly a part of Hippocratic medicine. The dilemma which Veatch and many others see in the conflict between research and patient care arises most acutely, however, in the application of scientific methods to medical problems — something that did not occur in the Hippocratic context and indeed did not occur in medicine systematically until the early part of this century.[39]

The dilemma, then, between research and patient care is one which is internal to medicine itself, and not simply one that pits individual *medical* good against the *social* good. We can resolve this conflict between these dual physician obligations by pushing our analysis of the medical duty to research one step further. Inasmuch as the body of medical knowledge is the condition for the possibility of the physician benefiting (and not harming) his or her patient, it follows that the duty to contribute to this knowledge logically precedes or is the condition of the possibility of the duty of benefiting the particular patient, just as the duty to educate oneself in medicine precedes the duty to treat actual patients medically. Patients cannot be the object of medical beneficence in the absence of a valid body of knowledge according to which a physician practices.

We have already observed that a person's right to be free of harm and to exercise autonomy is, in general, a negative constraint upon the research enterprise, and thus we cannot justify violating these rights except in peculiar circumstances in order to produce more and better medical knowledge.[40] It is generally considered a harm to withhold from a patient a medical treatment known to be a benefit, for the purpose of testing an unknown treatment.

Where the scientific validation of a treatment, procedure, or diagnostic test has already been established there is a duty for a physician to provide or make available to the patient such known benefits. To withhold a known benefit from a patient for the purpose of generating scientific knowledge is contrary to the goal for which this knowledge is generated in the first place: to benefit individual patients. This is one important reason why the Tuskegee syphilis study was wrong.

However, when medical knowledge is professionally unsure of the harms and benefits of its practice, the physician is under no obligation to take any particular action on behalf of a patient, such as providing unvalidated treatments. Positively, the profession has an obligation in such circumstances to conduct the appropriate research to determine the benefits and risks of these treatments.[41] Thus, although the FDA has made available to AIDS patients a number of unproven therapeutic treatments "off protocol," where such off-protocol use threatens sufficient enrollment in clinical trials or otherwise compromises their validity, off-protocol use may be limited.[42] The principle at work here is that when research conflicts with possible but unknown patient benefits, research must supersede the interests of individual patients for the greater good of producing valid medical knowledge that will be of benefit to all. Other conditions may arise in which possible benefits to individual patients or subjects may be subordinated to the exigencies of research: when the obligation to benefit patients competes for resources with the obligation to produce medical knowledge, it may be morally justifiable to privilege the production of medical knowledge over the possible benefits to individual patients.

A simple example will illustrate the point. Let us suppose we are back some thirty years when the only source of insulin available was from human cadavers, as the process of producing synthetic insulin was not yet available. Let us also assume for the sake of argument that the amount of insulin is very limited, perhaps due to a limited supply of donated cadavers. Research has already determined that human insulin is of great benefit to diabetic patients, but there are, of course, many more patients than there is insulin. It seems that we have two choices to explore in this situation: (1) we could use the limited supply of insulin for research purposes in hopes of discovering its molecular structure and ultimately finding a way to produce it synthetically; or (2) we could provide what little insulin is available to some very limited number of patients according to some allocation scheme, just or unjust.[43]

The classic analysis of this problem is a *utilitarian* calculation in which we weigh the relative benefits of each option. Although option (2) will be of great benefit to a few persons (and also not a benefit to the much larger number of persons who are excluded), and although option (1) carries some risk of failure, option (1) nevertheless holds a reasonable likelihood of bestowing a tremendous benefit upon a much larger group of people, both present and in the future. It would be hard to rationally justify any other course of action.

Let us note that this problem is not only one of balancing *social good* against *individual good*, though these are the terms most often used in the literature.[44] It is also a medically professional question of balancing medical benefits to individual patients against the good of producing medical knowledge. Even though the profession knows that this substance is of benefit to patients, since its supply is quite limited and the benefit of the drug cannot be equally shared by all those who are affected, the research project of developing a synthetic variety by studying the quite limited quantities of the drug available takes precedence over the benefits to the few patients who may profit by it individually. It is a mistake to view this dilemma simply in terms of the political conflict between society and the individual. Rather, the conflict arises first within the professional complex[45] of medicine itself, and the duty to research is grounded upon the prior commitment of physicians to the body of knowledge by which they are in turn able to benefit patients. The physician, or rather the profession, may make a utilitarian calculation when confronted with this dilemma and reason that a greater number of people may benefit in the long run by using the limited supplies for research. The obligation to make this calculation derives from within the professional complex of medicine itself. This obligation may also be encouraged and funded by the state for the purposes of promoting a common good, but the obligation is first and foremost medical.

The case of scarce insulin is not unlike the problem raised by the claims that researchers have an obligation to benefit their sources by providing the results of research to them and, in general, that research carries with it clinical obligations, or that, following Veatch, researchers should maximize the benefits patients receive, even at the expense of the research itself. The competing claim is that such obligations would be financially and administratively burdensome, drawing resources away from the production of knowledge and committing them to clinical care.

There are two constraints upon our judgment in this case. First, from the standpoint of medicine as a profession, the production of medical knowledge will outweigh the benefits realized by individual patients when these two activities compete for scarce resources, since in the long run many more patients may realize benefit through the prudent allocation of medical resources to research activities. This is the argument proposed above in respect to scarce insulin.

But a second factor enters in this case: researchers owe a fiduciary obligation to their funding sources which make the research possible. To commit significant amounts of these resources to other purposes, no matter how laudable, violates this obligation. It may well be that as a society we spend too much on research at the expense of the basic medical care of individuals and populations disenfranchised from the health care delivery system. But this, again, is a political judgment and the place to solve that problem is in the political arena, not through the reappropriation of research funds to clinical purposes for which they were not intended.

So, in general, I conclude that there is no obligation on the part of researchers using tissue samples to provide research results to tissue sources. This is a general principle which may well admit of exceptions in particular circumstances. For instance, we should observe that some research projects on linked specimens arise out of and feed directly back into the clinical practice of medicine. Linkage studies to map and clone particular disease genes often are undertaken by clinician/researchers who maintain ongoing clinical relationships with their patients/sources. My argument here would not preclude this practice. My only claim is that as a matter of research obligation it is not necessary.

Yet, when a physician is engaged in an ongoing clinical relationship with the source, there may well be an obligation to disclose all clinically relevant information.[46] But this duty is one that is incumbent upon the physician qua physician, not researcher qua researcher. Although these dual roles may be combined in the same person and in the same relationship, it is important to distinguish these roles because they entail different obligations. Confusing these obligations may well lead to inappropriately overgeneralizing the obligations of the one to the other. Though research arises out of a compassionate medicine and serves its goals, research is an activity which has its own principles separate and distinct from those governing medical practice. It is this distinction that gives rise to the conflicts analyzed here. Failure to maintain a keen awareness of these separate principles and goals can lead us either to compromise patient welfare on the one hand or to compromise the validity, value, or production of research on the other.

Having argued that providing research results to tissue sources is not obligatory, let me now explain why, in general, I think it is a bad idea and should be avoided, except in particular circumstances. What makes the above noted linkage study an appropriate situation to provide research results is an ongoing clinical relationship between the physician/researcher and the patient/source. The patient has presumably been well counseled about the risks of genetic research — that unexpected findings may arise, that the information is sometimes inconclusive, that family members may be implicated in the results, and that one may experience adverse economic and social consequences if the information becomes a part of the medical record.

Such advantages, however, are lacking when the tissue source is anonymous, anonymized, or linked but not in a clinical relationship with the investigator or her collaborators. In such cases, there is no way to have completed pretest counseling and there is no way to know whether the source wants to receive results of the research. Revealing clinical results to the source may in fact do as much harm as good. There is simply no way to know.[47]

One final reason for providing research results to sources needs to be examined. It may be argued that in general benefits to research subjects are necessary to compensate for the risks of harm that arise in the research process. Thus, IRBs are mandated to insure that risks are minimized and also to balance commensurately the possible benefits to the subject of participation against the potential risks.[48] The underlying assumption in finding an obligation of researchers to provide results to sources may be that such benefits (if in fact they are benefits) balance the risks of psychosocial harm that may result should their tissue or medical information be inadvertently leaked to the general public, insurance agencies, or employers. But these harms are not *clinical* risks of harm. Adding clinical responsibilities to the researcher in this context would fail to address these psychosocial risks and would fail to justify them. Clinical care of the tissue source cannot ameliorate these risks, nor ameliorate the conditions from which they arise. It is a category mistake to presume otherwise. One protects sources of tissue by limiting access to the tissue sample and the information derived from it. Indeed, passing on results from genetic research may in fact exacerbate these risks, particularly given the lack of precounseling and consequent lack of prior understanding between source and researcher.

We should therefore be circumspect about imposing clinical obligations upon researchers. In general they should be avoided when appropriate, as they run the risk of imposing substantial financial and administrative burdens on the research enterprise. This works to the detriment of the greater medical and social good to which research contributes. Some research is inherently clinical, particularly research involving linkage studies or patients whose condition remains obscure to the physician/investigator. But even where the investigator maintains an ongoing clinical relationship with the source as patient, the distinction between these roles should be kept clear. Much research on anonymous, anonymized, and many linked tissue samples, however, does not involve an ongoing relationship between an investigator and the source. A clear statement in the consent process that participation will not bring any clinical benefits to the subject will clarify these expectations for research participants.

Avoiding clinical responsibilities in the research process where appropriate will contribute to medical knowledge through its savings of financial and administrative resources.

Acknowledgments

I gratefully acknowledge the support of the Fellowship in the Program in Biomedical Ethics at the University of Iowa, School of Medicine.

Notes

1. Department of Health and Human Services, *Basic HHS Policy for Protection of Human Research Subjects.* Section 46.101, b (4); 56 FR 28003, June 18, 1991.

2. George J. Annas, Leonard H. Glantz, and Patricia A. Roche, *The Genetic Privacy Act and Commentary* (Boston: Boston University School of Public Health, 1995), 131(g).

3. I follow the recommendation made by Ellen Wright Clayton and her co-authors that persons from whom tissue samples are derived be referred to as "sources," rather than donors, which implies, in their words, "an intent to make a gift or to relinquish control that may not apply to any particular individual." See E. W. Clayton, K. K. Steinberg, M. J. Khoury, E. Thomson, L. Andrews, M. J. Kahn, L. M. Kopelman, and J. O. Weiss, "Informed Consent for Genetic Research on Stored Tissue Samples," *JAMA* 274 (December 13, 1995): 1786–1792.

4. See, for instance, Wayne W. Grody. "Molecular Pathology, Informed Consent, and the Paraffin Block," *Diagnostic Molecular Pathology* 4 (1995): 155–157.

5. See Philip R. Reilly, "Panel Comment: The Impact of the Genetic Privacy Act on Medicine," *Journal of Law, Medicine, and Ethics* 23 (1995): 378–381, who notes that technology is already being developed to screen samples for several hundred alleles simultaneously. For a description of high speed computer-based sequencing, see A. C. Pease, D. Solas, E. J. Sullivan, M. T. Cronin, C. P. Holmes, and S. P. A. Fodor, "Light Generated Oligonucleotide Arrays for Rapid DNA Sequence Analysis," *Proceedings of the National Academy of Sciences* 91 (1993): 5022–5026. For a description of the use of this computer-based sequencing technology to probe multiple genetic polymorphisms, see R. J. Lipshutz, D. Morris, M. Chee, E. Hubbell, M. J. Kozal, N. Shah, N. Shen, R. Yang, S. P. A. Fodor, and Affymetrix, Santa Clara, California, "Using Oligonucleotide Probe Arrays to Access Genetic Diversity," *Biotechniques* 19 (September 1995): 442–447.

6. Reilly, "Panel Comment: The Impact of the Genetic Privacy Act on Medicine," p. 379.

7. See, for instance, Maggie Scarf, "Keeping Secrets," *New York Times Magazine* (June 16, 1996): 37–40; D. A. B. Lindberg and B. L. Humphreys, "Medical Informat-

ics," *JAMA* 275 (1996): 1821–1822; George J. Annas, "Rules for Gene Banks: Protecting Privacy in the Genetics Age," in Timothy F. Murphy and Marc A. Lappe, eds., *Justice and the Human Genome Project* (Berkeley: University of California Press, 1994), pp. 75–90.

8. See Mark Green, "Compromising Your Drug of Choice: How HMOs are Dictating Your Next Prescription," a report by the Public Advocate for the City of New York, December 1996; and Michael W. Miller, "Patients' Records Are Treasure Trove for Budding Industry," *Wall Street Journal* (February 27, 1992). Also see Elyse Tanouye, "Merck to Exploit Medco's Database," *Wall Street Journal* (August 4, 1993); and Gina Kolata, "When Patients' Records Are Commodities for Sale," *New York Times* (November 15, 1995): A1, C14.

9. See Onora O'Neill, "Medical and Scientific Uses of Human Tissue," *Journal of Medical Ethics* 22 (1996): 5.

10. Charles Fried in *Medical Experimentation: Personal Integrity and Social Policy* (New York: North-Holland Publishing Co., 1974), p. 98, argues that the purpose of the physician in treating dying patients is not simply to preserve life, but rather that the physician is a servant of the life plans of the patient. We might generalize this principle to the effect that the physician serves not simply the health of the patient, but the health of the patient in the context of his or her life plans. The problem with recontacting putatively anonymous tissue sources is that we do not know what they would want to be informed of or if they would want to be informed at all.

11. See David C. Rubinstein et al., "Phenotypic Characterization of Individuals with 30–40 CAG Repeats in Huntington Disease (HD) Gene Reveals HD Cases with 36 Repeats and Apparently Normal Elderly Individuals with 36–39 Repeats," *American Journal of Human Genetics* 59 (1996): 16–22.

12. See Marleen Decruyenaere, Gerry Evers-Kiebooms, and Herman Van den Berghe, "Perception of Predictive Testing for Huntington's Disease by Young Women: Preferring Uncertainty to Certainty?" *Journal of Medical Genetics* 30 (1993): 557–561; Kimberly A. Quaid and Michael Morris, "Reluctance to Undergo Predictive Testing: The Case of Huntington Disease," *American Journal of Medical Genetics* 45 (1993): 41–45; A. Tyler, D. Ball, and D. Crauford, "Presymptomatic Testing for Huntington's Disease in the United Kingdom," *British Medical Journal* 304 (June 20, 1992): 1593–1596; and R. Williamson, "Testing for Huntington's Disease," *British Medical Journal* 304 (June 20, 1992): 1585–1586.

13. Manning Feinleib, "The Epidemiologist's Responsibilities to Study Participants," *Journal of Clinical Epidemiology* 44 (Suppl. 1, 1991): 73s–79s. The article also recommends, for those subjects who do not have a regular physician, that it "would be incumbent on the epidemiologist to arrange access to a qualified physician to explain the findings and arrange for appropriate follow-up care if needed."

14. For a discussion of the ethical issues surrounding the NHANES study, see Karen Steinberg et al.'s paper in this volume.

15. Kenneth J. Rothman, "The Rise and Fall of Epidemiology," *New England Journal of Medicine* 304 (March 5, 1981): 600–602. See also "Protecting Individuals; Preserving Data [editorial]," *Lancet* 339 (March 28, 1992): 784.

16. Wayne W. Grody, "Molecular Pathology, Informed Consent, and the Paraffin Block," *Diagnostic Molecular Pathology* 4 (1995): 155–157.

17. Vicki L. Hannig, Ellen Wright Clayton, and Kathryn M. Edwards, "Whose DNA Is It Anyway? Relationships between Families and Researchers," *American Journal of Medical Genetics* 47 (1993): 257–260 (p. 259).

18. Annas, "Rules for Gene Banks: Protecting Privacy in the Genetics Age," p. 85.

19. Feinleib, "The Epidemiologist's Responsibilities to Study Participants," p. 77s.

20. Reilly, "Panel Comment: The Impact of the Genetic Privacy Act on Medicine," p. 380.

21. The problem of how to proceed with existing tissue samples already stored either in hospital pathology labs or in the laboratories of researchers is more vexing. Obtaining consent for the future use of these tissues may be next to impossible, both administratively and financially, as well as practically since the sources will be difficult to find and contact, even if they could in the future be identified by matching genotypes against computerized medical records. Following the arguments presented here, I would recommend that research on these tissues no longer be conducted outside of full IRB review to ensure that special precautions are taken regarding the confidentiality of data and that specific ethnic and racial sensitivities be respected in conducting the research.

22. Edmund D. Pellegrino, *Humanism and the Physician* (Knoxville: University of Tennessee Press, 1979), p. 226.

23. Albert R. Jonsen, "Do No Harm," *Annals of Internal Medicine* 88 (1978): 828.

24. Charles Fried in *Medical Experimentation: Personal Integrity and Social Policy* finds the moral basis of medicine in the response to the disadvantage of the patient: "for morality is concerned to restrain the impulse to profit from natural disadvantage and to require justification for imposing greater burdens on others than we accept for ourselves. . . . Indeed the whole practice of medicine may be seen as an expression of this moral tendency to overcome the effects of the 'natural lottery' without which disease would be allowed to run its course, weeding out the weak and inept. By seeking to overcome the effects of the natural lottery, we affirm each person's equal dignity, the priority of his moral status as a person over his natural status as a sick person or a weak or handicapped person" (p. 65).

25. Hippocrates, "Precepts," in W. H. S. Jones, trans., *Hippocrates I* (Cambridge: Harvard University Press, 1923), p. 319.

26. Jonsen in "Do No Harm," p. 827, suggests on the advice of Temkin that the origin of the addition of the "primum" is probably Galen.

27. Ludwig Edelstein, "The Hippocratic Oath: Text, Translation and Interpretation," *Bulletin of the History of Medicine* (Suppl. 1, 1943): 3.

28. Hippocrates, "Epidemics," in Jones, *Hippocrates I*, p. 165.

29. The Hippocratic text "Ancient Medicine" includes the following passage: "medicine has long had all its means to hand, and has discovered both a principle and a method, through which the discoveries made during a long period are many and excellent, while full discovery will be made, if the inquirer be competent, conduct his researches with knowledge of the discoveries already made, and make them his starting point," as quoted in Jones, *Hippocrates I*, p. 15.

30. Such duty to expand the quality and quantity of medical knowledge has been recognized by a number of authors, modern and contemporary. See, for instance, Claude Bernard, *An Introduction to the Study of Experimental Medicine* (original 1865),

translated by H. C. Green (New York: Macmillan, 1927), p. 102: "So among experiments that may be tried on man, those that can only harm are forbidden, those that are innocent are permissible, and those that may do good are *obligatory*." See also Henry. K. Beecher, *Research and the Individual: Human Studies* (Boston: Little, Brown, 1970); H. Tristram Engelhardt, Jr., *The Foundations of Bioethics* (New York: Oxford University Press, 1986), pp. 290–292; Charles Fried, *Medical Experimentation: Personal Integrity and Social Policy*; J. P. Gilbert, B. McPeak, and F. Mosteller, "Statistics and Ethics in Surgery and Anesthesia," *Science* (1977): p. 689; F. H. K. Green, "The Clinical Evaluation of Remedies," *Lancet* 2 (1954): 1085–1091; Jonsen, "Do No Harm"; Talcott Parsons, "Research with Human Subjects and the Professional Complex," *Daedalus* 98 (Spring 1969): 325–360; L. W. Shaw and T. Chalmers, "Ethics in Cooperative Clinical Trials," *Annals of the New York Academy of Sciences* 169 (1970): 487–495; and D. P. Thomas, "Experiment versus Authority: James Lind and Benjamin Rush," *New England Journal of Medicine* 289 (1969): 932–933.

31. See, for instance, Samuel Hellman and Deborah S. Hellman, "Of Mice But Not Men: Problems of the Randomized Clinical Trial," *New England Journal of Medicine* 324 (May 30, 1991): 1585–1589.

32. Although there are many accounts of the principle of autonomy, they ultimately derive from Immanuel Kant's articulation of this principle in his *Groundwork of the Metaphysics of Morals*. For a good discussion of this principle in the contemporary context, see Gerald Dworkin, "Must Subjects Be Objects?" in Tom L. Beauchamp, Ruth R. Faden, R. Jay Wallace, Jr., and LeRoy Walters, eds., *Ethical Issues in Social Science Research* (Baltimore: Johns Hopkins University Press, 1982), pp. 246–254.

33. Bernard, *An Introduction to the Study of Experimental Medicine*, p. 102.

34. Hans Jonas, "Philosophical Reflections on Experimenting with Human Subjects," *Daedalus* 98 (1969): 245.

35. Jonas writes, "The destination of research is essentially melioristic. It does not serve the preservation of the existing good from which I profit myself and to which I am obligated. Unless the present state is intolerable, the melioristic goal is in a sense gratuitous, and not only from the vantage point of the present. Our descendants have a right to be left an unplundered planet; they do not have a right to new miracle cures. We have sinned against them if by our doing we have destroyed their inheritance — which we are doing at full blast; we have not sinned against them if by the time they come around arthritis has not yet been conquered (unless by sheer neglect). And generally, in the matter of progress, as humanity had no claim on a Newton, a Michelangelo, or a St. Francis to appear, and no right to the blessings of their unscheduled deeds, so progress, with all our methodical labor for it, cannot be budgeted in advance and its fruits received as a due. Its coming-about at all and its turning out for good (of which we can never be sure) must rather be regarded as something akin to grace" (p. 230).

36. Alexander M. Capron, "Protection of Research Subjects: Do Special Rules Apply in Epidemiology?" *Journal of Clinical Epidemiology* 44 (Suppl. 1, 1991): 81s–89s.

37. Dworkin, "Must Subjects Be Objects?" p. 247.

38. Robert M. Veatch, *The Patient as Partner: A Theory of Human-experimentation Ethics* (Bloomington and Indianapolis: Indiana University Press, 1987), p. 13.

39. See J. V. Brady and A. R. Jonsen, "The Evolution of Regulatory Influences on

Research with Human Subjects," in R. A. Greenwald, M. K. Ryan, and J. E. Mulvihill, eds., *Human Subjects Research* (New York: Plenum Press, 1982), pp. 3–18.

40. Veatch in *The Patient as Partner: A Theory of Human-experimentation Ethics*, p. 27, comes to a similar conclusion regarding the priority of individual autonomy over producing benefits in research. His argument is based upon the qualitative distinction between deontological and consequentialist arguments. Veatch concludes that while we may balance competing interests within each of these categories, deontological concerns always will take precedence over consequentialist concerns.

41. See Parsons, "Research with Human Subjects and the Professional Complex," for a discussion of the fiduciary obligations medicine as a profession owes to society and the state to maintain the quality of its knowledge, education, and practice.

42. Joseph Palca in "AIDS Drug Trials Enter New Age," *Science* 246 (October 6, 1989): 19–21, reports on the joint deliberations on this problem of the National Institute of Allergy and Infectious Disease and the National Cancer Institute: "While the statistical working group will consider changes in the way trials are conducted, there are some principles that appear inviolable." The integrity of the randomized clinical trial must be maintained because "that's our fastest way of getting reliable knowledge," says NCI's Byar. "No one spoke against that principle. In fact several people said that if the parallel track got in the way by screwing up recruitment, then too bad for the parallel track" (p. 20).

43. There is, of course, a third option: to increase the supply of insulin by increasing the supply of cadavers. This violates fundamental political rights as well as being contrary to the purposes of medicine, and such notions, incredible as they seem, have unfortunately been the historical basis of the implementation of research ethics codes, such as that of Nuremberg.

44. For instance, Hellman and Hellman, "Of Mice But Not Men: Problems of the Randomized Clinical Trial," observe that "randomized trials often place physicians in the ethically intolerable position of choosing between the good of the patient and that of society" (p. 1586); and Beecher in *Research and the Individual: Human Studies* similarly posits the dilemma as between individual and society: "In experimentation on man, is the individual subject the first to be considered, or does society have priority?" (p. 47). For other examples, see Brady and Jonsen, "The Evolution of Regulatory Influences on Research with Human Subjects," p. 14; Alex Capron, "Human Experimentation," in Robert M. Veatch, ed., *Medical Ethics* (Boston: Jones and Bartlett Publishers, 1989), p. 136; Leon Eisenberg. "The Social Imperatives of Medical Research," *Science* 198 (1977): 1106; Carol Levine, Nancy N. Dubler, and Robert Levine, "Building a New Consensus: Ethical Principles and Policies for Clinical Research on HIV/AIDS," *IRB* 13 (January/April 1991): 7; Edmund D. Pellegrino, "The Necessity, Promise and Dangers of Human Experimentation," in Stephen E. Lammers and Allen Verhey, eds., *On Moral Medicine: Theological Perspectives in Medical Ethics* (Grand Rapids, Mich.: William B. Erdmans Publishing Co., 1987), p. 600; Harold Vanderpool and Gary Weiss, "False Data and Last Hopes: Enrolling Ineligible Patients in Clinical Trials," *Hastings Center Report* 17 (1987): 17; and Veatch, *The Patient as Partner: A Theory of Human-experimentation Ethics*, p. 42.

45. For a discussion of the concept of the "professional complex," see Parsons, "Research with Human Subjects and the Professional Complex."

46. See Mary Z. Pelias, "Duty to Disclose in Medical Genetics: A Legal Perspective," *American Journal of Medical Genetics* 39 (1991): 347–354.

47. A number of commentators examining the related problem of reporting unexpected research results to family members of an affected individual in a linkage study have similarly concluded for the same reasons that the perils of reporting results outweigh any benefits unless the family member has explicitly consented in the first place to such reporting. It follows, of course, that with sources with whom a researcher has an even less substantial relationship reporting results is even more perilous. See Peter S. Harper, "Research Samples from Families with Genetic Diseases: A Proposed Code of Conduct," *British Medical Journal* 306 (May 22, 1993): 1391–1394; Lisa S. Parker, "Ethical Concerns in the Research and Treatment of Complex Disease," *Trends in Genetics* 11 (1995): 520–523; and Mary Z. Pelias, "The Duty to Disclose to Relatives in Medical Genetics: Response to Dr. Hecht," *American Journal of Medical Genetics* 42 (1992): 759–760.

48. Department of Health and Human Services, "Basic HHS Policy for Protection of Human Research Subjects." Section 46.111, a (1 & 2); 56 FR 28003, June 18, 1991.

Human Biological Samples and the Laws of Property: The Trust as a Model for Biological Repositories

Karen Gottlieb

The laws of property that apply in the United States today have ancient Roman, Anglo-Saxon, and Norman roots. Fee simple estates, equitable servitudes, and contingent remainders are not items of everyday discourse, but they still play a role in the transfer of property by inheritance, purchase, or gift. The common law[1] is rather timid and rarely goes out on a limb. When novel scenarios appear, judges will harken back to the past and apply "old" law with a twist to new situations that were never dreamt of by the original jurist. Although it is sometimes said that technology has outpaced the law, the law is able to evolve to answer new legal questions. Thus, the property laws pertinent to preembryos, DNA samples, and cord blood stem cells need not be fashioned out of whole cloth, but can be developed through analogy using the existent corpus of common law decisions.

In this essay I look at how courts have applied the laws of personal property to human biological samples and then review three models of property transfer — abandonment, bailment, and gifting — that are used for human biological samples. I propose the trust as the ideal model for property transfer of human biological samples to a repository. Along the way I consider a variety of types of tissue samples because biological sample repositories include everything from commercial and nonprofit tissue, blood, sperm, and cell line banks to preembryos in a laboratory freezer to criminal, public health, and military DNA databanks.

Property is a concept that is both concrete and abstract. We are most familiar with the concrete concept of property: a house, a car, a watch. A technically more precise (and abstract) definition of property would not be an "object," but "an aggregate of rights which are guaranteed and protected by the government."[2] Property rights consist of legal relations between persons with respect to the object. Ownership is the "collection of rights to use and enjoy property" and "the right to control, handle, and dispose."[3] As ownership is the entirety of all property rights, it is much more than mere possession, which does not include holding legal title to the object.

There are two types of property: real property and personal property. Personal property is everything that is the subject of ownership that is not real estate, and the rights or interests in things personal.[4] Personal property includes money, goods, chattels, and intangible things such as patents and copyrights. Does personal property include your tissues? Are your gametes your personal property? Are your blood, placenta, fingernail clippings, urine, bone marrow, and DNA your personal property? If they are not your personal property, whose property are they? Or are they not property at all?

Human Biological Samples: Are They Personal Property?

Several legal opinions that have considered the issue of human biological samples as property have either begun with the assumption that they are property or have found through legal analysis that they are property. The findings have included a property right in your feces,[5] preembryos,[6] and sperm.[7] But the law is unsettled, and there are some exceptions. One well-known exception is *Moore v. Regents of the University of California*,[8] a landmark case that refused to recognize property rights in spleen cells ostensibly excised for therapeutic purposes and later used in medical research. The unsettled state of the law possibly reflects the heterogeneity of the biological samples discussed, which range from waste material to genetic material to preembryos. Several cases are reviewed below to highlight the difficulties in treating human biological samples as property.

DEL ZIO V. PRESBYTERIAN HOSPITAL

Del Zio v. Presbyterian Hospital[9] is a case of first impression that involved a preembryo as property, and it demonstrates the difficulty of ascertaining damages for a destroyed preembryo. The Del Zios had been unsuccessful in their attempts to conceive due to problems with Mrs. Del Zio's fallopian tubes. In 1972 their physician informed them of a new procedure known as in vitro fertilization (IVF) that would circumvent the fallopian tubes and involve fertilization of her ova with his sperm in a test tube. After fertilization the preembryo would be implanted into Mrs. Del Zio's uterus and, they hoped, pregnancy would be achieved. At that time there had been no successful IVF attempts in humans; Louise Brown, the first "test tube" baby, was still six years in the future.[10]

The Del Zios decided to undergo the procedure, and IVF was performed by Dr. Landrum Shettles in 1973. On the day after the procedure, when the test tube and its contents were still in the incubator, the chief of the Obstetrical and Gynecological Service at Presbyterian Hospital ordered it removed from the incubator and placed in a deep freeze without consulting Dr. Shettles. These actions terminated the procedure and destroyed the preembryo. Because of numerous previous operations on Mrs. Del Zio's abdomen, it was not possible to attempt IVF a second time.

The Del Zios charged the hospital with extreme, outrageous, and shocking conduct that caused them severe emotional distress and with damaging and converting their personal property. Conversion, an action that dates back to medieval England, is an "unauthorized and wrongful exercise of dominion and control over another's personal property, to exclusion of or inconsistent with rights of owner." [11] The hospital contended that the chairman's actions were reasonable in light of the fact that the experiment had not been cleared by the hospital's review board. There was no dispute between the parties as to whether or not the contents of the test tube were the personal property of the Del Zios. The instructions to the jury assumed that the contents of the test tube were personal property and could be converted. However, the judge informed the jury that in awarding damages for the conversion claim: "When, as in this case, the property had no readily ascertainable market value, to determine the amount of plaintiffs' loss you may consider the replacement costs if any, of the specimen. You may not take into account the sentimental value of the property to the plaintiffs." [12]

The jury found for the Del Zios on the claim of intentional infliction of emotional distress and awarded Mrs. Del Zio $50,000. The jury found for the hospital on the conversion claim; the appellate judge speculated that the jury may have properly concluded that the Del Zios could have collected damages for the intentional infliction of emotional distress claim or the conversion claim, but not both. Although the hospital appealed the trial court's verdict, it was upheld.

DAVIS V. DAVIS

Davis v. Davis [13] is a 1992 Tennessee Supreme Court divorce case that garnered a great deal of media attention and underscored the question of whether preembryos were persons or property. The Davises had undergone unsuccessful IVF several times and during the last procedure had cryogenically preserved seven preembryos for later implantation. Not long after the last IVF attempt Mr. Davis filed for divorce, and the frozen preembryos were disputed in the property settlement. The trial court judge, who called the preembryos "children in vitro," [14] treated the case as a custody decision rather than a property division. The judge determined that it was in the best interests of the children to be born rather than destroyed and gave custody to Mrs. Davis, who professed a desire to implant them.

Mr. Davis appealed, and the Tennessee Court of Appeals found in 1990 that Mr. Davis had a constitutionally protected right not to beget a child where no pregnancy had taken place.[15] The appellate court sent the case back to the trial court with the instructions to enter a judgment giving Mr. and Mrs. Davis joint control of the preembryos and an equal voice over their disposition. Mrs. Davis then appealed to the Tennessee Supreme Court, not for a right to implant the preembryos, but for the authority to donate them to a childless couple.

The Tennessee Supreme Court considered the issue whether the preembryos should be considered "persons" or "property." They affirmed the Court of Appeals holding that the preembryos cannot be considered "persons" under Tennessee or federal law. The Tennessee Supreme Court further relied on the ethical standards put forth by the American Fertility Association:

> A third view — one that is most widely held — takes an intermediate position between the other two [the preembryo is a person versus the preembryo's status is no different than that of any other human tissue]. It holds that the preembryo deserves respect greater than that accorded to human tissue but not the respect accorded to actual persons. The preembryo is due greater respect than other human tissue because of its potential to become a person and because of its symbolic meaning for many people. Yet, it should not be treated as a person, because it has not yet developed the features of personhood, is not yet established as developmentally individual, and may never realize its biologic potential.[16]

The conclusion of the Tennessee Supreme Court was "that the preembryos are not, strictly speaking, either 'persons' or 'property,' but occupy an interim category that entitles them to special respect because of their potential for human life." [17] The court did not find that the Davises had a true property interest in the preembryos, but did allow that the decisional authority regarding their disposition resided in the Davises. Since the Davises disputed the disposition of the preembryos, the court held that, in the interests of preserving procreational autonomy, the party who wanted to avoid procreation should prevail as long as the party wanting procreation had a reasonable possibility of procreating by other means.

MOORE V. REGENTS OF THE UNIVERSITY OF CALIFORNIA

Although your high school health teacher told you that your body is only worth $1.27, John Moore's body may be worth much more due to biotechnology.[18] This case centered on whether a person had a property interest in his excised surgical tissue that was later developed into a patented cell line. Moore was treated for hairy cell leukemia in 1976 by Dr. David Golde, a physician and researcher, at UCLA Medical Center. As part of his treatment, Moore's spleen was removed. Dr. Golde developed a cell line from the spleen and other tissue (blood, serum, skin, bone marrow aspirate, and sperm) that produced nine patented pharmaceutical products. The researchers at UCLA continued to monitor Moore and take tissue samples from him for almost seven years without disclosing to him the commercial value of his cells.

Moore brought an action against the physician and the university alleging, among other things, that his blood and bodily substances were his tangible personal property and that they had converted his property. The Court of Appeals[19] agreed that Moore had a property interest in his tissues and that he enjoyed the unrestricted right to use, control, and dispose of his spleen. The court stated: "The rights of dominion over one's own body, and the interests one has therein, are recognized in many cases. These rights and interests are so akin to property interests that it would be a subterfuge to call them something else."[20] The court held that Moore could bring an action for conversion because, besides having a property interest in his tissues, he also had not abandoned his spleen as alleged by the university.

The California Supreme Court in a split opinion reversed the decision that Moore could bring an action for conversion.[21] Instead, the court found that the allegations stated a cause of action for breach of fiduciary duty or lack of informed consent. For public policy reasons, the court refused to find a property interest in tissues removed from the body. The court thought that if a patient could bring an action for conversion of his tissues medical research that uses cell repositories would be impeded. It gave three reasons why conversion was inappropriate: "First, a fair balancing of the relevant policy considerations counsels against extending the tort. Second, problems in this area are better suited to legislative resolution. Third, the tort of conversion is not necessary to protect patients' rights. For these reasons, we conclude that the use of excised human cells in medical research does not amount to a conversion."[22] But the majority did not deny that under other circumstances excised cells could be considered property.[23]

Current Models of Property Transfer for Human Biological Samples: Abandonment, Bailment, and Gifting

Assuming that human biological samples are personal property or something closely akin to personal property, what legal models characterize the transfer of human biological samples from the person to the repository? The great variety of biological samples (e.g., DNA, preembryos, pathological specimens, blood, sperm, and bone marrow) and great variety of reasons for storage (e.g., forensics, identification, assisted reproduction, genetic testing, transplantation, blood banking, and basic and applied research) might suggest that many different models of legal transfer are involved. But most transfers of human tissue can be characterized as abandonment, bailment, or gifting.

ABANDONMENT

Abandonment is "the voluntary surrender, relinquishment, disclaimer, or cession of property . . . with the intention of not reclaiming it."[24] This voluntary abandonment of property with the intention of not returning to it includes the idea that it may be appropriated by the next comer or finder. The finder of abandoned property generally is entitled not only to possession, but also to ownership against all others.[25] Abandonment is usually contrasted with lost, misplaced, or treasure trove property. With abandonment, however, the true owner is thought to remember where the personal property is, but to have given up his or her claim to it.

In a 1976 criminal case, *Venner v. Maryland*,[26] the Maryland Court of Special Appeals found that Charles Venner had abandoned balloons filled with hashish oil when he did not attempt to exercise any right of possession or control of them when they passed from his excretory system. The finder, the nursing staff, was then legally entitled to ownership of the balloons and could give them to the police. This evidence led to Venner being convicted of unlawfully possessing hashish oil in such quantity that there was an intent to manufacture or distribute it.

Venner alleged that the state had illegally obtained evidence from him without a warrant when it collected his feces that contained the balloons of hashish oil. He had been admitted to the hospital in a semiconscious state due to an overdose caused by one of the balloons breaking in his stomach. An X ray showed twelve to fifteen balloons still inside his stomach. Over a period of five days the police recovered a total of twenty-one balloons found in Venner's feces, plus a fragment of a broken balloon, with the nursing staff's help. The question posed on appeal was whether the nurses were legally entitled to take the feces and examine them and whether the police were legally entitled to receive them without a search and seizure warrant.

The Fourth Amendment of the United States Constitution protects the right of the people to be secure against unreasonable searches and seizures. However, the Maryland Court of Special Appeals found the Fourth Amendment not to be applicable in this case because it held that Charles Venner had "abandoned" his feces and had renounced any reasonable expectation of privacy in them. Also, it found that there had been no intrusion into his body to retrieve the balloons by the police. The court distinguished the *Venner* case from a 1975 California case where a woman was forced by the police to regurgitate balloons containing heroin.[27]

Although the court held that the balloons were lawfully seized because Venner abandoned the balloons when he did not attempt to exercise any right of possession or control over them in the bedpan, the court *in dicta* did consider his feces his property:

> It could not be said that a person has no property right in wastes or other materials which were once a part of or contained within his body, but which normally are discarded after their separation from the body. It is not unknown for a person to assert a continuing right of ownership, dominion, or control, for good reason or for no reason, over such things as excrement, fluid waste, secretions, hair, fingernails, toenails, blood, and organs or other parts of the body, whether their separation from the body is intentional, accidental, or merely the result of normal body functions.[28]

Had Venner asserted his property right in his feces when they passed from his body, then the police would have needed to obtain a warrant to seize the balloons.

In contrast, the California Court of Appeals in *Moore* found that John Moore had not abandoned his spleen as alleged by the university.[29] They stated that the consent to remove a diseased organ, or the taking of blood or other bodily tissues, does not necessarily imply an intent to abandon such organ, blood, or tissue: "We do not find that, as a matter of law, anyone who consents to surgery abandons all removed tissue to the first person to claim it. Certainly, in the example of an unconscious patient, the concept of abandonment becomes ridiculous."[30] On appeal, the California Supreme Court relied on Moore's original complaint and the California public health and safety laws and found that Moore did not expect to retain possession of his cells following the operation.[31] The issue of abandonment of surgical and pathological samples is perhaps best dealt with by using a surgical consent form and having the patient knowingly waive any rights to the excised tissue. John Moore aside, most people are not interested in preserving whatever property rights they have in surgical and pathological samples.

BAILMENT

Bailment is the delivery of personal property by one person (the bailor) to another (the bailee) for some particular use or mere deposit; after the purpose has been fulfilled, the property is redelivered to the bailor.[32] Common bailments are leaving your clothes at the cleaners or leaving a car with a parking valet. The dry cleaner and the valet, as bailees, are in possession of your personal property, but there is no transfer of legal title. In order to have possession, there must be physical control over the property and an intention to exercise that control. The understanding between the bailor and the bailee is based on an express or implied contract. The bailee has a legal duty to redeliver the property to the bailor on demand or at the end of the expiration of a fixed term. The bailee is liable for conversion if he or she wrongfully refuses to deliver to the bailee or delivers to the wrong party. The liability of the bailee is based on negligence if the property is lost, destroyed, or damaged during the bailment and the usual measure of damages for the complete loss of a bailment is the market value at the time of the loss.[33] Bailments are usually distinguished from custody, which occurs when the owner of personal property places the property in the actual physical control of another, but there is no possession. An example of custody would be giving someone a heavy bag to hold while you open a door.

In *York v. Jones*,[34] IVF patients alleged that the clinic would not release their cryopreserved preembryo to them. The Yorks underwent four unsuccessful IVF procedures at the Jones Institute in Virginia during 1986 and 1987. During the last procedure, all but one of the preembryos were transferred to Mrs. York's uterus. The remaining preembryo was cryogenically preserved according to a previous agreement to implant only five preembryos. In 1988 the Yorks attempted to have the cryopreserved preembryo transferred to an IVF facility in California, where they now lived. The Jones Institute refused to approve the transfer of the frozen preembryo, saying that the Cryopreservation Agreement did not address the issue of interinstitutional transfer.

The U.S. District Court for the Eastern District of Virginia found that the Jones Institute had defined itself in the Cryopreservation Agreement as a bailee of the preembryo by the following provision: "We may withdraw our consent and discontinue participation at any time without prejudice and we understand our pre-zygote will be stored only as long as we are active IVF patients at the [Jones Institute]."[35] As the bailee, the Jones Institute only had a possessory interest, not a property interest, in the preembryo and had no right to the preembryo once the Yorks demanded it. The court also found that the Jones Institute by the wording in the Cryopreservation Agreement fully recognized the Yorks' property rights in the preembryo. There were repeated references to "our [i.e., the Yorks] pre-zygote," and the agreement called for the legal ownership of the preembryos to be determined in a property settlement in the event of divorce. The court noted that this vesting of the property rights in the donors is consistent with the position of the American Fertility

Society's ethical statement on IVF that the gametes and concepti are the property of the donors, who have the right to decide their disposition within medical and ethical guidelines.[36]

A bailment does not characterize the majority of biological sample transfers because the originator of the biological sample does not usually keep legal title to the samples. Likewise, the biological sample repository does not usually have the duty to redeliver the property to the originator. Bailment is a good model for transfer of tissues such as sperm, preembryos, or blood that are meant to be used in the future by the bailee, but the fit is not perfect. Damages for the loss of a bailment are the market value of the property at the time of the loss, and there would be difficulty in putting a market value on human biological samples because they are not, as a rule, traded in the market economy. If a sperm bank lost all its stored vials in an earthquake, how could a price be calculated for sperm that cannot be replaced due to a vasectomy or orchiectomy? As the judge instructed the jury when assessing damages in the *Del Zio* frozen IVF culture case, "you may consider the replacement costs if any, of the specimen. You may not take into account the sentimental value of the property to the plaintiffs."[37]

GIFTING

A gift is the voluntary transfer of property to another made freely and without receiving anything in return.[38] The characteristics of a gift are that it is presently effective and not a promise to give personal property sometime in the future. There must be a delivery of the gift, and the delivery divests the owner of dominion and control over the property. A donative intent is necessary to constitute a valid gift. A gift *inter vivos* (i.e., not a gift *causa mortis*, a gift made in contemplation or apprehension of death) is absolute and unconditional, taking effect at the time of delivery. In addition, a gift must be accepted before the transfer is considered a gift.[39]

Gifts are distinguished from implied contracts and trusts. Giving personal property "with strings attached" is not a gift but an implied contract, sometimes called a conditional gift. For example, giving someone a piano on the condition that he or she take lessons does not constitute a gift. A trust is distinguished from a gift in that a trust requires a settlor, beneficiary, trustee, corpus, and intent to create a trust.

Hecht v. Superior Court of Los Angeles County[40] is a probate case centering around the question whether fifteen vials of sperm in a sperm bank were part of the decedent's estate or had been gifted to a girlfriend at the time of deposit. In 1991 William Kane deposited the sperm samples in the month preceding his suicide. In the event of his death, he instructed the sperm bank to store the specimens upon request of the executor of the estate or to release the specimens to the executor. He also authorized the sperm bank to release the vials to his live-in girlfriend, Deborah Hecht, although it is not clear whether this authorization only applied during his lifetime. His will named Hecht the executor of his estate and bequeathed "all right, title, and interest that I may have in any specimens of my sperm stored with any sperm bank or similar facility for storage to Deborah Ellen Hecht." [41]

Kane's adult children contested the will, which involved the disposition of other property. In the settlement agreement between Hecht and the Kanes, the sperm vials were not mentioned. When Hecht attempted to retrieve the sperm six months later, the sperm bank refused to release it to her. In a second settlement agreement, the estate assigned to Hecht any interest the estate might have in the decedent's sperm, but the agreement was not approved by the court and the matter of the sperm was set for trial. The adult Kane children filed a statement arguing that the sperm should be destroyed. Hecht argued that the sperm was not part of the estate because it was gifted to her at the time of deposit into the sperm bank either as a gift *inter vivos* or a gift *causa mortis*. In December 1992 the court ordered that the sperm be destroyed, and Hecht filed a petition to vacate the order.

The California Court of Appeals distinguished this case from *Moore* because the agreement with the sperm bank showed Kane's intent to control the sperm following deposit. The court found that Kane had an interest in his sperm that fell within the broad definition of property in the Probate Code. It cited the *Davis* decision at length and likened the sperm to the Davis pre-embryos: "The decedent's interest in his frozen sperm vials, even if not governed by the general law of personal property, occupies 'an interim category that entitles them to special respect because of their potential for human life' (see *Davis v. Davis* [Tenn. 1992] 842 S.W.2d 588, 597), and at the time of his death, decedent had an interest, in the nature of ownership, to the extent that he had decisionmaking authority as to the sperm within the scope of policy set by law." [42] The appellate court concluded that the trial court had abused its discretion in ordering the decedent's sperm destroyed. Although it was decided that the sperm was part of Kane's estate, the court declined to apply the personal property gift laws to this case. [43]

Some biological sample transfers to repositories can be considered to be gifts. The gift model describes the donation of blood and bone marrow for banking, as well as tissues given for basic research, such as DNA research done for the Human Genome Initiative. Other biological sample transfers are clearly not gifts. Although the word "donor" is used interchangeably with the originator of biological samples, often there is no donative intent. For example, when samples are being given for diagnostic purposes such as genetic testing, it is questionable whether donative intent exists. Also, many informed consent procedures would allow the transfer of the biological samples to be revocable, whereas a gift *inter vivos* is absolute.

The Trust as a Model for a Biological Sample Repository

The trust is a model of property transfer that is not currently used for the transfer of biological samples to a repository. A trust is a fiduciary relationship in which one person (the trustee) holds title to the property and has an obligation to keep or use the property for the benefit of another (the beneficiary).[44] In the analogy with the biological sample repository, the settlor is the originator of the sample, the corpus or *res* of the trust is the biological sample, the trustee would be the repository, and the beneficiary would be the patients or victims of crime who would benefit from use of the biological sample for therapeutic or forensic purposes. The settlor and the beneficiary can be the same person.

Can a repository for biological samples be a trust? A trust is created when the settlor, the person wishing to create the trust, expresses the intent for a trust to arise in writing or speaking and transfers the sample. The language used to convey the intent to establish the trust need not be any special "trust language." It is not even necessary that the words "trust" or "trustee" be used, but the purpose of the trust must be described.[45] Forms similar to current consent forms could be used to create a trust. It is required that the settlor own or have a power of ownership over the trust property, the biological sample.[46] This could be problematic in jurisdictions such as California that do not recognize a proprietary interest in excised tissues used for medical research. There would be an impossibility of trust creation then because what is actually transferred in a trust is a property interest. But, in general, property interests are recognized in human biological samples.

Another requirement of trust creation is that the beneficiaries must be named and described in certainty with no vagueness or indefiniteness.[47] A private trust will fail if there is no beneficiary described because there can be no transfer of property without a person to receive it. This would be a problem for the biological sample repository analogy but for the existence of *charitable* trusts that do not require the beneficiaries be named. A charitable, or public, trust has as its objective the betterment of society.[48] Examples of charitable trusts are trusts for the support of religious institutions, construction or maintenance of cemeteries or monuments, public education, relief of poverty, and promotion of health and aid to the sick, disabled, and aged. A biological sample repository fits easily into the last category. The only requirement would be that the repository must be nonprofit, although it may charge for services to assist in paying its operating expenses.[49]

DUTIES OF THE TRUSTEE

The core of the trust model is the fiduciary relationship between the trustee and the beneficiary. The trust model imposes a fiduciary duty, that is, a higher standard of care and loyalty, upon the trustee.[50] This is the advantage of the trust model of property transfer for biological samples over the other models of property transfer — abandonment, bailment, and gifting. The trustee is held to a very high standard of conduct in managing the trust property and is under a duty to administer the trust solely in the interest of the beneficiaries. Fiduciary law has evolved in response to the recognition that there are legal relationships that are inherently unbalanced in terms of power, and the more vulnerable party (the beneficiary) needs to be protected from the more powerful party (the trustee).[51] When the fiduciary duty of loyalty is applied in the repository analogy, the trustee must determine if the proposed use of the biological sample is consistent with the trustee's fiduciary duty.

Another duty of the trustee is a duty to use reasonable care in making the trust property productive.[52] The net income of the trust can be seen literally as profit from selling licenses to patents that can then be plowed back into the trust or figuratively as the biological sample needed by the beneficiary. Presently, under the other models of property transfer, the repository has no duty to care for the biological samples or to make the property productive. From a public policy perspective, the trust is a better model and would obviate the need to put a regulatory framework in placc to achieve a proper balance between the private and public good.

CAN THE TRUST MODEL ACCOMMODATE THE TRANSFER
OF THE WIDE RANGE AND VARIETY OF HUMAN
BIOLOGICAL SAMPLES TO REPOSITORIES?

The trust model can accommodate the transfer of a wide range and variety of human biological samples to repositories, but not all. Hospital tissue archives, sperm banks, and research biological sample repositories would be well served by functioning as a trust. Others, like criminal DNA databanks, do not fulfill the spirit of a trust. But all repositories can benefit by incorporating the fiduciary concept in their structure.

A large percentage of the stored tissues in the United States today can be found in pathology laboratory archives in hospitals. The source here is the surgical excision of tissue in operating and autopsy rooms. Although some of the specimen is studied for diagnostic purposes, the excess tissue is archived in the form of paraffin-embedded blocks or glass slides for future clinical, educational, or research use. The usual practice is for the patient to sign a surgical consent form that states that the hospital will dispose of the tissue (as it is required to do by public health law) at the conclusion of its scientific use. What most patients do not realize is that some of the tissue will be kept, virtually forever.

The hospital appears to be a likely candidate for the trust model repository because the fiduciary relationship that is the core of the trust model already exists in the physician-patient relationship. The surgical consent form could be altered to include trust creating language for the excess tissue samples. The head of the pathology laboratory would be the trustee of the samples and have the duty to preserve and protect the trust for the benefit of the beneficiaries (i.e., the community). Since the beneficiaries would not be named in the creation of the trust, the repository would have to be a public, nonprofit trust. This may be a problem at for-profit hospitals but not at nonprofit hospitals. If UCLA hospital's pathology laboratory had been functioning in the trust model mode at the time of John Moore's splenectomy, it is unlikely that events would have transpired as they did.

SPERM BANK REPOSITORIES

Sperm bank repositories serve two functions: as a storage facility for persons who will be claiming their own sperm in the future and as a sperm bank for assisted reproduction. The first type of depositor uses the repository in a bailment relationship: he keeps legal title to his sperm, and he expects to have it returned to him at some time in the future. He is both the settlor of the trust and the beneficiary. The second type of depositor uses the repository in a gift relationship and does not expect to have it returned to him in the future. He is only the settlor of the trust and not the beneficiary. A trust can be revoked if the power of revocation is reserved in the creation of the trust. So the two different types of depositors would be creating different trust structures, one revocable and one irrevocable. Both types of depositors, though, would benefit from the trust model because, whether or not the depositors expected to have the sperm returned to them, both men would want the trustee to preserve and protect the samples for the beneficiaries. The trust model's strength is apparent in that it can manage both bailment-type and gift-type deposits. A problem, as in the hospital example above, would arise if the sperm bank repository was a for-profit institution.

Preembryo repositories are similar to sperm repositories in that some depositors expect to have their biological sample(s) retrieved and used, and others may expect to transfer excess preembryos to be used by others. Once again, both would benefit from the trust model because of the trustee's duty to preserve and protect the samples.

HUMAN GENOME DIVERSITY PROJECT

The Human Genome Diversity Project is a proposed offshoot of the Human Genome Initiative.[53] The plan is to gather biological samples from various populations around the world and create immortal cell lines that can be used by researchers to study human genetic diversity. The trust model is an excellent vehicle for this project because the power positions of the various players are not equal. Many of the populations to be studied are in a vulnerable position vis-à-vis scientists from the United States, who appear to be the primary, or at least the first-string, beneficiaries of the databank. In a twist on the usual relationships between settlor, trustee, and beneficiary, here the settlor is in the most defenseless position. A strong trustee would be a positive force here in remembering and reinforcing the true beneficiaries of the project: humankind in general.

CRIME LABORATORY DNA DATABANKS

The mode of transfer for deposits in crime laboratory DNA databanks currently is seizure predicated on probable cause. Depending on the state, DNA samples are often collected from alleged or convicted criminals, usually those involved in sexual offenses. The state crime laboratories currently do not owe a fiduciary duty to alleged or convicted criminals. Given the potential for abuse of the crime laboratory DNA databank (e.g., sociological or behavioral genetic research on the databank population), the depositor in such a databank would have more protection under the trust model. However, it is doubtful that alleged or convicted criminals will voluntarily transfer their DNA to a crime laboratory databank via a trust model — or any model, for that matter.

Conclusion

Although the trust model of property transfer is not a perfect fit for the multitude of biological sample types and reasons for storage, it is an improvement over the current models of human biological sample property transfer because of the concept of fiduciary duty that is the heart of the trust model. The trust as a model for property transfer of biological samples will protect the depositor of the biological sample and at the same time increase the availability of biological samples for beneficiaries.

Notes

1. The common law is the system of law that originated in England and is also used in the United States. It is based on written opinions of judges rather than statutory laws which are legislative enactments.

2. *Black's Law Dictionary* (6th ed., 1990): 1216.

3. *Black's Law Dictionary* (6th ed., 1990): 1106.

4. *Black's Law Dictionary* (6th ed., 1990): 1217.

5. *Venner v. Maryland*, 354 A.2d 483 (Md. Ct. Spec. App. 1976).

6. *Del Zio v. Presbyterian Hospital*, No. 74 Civ. 3588 (S.D.N.Y. Nov. 9, 1978); *York v. Jones*, 717 F. Supp. 421 (E.D. Va. 1989).

7. *Hecht v. Superior Court of Los Angeles County*, 20 Cal. Rptr.2d 275 (Ct. App. 1993).

8. 793 P.2d 479 (Cal. 1990), *cert. denied*, 111 S.Ct. 1388 (1991).

9. *Del Zio v. Presbyterian Hospital*, No. 74 Civ. 3588 (S.D.N.Y. Nov. 9, 1978).

10. Ironically, Louise Brown was born in England on July 25, 1978, during the Del Zio trial.

11. *Black's Law Dictionary* (6th ed., 1990): 332.

12. *Del Zio v. Presbyterian Hospital*, No. 74 Civ. 3588 (S.D.N.Y. Nov. 9, 1978).

13. 842 S.W.2d 588 (Tenn. 1992).

14. *Id.* at 594.

15. *Davis v. Davis*, No. 180 C/A, 1990 Tenn. App. LEXIS 642 (Ct. App. E.D. Sept. 13, 1990), *aff'd* 842 S.W.2d 588 (Tenn. 1992).

16. *Davis v. Davis*, 842 S.W.2d 588, 596 (Tenn. 1992) *citing* the Ethics Committee of the American Fertility Society, "Ethical Considerations of the New Reproductive Technologies," *Fertility and Sterility* 53 (1990): 34S–35S

17. *Id.* at 597.

18. *Moore v. Regents of the University of California*, 793 P.2d 479 (Cal. 1990), *cert. denied*, 111 S. Ct. 1388 (1991).

19. *Moore v. Regents of the University of California*, 249 Cal. Rptr.2d 494 (Ct. App. 1988), *aff'd in part and rev'd in part*, 793 P.2d 479 (Cal. 1990).

20. *Id.* at 505.

21. *Moore v. Regents of the University of California*, 793 P.2d 479 (Cal. 1990), *cert. denied*, 111 S. Ct. 1388 (1991).

22. *Id.* at 502–503.

23. *Id.* at 493.

24. *Black's Law Dictionary* (6th ed., 1990): 2.

25. R. E. Boyer, *Survey of the Law of Property*, 3d ed. (St. Paul: West Publishing Co., 1981), p. 680.

26. *Venner v. Maryland*, 354 A.2d 483 (Md. Ct. Spec. App. 1976).

27. *People v. Bracamonte*, 124 Cal. Rptr. 528 (Cal. 1975).

28. *Venner*, 354 A.2d 483 at 498 (footnote omitted).

29. *Moore v. Regents of the University of California*, 793 P.2d 479 (Cal. 1990).

30. *Id*. at 509.

31. *Moore v. Regents of the University of California*, 793 P.2d 479, 489 (Cal. 1990), *cert. denied*, 111 S. Ct. 1388 (1991).

32. *Black's Law Dictionary* (6th ed., 1990): 141.

33. Boyer, *Survey of the Law of Property*, pp. 689–691.

34. 717 F. Supp. 421 (E.D. Va. 1989).

35. *Id*. at 426.

36. *Id*. at 427 *citing* the Ethics Committee of the American Fertility Society, "Ethical Considerations of the New Reproductive Technologies," *Fertility and Sterility* 46 (1986): 89S.

37. *Del Zio v. Presbyterian Hospital*, No. 74 Civ. 3588 (S.D.N.Y. Nov. 9, 1978).

38. *Black's Law Dictionary* (6th ed., 1990): 688.

39. Boyer, *Survey of the Law of Property*, pp. 698–699.

40. *Hecht v. Superior Court of Los Angeles County*, 20 Cal. Rptr.2d 275 (Ct. App. 1993).

41. *Id*. at 276.

42. *Id*. at 281.

43. *Id*. at 283.

44. G. T. Bogert, Trusts, §1 (1987).

45. *Id*. at §11.

46. *Id*. at §25.

47. *Id*. at §34.

48. *Id*. at §45.

49. *Id*. at §124.

50. *Id*. at §95.

51. T. Frankel, "Fiduciary Law," *California Law Review* 71 (1983): 795.

52. G. T. Bogert, Trusts, §95 (1987).

53. See, e.g., P. Kahn, "Genetic Diversity Project Tries Again," *Science* 266 (1994): 720.

DNA Banking: An Empirical Study
of a Proposed Consent Form

Jon F. Merz and Pamela Sankar

DNA banking — the storage of blood and other human tissues from which genetic materials may be derived — is ongoing in many places. The analysis and circulation of genetic information presents complex, and often novel, consent issues. Yet researchers have rarely obtained express consent from the donors (or, perhaps more appropriately, sources, inasmuch as there has been little donative intent or even knowledge that tissues have been stored)[1] to store and use their biological specimens.[2-3] This raises serious concerns regarding source privacy and the confidentiality of the information gained in genetics research, primarily because laws protecting people from the harms of genetic discrimination are inadequate.[4]

Recent attention to this problem has led to several proposals for fairly elaborate consent forms.[5-8] Commentators have suggested that consent forms address numerous issues, including (1) the risks and benefits to individuals, groups, and society at large of research; (2) the scope of research uses (e.g., research on specific diseases or conditions and uses that may yield commercial products or intellectual property); (3) the right to refuse and right to withdraw without affecting care; (4) assurances of privacy and confidentiality; (5) future access to information, both by donors and by others (e.g., family members, research sponsors, and government agencies); (6) ownership of tissues and the associated data, as well as derivative information and products; and (7) assignment of surrogates and agents to make future decisions about uses and disposition of tissues and information, in case the principal is unable due to disability or death.

Nonetheless, little has been done to examine potential donors' concerns and preferences about banking their genetic materials or the effectiveness of the suggested consent forms. To study the opinions and preferences of laypersons regarding research involving genes, we developed a consent form and questionnaire and have begun to pilot it with different subject populations. This essay presents our development effort to date, including a large-scale pilot of a DNA banking consent form and questionnaire with a convenience sample of prospective jurors waiting for selection at the local courthouse. All studies involving human subjects presented here were approved by the

University of Pennsylvania Committee on Studies Involving Human Beings. Funding has been provided by the Annenberg Public Policy Center.

Consent Form Development

We initially wrote a consent form, which we will refer to as the initial version, incorporating many of the suggestions found in the literature.[4-6] The initial version of the consent form presents potential donors with detailed information about genes, genetic research, commercialization, and other material required under the federal regulations.[9] This initial form also gives subjects who choose to donate a choice about keeping a link between their name and the research samples, such that research information could potentially be provided back to them. For those choosing to keep their identity linked with their samples, we also asked them to indicate acceptable uses, including: to be used for their clinical care; to be used at the request of immediate family members if the donor is incapable of giving permission; to be used for research by investigators at the hospital; and to be used by researchers at university or company laboratories other than the hospital, provided their identities would not be given out. For the last three options, we also asked if they would want the results of research given back to them or their family.

We also developed a questionnaire to accompany the form, designed to (1) study comprehension of the consent form, coherence of responses on the consent form and questionnaire, and attitudes about the risks and benefits of genetics research; (2) solicit comments on the form's content and format; and (3) elicit demographic information, including age, gender, education, race, and religion. A copy of the initial version of the consent form and questionnaire is available from the authors.

The consent form has a Flesch reading level of about the ninth grade. We piloted these initial documents with a convenience sample of students taking a health law class in the Wharton School at the University of Pennsylvania. The students had just completed a section on informed consent, and we hoped to elicit their responses as well as comments about the purpose, content, and format of the documents. Ten of thirty students responded, eight of whom were female and two of whom were medical professionals. Responses showed great variability in preferences and exhibited some difficulties with understanding the format and wording of some of the questions that attempted to test comprehension and coherence of responses on the consent form. No students expressed problems with comprehension or made suggestions for substantive improvement of the form.

Consent Form Revision

During this process, we discussed the practical problems of implementing a consent form that gave donors different levels of choice regarding acceptable uses of their DNA. This presents unique challenges to fulfilling the goal of informed consent and complicates the management systems needs for data management of the DNA Bank. One of us (JFM) has also been working with the National Biological Resources Tissue Banks Working Group of the National Action Plan on Breast Cancer. From these discussions, we developed a model for protecting donors to apply to the DNA Bank.[10] Essentially, we characterize the DNA Bank as a trustee, whose obligation is to protect the privacy of donors and ensure the confidentiality and proper use of all information flowing into and through the bank. The bank may develop an identified database which can be updated by surveys of donors or by drawing data from medical records or disease registries. While the bank has donor identifiable data, it would provide only unlinked data and DNA to researchers; that is, all identifying and linking codes would be removed from materials given to researchers.

Based on this model of a DNA bank, we revised the consent form and questionnaire. The revised form is much simpler; it has a less comprehensive discussion of the risks of stigmatization and discrimination that could result from breaches of confidentiality; it discusses the delinking procedure and the purposes of it with assurances of confidentiality; and we make clear that no research information will be available for use in the care of the donor, other than as a matter of general scientific knowledge resulting from the research. Because of the desirability for some research protocols to use current outcomes or survey information, we ask donors whether they will permit the DNA Bank personnel to contact them in the future to solicit their participation in a specific research project. That is, if an investigator wishes to use current data or to incorporate data in a study that is not available in the DNA Bank records, then a specific proposal to the DNA Bank must be made requesting that donors be solicited to consent to more comprehensive data collection or to respond to surveys (which may be anonymous or not, depending upon the protocol).

We convened a focus group in the General Clinical Research Center at the Hospital of the University of Pennsylvania to elicit feedback on the content of the form and the revised structure of the bank. Participants included hospital nonmedical staff, one nurse, and laypersons identified and solicited for participation by the nursing staff in the GCRC. Participants were predominantly women (9 of 11) and African American (9 of 11). They were paid $30 for an hour and a half discussion. We gave participants a brief introduction to our work and the topic of DNA banking. We then gave them the consent form and questionnaire, and left the room for twenty minutes while they read the form and filled out the questionnaire.

The ensuing discussion was consistent with responses and written comments we received on the documents. The group expressed concerns about (1) lack of information about how much blood was needed, how often it would be taken, and how long it could be stored; (2) assurances of confidentiality, including the exception "as required by law," the apparent inconsistencies between asserted anonymity and the need for identities in order to make future contacts, and concern about who would make contact in the future (as well as concern about what might be inferred about genetic disease status if contacted); and (3) the role of proprietary funding in sponsoring the DNA Bank, and whether pharmaceutical firms would make huge profits using their DNA. Overall, the group (and individual responses on the questionnaires) stated that the consent form was well written and relatively easy to understand, although we found that people had problems with the questions that test recall and comprehension of the consent form.

We again revised the consent form and questionnaire, addressing the concerns people raised, incorporating more details about the blood draw and duration of storage, clarifying the confidentiality statements and identifying who might recontact people if they approved it, and modifying the questionnaire to be clearer. Copies of the revised consent form and questionnaire are included at the end of this essay. The remainder of the essay presents the results of a pilot test of the revised consent form and questionnaire with prospective jurors waiting in a holding room at the Philadelphia County Courthouse in Center City, Philadelphia.

Method

The consent form and questionnaire were taken by a research assistant to the courthouse on five different days in April and early May 1996. Prospective jurors normally have several hours of idle time, waiting in a holding room. The court has approved our solicitation of jurors in survey research. An announcement was made to prospective jurors, telling them about the general purpose of the study and asking for volunteers to read and complete the consent form and fill out the questionnaire. A candy bar was given to respondents as a token of appreciation. No identifying information was elicited.

We planned to examine respondents' responses about the consent form and questionnaire, looking for correlations between factors such as risk and benefit perceptions, correctness of responses, and demographic measures and stated willingness to donate. Chi square and linear and logistic regression analyses were planned.

The questionnaire elicits responses in several areas, which are analyzed separately. First, we presented a series of twenty-one yes/no and true/false questions testing comprehension and understanding of the consent form and asked two questions about perceptions of the ease of reading and sufficiency of the information content. We hypothesized that there would be some educational effects on comprehension. We also intend to study the questions themselves, to test their relevance and validity.

Second, we inquired whether respondents think they would be willing to donate a sample for research if the situation were real, and whether those willing to donate would be willing to be contacted for future studies. We also elicited perceptions of the risks and benefits of genetic research and DNA banking and asked for reasons why respondents chose as they did. We hypothesized that those who perceive greater risks would be less likely to donate and those perceiving greater benefit would be more likely to donate. In addition, we hypothesized that those persons identifying confidentiality or discrimination concerns as reasons for saying they would not donate would identify the risks as greater. Further, we inquired about whether subjects believed any genetic diseases ran in their families and hypothesized that those saying yes would see greater benefit in donation than others. We also anticipated that there might be associations between comprehension/recall and stated willingness to donate, but had no prior hypotheses about the directions of any such effects.

Third, we asked respondents to consider an alternative model of DNA banking, a "linked model," where a link can be maintained between DNA given to researchers and their identities. This permits research findings to be provided back to them, and we asked whether they would be willing to donate under this model and, if so, whether they would want to be given feedback from the bank about research results. We also asked if they would want their names provided directly to researchers to permit the researchers to contact them with research results.

Fourth, because of suggestions that donors should have choices to limit the types of research (particularly in socially sensitive areas such as alcoholism and criminality),[1] we asked respondents if they would wish to limit the types of diseases that could be studied with their DNA and presented a list from which they could choose.

Fifth, we asked four questions about commercial interests in genetics, including whether respondents would wish to restrict access by pharmaceutical companies or by academic researchers funded by pharmaceutical companies, whether they would be offended by patenting of products resulting from research with their DNA, and whether they believed they should share in the profits resulting from potential commercial products developed with their DNA.

Results

Ninety-nine prospective jurors volunteered to read the consent form and complete the questionnaire. It is estimated that between 10 and 20 percent of prospective jurors who were solicited actually volunteered, which is consistent with response rates to other surveys in this setting. The demographic breakdown of respondents is presented in table 1.

CONSENT FORM COMPREHENSION

We asked three questions to test respondents' comprehension of the contents of the consent form. Question 1 asks about the purposes for which the DNA Bank is soliciting blood donations, presenting five uses with yes/no choices. Question 4 asks about the risks that might be presented if the bank did not protect subjects' identities and presents eight potential outcomes with yes/no choices. Question 7 presents a series of eight statements on a variety of topics and asks respondents to mark each statement as true or false. Responses are summarized in table 2.

In addition, we asked respondents to rate how easy to understand they found the consent form (1 = very easy, 7 = too hard) and whether the form gave them too little or too much information (1 = too little, 7 = too much). Respondents ranked the form as relatively easy to understand ($\hat{\mu}$ = 3.2, $\hat{\sigma}$ = 1.6), but overall responded that the forms provided them with too much information ($\hat{\mu}$ = 4.2, $\hat{\sigma}$ = 0.9). These responses were correlated (r = 0.24, p = 0.02), reflecting that respondents who found the forms easier to understand also found the amount of information more acceptable.

On average, respondents provided answers on 18.5 of the 21 questions. On average, 15.6 of 99 (range 7–20) respondents left blanks on the 5 questions in question 1, 13.9 (range 11–19) respondents left blanks on question 4, and 7.0 (range 5–8) respondents left blanks on question 7. The difference in rate of nonresponses between the yes/no and true/false questions is highly significant (F^* = 25.8 with 1,19 df, p < 0.0001). This suggests that there may be some problem in the specification of the yes/no questions, which test knowledge of

TABLE 1. *Respondent Demographics*

Age, mean (standard deviation), years		40.9 (13.6)
Gender:	Male	33
	Female	61
	Nonresponse	5
Education:	Did not graduate high school	7
	High school graduate	29
	Some college	23
	College graduate	20
	Some graduate school	3
	Graduate degree	12
	Nonresponse	5
Race:	African American	38
	Caucasian	48
	Other	9
	Nonresponse	4

Religious affiliation:	N	Importance of religion in your life, mean (SD) (0 = not at all important; 6 = extremely important)
Catholic	27	4.2 (1.4)
Jewish	9	3.6 (1.3)
Protestant	11	3.9 (2.0)
None	9	2.1 (1.8)
Other	11	4.6 (1.2)
Nonresponse	32	4.7 (1.7)
Total		4.1 (1.7)

TABLE 2. *Responses to Test Questions*

1. Why does the DNA Bank wish to store your blood?	*Yes*	*No*	*N/R*
(a) To use it for your medical care.	28 (34)	**54 (66)**	17
(b) To use it to research the role of genes in causing disease.	**90 (98)**	2 (2)	7
(c) To sell to other people for transfusions.	6 (8)	**73 (92)**	20
(d) To give to researchers with other information about you.	**33 (40)**	49 (60)	17

TABLE 2. *Continued*

(e) To give to researchers without identifying you.	**65** (79)	17 (21)	17
4. If the DNA Bank did not protect your anonymity, the storage and research of genes could possibly cause:	*Yes*	*No*	*N/R*
(a) Loss of employment.	**69** (78)	19 (22)	11
(b) Disease.	17 (21)	**63** (79)	19
(c) Discrimination against family members.	**70** (80)	18 (20)	11
(d) Refusal of a doctor to care for you.	48 (59)	**34** (41)	17
(e) Loss of health insurance.	**70** (80)	17 (20)	12
(f) Distress about becoming ill.	**68** (78)	19 (22)	12
(g) Loss of your medical records.	14 (17)	**67** (83)	18
(h) Disclosure of your identity.	**69** (78)	19 (22)	11
7. Please mark each of the following as true or false:	*True*	*False*	*N/R*
(a) The hospital has agreed to share with you any profits resulting from research with your blood.	7 (7)	**87** (93)	5
(b) Genes are chemicals contained in the cells in your body.	**72** (79)	19 (21)	8
(c) The DNA Bank will only disclose your identity if you permit it or if required by a court of law.	**60** (66)	31 (34)	8
(d) Genes from a person can tell us nothing about that person's family members.	12 (13)	**80** (87)	7
(e) The hospital will own the blood and genes that you donate.	**87** (94)	6 (6)	6
(f) Insurers might use genetic information to deny insurance to people.	**63** (68)	29 (32)	7
(g) The DNA Bank will return your blood to you if they decide to no longer store these materials.	13 (14)	**79** (86)	7
(h) You have the right to require the DNA Bank to remove or destroy your genes at any time.	**55** (60)	36 (40)	8

Notes: N = 99; "correct" responses are shown in bold; parenthetical values are percentage of responses; and N/R is nonresponse.

planned uses and risks, respectively. There also might be a preference for true/false questions by respondents.

For each question, we had preconceived notions of "correct" responses. By our measures, respondents averaged 14.2 of 21 (68%) correct; 77% of the questions actually answered (as opposed to left blank) were answered correctly, but there was a good deal of variability in rates of both nonresponse and correctness. As shown in table 2, several questions were particularly problematic, as reflected by high nonresponse (N/R) rates and by high error rates. Item-total correlations across subjects for each test question with the total number of correct responses suggest that respondents had particular problems with questions 1d, 4d, 7c, and 7h. A factor analysis was consistent with this observation, suggesting that these questions need to be studied further and addressed in the next version of the consent form and questionnaire.

We also repeated several questions in different forms to test consistency. Questions 4e and 7f both require respondents to positively identify the risk of insurance loss, and 15 (18%) of 83 respondents who answered both questions were inconsistent. Questions 4h and 7c asked respondents about the potential for disclosure of information about them by the DNA Bank: 35 (42%) of 84 respondents answered these inconsistently; 23 who identified the risk on 4h did not do so in 7c, and 12 who initially did not identify the risk did so on 7c. Question 6 also presented a scale response, asking respondents to rate the likelihood of disclosure. There was no significant difference in likelihood ratings based on responses to the test questions.

For further analysis purposes, we calculated individual counts of "correct" and "incorrect" responses and nonresponses across all test questions. We performed best subsets linear regression analyses to see if there were any differences in these global test measures based on our sociodemographic factors. Analysis of the total correct responses found two similar but alternative models. The best fit model ($F* = 9.38$ with 3,89 df, $p < 0.0001$) showed that the number of correct responses was higher for respondents who rated the risks higher ($\beta = 0.53$, $t = 2.66$, $p = 0.009$), who rated the consent form easier to understand ($\beta = -0.58$, $t = -2.60$, $p = 0.011$), and who identified themselves as Caucasian ($\beta = -2.39$, $t = -3.30$, $p = 0.001$). An alternative model ($F* = 7.71$ with 3,88 df, $p = 0.0001$) again showed more correct responses for those giving higher risk ratings ($\beta = 0.45$, $t = 2.20$, $p = 0.03$), indicating greater ease of understanding ($\beta = -0.68$, $t = -2.97$, $p = 0.004$), and for those reporting having a college degree or postgraduate education ($\beta = 1.96$, $t = 2.60$, $p = 0.01$).

A best subsets regression of total incorrect responses yielded a single best model ($F^* = 10.10$ with 4,85 df, $p < 0.0001$). This model shows that the total number of incorrect responses increased for those ranking the benefits of genetics research lower ($\beta = -0.48$, $t = -2.62$, $p = 0.01$), for those rating the consent form as more difficult to understand ($\beta = 0.48$, $t = 3.03$, $p = 0.003$), for those of younger age ($\beta = -0.051$, $t = -2.69$, $p = 0.009$), and for those reporting an education level of less than completing a college degree ($\beta = -1.88$, $t = -3.58$, $p = 0.0006$).

Similarly, a best subsets model of the total nonresponses out of the possible 21 questions yielded one significant model ($F^* = 9.58$ with 1,94 df, $p = 0.003$), showing that older respondents were more likely to leave individual questions blank ($\beta = 0.1$, $t = 3.10$, $p = 0.003$).

ANALYSIS OF CHOICES

After presenting the forms to the first group of subjects ($N = 17$), we realized that we did not expressly ask subjects to indicate whether they would agree to donate (i.e., would they sign the consent form) and that respondents were not filling in an answer on the consent form addressing permission for future contact by bank personnel. For subsequent surveys, we added a page between the consent form and questionnaire, clearly differentiating the forms and asking these two questions explicitly.

Of 82 subjects given the express choice to donate or not, 49 (60%) stated they would donate, 26 (32%) indicated they would not, and 7 (8%) did not indicate a choice. Of those choosing to donate, 41 (84%) stated they would permit the DNA Bank personnel to contact them in the future, and 8 (16%) stated they would not. There were no inconsistent responses indicating unwillingness to donate but willingness to be contacted in the future.

Our initial hypothesis was that perceptions of risks and benefits would be related to individuals' stated willingness to donate. Respondents were asked to rate the benefit of research of the role of genes in causing disease (1 = not at all beneficial, 7 = extremely beneficial) to them personally ($\hat{\mu} = 5.3$, $\hat{\sigma} = 1.6$) and to society ($\hat{\mu} = 5.7$, $\hat{\sigma} = 1.4$). The two benefit ratings were highly correlated ($r = 0.45$, $p < 0.0001$). Respondents also rated the riskiness of storage and use of DNA, absent adequate precautions to ensure anonymity by the DNA Bank (1 = not at all risky, 7 = extremely risky). Ratings were relatively high, but exhibited large variability ($\hat{\mu} = 5.1$, $\hat{\sigma} = 1.8$). We also asked respondents to rate the likelihood that their identity would be disclosed to third parties (1 = extremely unlikely [never], 7 = extremely likely [always]). Ratings of the chance of identity disclosure were lower than ratings of risk ($\hat{\mu} = 3.5$, $\hat{\sigma} = 1.6$). As with the benefit judgments, the two risk judgments were significantly correlated ($r = 0.39$, $p = 0.0002$). Contrary to our expectation, we found that the ratings of the risks and benefits were not significantly correlated at an $\alpha = 0.05$ level.

Linear and logistic regression models and one-way analysis of variance (ANOVA) suggest only a very weak relationship between respondents' risk judgments and stated willingness to donate to the bank. Respondents' assessments of the riskiness of storage and use of DNA were not significantly related to stated willingness to donate. Linear regression of the likelihood that one's identity would be disclosed by the bank shows respondents' judgments to be weakly associated with their willingness to donate ($\beta = 0.07$, $t = -1.98$, $p = 0.052$). Similarly, a logistic regression model showed that those who thought the risk of disclosure was higher were less likely to state a willingness to donate (model $\chi^2 = 3.9$ with 1 df, $p = 0.049$; $\beta = -0.31$, $z = 1.92$, $p = 0.055$). There were no significant associations with perceptions of the personal or social benefit of genetics research, with total test scores, or with any of the sociodemographic factors we measured. Furthermore, multiple linear regression analysis found that none of the factors measured were related to respondents' choices to be contacted for future research.

We also examined individuals' assessments of the risks. Using a best-subsets search routine, we found two alternative linear regression models. The most variance in the risk judgment ($R^2 = 0.251$) was explained by a model ($F^* = 9.48$ with 3,85 df, $p < 0.0001$) showing that risk judgments are positively associated with respondents' assessments of the likelihood that their identity would be disclosed to third parties ($\beta = 0.38$, $t = 3.70$, $p = 0.0004$), negatively related to whether respondents believe that they have any diseases that run in their families ($\beta = -0.79$, $t = -2.37$, $p = 0.02$), and positively related to the total number of correct test responses ($\beta = 0.12$, $t = 2.82$, $p = 0.006$). An alternative model ($F^* = 8.73$ with 3,85 df, $p < 0.0001$) again shows that risk judgments are significantly positively related to respondents' assessments of disclosure likelihood ($\beta = 0.32$, $t = 2.98$, $p = 0.004$), are lower for respondents who believe that they have any diseases that run in their families ($\beta = -0.67$, $t = -2.02$, $p = 0.047$), and are higher for respondents ($N = 29$) who mention a privacy or confidentiality-related concern as a reason they would not donate to the bank or permit the bank staff to contact them in the future compared to all other respondents ($\beta = 0.92$, $t = 2.47$, $p = 0.015$).

A similar analysis yielded a multiple linear regression model ($F^* = 6.07$ with 2,89 df, $p = 0.003$) showing that respondents' judgments of the likelihood of their identities being disclosed to third parties were related to their mentioning of privacy or confidentiality concerns, as above ($\beta = 1.01$, $t = 2.89$,

p = 0.005), and to higher assessments of the difficulty of understanding the consent form (β = 0.23, t = 2.27, p = 0.026). An alternative model (F^* = 5.76 with 2,89 df, p = 0.004) shows that likelihood ratings are higher for those mentioning privacy concerns (β = 1.12, t = 3.11, p = 0.002) and increase with the total number of incorrect test responses (β = 0.128, t = 2.14, p = 0.03), reflecting the relationship between difficulty of understanding and incorrect test responses found in the prior section.

We also used best-subsets multiple linear regression to examine benefits judgments. A single best fit model for personal benefit judgments (F^* = 14.89 with 2,88 df, p < 0.0001) showed that respondents' responses were positively related to their judgment of the benefit to society (β = 0.54, t = 5.16, p < 0.0001) and that those respondents (N = 9) stating they had no religious affiliations gave significantly lower personal benefit judgments than others (β = −1.16, t = −2.41, p = 0.02). A similar analysis of social benefit yielded a single model (F^* = 6.92 with 1,92 df, p = 0.01) showing that judgments of social benefit are inversely related to the total number of incorrect test responses (β = −0.13, t = −2.63, p = 0.01).

ALTERNATIVE MODEL FOR A DNA BANK

A separate set of questions asked whether respondents would be willing to donate to a DNA bank that would maintain a link (a "linked model") between the DNA provided to researchers and their identity, permitting information to be provided back to them. Of 93 responses, 33 (35%) said yes, 33 (35%) said no, 27 (29%) stated they did not know, and 1 responded that she or he did not understand the question. Of these 93, 71 had provided initial choices about whether they would donate under the consent form. Of the 47 who initially stated that they would donate, only 24 (51%) stated they would donate under the alternative linked model, 11 (23%) stated that they would not, and 12 (26%) said they did not know. Of the 24 respondents who initially stated that they would not donate, 5 (21%) stated that they would donate under the linked model, 13 (54%) stated that they would not, 6 (25%) said they did not know, and 1 (4%) stated she or he did not understand the question. The percentage of respondents who indicated a willingness to donate under the alternative model was significantly different based on their initial choices by test of proportions (χ^2 = 9.08 with 3 df, p = 0.02).

We also asked whether respondents agreeing to maintain a link would want research results given back to them by the bank and whether they would want researchers to be given their names so they could be contacted directly by the researchers to be given the results of studies. Of the 33 respondents who stated that they would donate under the linked model, 26 (79%) expressed a desire for feedback, while 7 (21%) did not. Of these 33, 20 (61%) stated that they would permit their names to be given to researchers, while 13 (39%) did not. Of the 33 respondents who stated that they would not donate under a linked model, 1 indicated a desire for this type of information, and none wanted their names given to researchers. Of the 27 who said that they did not know whether they would donate, 5 (19%) stated that they would want feedback of research information, and 4 (15%) stated that they would permit researchers to be given their names.

Of 33 respondents who indicated that contact by the bank was acceptable, 12 (36%) stated that giving their names to researchers for contact by the researchers was unacceptable; 4 respondents made somewhat inconsistent choices, indicating that they would not want to be provided information by the bank but that their names could be given to researchers so that the researchers could provide the information back to them. In addition, 9 of 27 (33%) respondents who indicated initial preferences that they not be contacted by the bank for participation in future research stated that they would permit contact by the bank for feedback of research results, and 6 of 27 (22%) would permit identification and feedback from researchers directly.

Exploratory regression analyses yielded a multiple logistic regression model suggesting that those stating that they would donate under the linked model were more likely to state that they would donate under the Consent Form model ($OR = 3.6$, $z = 2.01$, $p = 0.04$) and were more likely to leave more test questions unanswered ($OR = 1.4$, $z = 2.25$, $p = 0.02$).

RESTRICTING RESEARCH

We asked respondents, assuming they would donate, whether they would want to limit the types of diseases or conditions that could be studied. For those indicating yes, we also presented a list of diseases and conditions from which they could select those they would like to have excluded. Of 93 respondents, 12 stated that they would put some limit on uses; 2 of these checked all or all but one of the listed diseases/conditions, suggesting that they misread the directions. There was no pattern to the choices by others, such as exclusion of behavioral or stigmatizing conditions.

We also performed exploratory analyses to examine whether any socio-demographic factors were related to preferences to limit uses. This analysis found that 10 (83%) of the 12 respondents who would limit uses were non-whites, a significant difference by test of proportion (continuity corrected $\chi^2 = 4.9$ with 1 df, $p = 0.03$). Further, for the 73 respondents who made initial choices about donation, we found that of 10 respondents indicating they would limit uses, 7 would not donate and 3 would, while of the 63 individuals who would not put limits on research, 17 would not donate and 46 would ($\chi^2 = 7.24$ with 1 df, $p = 0.007$). This suggests that the potential uses of DNA might lead some fraction of potential donors to refuse to donate.

COMMERCIAL INTERESTS

We asked respondents four questions addressing proprietary interests in performing and funding research, patenting of the fruits of genetics research, and sharing profits from commercial products developed from individuals' DNA. First, we asked whether respondents would wish to restrict access by pharmaceutical companies to their DNA for use in research; 28 (31%) of 91 respondents said yes, and 63 (69%) said no. Second, we asked whether they would want to restrict access by academic researchers funded by pharmaceutical companies; 23 (25%) of 91 said yes, and 68 (75%) said no. Third, we asked whether they would be offended by patenting of products resulting from research with their DNA, finding that 29 (32%) of 91 said yes, and 62 (68%) said no.

Fourth, we described the process by which pharmaceutical products derived from DNA might be created and asked respondents whether they believed they "deserved" a share in the profits resulting from sales of any such products developed with their DNA: 38 (41%) of 92 respondents said yes, and 54 (59%) said no. A contingent question was also posed for those who said yes to the fourth question, asking whether they thought they would deserve a share of profits even if they had been paid $5 at the time of donation: 35 of the 38 respondents completed this question, with 23 saying yes and 12 saying no. In addition, 1 respondent who said no on the fourth question responded yes to this dependent question.

Responses on the four commercial interest questions were highly correlated. Of 85 respondents who answered all four questions, 36 (42%) answered all negatively, 16 (19%) answered yes to one question, 16 answered yes to two questions, 11 (13%) responded yes to three questions, and 6 (7%) said yes to every question. Exploratory logistic regression analyses showed that the 36 respondents who answered no to all four commercial interest questions rated the likelihood of disclosure of their identity as lower than did those responding yes to any of the questions ($OR = 1.75$, $z = 3.1$, $p = 0.0002$) and were more likely to report having a college degree or more education ($OR = 0.28$, $z = 2.4$, $p = 0.02$). An alternative model showed that those rating the risks of genetics research lower absent adequate protection of confidentiality were likewise more likely to answer all four commercial interest questions negatively ($OR = 1.4$, $z = 2.4$, $p = 0.02$) and were again more likely to report higher educational attainment ($OR = 0.31$, $z = 2.3$, $p = 0.02$). No analyses of responses to individual commercial interest questions were performed.

Discussion

This study presumes that the form and content of informed consent to blood donation for DNA banking purely for research purposes must conform to the processes implemented by the bank for protecting donor privacy and confidentiality. We believe it is essential that the DNA Bank be absolutely responsible to donors, that this responsibility must be contractual in nature (by the terms of the consent form), and that the DNA Bank must be held accountable to a duly authorized institutional review board (IRB) to secure approval of its procedures and oversight of its practices.

Essentially, we believe that the level of detail needed to secure informed consent to genetics research must be commensurate with, or preferably exceed, the identifiability of the subjects of such research. In this study, we have examined a minimal level of consent, reflecting maximal protections of donor privacy by the DNA banking trustee. If links between researchers and subjects are maintained, we believe much more comprehensive informing is needed, because the risks to subjects and potential uses of research results in unplanned or unacceptable ways would be much greater.

Our results suggest that a consent form describing genetics research with stored DNA can be written to convey important information to laypeople. Our test results suggest, however, that there may be problems in effectively communicating information to everyone; we find that those reporting less advanced education had greater difficulty with the forms and that older subjects had a tendency to leave more of the test questions blank, although we do not know why. We also found some inconsistencies in responses, suggesting that some respondents were confused either by the material or by the wording of the questions. Several respondents commented that the consent form was easier to read than the questionnaire. While a consent form could be written in simpler terms, our subjects on average found the existing document to be written at a reasonable level. Those who had difficulty understanding the form recognized that in their ratings of ease of understanding. Ratings indicating that the form was relatively easy to understand were associated with a greater number of correct test responses, and those who rated the form more difficult to understand generally got more wrong responses.

It may be that more can be gained by focusing on the process of informing, by giving people more time, and perhaps by having forms read aloud. Informed consent should not be viewed as simply reading and signing a form; while this study suggests that many people may be able to understand the information, more effort is necessary to help potential research subjects understand what they are volunteering for. How that process should occur to best enable all potential subjects to understand the information requires more exploration.

Our study, using a subject pool of prospective jurors, suggests that many persons (60% in this study) who volunteer to fill in a survey on research state a willingness to donate blood to a DNA Bank that would provide unlinked DNA for research purposes. Of course, we did not actually ask to draw blood, and it is likely that some persons would refuse to donate when faced with an actual request. Nonetheless, it may be that patients approached in clinics or hospitals, particularly when blood is being drawn for other purposes, may be more likely to donate than this population. Altruism in a sick population may also be greater; arguably, sick people are more vulnerable, justifying a greater effort by researchers to communicate needed information and negotiate consent.

Contrary to our expectations, individuals' assessments of the risks and benefits of genetics research were not significantly related to their stated willingness to donate. Our results show that individuals' assessments of the risks and benefits vary greatly. We find that ratings of the riskiness of donation, if the bank were not to protect donor identities, were higher for those who believed they had diseases that ran in their families, and risk judgments were also higher for those who got a greater number of correct test responses and for respondents who mentioned a privacy or confidentiality-related concern as a reason they would not donate to the bank or permit the bank staff to contact them in the future. Similarly, assessments of the likelihood of disclosure of one's identity by the DNA Bank, despite the assurances of anonymity given in the consent form, were higher for those respondents mentioning privacy or confidentiality concerns, as above, and were higher for those reporting difficulty understanding the consent form or having a greater number of incorrect test responses.

Assessments of benefit showed that individual benefit judgments were significantly lower for those respondents stating that they had no religious affiliation, and social benefit judgments were lower for those having more incorrect test responses. Thus, subjects who correctly answered more of our test questions were more likely to rate the risks of nonanonymous genetics research higher, and subjects who got more test questions wrong were more likely than others to say that their anonymity would not be protected and that the benefits to society were not as great.

While assessments of risks and benefits were not directly related to respondents' stated willingness to donate under the unlinked Consent Form model of the DNA Bank, the data suggest that anonymity is important to many persons. We asked respondents if they would donate under a linked model, and only half of those who stated that they would donate under the unlinked model stated that they would. Nonetheless, the availability of research information from studies would also be important to some people, which would require that some link be maintained. Of 33 respondents indicating a willingness to donate under a linked model, most (79%) indicated a desire to receive research results and 60% indicated a willingness to have their names disclosed to researchers. This suggests that the availability of research information may be a motivating factor in some individuals' decisions to donate, although it would not be determinative because most of these people stated that they would also donate under an unlinked model.

It remains contentious whether and under what circumstances recontact of patients or donors to tissue and DNA banks for the purpose of providing them with individual results from research is appropriate. On the one hand, the present study suggests that a minority of people given the option of donating and receiving research information feedback may agree to do so, particularly if they have only the option of anonymous donation and are fairly completely informed of the risks and benefits of the research. On the other hand, it has been shown that such findings may have clinical relevance, and providers often want to ensure that their patients who have donated their tissues and information for scientific purposes have access to individually beneficial information.

One potential ramification of our results is that persons offered only the linked model might be more "willing" to donate under it. This possibility has serious implications for the legitimacy of the informed consent, because the availability of different options might influence peoples' choices, decisions may degrade as more options are offered, and the order of offering options is likely to influence choices. Thus, we could expect that expressed choices in this study would be different if respondents were initially asked to donate under a linked model and only then asked about their willingness to donate under an unlinked model. These issues need further exploration.

Our results suggest that only a minority of people would want research information provided back to them, but that the potential availability of such information is not determinative of their decisions to donate. Thus, there may be no practical need to make such information available as an inducement to potential donors. In addition, there are several reasons why such results should not be offered back to patients and donors.

First, investigators or others with access to research results must keep a link with patient identities, creating the risk of a breach of confidentiality and misuse of information. Second, research results are often uncertain, not having been confirmed by other studies and not normally having the benefit of quality controls typical of clinical laboratory services. Third, it is not clear whether people would want the information generated by a specific research study, how they would respond to it, and how counseling would be provided. One problem is that counseling simply cannot be provided until donors or patients get a phone call or letter informing them that potentially clinically relevant information has been learned about them, and a number of our focus group and pilot study participants stated their concern about the meaning of any future contact.

Fourth, the clinical relevance of information may be quite uncertain, making it a subjective decision about what results should be provided, when, and how. One published report explains how a specially convened ethics panel recommended against providing findings from a p53 prevalence study in osteosarcoma patients back to patients' providers because of the clinical uncertainty of the research findings.[11] There are two problems with this general approach: the potentially damaging information has already been created and can be linked by the researchers to individual subjects; and the resolution fails to address what might occur in the future. The information created now could become clinically relevant later, and the investigators have not finally disposed of the issue unless they have destroyed the linking file. If they did destroy the link, this begs the question why the link was maintained in the first instance.

Fifth, research is performed primarily to generate generalizable knowledge. We have found in this study that many persons appear to be willing to make a donation purely for research purposes, even though they stand to gain nothing personally from the studies. Most of the respondents were not troubled by the role of commercial firms in performing or funding research or in patenting the results of research. Also, a large proportion of our respondents did not believe that they would deserve a share of profits that might result from research performed with their DNA. Similarly, when asked if there were any limits on the types of diseases or conditions that could be studied with their DNA, only a small fraction of those who stated a willingness to donate would place such limits. While this study suggests that some people may have concerns about uses or commercial research activities, there is only weak evidence that such concerns would lead any individuals not to donate if asked. If such concerns are not material enough to cause significant numbers of potential donors to refuse to volunteer, then it may be asserted that choices on those issues need not be presented to facilitate choice by a small number of donors at the expense of making the informed consent process and the data management process much more complex.

Conclusion

We believe that we can appeal to individuals' altruism to promote research as long as we recognize our obligations, ethically and under the federal rules,[12] to minimize the risks of participating in research, including the risks resulting from breaches of confidentiality and potential misuse of information. This study presented jurors with a hypothetical situation, asking if they would be willing to donate a blood sample purely for research purposes, where they stood no chance of getting information, compensation, or anything else from the research except for the feeling that they might be helping to advance medical science. Most respondents who agreed to read the consent form and work through the questionnaire stated a willingness to do so; despite the length of the forms, many found them to be reasonably understandable. Further research is needed to continue to simplify and refine the consent form and questionnaire and to study the forms with different populations of potential blood donors, as well as to examine different processes for presenting these documents to individuals to best enable them to understand the information and make knowledgeable decisions about whether they wish to donate to the bank.

Acknowledgments

We thank Emma Meagher and Linda Knox for their assistance in organizing the focus group and revising the consent form and questionnaire; Garret Fitzgerald, Arthur Caplan, Edward Holmes, Barbara Weber, Mildred Cho, and Peter Ubel for comments on the documents; and Christine Weeks for running the surveys at the courthouse. The first author also thanks the Obermann Center for Advanced Studies at the University of Iowa for sponsoring the analysis and writing of this manuscript during the 1996 Obermann Faculty Seminar.

Notes

1. E. W. Clayton, K. K. Steinberg, M. J. Khoury, E. Thomson, L. Andrews, M. J. E. Kahn, L. M. Kopelman, and J. O. Weiss, "Informed Consent for Genetic Research on Stored Tissue Samples," *JAMA* 274 (1995): 1786–1792.

2. J. E. McEwen and P. R. Reilly, "A Survey of DNA Diagnostic Laboratories regarding DNA Banking," *American Journal of Human Genetics* 56 (1995): 1477–1486.

3. D. E. Goldgar and P. R. Reilly, "A Common BRCA1 Mutation in the Ashkenazim," *Nature Genetics* 11 (1995): 113–114.

4. G. J. Annas, L. H. Glantz, and P. A. Roche, "The Genetic Privacy Act and Commentary," Boston University School of Public Health, 1995.

5. B. M. Knoppers and C. Laberge, "DNA Sampling and Informed Consent." *CMAJ* 140 (1989): 1023–1028.

6. R. L. Gold, R. R. Lebel, E. A. Mearns, R. B. Dworkin, T. Hadro, and J. K. Burns, "Model Consent Forms for DNA Linkage Analysis and Storage," *American Journal of Medical Genetics* 47 (1993): 1223–1224.

7. R. F. Weir and J. R. Horton, "DNA Banking and Informed Consent — Part 1," *IRB* 17 (1995): 1–4.

8. R. F. Weir and J. R. Horton, "DNA Banking and Informed Consent — Part 2," *IRB* 17 (1995): 1–8.

9. 45 C.F.R. $46.116 (1995).

10. J. F. Merz, P. Sankar, S. Taube, V. Livolsi, "Clarifying Permissible Information Flows in the Use of Tissue Banks for Research: Understanding Clinician and Researcher Roles and the (Mis)Use of Research Results," in preparation.

11. E. Kodish, T. H. Murray, and S. Shurin, "Cancer Risk Research: What Should We Tell Subjects?" *Clinical Research* 42 (1994): 396–402.

12. 45 C.F.R. $46.111(a)(1) (1995).

Consent Form

CONSENT FOR BLOOD DONATION FOR RESEARCH

I have been asked to give a blood sample to the DNA Bank at the Hospital of the University of Pennsylvania (Hospital) for storage and use in research. If I agree to this, about 1 teaspoonful of blood will be taken through a needle put in my arm.

WHAT ARE GENES?

My blood contains cells. Inside the cells is a substance called DNA. DNA is made up of smaller chemical parts called genes. My genes are unique to me.

I got my genes from my parents. They got theirs from their parents. And my children get theirs in part from me. In this way, my family shares genes. These shared genes are the reason family members often look alike or share similar traits—such as hair color.

Genes may also cause illness. Genes may make it more likely that one person will get sick while another person does not. Because of our genes, people have different risks of getting sick from poisons, bacteria, or viruses to which they are exposed. How this happens is not well understood.

Doctors are learning more every day about the role of genes in causing illness. The number of diseases that can be detected is growing quickly. Doctors are specially curious about illnesses that occur in some families more often than in others, because this pattern hints that genes play a role. Despite growing knowledge, there is much we do not know. Researchers need to study genes from many people to continue learning and hopefully to someday cure or prevent diseases such as cancer.

BENEFITS OF RESEARCH WITH GENES

Doctors need blood samples from many people in order to discover genes, to learn how genes work, and to develop treatments for diseases caused by genes. Doctors can learn more about how genes cause disease by comparing the genes of many people or families.

If I decide to donate my blood and permit use of information about me, many researchers may be able to study my genes. Research may be carried out by physicians at the Hospital, as well as by researchers at other laboratories or companies.

Research is done to develop general knowledge. Thus, research with my genes may help doctors understand how genes work, how they cause disease, and hopefully how to prevent some diseases.

If I donate blood to the DNA Bank, I understand that I will not be paid, and that I will get no direct benefit from my donation or from the research.

THE DNA BANK

The DNA Bank is a unit of the Hospital. The DNA Bank will provide genes and information from people like me to researchers, and the Bank will protect my privacy and prevent the disclosure or misuse of information about me. Researchers will not be given information that identifies me.

If I give a blood sample to the DNA Bank, my genes will be taken from my cells. By doing this, the DNA Bank may be able to store my genes for a long time, perhaps forever.

Information about me. To learn about genes, researchers also need information about me, such as my age, sex, race, medical and surgical history, and my family history. I agree that information from my medical records kept at the Hospital may be recorded and stored with my genes by the DNA Bank. I understand that no identifying information (such as my name or address) will be given to researchers who use my genes.

Risks. Research with my genes could show that I and my family are at risk of getting ill in the future. This information, if told to me or my family, could be upsetting; it could cause depression, anxiety, anger, fear, and stress between us. Also, if this information were learned by my insurers or employer, it could lead to cancellation of insurance policies, difficulty in getting insurance, or loss of my job.

Research is anonymous. Because of these risks, the DNA Bank will not give my name or identity to any researchers who use genes in their studies. The DNA bank will not identify me or give information about me to anyone without my permission, unless required by law. All research will be anonymous, and all data will be kept confidential.

No feedback of research findings. No one, including me, my family, my doctors, or anyone else, will learn anything specific about me or my family from this research. Thus, I will not directly benefit from donating my genes for use in research.

RISK OF BLOOD DRAW

The needle inserted into my arm may cause some pain and redness at the site, and I may get a bruise at the site.

DONATIONS ARE VOLUNTARY

My donation of blood for storage is voluntary. I may change my mind at any time and require that my genes and information stored in the DNA Bank be removed or destroyed.

Whether I choose to donate blood or permit future contact of me or change my mind in the future, my current and future health care at the University of Pennsylvania will not be affected by my choice.

DONATION IS A GIFT

My donation of blood and genes is a gift to the Hospital to enable researchers to study the genetic causes of disease. The DNA Bank is sponsored by the

Hospital and by _____ (a drug company). In the future, researchers who use genes from the Bank will help pay the costs of storage and handling.

Sometime in the future, my family or I may want to access my genes stored in the DNA Bank, for testing of me or my family. The DNA Bank will attempt to fulfill my request, but may not be able to because my genes may be lost, ruined, or used up. Also, the DNA Bank may stop storing my blood and genes at any time without notice to me or my family.

HOSPITAL OWNS THE MATERIALS I DONATE

If I permit the storage of my blood and genes, it becomes the exclusive property of the Hospital. Neither I nor my family or heirs have any right to ownership or possession of the blood or genes taken from it. If I approve research uses of my genes, commercial uses or products may result from this research. I will not receive any money or other compensation from any possible business ventures or revenues derived from the analysis, testing, and development of my blood or my genes.

FUTURE RESEARCH PROJECTS

Sometimes researchers may need more information about people for a study. If so, they will ask the DNA Bank to contact people like me for more information. If I approve of this, I may be called or sent a letter by DNA Bank personnel asking me to fill out a survey or to participate in a study. If I say now that the DNA Bank may contact me in the future, I will not be obligated to participate. I will be fully informed when contacted about the research, and I may refuse to participate.

I permit someone from the DNA Bank to contact me in the future to ask me to take part in a research project (please check one):

_____ YES   _____ NO

If I checked YES above, I will let the DNA Bank know if my address changes in the future by contacting Dr. _____, at _____.

READ THIS FORM AND ASK QUESTIONS

I have read this consent form. I understand that knowledge about genes and what may happen with this knowledge is uncertain. I also understand the benefits and risks of blood storage and genetic research. Any questions I have have been answered to my satisfaction. By signing below, I permit the DNA Bank to store and use my blood and genes.

If I have any further questions about this consent form, or the research that may be performed with my genes, I may contact _____ at _____.

If I have any questions about my rights as a research subject, I may contact the Executive Director in the Office of Research Administration at the University of Pennsylvania at ⎯⎯⎯⎯⎯⎯⎯⎯⎯⎯⎯⎯⎯⎯ .

Signatures:

⎯⎯⎯⎯⎯⎯⎯⎯⎯⎯⎯⎯⎯⎯⎯⎯	⎯⎯⎯⎯⎯⎯⎯⎯⎯⎯
Donor	Date
⎯⎯⎯⎯⎯⎯⎯⎯⎯⎯⎯⎯⎯⎯⎯⎯	⎯⎯⎯⎯⎯⎯⎯⎯⎯⎯
Physician or counselor	Date
⎯⎯⎯⎯⎯⎯⎯⎯⎯⎯⎯⎯⎯⎯⎯⎯	⎯⎯⎯⎯⎯⎯⎯⎯⎯⎯
Witness	Date

Questionnaire

We'd first like to ask you a few questions about the Consent for Blood Donation for Research.

1. Why does the DNA Bank wish to store your blood? (please check √ Yes or No for each)
   (a) To use it for your medical care. ⎯⎯ YES ⎯⎯ NO
   (b) To use it to research the role of genes in causing disease. ⎯⎯ YES ⎯⎯ NO
   (c) To sell to other people for transfusions. ⎯⎯ YES ⎯⎯ NO
   (d) To give to researchers with other information about you. ⎯⎯ YES ⎯⎯ NO
   (e) To give to researchers without identifying you. ⎯⎯ YES ⎯⎯ NO

2. How beneficial do you think research of the role of genes in causing disease is to you? (please mark with a slash "/" on this scale)

   1 - - - - - - 2 - - - - - - 3 - - - - - - 4 - - - - - - 5 - - - - - - 6 - - - - - - 7
   not at all   extremely
   beneficial   beneficial

3. How beneficial do you think research of the role of genes in causing disease is to society?

   1 - - - - - - 2 - - - - - - 3 - - - - - - 4 - - - - - - 5 - - - - - - 6 - - - - - - 7
   not at all   extremely
   beneficial   beneficial

4. If the DNA Bank did not protect your anonymity, the storage and research of genes could possibly cause: (please check √ Yes or No for each)
   (a) Loss of employment. ⎯⎯ YES ⎯⎯ NO
   (b) Disease. ⎯⎯ YES ⎯⎯ NO
   (c) Discrimination against family members. ⎯⎯ YES ⎯⎯ NO
   (d) Refusal of a doctor to care for you. ⎯⎯ YES ⎯⎯ NO

(e) Loss of health insurance.   ____ YES   ____ NO

    (f) Distress about becoming ill.   ____ YES   ____ NO

    (g) Loss of your medical records.   ____ YES   ____ NO

    (h) Disclosure of your identity.   ____ YES   ____ NO

5. With these risks in mind, how risky do you think research could be to you, using your genes, if the DNA Bank did not ensure your anonymity?

1 - - - - - - - 2 - - - - - - - 3 - - - - - - - 4 - - - - - - - 5 - - - - - - - 6 - - - - - - - 7

not at all   extremely

risky   risky

6. How likely do you think it is that your identity would be disclosed by the DNA Bank to others (anyone outside of the DNA Bank)? (please put a slash "/" on this scale)

1 - - - - - - - 2 - - - - - - - 3 - - - - - - - 4 - - - - - - - 5 - - - - - - - 6 - - - - - - - 7

extremely   extremely

unlikely   likely

(never)   (always)

7. Please mark each of the following as true or false:

                                          (please check √ T or F for each)

    (a) The Hospital has agreed to share with you any profits resulting from research with your blood.   ____ TRUE   ____ FALSE

    (b) Genes are chemicals contained in the cells in your body.   ____ TRUE   ____ FALSE

    (c) The DNA Bank will only disclose your identity if you permit it or if required by a court of law.   ____ TRUE   ____ FALSE

    (d) Genes from a person can tell us nothing about that person's family members.   ____ TRUE   ____ FALSE

    (e) The Hospital will own the blood and genes that you donate.   ____ TRUE   ____ FALSE

    (f) Insurers might use genetic information to deny insurance to people.   ____ TRUE   ____ FALSE

    (g) The DNA Bank will return your blood to you if they decide to no longer store these materials.   ____ TRUE   ____ FALSE

    (h) You have the right to require the DNA Bank to remove or destroy your genes at any time.   ____ TRUE   ____ FALSE

8. The DNA Bank will assure that no one can identify you. This will prevent anyone from ever linking research findings with your name. The Bank has

done this to make sure that information about you and your family is kept secret. This means that you will not learn anything about your own genes from any research.

As an alternative, a DNA Bank could be set up so that data could be linked with your name. If it were done this way, and if you wanted the information, research results could be given back to you or to your family, but secrecy could not be guaranteed.

If this alternative DNA Bank were set up, would you donate blood to the Bank?

_____ YES _____ NO _____ I don't know. _____ I don't understand this question.

If you said YES, would you:

(a) want research results given back to you by
    the Bank?   _____ YES _____ NO

(b) want researchers given your name so they could
    contact you directly to give you the results of
    their studies?   _____ YES _____ NO

9. Do you think the consent form is easy or hard to understand? (please put a slash "/" on this scale)

1 - - - - - - - 2 - - - - - - - 3 - - - - - - - 4 - - - - - - - 5 - - - - - - - 6 - - - - - - - 7

very easy   too hard to
to understand   understand

10. To help us write the Consent Form so it addresses your needs for information, can you tell us whether you thought the form had too little or too much information?

1 - - - - - - - 2 - - - - - - - 3 - - - - - - - 4 - - - - - - - 5 - - - - - - - 6 - - - - - - - 7

too   just   too
little   right   much
information   information

11. If you permit research to be performed with your
    blood, would you want to limit the types of diseases
    or conditions that could be studied?   _____ YES _____ NO

    If YES, please check (√) any diseases or conditions that you would NOT want to have studied by researchers using your blood:

_____ heart diseases   _____ cancer
_____ infectious diseases (e.g., viruses)   _____ depression
_____ schizophrenia   _____ liver disorders
_____ skin diseases   _____ alcoholism
_____ kidney diseases   _____ bowel diseases

_____ violence   _____ bone diseases

_____ nerve diseases   _____ learning disabilities

_____ diabetes   _____ eye diseases

_____ AIDS   _____ reproductive disorders

_____ others? _____

12. If you will not allow your blood to be stored for use in research, can you say what the most important reason or concern you have is?_____

_____

_____

_____

13. If you do not want staff from the DNA Bank to contact you in the future to ask you to participate in other research, can you say what the most important reason or concern you have is? _____

_____

_____

14. Assuming you were to permit research to be performed with your blood, would you want to prevent drug companies from using your blood in their studies?   _____ YES _____ NO

15. Assuming you were to permit research to be performed with your blood, would you want to prevent researchers at universities from using your blood in studies that are paid for by drug companies? _____ YES _____ NO

16. Assuming you were to permit research to be performed with your blood, would you be offended if researchers patent inventions resulting from this research (which gives them the ability to prevent others from making, using, or selling those inventions)?   _____ YES _____ NO

17. Some people have genes that could be developed into useful products, such as drugs. Researchers can't tell whose genes would be useful in this way without studying the genes of hundreds or thousands of people. The costs of this research and of developing and making a possibly valuable product may be several million dollars. Most times this research does not yield a successful product, but that is learned only after spending the money. If your genes were found to be useful in this way, do you believe you would deserve a share of the profits made from sale of the product?

                                                   _____ YES _____ NO

If you said YES, do you believe you would deserve a share if you had been paid a small amount, say $5, at the time you agreed to donate your blood?

                                                   _____ YES _____ NO

18. Do you have any comments or suggestions for improving our consent form? _____

_____

_____

_____

19. Do you have any questions about the benefits and risks of blood storage and research that we did not answer in the Consent Form? _____

_____

_____

_____

20. Do you believe there are any diseases that run in your family?

_____ YES _____ NO _____ Don't know

If YES, can you tell us which one(s) and why you think so? _____

_____

_____

Now, we'd like a little information about you. **Again, we will keep your answers secret.** (please fill in blanks or check (√) boxes)

21. What is your age? _____ years

22. And your sex? _____ Male _____ Female

23. How many years of education do you have?

_____ did not graduate high school

_____ high school graduate

_____ some college

_____ college graduate

_____ some graduate school

_____ graduate degree(s): _____

24. What is your occupation? _____

25. What is your race?

_____ African-American

_____ Asian

_____ Caucasian

_____ Hispanic

_____ Other: _____

26. What is your religious affiliation?

_____ Catholic

_____ Jewish

_____ Protestant

_____ None

_____ Other: _____

27. How important is religion in your life? (please put a slash "/" on this scale)

1 - - - - - - - 2 - - - - - - - 3 - - - - - - - 4 - - - - - - - 5 - - - - - - - 6 - - - - - - - 7

not at all   extremely

important   important

THANK YOU VERY MUCH!

Human Genetic Material: Commodity or Gift?

Bartha Maria Knoppers

The Canadian project on Persons, Property, Patents and Policies examined the ethical and legal implications of the protocols and procedures employed in the collection and banking of human genetic material. The legal principles examined included the notion(s) of property under the common law and civil law as well as DNA banking and patenting issues. The ethical issues covered aspects of recruitment, informed consent, storage, sample sharing, and record linkage.

Our findings demonstrate the need to adopt nationally acceptable policies for the collection and banking of human genetic material. These policies must conform with ethical principles as well as legal obligations. Our findings also demonstrate the difficulty, if not artificiality, of the property-versus-person debate on the legal characterization of DNA samples, as well as the possible emergence of a trend toward a system of rewards for participation in genetic research. What *is* at issue is respect for human dignity and integrity as expressed through personal choices over genetic material and information. Thus, there is a need not only to move beyond the issue of characterization of human genetic material but to halt the increasing "commodification" of the human body and its parts by adopting a conditional-gift approach.

Beyond Characterization?

Even though the notions of property and ownership of human genetic material may seem to commodify the human person, under the common law, property considerations, when seen as offering rights of control, may have a "proper place in the recognition of research and as a mechanism to protect the interests of patients/participants."[1] Yet the policy considerations are such that M. Litman and G. Robertson conclude that "rather than focusing on the legal characterization of genetic material and information, and trying to assign them to specific juridical categories such as property and persons, courts should view them as legally unique, and utilize the flexibility of the *sui generis* approach to fashion whatever rights, obligations and remedies, policy demands in the particular context and circumstances of each case."[2]

The civil law position also foresees "the possibility of a right of control through an expanded informed consent process under the law of persons — that is, a personality rights — approach."[3] M. Hirtle concludes:

> There is no legal concept that readily applies to the human body and its parts. This may be because the human body is indissolubly both person *and* thing. . . . In practice, body parts and products permanently removed from the body are considered to be commodities that enter legal commerce even though gratuity remains the rule. . . . It seems that a personal rights approach through the obtaining of an informed consent to the actual and eventual use(s) of body tissues, fluids, products and cells would not necessarily hinder a property rights approach once the body part is separated from that person.[4]

Finally, because so much time, effort, and money are involved in genetic research, and because there is a belief that a significant percentage of this research will be essential to the development of highly lucrative commercial products or processes, researchers and the entities that fund them have a desire to protect the fruits of their labor. To date, obtaining a patent has been the preferred method of protection. Indeed, despite the continuing and explicitly unresolved nature of the question of ownership, the patenting of human DNA has continued unabated. T. Caulfield, K. Cherniawsky, and E. Nelson conclude:

> As with the growth of genetic technology itself, the current legal and administrative practice of simply applying the traditional patent law principles has progressed in a largely unchecked and ad hoc manner. Therefore, a re-examination and clarification of these principles, and the effect of their application, is clearly warranted. To this end, it is submitted that any patent policy should consider a broad range of issues including, *inter alia*: the purpose behind intellectual property regimes; the various mechanisms which could be used to modify the current system; the ramifications of any policy on past and future patents; the influence of the policy on research and industry; the legal loopholes which may undermine the implementation of any policy; and, perhaps most importantly, how ethical and moral concerns can be addressed.[5]

In 1995, to investigate how issues pertaining to DNA banking and control by research participants and researchers are handled in Canada, our project also conducted separate surveys of investigators using human DNA, institutional research administrators, research ethics boards (REBs), and existing consent procedures.[6]

Administrators, REBs, and DNA investigators gave mailed survey response rates of 76 percent (69/91), 68 percent (106/156), and 57 percent (132/230), respectively. In each group, fewer than one-third of respondents were aware of local institutional policies for DNA banking. Roughly three-quarters (74%) of DNA investigators indicated satisfaction with local policies for recruitment and informed consent, with a range of 42 percent to 52 percent for policies concerning sample control, sharing, storage, and nominal linkage. In contrast, responses from REBs indicated lack of satisfaction ranging from 45 percent to 72 percent for the same banking procedures.

Those who maintained DNA banks ($N = 75$) were asked about their consent forms for acquisition of human genetic material. Ownership/control options were specified by 21 percent and duration by 8 percent; 25 percent of DNA bankers did not answer these questions.

Sample sharing was reported by 61 percent of DNA bankers. Overall, 47 percent obtained informed consent from donors for sample sharing, and 63 percent of these restricted further research to the donors' disease(s). Anonymous linkage of donors with shared samples was used by 63 percent of DNA bankers, but nominative linkage was used by 15 percent. Of those 46 bankers who shared DNA specimens with external banks, 33 percent reviewed the regulations of external bankers, 33 percent did not review, and 33 percent did not answer the questions.

These data led M. J. Verhoef, R. M. Lewkonia, and T. D. Kinsella to conclude that most Canadian academic health centers and research institutions have not established satisfactory policies for DNA banking. Most respondents felt that such policies are desirable. In addition, such procedures that were in place often appeared to have potential ethical deficiencies or not to comply with existing policy guidelines. A separate qualitative analysis by B. Godard and M. J. Verhoef of the comments found on the questionnaires underscores these findings and conclusions.[7]

While the analysis of the consent forms currently in use for DNA banking in Canada reveals a certain consensus on the need to obtain consent, ensure confidentiality, permit withdrawal without prejudice, and define the type of sample as well as the fact of storage, there is a lack of consensus (if not ignorance) not only on the need to provide for certain choices that respect personal values, but also on intellectual property issues.[8] According to B. M. Knoppers and C. M. Laberge, standardization and simplification of forms are essential.[9]

In short, the wide diversity of positions found both in the responses to the questionnaire and in the qualitative study of the commentaries received and the analysis of the consent forms illustrate a lack of direction and consensus on certain issues of DNA banking. As demonstrated by Hirtle,[10] there is agreement on the internationally shared principles of autonomy, privacy, justice, equity, and quality assurance, but not on their translation in the more controversial areas of choice, control, and commercialization.

Neither the proposed UNESCO "Universal Declaration"[11] nor the draft bioethics "Convention"[12] of the Council of Europe specifically addresses DNA banking issues. The "Convention," however, does mandate:

> Article 21: The human body and its parts shall not, as such, give rise to financial gain.
>
> Article 22: When in the course of an intervention any part of a human body is removed, it may be stored and used for a purpose other than that for which it was removed, only if this is done in conformity with *appropriate information and consent procedures.* (emphasis added)

The 1996 Human Genome Organization (HUGO) "Statement on the Principled Conduct of Genetic Research"[13] is more specific when it mandates that "undue inducement through compensation for individual participants, families and populations should be prohibited. This prohibition, however, does not include agreements with individuals, families, groups, communities or populations that foresee technology transfer, local training, joint ventures, provision of health care or of information infrastructures, reimbursement of costs, or the possible use of a percentage of royalties for humanitarian purposes."[14]

If such a return to the community or to the population were to become part of genetic research protocols and contracts, what of the original "contributor"? Can such a contribution be considered a gift?

Conditional Gift?

An editorial in *Nature* included this comment: "In the past, the prospect of novel treatment resulting from a better understanding of disease has generally been seen as sufficient reward. This formula is no longer sufficient, chiefly because it does not provide any mechanisms for ensuring that other potential benefits are made available to contributors."[15] In this vein, a 1995 American study of twenty-three consent forms for sampling and banking concludes that

> individuals who contribute tissue samples for genetics-related research projects have a legitimate claim to partial ownership of the stored biological materials, as well as to some of the commercial profits resulting from patenting an immortalized cell line in the unlikely event that profits are to be

made from the research. . . . [The authors suggest] that the original owners in this sequential ownership be promised in consent documents they sign that they will receive 10–25% of any profits gained from a cell line created from their DNA sample (including profits made by subsequent investigators at other institutions).[16]

While tissues and blood are no longer considered to be abandoned or to be waste, surely promises of eventual financial rewards are not the answer. The ethical propriety and workability of such a "commodification" through royalties has already been questioned.[17] If DNA is neither "person" nor "thing" but rather requires a *sui generis* approach, it may be more respectful of its unique status and qualities to consider its use in genetic research as a gift — a gift conditional on the individual choices made.

Black's Law Dictionary defines "gift" as "a voluntary transfer of personal property without consideration. . . . A voluntary conveyance of land, or transfer of goods, from one person to another, made gratuitously, and not upon any consideration of blood or money. . . . Essential requisites of 'gift' are capacity of donor, intention of the donor to make a gift, completed delivery to or for donee, and acceptance of gift by donee." "Consideration" is defined as an "inducement to a contract." Under a conditional gift approach, then, there is neither payment for the voluntary transfer of DNA nor a promise of individual percentages of future royalties. What is required is a clear delineation of choices, of institutional policies, and a statement (where applicable) of commercial investment or possible future commercial benefits. While such an approach encourages "the development of useful inventions and products for promoting human health and well-being,"[18] it does not eschew the possibility of "an appropriate share of the economic and commercial returns derived from medical investigations, including both clinical trials and genetic epidemiological studies, using biological material derived from their population groups"[19] returning to the health care infrastructure that made participation possible.[20] In other words, a conditional-gift approach may only be possible in countries with such a health care infrastructure.

Conclusion

As the Human Genome Project moves from mapping into the DNA sequencing phase and then to the search for function, attention will turn to "interesting" populations.[21] International collaboration and "free" exchange of genetic material have long been the hallmark of genetic research.[22] Only a halt to increasing commercialization at the level of the sampling of individuals or populations, together with respect for personal and cultural values as expressed through choices within the consent process, can serve to maintain this tradition. Recognition of this gift, however, requires some sharing of eventual profits for humanitarian purposes with the contributing communities and populations.[23] The search for mechanisms to make this possible should begin.

Acknowledgments

This essay is a slightly revised version of the concluding chapter of a Canadian study supported by the Canadian Genome Analysis and Technology Program (CGAT) found in B. M. Knoppers, T. Caulfield, and T. D. Kinsella, eds., *Legal Rights and Human Genetic Material in Canada* (Toronto: Emond Montgomery Publishers, Ltd., 1996), pp. 171–180.

Notes

1. B. M. Knoppers, T. Caulfield, and T. D. Kinsella, "Introduction," in B. M. Knoppers, T. Caulfield, and T. D. Kinsella, eds. *Legal Rights and Human Genetic Material in Canada* (Toronto: Emond Montgomery Publishers, Ltd., 1996), p. 3.

2. M. Litman and G. Robertson, "The Common Law Status of Genetic Material," in Knoppers, Caulfield, and Kinsella, *Legal Rights*, p. 84.

3. Knoppers, Caulfield, and Kinsella, *Legal Rights*, p. 3.

4. M. Hirtle, "Civil Law and the Status of Human Genetic Material," in Knoppers, Caulfield, and Kinsella, *Legal Rights*, p. 116.

5. T. Caulfield, K. Cherniawsky, and E. Nelson, "Patent Law and Human DNA: Current Practice," in Knoppers, Caulfield, and Kinsella, *Legal Rights*, p. 147. See also B. M. Knoppers, "Patenting 'Human Life': A Misdirected Concern?" *Policy Options* 17 (1996): 3.

6. M. J. Verhoef, R. M. Lewkonia, and T. D. Kinsella, "Ethical Implications of Current Practices in Human DNA Banking in Canada," in Knoppers, Caulfield, and Kinsella, *Legal Rights*, pp. 5–16.

7. B. Godard and M. J. Verhoef, "DNA Banking: Current and Ideal Practices," in Knoppers, Caulfield, and Kinsella, *Legal Rights*, pp. 17–31.

8. B. M. Knoppers and C. M. Laberge, "DNA Banking/Collecting: A Canadian 'Sample' of Consent Forms," in Knoppers, Caulfield, and Kinsella, *Legal Rights*, pp. 33–49.

9. See a proposed model consent form at the end of this essay.

10. M. Hirtle, "International Policy Positions on the Banking and Further Use of Human Genetic Material," in Knoppers, Caulfield, and Kinsella, *Legal Rights*, pp. 85–115.

11. UNESCO, "Universal Declaration on the Protection of the Human Genome and Human Rights," March 1996.

12. Council of Europe, "Convention for the Protection of Human Rights and Dignity of the Human Being with Regard to the Application of Biology and Medicine: Convention on Human Rights and Biomedicine," June 1996.

13. Human Genome Organization (HUGO), "Statement on the Principled Conduct of Genetic Research," *Genome Digest* 3 (1996): 2–3 (p. 3).

14. This statement establishes the core principles for genomic research. See also the recent proposed guidelines of the Indian Health Services, which are published in this volume at the end of William L. Freeman's essay.

15. Editorial, "Gene Donors' Rights at Risk," *Nature* 381 (May 2, 1996): 1.

16. R. Weir and J. Horton, "DNA Banking and Informed Consent," *IRB* 7 (5 and 6) (1995): 1–8. In contrast, and closer to our position, is the view held by Jon Merz and Pamela Sankar: "We believe it is essential that the DNA bank be absolutely responsible to donors, that this responsibility must be contractual in nature (by terms of the consent form), and that the DNA bank be held accountable to a duly authorized Institutional Review Board to secure approval of its procedures and oversight of its practices. . . . We have found in our studies that many persons are willing to make a donation purely for research purposes, even if they stand to gain nothing personally from the studies. We can appeal to individual's altruism to promote research, while recognizing our obligations, ethically and under the Federal Rules, to minimize the risks of participating in research including the risks resulting from breaches of confidentiality and potential misuse of information."

17. Knoppers and Laberge, "DNA Banking/Collecting," pp. 33–49.

18. A. L. Caplan and J. Merz, "Patenting Gene Sequences," *British Medical Journal* 312 (1996): 926. See also Knoppers and Laberge, "DNA Banking/Collecting"; and S. M. Thomas, A. R. W. Davies, N. J. Birtwistle, S. M. Crowther, and J. F. Burke, "Ownership of the Human Genome," *Nature* 380 (1996): 387–388, where they state: "attention and energy must be given to restricting the scope of patents so that the prospect of one company having proprietary rights over an entire gene and its mutations for all diagnostic and therapeutic purposes is no longer a reality. Public interest would be better served by policies encouraging competitiveness for improved second-generation healthcare products."

19. S. Grisolia, "'Gene Hunting' in India [letter]," *Nature* 380 (1996): 664.

20. D. Dickson, "Whose Genes Are They Anyway?" *Nature* 381 (1996): 11–14 (p. 13): "Researchers in Finland, for example, whose stable and well-documented social structure has provided a valuable resource for genetic studies, point out that the willingness of families to participate is based partly on trust in the state-run health-care system — as well as knowledge of its cost — and that this trust could be lost if the family data was to be 'sold off' to some drug company."

21. "The stakes involved in the quest for genetic information are high. Those already caught up in this new gold-rush include virtually any group considered sufficiently homogeneous to provide tissue or blood samples from which information leading to the eventual identification of disease-related gene or genes can be identified. Such groups range from isolated populations distinguished by certain medical characteristics (which could be resistance to a particular disease) to sets of families

suffering from a common illness, such as diabetes, who agree to assist researchers in the hope of developing improved treatment": editorial, "Gene Donors' Rights at Risk," p. 1.

22. D. Balasubramanian, " 'Gene Hunting' in India [letter]," *Nature* 380 (1996): 664: "I would like to add that international collaboration between medical researchers, including collaboration that requires the exchange of genetic material, is a noble, uncommercial activity."

23. Dickson, "Whose Genes Are They Anyway?" See also B. Cohen, "Population Groups Can Hold Critical Clues," *Nature* 381 (1996): 12.

Proposed Model Consent Form for DNA Sampling and Storage for Medical Research

© Bartha Maria Knoppers (LL.D.), Claude Laberge (Ph.D., M.D.);
Kathleen Cranley Glass (LL.D.); Beatrice Godard (Ph.D.)

Family Name: _____

First name: _____

Birth date: ___/___/___   Sex: F ___ M ___

_____ Project researchers have asked me to participate in a study based on the possible contribution of genetic factors to _____. After having read the information pamphlet/video, and having been informed that I can obtain counseling upon request, I am willing to participate in this study and to be registered in the Project's data bank under the following conditions:

I agree:	YES	NO
— to undergo a medical exam, if necessary. Such an exam may entail physical or diagnostic tests;	___	___
— to permit consultation of my medical record for any information related to _____;	___	___
— to provide a blood/tissue sample;	___	___
— that such sample be used as a source of DNA for the specific aims of the _____ Project;	___	___
— that my DNA be preserved in a permanent, viable state using cell cultures;	___	___
— that my DNA be used in coded form in research into _____;	___	___
— that genetic information pertaining to me be used confidentially by my family members for their personal risk assessment, should they request it (and this even after my death);	___	___

— that I agree to be contacted and receive counseling if   ___   ___
   my risk of developing _____ becomes significant because of new findings;

— that I agree to be contacted and receive counseling if   ___   ___
   other genetic disorders are discovered;

— that I be informed of the results concerning my medical exam or DNA analysis by _____ or his/her representative: ___   ___

Name: _____

Address: _____

_____

_____

_____

I agree to inform the _____ Project's researchers of any change of address and to reaffirm my continuing interest in receiving genetic counseling according to my choices indicated above.

I understand that the _____ Project's researchers are available to answer my questions or concerns.

I understand that any information identifying me will be kept confidential.

I am satisfied with the answers to my questions and with the information made available to me.

My decision to participate in this study on _____ is both voluntary and informed.

I understand that I may withdraw from the study at any time without prejudice whatsoever to myself or my family.

I hereby donate my DNA subject to the conditions indicated above.

Signature: _____ Date: ___/___/___
 (Participant or legal representative)

Name: _____ Phone number: _____

Address: _____

Signature: _____ Date: ___/___/___
 (Project's representative)

Name: _____ Phone number: _____

Address: _____

The use of this model as a communication tool, as part of the consent process, and as a basis for developing a consent form, implies the prior preparation of an information video/pamphlet in understandable language explaining the goals of the research project and the means taken to protect confidentiality and privacy. The video/pamphlet should also warn potential participants of the possibility of detecting and communicating (or not) nonpaternity, of policies concerning disposal of samples (length of storage, storage failure, withdrawal, destruction, etc.), and of any commercial interests. The participant should receive a copy of the signed form. This model is an evolving product of the original paper of B. M. Knoppers and C. Laberge, "DNA Sampling and Informed Consent," *Canadian Medical Association Journal* 140 (1989): 1023–1028.

Advance Directives for the Use
of Stored Tissue Samples

Robert F. Weir

In recent years considerable controversy has developed over the collection, storage, and use of fluids and tissues removed from individuals in clinical and research settings. With the continually expanding abilities of genetics investigators in the era of molecular biology, body fluids (e.g., blood, urine, amniotic fluid) and tissues (e.g., cheek swabs and skin biopsies) that have traditionally been collected by physicians and biomedical researchers for diagnostic and investigative purposes can now be used for the multiple purposes of genetic analysis. The result, depending on many factors, is a potentially serious threat to the personal interests and values of the persons who provided the fluid(s) and tissue(s). Given the ensuing controversy over genetics and privacy issues, a secondary result is a series of ethical and legal recommendations regarding individual choice and stored tissue samples that represents a potentially serious threat to the traditional practices of some physicians and biomedical researchers (e.g., pathologists) outside of genetics.

The debate over the appropriate use of blood and other human tissues that can be stored for long periods raises questions about previously routine *clinical* practices. For example, some persons are convinced that, given the personal and familial information hidden in a DNA sample, there may no longer be "a simple blood draw" in contemporary medicine. The debate also raises questions about some of the traditional *research* practices by pathologists and other biomedical investigators who often work with archival biological materials (e.g., paraffin-embedded tissue blocks, histological slides, frozen tissue) for which no informed consent was ever given by the individual sources of the materials other than, one assumes, a consent for surgery. In addition, the debate raises questions about currently acceptable practices that cut across any neat *clinical/investigative* distinction, such as the cryopreservation of human preembryos, the collection of neonatal blood spots, and the study of blood and other tissue samples in a cytogenetics laboratory.

Although neither widely publicized nor generally known by the public, this debate has enormous implications for biomedical investigators in many fields, for physicians who depend on diagnostic tests using stored tissue samples, and, potentially, for every person who in the future will be asked by a physician or biomedical investigator to supply blood or some other tissue sample for diagnostic or investigative purposes. My purposes in this essay are four-fold: to identify the important questions that currently characterize this debate, to describe the origin and positions in the debate, to discuss alternative solutions, and to make a proposal for using a new type of advance directive to communicate personal preferences about the storage and use of human tissues with personal and familial implications.

Questions in the Debate

In multiple settings — clinical medicine, biomedical research, and numerous combinations of diagnostic, therapeutic, educational, and investigative endeavors — serious questions are now being raised about the process of informed consent and its applicability to the collection and use of tissue samples that can be stored in a number of ways for long periods. Some of the questions are new, some are threatening to biomedical investigators in some fields, and all of them indicate that some traditional practices in biomedicine and some traditional assumptions on the part of patients and research participants are going to have to be reexamined as medicine and the biomedical sciences become increasingly geneticized.

A number of questions pertain to the role of informed consent in *prospective* scientific studies, whether those studies are primarily diagnostic or investigative in nature. For example, should patients and potential research participants be told about the possibilities of (1) long-term storage of their tissue sample(s) and (2) subsequent biomedical research on the sample(s)? What information, if any, should they be given about the *likely nature of the planned storage* of their tissue samples, including, perhaps, the cryopreservation of the tissue samples, or the biological transformation of the tissue samples into immortalized cell lines, or the computerized storage of their personal genetic information in a DNA database? Should they be informed about the ways in which the confidentiality and privacy of their personal genetic information (derived from a DNA sample) will be protected, or about the possibilities of future secondary use of the stored tissue sample for different scientific purposes than the purposes for which it was obtained? Should they be given information about the *planned identity status of their stored sample* in terms of whether it will be (1) identified as their sample, (2) linkable (by breaking an identifying code) to them as the source of the sample, (3) completely anonymous as to individual origination, or (4) anonymized after collection? If identified or linkable genetic information about them is likely to be entered into a DNA database, should individuals be given written assurances that this information will not be disclosed to governmental officials who might request it for forensic purposes? And what information, if any, should they be given by physicians or biomedical investigators about planned scientific uses of the tissue sample(s) so that they can *communicate personal choices* about the control and ownership of the biological materials, future personal access to the information derived from the banked materials, the access of third parties (including employers and health insurance companies) to the same information, the remote possibility that a particular DNA sample might become commercially valuable, and the possibility that they might subsequently want to withdraw their tissue sample (and/or derivative DNA data) from scientific storage?[1]

The questions related to *retrospective* studies on stored tissue samples are different, but equally important. Should archival tissue samples (e.g., paraffin blocks in pathology departments, neonatal blood spots in newborn screening laboratories) have a planned, limited lifespan in terms of a specified number of years for storage, or should they be retained essentially forever? As an alternative, should all stored tissue samples (whether banked for biopsy tests, autopsy studies, epidemiological studies, or genetic studies) be destroyed after the planned testing has been done? For that matter, how broadly or narrowly should "genetic studies" be defined in order to establish guidelines for the appropriate use of various molecular research methods with stored tissue samples?[2] In terms of the *identity status* of the stored samples, should all such tissue samples be anonymized as a condition for long-term storage, or should some or all of the samples be retained as identified or, more likely, linkable samples in the event that potentially relevant clinical information is discovered and could be disclosed by appropriate clinicians to the individual sources of the samples? If some identified or linkable samples are stored, should the persons from whom those samples came be contacted again (assuming they are still alive) for consent in the event that new diagnostic tests become possible, the tests are promising in terms of possible benefit, and the tests are wanted by physicians or scientific investigators? In the same kind of situation, should individuals (the sources of the samples) be contacted again for consent in the event that promising new research possibilities come into being that did not exist when the samples were originally collected and stored? If the residual stored samples are *anonymous*, does that status mean that investigators who have the samples can use them in whatever ways they regard as appropriate (e.g., as positive or negative controls, as biopsy specimens, as materials for virtually any kind of biomedical research) without ongoing review? Does the status of anonymity mean that such samples, including cell lines, can be accessible to virtually any biomedical investigator (in any university, any commercial firm, any country) who gets them in collaboration with other scientists and that the samples can then be used for any scientific purpose, without regard to whether it might have been offensive or harmful in some other way to the (now unknown) individual from whom they came?

Origins of the Debate

The debate over the appropriate use of stored tissue samples has been simmering for a number of years. National publicity at various times has focused on parental disputes over cryopreserved preembryos in assisted reproduction programs, the use of stored neonatal blood spots for anonymous epidemiological studies of HIV prevalency, and the federal government's requirement that military personnel provide blood samples and cheek swabs for military identification purposes to the Department of Defense's DNA databank.

However, for biomedical scientists and for members of institutional review boards (IRBs), the important implications of the debate over stored tissue samples were first seen most clearly in an otherwise noncontroversial series of studies carried out by the Centers for Disease Control and Prevention (CDC). Since 1966 more than 70,000 persons have participated in the National Health and Nutrition Examination Surveys (NHANES). The third National Health and Nutrition Examination Survey (NHANES III) is different from the previous two surveys in that it is the only national survey in which physician examinations are performed to measure an individual's health. Beginning in the 1980s, NHANES III had multiple purposes: to provide a natural history of diseases in the population, to give an accurate description of the distribution of diseases in the country, to monitor changes in the health of the population, to study the etiology of diseases, and to establish empirical data for recommended changes in health policy (e.g., unleaded gas).

The NHANES III methodology consisted of identifying 40,000 sample persons in 26 states; selecting high sample rates for certain groups (e.g., children, older adults, racial minority groups); interviewing 30,000 of the persons regarding nutrition, reproductive health, physical activity, mental health, and health habits; giving them an extensive physical examination with multiple lab tests of blood and urine; doing a home study examination regarding socioeconomic status, demographic information, and environmental influences; and promising a long-term follow-up (the NHANES consent document stated: "After several years, we will check back with you to note any changes in your health").[3] All of the medical and health data were linked to other personal information to facilitate the multiple purposes of the study and to make long-term follow-up more valuable. By the mid-1990s the CDC scientists had also produced an archive of approximately 19,500 tissue samples stored in liquid nitrogen and immortalized cell lines from approximately 8,500 persons.

To meet the ethical and legal requirements for informed consent, the NHANES III administrators, working with the IRB at the CDC, initially prepared a very detailed and technical statement on consent to be given to prospective participants in the study. That document was later judged to be too technically difficult, and it was replaced by a simple six-page booklet with descriptive text and pictures about NHANES III. The only language in the booklet that pertains to informed consent for banked samples is a one-sentence descriptive statement: "A small sample of your blood will be kept in long-term storage for future testing."[4]

In early 1994 some officials at the CDC faced a major problem. On the one hand, they possessed an invaluable "national treasure chest" of health information on a cross-section of the U.S. population and an unmatched archive of nationally representative DNA samples for biomedical research. On the other hand, they wondered (in the light of recent professional literature on molecular genetics and ethics) if the CDC scientists had adequately informed the sample population regarding the planned storage and scientific uses of their blood samples, if persons in the study population had understood themselves to be consenting to long-term research on their banked blood samples, and if the CDC would need to get additional, more specific consent (at an estimated cost of $2 million) from these persons before carrying out the planned research with the stored samples.

Because of this concern at the CDC, a meeting was held at the National Institutes of Health (NIH) in July 1994 to address questions related to "Informed Consent for Genetic Studies Using Stored Tissue Samples." The meeting was jointly planned by representatives from the CDC and the National Center for Human Genome Research (NCHGR; renamed the National Human Genome Research Institute or NHGRI in 1997) at the NIH. Several persons invited to participate in the meeting had previously received funding from the ELSI (ethical, legal, and social implications of genetics) Branch of the NCHGR. The planned purpose of the meeting was to produce a consensus statement regarding informed consent and the use of stored tissue samples in genetics, whether at the CDC or elsewhere. An initial version of the statement was drafted by a small group under the leadership of Ellen Wright Clayton, M.D., J.D., who chaired the meeting. However, the desired "consensus" proved difficult to accomplish, with the group expressing important differences over traditional research uses of stored tissue samples, the meaning and necessity of informed consent in the context of archival samples, the ownership and control of stored samples, the impracticability of recontacting persons for consent to anonymize stored samples, and the limits to be placed on the use of anonymized samples. As it turned out, this group discussion at the CDC/NIH meeting foreshadowed much more specific positions in the debate that appeared the following year.

Positions in the Debate

In early 1995 George Annas, J.D., along with Leonard Glantz, J.D., and Patricia Roche, J.D., began distributing a model piece of legislation that had been drafted with ELSI funding through the Department of Energy. Called the Genetic Privacy Act (GPA), the model act is intended as a proposal for federal legislation, although it could be and has been proposed as well for state legislation.[5] The GPA is based on four premises: genetic information is different from other types of personal information; the genetic information contained in DNA is like a "coded probabilistic future diary"; this information can be accessible to many parties in the era of molecular biology; and, because of the highly personal nature of the information and its accessibility, individually identifiable DNA samples need to be protected by law. Consequently, the overarching premise of the GPA "is that no stranger should have or control *identifiable* DNA samples or genetic information about an individual unless that individual specifically authorizes the collection of DNA samples for the purpose of genetic analysis, authorizes the creation of that private information, and has access to and control over the dissemination of that information" (emphasis added).[6]

The proposed GPA addresses several of the concerns mentioned earlier, with most of the proposed legislation depending on the identity status of stored DNA samples. The central claim in the GPA is that individually identifiable DNA samples are the property of the person from whom they come (identified as the "sample source"). Therefore, if tissue samples will be individually identifiable, the act states that the sample source must grant advance authorization in writing for the collection, storage, and proposed use(s) of the samples, as well as for the possible disclosure of private genetic information gained from genetic analysis. In addition, the sample source (or that person's representative in the event of incompetency or death) has a number of rights: to revoke consent to genetic analysis at "any time prior to the completion of the analysis," to inspect records that contain information derived from a genetic analysis, to prohibit the use of the DNA sample for research or commercial purposes "even if the sample is not in an individually identifiable form," to consent (with forty-five days' advance notice) to the transfer of a DNA sample to other scientists for secondary research purposes, and to order the destruction of the DNA sample upon the research study's completion or the withdrawal of the sample source from the study.

By contrast, the GPA would permit *anonymous* tissue samples to be used for research purposes if such use was not previously prohibited by the sample source. The authors emphasize: "Nothing in this Act shall be construed as prohibiting or limiting research on a DNA sample that cannot be linked to any individual identifier."[7] Moreover, research by pathologists, geneticists, and other medical investigators can be done on *archival* tissue samples, even if the stored samples are individually identifiable, as long as the samples were stored "prior to the effective date of this Act." However, no individually identifiable genetic information may be disclosed without the authorization of the sample source's representative.

In late 1995 two published papers staked out additional positions in the developing debate. The first paper was a position statement of the American College of Medical Genetics (ACMG), written by John Phillips, M.D., and other members of the ACMG Storage of Genetics Materials Committee.[8] Emphasizing the importance of informed consent, the authors make several recommendations regarding the storage and use of genetic materials that are obtained for *clinical* tests. They recommend that patients be informed about the purpose and possible outcomes of the genetic test, the anticipated use of the blood or other tissue samples (including whether the sample will be stored for additional scientific purposes), and their options regarding future access to the genetic information and the possibility of subsequently requesting that the samples be destroyed. They also recommend that if samples are going to be stored patients should be asked for permission to use the samples and the derivative genetic information in counseling and testing their relatives and for permission to anonymize the samples for the purposes of additional scientific research.

In terms of tissue samples that are obtained for *investigational* purposes, the ACMG committee recommends that potential participants in research be informed about the purpose and possible outcomes of the current research study, the investigator(s)' policy regarding the length of storage time for samples and subsequent destruction of samples, and the possibility that the research may lead to the development of diagnostic tests having several related issues (e.g., the possible need to disclose personal genetic information in a family setting and the remote chance that diagnostic tests will be commercially profitable). It also recommends that research participants be asked for permission to anonymize their tissue samples for other types of research and to recontact them for additional consent for (currently unknown) future research efforts with their stored samples. As to research on archival samples, the committee simply points out the inherent conflict between the desirability (in terms of ethics and law) of recontacting individuals to secure their informed consent for ongoing research studies and the impracticability (in many research settings) of recontacting persons from whom samples were previously collected, but makes no specific recommendations regarding how this conflict can or should be resolved.

The second paper, the report coming out of the CDC/NIH meeting, was controversial before and after its publication. Written by Ellen Wright Clayton and several other persons with diverse professional backgrounds, "Informed Consent for Genetic Research on Stored Tissue Samples" was supported by most of the individuals who attended the 1994 meeting, including me.[9] However, portions of the paper were unacceptable to some geneticists at the meeting who work with archival tissue samples, and they refused to be signatories of the document.

The Clayton et al. document emphasizes the importance of conducting research with stored tissue samples within the ethical and legal framework provided by federal regulations for the protection of human subjects and by local review by IRBs. The document addresses a range of situations and questions pertaining to genetic research on stored tissue samples: (1) whether anonymous samples for research are exempt from federal regulations regarding informed consent, (2) whether removing identifiers from existing samples can be done without the consent of the individual "source" of the sample, (3) whether limits (related to the preferences of sources or the psychosocial risks of the research) need to be placed on the use of linkable or identified samples for research, (4) whether genetic research can be done on samples (in pathology or elsewhere) obtained from persons who subsequently died, (5) whether tissue samples from children can be used in genetic research, and (6) whether public health investigations involving genetic studies can be done without the consent of the tissue sources.

The consensus document makes several specific recommendations. In terms of tissue samples that have *already been collected*, the document emphasizes the distinction between anonymous samples and samples that are identifiable or linkable at the time a research project is proposed. Samples that are *already anonymous* (e.g., anonymous pathological samples that might be used for a genetics study) do not require informed consent for the obvious reason that it is impossible to identify the individual source directly or indirectly. Even genetic studies with anonymous samples, however, should be reviewed by IRBs, at least in part to determine if the desired scientific information could be obtained in a protocol that allows individuals to consent. By contrast, stored samples that are *currently identified or linkable* to the individual source (e.g., samples originally obtained for diagnostic purposes, numerous kinds of pathological samples) require informed consent by that person if investigators plan to do genetic studies on the samples without anonymizing them.

What about the fairly common practice whereby investigators take existing identified or linkable samples and make them anonymous for use in research by removing all identifiers or linking codes? Current federal regulations permit this practice of anonymizing samples without the consent of the individual source. For the writers of this document, this practice is problematic, sometimes disingenuous, and occasionally deceptive when, for example, clinician investigators obtain a tissue sample for diagnostic purposes, know that they plan later to anonymize the sample for research purposes, do not convey that information to the source of the sample, and subsequently remove the identifiers without consent. Consequently, the writers recommend that this practice be curtailed by changing the federal regulations and by having IRBs weigh the benefits of any such proposed research with to-be-anonymized tissues against the difficulty of requiring the investigators to recontact the individual sources for their consent for such anonymization.

In terms of *collecting samples in the future*, the document is quite clear: "People should have the opportunity to decide whether their samples will be used for research." [10] In clinical and in research settings, information about possible research studies with tissue samples should be provided to individuals when their tissue samples are collected. Whenever individuals agree to such research use of their tissues, the writers of this document recommend that they be given the following options: (1) whether they are willing to have their samples used in identifiable or linked research (with appropriate information about confidentiality, psychosocial risks, and possible withdrawal from the study) and (2) whether they prefer or are willing to have their samples stripped of identifiers and linking codes for use in research (again, with appropriate information about the investigators' personal interests, possible commercial benefit, and so on). Additional recommendations involve giving research participants other choices about the research use of their tissue samples: whether they are willing to have their tissues shared with other scientists for secondary research purposes, whether they want to limit their tissue samples to certain kinds of research studies, and whether they want to restrict their tissue samples from being used in scientific studies they do not want to support.

Critical responses to the Clayton et al. consensus statement began even before the paper was published. Wayne Grody, M.D., Ph.D., wrote a sharply critical editorial in *Diagnostic Molecular Pathology* about the consensus statement when the paper was still in final draft form, arguing that the traditional practices ("as long as anyone can remember") of pathology were threatened by an undue ELSI emphasis on informed consent.[11] Stating incorrectly that the paper had been written by members of the ELSI Working Group, a group "too heavily weighted toward the ethicists and lawyers at the expense of the views of working geneticists," he said that the recommendations of the consensus document "would severely restrict access to archival clinical specimens for molecular genetic research and other purposes."[12] The recommended choices to be given patients about the uses of their tissue samples would require "a multitiered consent form with more options and permutations than an airline frequent-flyer program." Moreover, the same lengthy consent form would have to be administered to patients in all sorts of settings: "every phlebotomy, urinalysis, sputum collection, and even haircut." If actually put into practice, "these restrictive and burdensome policies . . . would seriously impede, or completely block, a major proportion of molecular research on human disease, especially impacting those research questions that can be addressed in no other way" than through retrospective study of large numbers of archival specimens.[13]

Soon thereafter, a "Rapid Action Task Force" (RATF) of the American Society of Human Genetics (ASHG) circulated a draft proposal regarding "Informed Consent for Genetic Research."[14] Chaired by Edward McCabe, M.D., and comprised of ten members (including John Phillips and Wayne Grody), the RATF in its draft criticizes the Clayton et al. document by affirming the "traditional research practices in human genetics" and calling for the development of consent forms that are "as clear and brief as possible." Accepting virtually all of the consensus statement's recommendations regarding *prospective* genetic research, the RATF's important differences with the earlier document pertain to *archival samples*, such as those contained in pathological laboratories and newborn screening laboratories.

The RAFT draft was subsequently revised by the Board of Directors of the ASHG and published as a policy statement in the *American Journal of Human Genetics*. The published version differs significantly from the Clayton et al. document and the RAFT draft, most notably by stating, in specific contrast to the RAFT draft, that *informed consent is not necessary* in *prospective* genetic studies using (1) *anonymous* samples ("biological materials [that] were originally collected without identifiers and are impossible to link to their sources") or (2) *anonymized* samples ("biological materials that were initially identified, but have been irreversibly stripped of all identifiers and are impossible to link to their sources [but may be linkable] with clinical, pathological and demographic information [gained] before the subject identifiers are removed").[15] The ASHG policy statement also affirms the practice of anonymizing samples without consent in *retrospective* studies, because the practice has two important benefits for investigators: it reduces the "chance of introducing bias" in a study by means of an incomplete study sample (some persons may refuse to consent, and others may be impossible to contact for additional consent), and "importantly, making samples anonymous will eliminate the need for [investigators to] recontact [sources] to obtain informed consent." [16]

In January 1996 additional concerns were expressed by some geneticists and pathologists attending a meeting convened by the NCHGR on "Genetics Research on Human Tissues: Conflicting Implications for Scientific Discovery, Informed Consent, and Privacy." As Richard Lynch, M.D., observed at the meeting, the role of pathologists as legal custodians of stored diagnostic tissue samples largely involves noncontroversial investigations of anonymous, anonymized, and identifiable tissue samples, with biomedical benefits arising from each kind of research. He commented: "99 percent of what pathologists do with stored tissues is just aimed at better characterizing a lesion that already exists and has been excised by the surgeon." [17] But as pointed out by privacy advocates at the meeting, problems arise when the tissue samples are subjected to genetic tests that may reveal personal genetic information that was neither known nor anticipated by the patient, the surgeon, or the pathologist and that may now involve substantial psychosocial risks for the source of the tissue sample and relatives of that person.

Later that year the College of American Pathologists (CAP) drafted a position paper entitled "Uses of Human Tissue" that was approved by fifteen pathology societies. The document states that general consent for research (not "separate patient consent for each research study") is sufficient to protect the rights of patients. Written as a general response to the papers on genetics research and informed consent by the ACMG, the CDC/NCHGR, and the ASHG, the unpublished paper says that such "general consent [will have to] be obtained for research and educational uses of tissues collected after January 1, 1998." [18]

Alternative Solutions

What should be done to address the competing interests and values at stake with stored tissue samples? What possible solutions are available that can help us manage the complexities and conflicts over stored tissue samples in the era of molecular genetics?

As indicated by the chronological developments and positions just described, six possible solutions have been suggested and/or tried. One possible solution is to *retain as many traditional research practices as possible*, especially regarding retrospective research on archival samples. As illustrated by Wayne Grody's editorial, the CAP policy statement, and the ASHG policy statement, there are some pathologists and geneticists who want to downplay the importance of informed consent with stored tissue samples and thereby to continue traditional research practices, especially the practice of anonymizing samples without consent in pathology laboratories, newborn screening laboratories, and other locations for archived specimens. The ASHG policy statement, while emphasizing the importance of informed consent in prospective studies using *identifiable* or *identified* samples, clearly favors placing greater weight on traditional research practices than on considerations of informed consent when the stored samples in question have been and could continue to be anonymized without the consent of the sample sources or their relatives or surrogates. No mention is made of possible ways of anonymizing samples in an expanded context of informed consent, either (1) by recontacting the still-identifiable adult sources before anonymizing the samples (as had been discussed in the CDC/NIH meeting and Clayton et al. paper) or (2) by initiating a request to an adult sample source (or the parent[s] of a neonatal sample source) for consent to anonymize samples for research purposes before the samples gain the status of "existing" or archival samples.

A second possible solution is to *recommend new professional society guidelines* that can update and change professional practices in the light of new technological developments and new ethical and legal concerns about stored samples. The strongest feature of this possible solution is the importance placed on self-governance and change from within professional ranks, with the hope that choosing to adopt peer-influenced change will preclude imposed change from forces outside the profession (e.g., by law, federal regulations, or patient-advocacy groups).

Thus the Storage of Genetics Materials Committee produced a position statement for the ACMG that briefly interpreted the concept of informed consent in the context of stored tissue samples, and then gave a series of recommendations regarding the collection of tissue samples for prospective genetic tests in clinical and research settings, and the currently acceptable uses of stored DNA or genetic materials. Somewhat similarly, the RATF made a proposal to the American Society of Human Genetics regarding the application of informed-consent considerations to prospective and retrospective studies that could have been helpful in modest ways in changing the practices of genetics investigators. However, the ACMG document failed to make several needed recommendations pertaining to DNA banking and informed consent, and the RATF document, already primarily protective of the research interests of some of its authors, became even more protective of the research interests of investigators who use anonymized samples without consent in the revised form published by the ASHG.

A third possible solution is to *try to arrive at consensus about acceptable research practices through special meetings of interested parties* who have conflicting interests and concerns about stored DNA samples. This is the solution that has been favored by the NCHGR at the NIH, as illustrated by the multidisciplinary meetings it planned and hosted in July 1994 and January 1996. In the first of these meetings, representatives from the CDC and NCHGR met with invited genetics investigators, ethicists, attorneys, and patient advocates in the hope of reaching agreement on whether the CDC could proceed to do research on its 19,500 tissue samples or whether investigators at the CDC and elsewhere needed to gain more specific consent of individual sources before carrying out research on identifiable and/or anonymized tissue samples. In the 1996 meeting several leading pathologists were invited to meet with NCHGR representatives, ELSI representatives, advocates for physicians and biomedical investigators, and patient advocates in order to enable the pathologists to express professional concerns over the issue of informed consent and stored tissues. Neither meeting resulted in unanimous agreement of the participants, but both meetings were educationally and politically beneficial. Both meetings also ended with a renewed sense that compromise was possible on at least some of the issues in question, with several participants voicing hope for soon achieving a reasonable balance (e.g., in improved consent forms) between the rights of individual patients and research participants and the practices and interests of biomedical professionals. How much compromise is actually achieved remains to be seen, given the vested interests and high stakes involved in the debate.

A fourth possible solution is to *recommend changes in the federal regulations and IRB review practices* pertaining to genetic studies using human participants and stored tissue samples. The clearest example of this approach is the Clayton et al. paper published in *JAMA*. This document states that the authors place considerable weight on the federal regulations regarding the protection of human subjects (and related publications by the federal Office for Protection from Research Risks) because the regulations "are legally enforceable and because they are the embodiment of an attempt to strike a balance between the desire to increase knowledge and the protection of individual interests." [19] The document therefore quotes the federal regulations in numerous places and sometimes goes to considerable lengths to show how the regulations can and should apply to some important research issues that have developed since the regulations were written—namely, the emerging questions about the collection and use of stored tissue samples.

Nevertheless, this proposed solution depends on professionals in multiple fields not merely being able to know, interpret, and apply the federal regulations to state-of-the-art concerns about the collection and use of stored DNA samples, but more importantly being able to bring about changes in the regulations (and their use by IRBs) so that they will continue to balance the competing interests of scientific investigators and individuals (and families) who participate in research studies. Therefore the Clayton et al. paper indicates several ways in which the regulations need to be updated, clarified, and changed to provide needed guidance for investigators and the IRB members who review their research proposals: the appropriate limits to be placed on genetics studies with anonymous samples, IRB review of studies using anonymous samples, the practice of anonymizing existing samples, the limits of impracticability in securing consent, and the degree of deference to be given to individuals' preferences not to have their tissue samples used for specific types of genetic research. The essay by William L. Freeman in this volume is another example of this approach, with his emphasis being placed on changing IRB review practices concerning informed consent to protect the preferences, beliefs, and values of minority communities participating in research studies.

A fifth possible solution is to *produce updated consent forms* in clinical and research settings that more accurately describe current research practices with stored samples and more adequately enable individuals to make informed choices about how their DNA samples (and personal genetic information contained therein) are to be used. The ACMG committee, the Clayton et al. group, and the RATF group all seem to assume that most of the conflicts over stored samples can be addressed by means of (1) more appropriately worded consent documents and (2) improved IRB review of research protocols using identified, linkable, anonymous, or anonymized tissue samples. The catch, of course, is whether updated consent forms will be more protective of the rights of individual sources to make informed-consent choices about their banked tissues or of the professional interests of biomedical investigators, who frequently write the documents. The challenge will be to see if multidisciplinary interests can be reflected in updated consent documents that contain workable compromises, such as providing modest amounts of information to patients about pathological research practices in surgical consent forms before any biological samples are collected as part of the surgery.[20] Two examples of updated consent documents appear in the Merz/Sankar and Knoppers essays in this volume.

The sixth possible solution is to *mandate by law* the changes in the era of genetic medicine that are necessary to protect individuals from unauthorized analysis of their DNA samples, unauthorized disclosure of personal genetic information resulting from genetic studies, and unauthorized transfer of their stored biological materials to other investigators. The clearest and most comprehensive attempt to work on this solution is the proposed GPA written by Annas, Glantz, and Roche. According to this model piece of legislation, an individual "sample source" has property rights to his or her DNA samples and therefore can determine who may collect and analyze a blood or other tissue sample, limit the purposes for which a DNA sample can be analyzed, know what information can reasonably be expected from the genetic tests, order the destruction of stored DNA samples, delegate authority to a surrogate to order the destruction of stored DNA samples, prohibit even the anonymous use of the samples in research, refuse to permit the use of the DNA sample(s) for research or commercial activities, and inspect (and obtain) copies of records containing information derived from genetic analysis of the DNA sample(s).[21]

This proposed solution is, of course, quite different from the other strategies. Rather than relying on peer-influenced change, consensus-driven change, or updated changes in regulations and consent forms, this approach would force change through the power of law and the threat of legal penalties. Thus the proposed GPA has a section on civil remedies according to which a person (e.g., a clinician, a biomedical investigator, a professional in a biomedical lab) who violates the provisions of the GPA through negligence would be liable for a $25,000 fine plus other monetary damages, and a person who willfully violates the GPA would be liable for a $50,000 fine plus other monetary damages.

As with the other proposed solutions, it remains to be seen whether this proposal will actually work. At the present time, the GPA remains a controversial proposal for a model law that has been frequently discussed and often praised, but also frequently rejected as unnecessary and counterproductive for biomedical progress.[22-24]

A New Type of Advance Directive

I propose an alternative solution that can supplement several of the alternatives just described. In addition to trying to change practice patterns in biomedical groups regarding stored tissue samples, update regulations and consent documents to accommodate the interests of individual sample sources and the professionals who work with their DNA samples, and/or protect personal genetic information through legislation, I propose that we develop and use a new kind of *advance-consent directive* that will focus on blood and other tissue samples that can be stored for future research purposes. This kind of advance directive, in contrast to other advance directives in health care, will enable individuals to give advance or prospective consent (or refusal) regarding acceptable research uses of their to-be-stored tissue sample(s) to physicians, biomedical researchers, and other professionals in hospitals, clinics, and research labs. In addition, this kind of advance directive will enable the potential sources of tissue samples to communicate their personal preferences and choices regarding possible use(s) of their stored tissue samples for any future situations in which they would not be able to give or withhold consent. Three such future situations are possible: these persons could become impossible to contact for additional consent by current biomedical investigators, they could become mentally disabled and unable to exercise choice about their stored samples, or they could die.

The first generation of advance directives in health care began with the development of the "living will" in the early 1930s by a Chicago attorney concerned about the barbaric medical treatment administered against the protests of a dying friend. Later, in the 1960s, an organization called the Euthanasia Educational Council revised the document and began distributing it. By the mid-1980s more than 7 million copies of the document had been distributed, and similar kinds of nonstatutory documents had been developed by the Catholic Health Association, the American Protestant Hospital Association, and other organizations interested in providing individuals with written forms that could be used to communicate personal choices and provide guidance to physicians and relatives regarding the medical treatments they wanted or, more commonly, did not want should they become critically or terminally ill.[25] In the 1990s there are numerous versions of *nonstatutory* (not backed by state law) advance directives that enable individuals to communicate personal choice about life-sustaining medical treatments years in advance by signing published forms distributed by Choice in Dying and other organizations, checking off options on "The Medical Directive" form, or drafting their own personalized documents.[26]

A second generation of advance directives for health care began in 1976 when the California Assembly passed into law the nation's first *statutory* advance directive. The advance directive connected with the California Natural Death Act subsequently became a model for "living will" legislation in other states that enabled adults to exercise their moral and legal right to refuse medical treatment. By the late-1980s several states had also enacted a second kind of statutory advance directive aimed at enabling adults not so much to make choices about life-sustaining medical treatments as to make choices about trusted surrogate decisionmakers who could be designated in writing to make decisions about life-sustaining treatments on their behalf. These documents give designated surrogates "durable" powers of attorney to make health-care decisions for the signers of the documents at a future time if they no longer have the capacity to make such decisions themselves.

All adult citizens in the United States now have access to one or both of these statutory advance directive options pertaining to medical treatments, with the directives usually dealing with possible medical treatments toward the end of life. The residents of the District of Columbia and forty-seven states (exceptions are Massachusetts, Michigan, and New York) have the option of using treatment-oriented directives backed by "living will" laws. The residents of D.C. and forty-eight states (exceptions are Alabama and Alaska) have the option of designating surrogates to make such decisions on their behalf and empowering these surrogates by means of state durable-power-of-attorney legislation. Since the passage of the federal Patient Self-Determination Act in 1991, all hospitals, nursing homes, and other health-care institutions have had a mandate to provide patients with information about advance directives and to see if individual patients have advance directives that they wish to be used, should the need arise, in decisions about their medical treatment while in the institution.[27]

Similar advance directives can and should be developed to enable individuals to communicate their personal choices regarding the use(s) of their stored tissue samples and the personal genetic information contained in those samples. Earlier proposals for advance-consent directives have included an "advance directive for experimental intervention," a "research living will," and a "generic consent form for genetic screening," but none of these proposals addressed the issue of stored tissue samples.[28–31]

As has been the case with "regular" advance directives aimed at possible end-of-life decisions, advance-consent directives for stored tissue samples can function as important written statements according to which individuals exercise prospective autonomy. Like other advance directives, these new advance directives can be instruments (probably written, but possibly electronic or video) that enable individuals to communicate portions of their value systems to relatives, personal physicians, and future strangers in biomedical settings (e.g., physicians and biomedical investigators in any number of clinical and laboratory locations, here and abroad). As has been the case with advance directives focused on the range of hypothetical and largely unknown future circumstances of critical or terminal illness, these new advance directives can be targeted toward current and projected future circumstances involving the banking of blood and other tissue samples in a range of largely unknown settings: clinical, investigational, commercial, and governmental.

Advance directives for stored tissue samples will share some of the limitations and benefits of end-of-life advance directives. These older directives, the advance directives spawned by the right-to-die movement, are the subject of substantial and repeated criticism. In abbreviated form, the criticisms are as follows:

1. advance directives, especially treatment directives or "living wills," are often written in such vague language that they are basically useless in clinical settings;
2. by contrast, some advance directives are so detailed that they prevent physicians from having sufficient discretionary flexibility to provide appropriate medical care;
3. treatment directives, especially those developed and signed years in advance, do not anticipate changes that are likely to occur over the intervening years;
4. treatment-oriented advance directives can be used to request or demand extreme measures without providing an attending physician with the rationale behind the stipulated choices;
5. advance directives that focus only on treatment preferences, with no selection of a surrogate, can be problematic because they tend to place the patient's family "outside the loop"; and
6. surrogate-oriented advance directives can be signed without sufficient information being given to the surrogate to enable him or her later to make informed choices on the behalf of the now-nonautonomous patient.

Nevertheless, we live in an age of advance directives in health care, at least in a formal and legal sense. Federal law, statutes in all fifty states and D.C., numerous academic publications, hospital policies, countless stories in the media — all suggest that the use of advance directives can be beneficial in bringing about medical-treatment decisions at the end of an individual's life that were earlier judged to be appropriate by that person (and, perhaps, a designated surrogate). Therefore, in the signing or drafting of an advance directive aimed at treatment decisions, an individual is trying to do a simple yet profound thing: put into effect *an instrument of moral persuasion* that will, if need be, convince relatives, physicians (who may be strangers in white coats), and possibly friends in a future situation of critical or terminal illness to make decisions about medical interventions that are consistent with the expressed preferences and desires of that individual.[32]

How and why does this sometimes happen? Given the limitations of advance directives, what is it about advance directives aimed at end-of-life decisions that sometimes gives them the power of moral persuasion, even if they may not be backed by state law? To be more specific, what are the beneficial features of end-of-life advance directives that convince numerous persons to sign or draft them and, at least in some cases, convince physicians to abide by their expressed wishes? Again in abbreviated form, the benefits are as follows:

1. advance directives, depending on their formulation, can provide significant information about an individual's value system that aids in the decisionmaking process about medical treatments;
2. advance directives can be helpful in communicating the autonomous choices made by patients regarding specific kinds of medical-treatment options toward the end of life;
3. advance directives can alleviate psychological and moral problems that patients may have, such as fears about overtreatment, anxiety about "ending up like Nancy Cruzan," and concerns about protracted hospitalization that could cause financial ruin for patients' families;
4. advance directives, even if not backed by state law, can bring about important conversations between physicians and patients that would otherwise not take place; and
5. advance directives can, when followed in clinical settings, actually make a difference in individual cases regarding the treatment decisions made toward the end of a patient's life (however, the results of the Study to Understand Prognoses and Preferences for Outcomes and Risks of Treatments [SUPPORT] do not encourage optimism on this point).[33]

In a similar fashion, advance-consent directives for the use of stored tissue samples will have some limitations and at least the promise of important benefits to the individuals who formulate and/or sign them, and some of the benefits may accrue to their relatives as well. First, the limitations. These research-oriented advance directives will be subject to the following criticisms:

1. these advance directives will *impede the progress of biomedical research* because, when used in clinical or investigational settings, they will place unprecedented limits on the kinds of scientific studies that can be done

with stored samples (including stored samples originally obtained for diagnostic purposes);

2. these advance directives are *not necessary* because supplying *identified* or *linkable* tissue samples is a common, *voluntary* practice by patients in multiple clinical settings and by research participants in scientific studies;

3. such directives are also not necessary because the use of *anonymous* or *anonymized* tissue samples poses no risk of harm to the sources of the samples or their relatives;

4. such directives may contain such *vague wording* that they will be subject to diverse interpretations and prove to be basically useless; and

5. such directives would *not apply to pediatric situations* in which tissue samples are collected and stored because the sources of the samples (e.g., neonates, young children) could not possibly understand the meaning of the documents.

This is not the place to develop responses to each of these criticisms, but it can be done. Rather, I suggest that advance directives for stored tissue samples will also have a number of benefits to the persons who sign or formulate such documents. Simply put, the likely benefits will include the following:

1. use of these advance directives will *alleviate some of the psychological and moral problems* that some persons have about genetic research and the personal genetic "secrets" that might be discovered about them without their consent;

2. use of these advance directives will, depending on the wording of the documents, *increase the sense of control* that an individual source of a tissue sample can have about the kinds of *prospective* scientific studies that will be done with the sample, the scientific purposes for which the sample will be used, and the possible commercial gain that might (in rare circumstances) accompany scientific research using the sample;

3. these advance directives will enable thoughtful individuals to *make autonomous choices* about the collection of their DNA samples, the scientific analysis of those samples, the storage of those samples, and the distribution of those DNA samples and derivative personal genetic information to other parties;

4. these advance directives will enable individuals to *determine the limits they want to place on their participation in genetic and molecular studies*, such as participating (by means of their tissue samples) as identifiable persons, or through anonymized samples in one scientific study only, or through anonymized samples in numerous secondary

studies, or with personally important restrictions regarding the kinds of genetic studies being done;

5. these advance directives will *supplement context-specific consent documents*, thereby providing a *generic and global consent form* that could apply to entire health-care institutions (as current end-of-life advance directives do) and transcend institutional and national boundaries (as regularly happens with the transfer of immortalized cell lines to genetics investigators in other places);

6. the use of these advance directives will enable individuals, with some legal and practical constraints, to *protect themselves and their relatives* (and, to some extent, larger groups with which they identify) from some of the psychosocial risks connected with genetics research, including the kind of psychological harm that can come to individuals when they suspect or find out that their tissue samples are being used without consent for scientific purposes they do not support;

7. these advance directives will be, perhaps, *morally persuasive instruments* with which individuals can communicate to physicians and biomedical investigators their sense of self-determination and personal well-being as these values extend to tissue samples no longer in their possession;

8. these advance directives will enable individuals to make prospective decisions that can be acted on by scientific investigators and thereby *avoid other impracticable alternatives,* such as trying to contact a previous sample source for consent to anonymize currently identifiable samples, or for consent to use the samples for previously unanticipated scientific purposes, or for research that might possibly have commercial implications;

9. these advance directives will provide some adults in their roles as potential parents (during pregnancy) and parents with a document that may *bring about conversations with physicians* in which the parents can communicate their permission, preferences, and reservations regarding proposed storage of *tissue samples from their children* (e.g., cord blood, neonatal blood spots); and

10. these advance directives will, as have treatment-oriented advance directives, *provide written documentation for a court* (in the unlikely event of a legal dispute between the surrogate of a no-longer-autonomous individual and physicians or biomedical investigators) of an individual's previous thinking and communicated preferences regarding tissue samples obtained from his or her body.

Three Types of Advance Directives
for Stored Tissue Samples

In conclusion, I present three advance-consent directives that might be used to give or withhold consent in various clinical and research settings. Each of the documents, if used in the real world of biomedical research, increases the chances that the signer(s) will actually be able to make informed choices about their participation in research studies using stored tissue samples and exercise at least some control over how their stored tissue samples will be used in those studies. At the same time, the documents also present some real problems related to data management in multiple hospitals and research laboratories, the transfer of stored tissue samples from one clinical or research setting to other locations (down the hall or across the world), and the difficulty in terms of logistics and informatics of retaining and/or linking such personal choices with the stored tissue samples to which they apply.

A COMPREHENSIVE ADVANCE-CONSENT DIRECTIVE

Just as there are several versions of a comprehensive advance directive for possible end-of-life decisions, including advance directives written by individuals, so there could be several versions of an advance directive for stored tissue samples. One example of such a document appears at the end of this essay.

The benefits of drafting or signing such a document would be several. This comprehensive form could communicate a series of personal choices regarding the use(s) of stored tissue samples identified with or linkable to the signer of the document. It would be most easily used to communicate one's personal preferences to an individual physician or scientific investigator. The document might also be applicable to multiple clinical and research settings within an institution (and beyond an institution) if the data management problems can be handled (e.g., by using bar codes) that relate to the retention of individual choices by the source of a stored sample that has been anonymized, especially when tissue samples are sometimes stored in and often transferred among different clinical and research locations. Moreover, the form could name one or more surrogate decisionmakers in the event the signer cannot be contacted, becomes cognitively impaired, or dies. Although not a statutory document, the form might carry some legal weight as written evidence of earlier, autonomous choices made by an individual while able to make such decisions, in the unlikely event of a judicial decision about the appropriate use of stored tissue samples identified with that individual.

This kind of comprehensive advance directive also presents problems. Because of its comprehensiveness, the document may include too many options and be difficult to use in the real world. Unlike a comprehensive end-of-life advance directive, this advance directive for stored tissue samples cannot simply remain with the signer, be attached to the signer's hospital chart, or be copied to accompany a blood sample or other tissue sample to multiple clinical or research settings. In addition, the choices provided in the document would seem to require the signer to be well educated, reasonably familiar with biomedical research practices, and reasonably knowledgeable about genetics studies.

AN ADVANCE-CONSENT DIRECTIVE FOR PARENTS OF NEWBORNS

All states, with the exceptions of Delaware and Vermont, now do legally mandated screening tests on the blood and/or urine of neonates, with the specific conditions being screened varying somewhat from state to state. Only two states (Maryland and North Carolina, plus the District of Columbia) require that parents be given the opportunity of granting permission or refusing permission for such newborn screening tests on their infants. In other states, parents of newborns may or may not be told about the screening tests that will be done, be given an explanation of the importance of the testing, be provided with an information brochure, be required to sign a waiver if they refuse the testing, and/or be informed that the stored tissue samples will be used for additional research studies. Because of these differences in practice, some knowledgeable and concerned parents or potential parents might want to be given more information about the research studies planned for the tissue samples taken from their children soon after birth. They might also want to have a conversation with the physician(s) about the mandated tests and projected research studies or be able to communicate their preferences and choices about the genetic studies that might be done using a stored tissue sample that came from their child. An example of an advance directive pertaining to stored neonatal blood spots (or other tissue samples) appears at the end of this essay.

The benefits of such an advance directive would be threefold. First, if potential parents (during pregnancy) were going to sign or draft such a document, they would necessarily have to give more thought to state-mandated screening tests and the possibility of additional research studies on their child's blood than most prospective parents now seem to do. Second, having signed or drafted such a document, new parents would be better prepared to participate in conversations with their baby's physician(s) and be able to give more informed consent concerning the state-mandated tests and proposed future research studies using their child's blood. Third, having signed or drafted such a document, new parents would also be better positioned to limit the use of their child's blood spots to the mandated tests and avoid additional, unspecified research studies using their child's blood, if that should be their choice.

The limitations and potential problems connected with such a document are fairly straightforward. At worst, the attempted use of this kind of document by parents in a neonatal setting would probably complicate their relationship with the physician(s) and nurses in the unit and generally be regarded by those persons as a waste of time and effort, especially since most new parents seem to accept the mandated tests and future research studies without much concern. At best, the use of this kind of document would probably interest only a small percentage of new parents or potential parents, and the document's effectiveness in the real world of newborn nurseries and neonatal intensive care units would probably depend in large part on the personal views about parental choice held by the physician(s) and nurses involved in the case.

A SIMPLIFIED ADVANCE-CONSENT DIRECTIVE

A comprehensive advance directive pertaining to stored tissue samples may be regarded as unacceptable and unworkable by some physicians, biomedical researchers, and other professionals who work in complex clinical and research institutions, just as end-of-life advance directives are regarded as "worthless pieces of paper" by some physicians in critical care units. Given this "reality check," an alternative is to develop a simplified advance directive that would enable interested persons to communicate choices about the possible use(s) of their stored tissue samples, yet would be more acceptable to the physicians and biomedical investigators who would actually be working with those stored samples. An example of a simplified form is included at the end of this essay.

A simplified advance-consent directive, like the other directives pertaining to stored tissue samples, would offer both benefits and problems. The major benefit is that it could actually work. Blood banks, pathology labs, and other locations for stored tissue samples already have several reasons for using bar codes on containers holding blood and other tissue samples: to code individual samples, to place stored samples in different categories, and to indicate any limitations on the possible use(s) of individual samples. When read by a computerized scanner, the bar codes quickly and easily communicate information about the individual tissue samples that is important to the professionals working with the samples. In a similar manner, bar codes could be placed on containers holding individual tissue samples in order to communicate the choices about possible research use(s) made earlier by the persons who are the sources of the tissue samples. In large research institutions, a centralized institutional tissue registry could keep track of the bar code information and the distribution of tissue samples to multiple investigators.

The major problem with this proposal is that even a simplified advance directive would complicate the work that biomedical scientists do with stored tissue samples. Data management with stored tissue samples would obviously be more complex when the earlier consent and preferences of the sources of some of the samples are considered, compared to the common practice of using linked or anonymized samples without consideration for the consent or choices of the persons from whom the samples came.

Two kinds of responses from scientific investigators can be anticipated. For some investigators, the response will be to regard even simplified advance directives as being too much of a hassle and too much of an impediment to biomedical research for practical use. These investigators will reject even simplified advance directives with critical comments along the lines of Wayne Grody's "frequent-flyer program" comments quoted earlier. For other investigators, the response will be a weighing of the possible benefits of a simplified advance-consent directive against a realistic assessment of the data-management and logistical problems that such directives would cause. These investigators will conclude, I hope, that with the use of bar codes and computers at least simplified versions of advance-consent directives are workable — and that the benefits of giving the sources of stored tissue samples the option of informed consent regarding the possible use(s) of those samples are worth the costs of doing so.

Acknowledgments

Some of this essay appears in revised form in a paper that I was commissioned to write for the National Bioethics Advisory Commission (NBAC). That paper, "The Ongoing Debate about Stored Tissue Samples, Research, and Informed Consent," is to be included in the NBAC's publication on stored tissue samples.

Notes

1. Robert F. Weir and Jay R. Horton, "DNA Banking and Informed Consent," *IRB* 17 (July–August 1995): 1–4.

2. Wayne W. Grody, "Molecular Pathology, Informed Consent, and the Paraffin Block," *Diagnostic Molecular Pathology* 4 (1995): 156.

3. Centers for Disease Control and Prevention, Department of Health and Human Services, "National Health and Nutrition Examination Survey III," January 1994, p. 3.

4. CDC, "National Health and Nutrition Examination Survey III," p. 3.

5. George J. Annas, Leonard H. Glantz, and Patricia A. Roche, "The Genetic Privacy Act and Commentary," February 1995.

6. "Genetic Privacy Act," p. 6.

7. "Genetic Privacy Act," p. 24.

8. American College of Medical Genetics, Storage of Genetics Materials Committee, "Statement on Storage and Use of Genetic Materials," *American Journal of Human Genetics* 57 (1995): 1499–1500.

9. Ellen Wright Clayton et al., "Informed Consent for Genetic Research on Stored Tissue Samples," *JAMA* 274 (December 13, 1995): 1786–1792.

10. Clayton, et al., "Informed Consent," p. 1791.

11. Grody, "Molecular Pathology," pp. 155–156.

12. Grody, "Molecular Pathology," p. 155.

13. Grody, "Molecular Pathology," p. 156.

14. Edward R. B. McCabe et al., American Society of Human Genetics Rapid Action Task Force, "Report on Informed Consent for Genetic Research," unpublished document, pp. 1–10.

15. American Society of Human Genetics, "Statement on Informed Consent for Genetic Research," *American Journal of Human Genetics* 59 (1996): 471–474.

16. American Society of Human Genetics, "Statement on Informed Consent," p. 474.

17. Joan Stephenson, "Pathologists Enter Debate on Consent for Genetic Research on Stored Tissue," *JAMA* 275 (February 21, 1996): 504.

18. College of American Pathologists, "Uses of Human Tissue," unpublished policy statement, August 1996.

19. Clayton, et al., "Informed Consent," p. 1787.

20. Stephenson, "Pathologists Enter Debate," p. 504.

21. George J. Annas, Leonard H. Glantz, and Patricia A. Roche, "Drafting the Genetic Privacy Act: Science, Policy, and Practical Considerations," *Journal of Law, Medicine, and Ethics* 23 (1995): 361.

22. Ellen Wright Clayton, "Panel Comment: Why the Use of Anonymous Samples for Research Matters," *Journal of Law, Medicine, and Ethics* 23 (1995): 375–377.

23. Neil A. Holtzman, "Panel Comment: The Attempt to Pass the Genetic Privacy Act in Maryland," *Journal of Law, Medicine, and Ethics* 23 (1995): 367–370.

24. Philip R. Reilly, "Panel Comment: The Impact of the Genetic Privacy Act on Medicine," *Journal of Law, Medicine, and Ethics* 23 (1995): 378–381.

25. Robert F. Weir, *Abating Treatment with Critically Ill Patients* (New York: Oxford University Press, 1989), p. 181.

26. Linda Emanuel and Ezekiel Emanuel, "The Medical Directive," *JAMA* 261 (June 9, 1989): 3288–3293.

27. Patient Self-Determination Act: Omnibus Budget Reconciliation Act of 1990, 1990: 4206, 4751. Pub. Law 101-508.

28. American College of Physicians, "Cognitively Impaired Subjects," *Annals of Internal Medicine* 111 (November 15, 1989): 843–848.

29. Robert J. Levine, *Ethics and Regulation of Clinical Research*, 2nd ed. (New Haven: Yale University Press, 1986).

30. Sherman Elias and George J. Annas, "Generic Consent for Genetic Screening," *New England Journal of Medicine* 330 (June 2, 1994): 1611–1613.

31. Rebecca Dresser, "Mentally Disabled Research Subjects," *JAMA* 276 (July 3, 1996): 67–72.

32. Robert F. Weir, "Advance Directives as Instruments of Moral Persuasion," in Robert H. Blank and Andrea L. Bonnicksen, eds., *Medicine Unbound* (New York: Columbia University Press, 1994), pp. 171–187.

33. SUPPORT Principal Investigators, "A Controlled Trial to Improve Care for Seriously Ill Hospitalized Patients," *JAMA* 274 (November 22/29, 1995): 1591–1598.

A Comprehensive Advance-consent Directive

ADVANCE DIRECTIVE FOR MY STORED TISSUE SAMPLES

INTRODUCTION: To my family, the physicians responsible for my care, geneticists and other biomedical scientists, and any administrators of a laboratory or facility that stores human tissues:

PERSONAL STATEMENT: I, _____ , am of sound mind, capable of making personal decisions, and under no pressure from other individuals. I am a beneficiary of modern biomedical research, in terms of both the discoveries and medicines produced by biomedical scientists and the voluntary participation in scientific studies by numerous persons around the globe. I realize that I am able to live longer and healthier because of the partnership between biomedical scientists and research participants now and in the past. I know that some of this research has been done with human tissue samples collected in clinical and research settings and then stored for scientific studies.

Nevertheless, I am concerned about contemporary genetic studies and other scientific studies using stored tissue samples. I am especially concerned that genetic analysis and other molecular studies of my blood and other tissues may be conducted without my consent, with samples identifiable with me, with inadequate protection of the confidentiality and privacy of the personal genetic information contained in my DNA samples, or with negligent or willful disclosure of that uniquely personal information to parties (e.g., my employer, health insurance company, or governmental officials) to whom I may not want it revealed.

I am also concerned that genetic studies and other molecular studies may be done with my tissue samples (including anonymized samples that came from me) for scientific purposes that I do not support, or for purposes of commercial gain that will neither be shared with me or my family nor be donated to a charitable cause. In addition, I am concerned that the personal genetic information gained about me from my identifiable DNA samples may have harmful implications for my family if disclosed to the wrong persons.

DECLARATION OF RIGHTS: I believe that I have a moral right to control what is done with the tissue samples collected from my body. In addition, I believe that I have the right to exercise self-determination in matters of personal biological materials and personal genetic information, to promote my individual well-being as it pertains to the scientific use of my tissue samples, and to protect the genetic privacy of my relatives. I now plan to exercise these rights by communicating a series of choices regarding the scientific uses of any tissues samples collected from my body by physicians, biomedical investigators, or governmental officials. I intend these choices to be followed unless I subsequently sign a consent document in a specific clinical or research setting that disagrees with and overrides these choices, or unless a specific choice is against federal or state law. In the event I can no longer defend these rights or discuss these choices, I expect my surrogate to use legal means if necessary to carry out these choices.

STATEMENT OF CHOICES: When blood and other tissues are removed from my body for diagnostic, surgical, or research reasons, I want my family, physician(s), and any biomedical researchers to know my preferences.

These are my preferences and choices regarding possible scientific uses of my stored tissue samples:

	I consent	I do not consent
1. my tissue samples may be used for *any kind* of genetic research	_____	_____

[If I give consent to #1, I need not indicate consent to the following items.]

2. *diagnostic studies* intended to *benefit me or my family*	_____	_____
3. *research studies* intended to *benefit me or my family*	_____	_____
4. genetic and other research studies using tissue samples *identified* with me	_____	_____
5. genetic and other research studies using tissue samples *linkable* to me	_____	_____
6. genetic and other research studies using *anonymized* samples that came from me, but cannot be linked to me	_____	_____

7. research studies intended to gather
   statistical data about the population   _____   _____
8. my tissue samples may be
   transformed into anonymized
   cell lines that can exist forever   _____   _____
9. my tissue samples may be
   transformed into anonymized
   cell lines and *sent to other*
   researchers   _____   _____
10. although it is unlikely, my tissue
    samples may be used for
    commercial gain by the
    investigators or institution   _____   _____

ACCESS TO PERSONAL GENETIC INFORMATION: I know that genetic studies of my stored tissue samples can reveal important information about my genetic heritage, my carrier status for genetic conditions and traits, and my presymptomatic status for genetic diseases.

If I am unable to give or refuse consent regarding access to this information in the future, these parties may have access to genetic information about me derived from my DNA samples:

	YES	NO
• my spouse	____	____
• my adult children	____	____
• my physician	____	____
• my employer	____	____
• my health insurance company	____	____
• the government	____	____

SURROGATE DESIGNATION: If I am no longer able to discuss the choices made for the use of my stored tissue samples, or if I am no longer alive but still have tissue samples in storage, I hope that my surrogate will abide by my wishes regarding the use of my tissue samples.

In the event I can no longer discuss my choices, or in the event of my death, I designate the following person to act on my behalf in making decisions about my stored tissue samples:

Name _____

Address _____

_____

SIGNATURE AND WITNESSES:

Signed: _____   Date: _____

Witness: _____   Witness: _____

An Advance-consent Directive for Parents of Newborns

ADVANCE DIRECTIVE REGARDING MY/OUR CHILDREN'S TISSUES

INTRODUCTION: I/we know that tissue samples are collected in clinical and research settings from pregnant women, fetuses, newborns, and children in their early years. I/we know that these DNA samples can be used for multiple scientific purposes. I/we expect, in these kinds of situations, to be asked to give permission for the collection and use of my/our children's DNA samples, but know that DNA samples are sometimes collected without parental permission.

STATEMENT OF CHOICES: I/we hereby establish the limits within which my/our children's DNA samples can be collected and used:

	I/we grant permission	I/we withhold permission	we disagree
1. my/our children's DNA samples may be used for *any kind* of genetic research	_____	_____	_____

[If I/we give permission to #1, there is no need to respond to the following items.]

	I/we grant permission	I/we withhold permission	we disagree
2. *diagnostic studies* intended to *help my/our children*	_____	_____	_____
3. *research studies* intended to *help my/our children*	_____	_____	_____
4. genetic and other research studies using tissue samples with *personal identifiers*	_____	_____	_____
5. genetic and other research studies using tissue samples *linkable* to a specific child	_____	_____	_____
6. genetic and other research studies using *anonymized* samples that cannot be linked to my/our children	_____	_____	_____
7. research studies intended to gather *statistical data* about the population	_____	_____	_____

SIGNATURE(S) AND WITNESSES:

Signed: _____ Date: _____

Signed: _____ Date: _____

Witness: _____ Witness: _____

A Simplified Advance-consent Directive

ADVANCE DIRECTIVE FOR STORED TISSUE SAMPLES

INTRODUCTION: I, _____, realize that I am able to live longer and healthier because of the successes of biomedical research. I know that some of this research has been done with human tissue samples collected in clinical and research settings and then stored for scientific studies.

Nevertheless, I am concerned about genetic studies and other scientific studies using stored tissue samples. I am specifically concerned about the following possibilities:

- genetic tests may be done with my blood and other tissues without my consent,

- someone may disclose information gained from my DNA to third parties (my employer, health insurance company, or government) to whom I may not want it revealed, and

- someone may use my tissue sample for scientific purposes that I do not support.

STATEMENT OF CHOICES: I therefore make the following choices about genetic and other research studies that might be done with my stored tissue samples:

	I consent	I do not consent
1. my tissue samples may be used for *any kind* of scientific research	_____	_____

[If I give consent to #1, I need not give consent to the other items.]

	I consent	I do not consent
2. genetic studies using tissue samples *identified with me*	_____	_____
3. genetic studies using tissue samples *linkable to me*	_____	_____
4. genetic studies using *anonymized* tissue samples that came from me, but are not linked to me	_____	_____
5. my tissue samples may be shared with other scientists for *other scientific studies*	_____	_____

SIGNATURE AND WITNESSES:

Signed: _____   Date: _____

Witness: _____   Witness: _____

The Role of Community in Research
with Stored Tissue Samples

William L. Freeman

This essay presents the ethical bases for the proposed Indian Health Service's *Guidelines for the Collection and Use of Research Specimens*, which are included at the end of the essay. The guidelines were designed to be a concise working document for multiple groups, including American Indian and Alaska Native (AI/AN)[1] communities and people. However, the ethical principles and social bases for the guidelines were not explicitly discussed. I believe the guidelines are relevant to most U.S. people, researchers, and policy makers; if researchers and ethicists are to see them as relevant, however, the ethical rationale for the guidelines must be clarified and convincing.

I begin by explaining the context of the guidelines: the IHS itself; Tribal sovereignty and self-determination, and their implications for research; and strong core values held by most AI/AN Tribal communities. Next I discuss the importance of Tribal communities, including the values and concerns of minority and other lay communities that differ from those of researchers and health professionals, the nature of those values and concerns, and the ways in which those values and concerns can be sufficiently compelling that communities seek to have an active "voice" in — rather than being passive "subjects" of — research. I then discuss the role of that voice (i.e., community participation) in the research process: its desirable characteristics, its limitations, and its place in the Indian Health Service research program.

The Context of the Guidelines

THE INDIAN HEALTH SERVICE (IHS)

In the 1990 U.S. Census, about 1.7 million people (0.7 percent of the population) were AI/AN by self-declaration. There are more than 500 federally recognized AI/AN Tribes; they are diverse in size, geography, culture, and interests. One Tribe, the Navajo Nation, has more than 200,000 members living on or near the Navajo Reservation, and several Tribes have 10,000 to 20,000 residents; the great majority of Tribes, however, have fewer than 5,000 members. Almost half of AI/AN people live in urban areas, while most reservations are rural. Tribal communities range in location from Barrow (well north of the

Arctic Circle in Alaska), to the arid desert Southwest near Phoenix, to the Everglades in Florida. Due to that diversity, the one accurate generalization about AI/AN Tribes, communities, and peoples is that most universal statements about "Indians" or "Native Americans" are inaccurate.

U.S. law is the basis for federal health services to AI/AN people.[2] The Indian Health Service of the Public Health Service has primary responsibility for those services. The IHS provided care to about 1 million AI/AN people in 1990, all of whom were enrolled members of a federally recognized AI/AN Tribe.

The IHS goal is to raise the health status of AI/AN people to the highest possible level. Its missions are to ensure equity, availability, and accessibility of a high-quality comprehensive health care system and to maximize the involvement of AI/AN people in defining their health needs, setting health priorities for their local areas, and managing and controlling their health programs. Tribes can and do manage the IHS programs in their communities under Public Law 93–638, the Indian Self-Determination Act of 1975. Tribes also can and do take over the entire IHS-funded health programs under the process of self-governance.

IHS provides and supports a broad set of preventive, curative, rehabilitative, and environmental services. As of October 1995 IHS had twelve regional administrative units called area offices. IHS operated 68 local administrative units called service units, 38 hospitals, 61 health centers, 4 school health centers, and 47 health stations; Tribes operated 76 service units, 11 hospitals, 129 health centers, 3 school health centers, 73 health stations, and 167 Alaska village clinics.[3] More than 1 million enrolled members of federally recognized AI/AN Tribes received services in those facilities in 1995. Most research in AI/AN communities is done by outsiders such as universities; only a small proportion is done by Tribes or by IHS service units or the IHS research program.

The IHS has twelve institutional review boards (IRBs), one for each area or region and the Headquarters IHS IRB. The Navajo Nation has its own IRB, whose members the IHS has appointed to the Navajo Area IHS IRB as a combined IRB. IHS IRBs help ensure that all research observes three principles of ethics: (1) *respect* for persons, (2) *beneficence* (to do no harm, and to maximize benefit), and (3) *justice*.[4] IRBs look closely at the "informed consent process" — the negotiation between the researcher and each potential volunteer.

TRIBAL SOVEREIGNTY AND RESEARCH

To understand how IHS views research, one must know about the sovereignty of AI/AN Tribes. Tribal sovereignty was recognized before and in the

Constitution, and in the past thirty-five years has become stronger as the result of federal law, case law, and U.S. Supreme Court decisions.[5] For instance, reservation land is generally controlled by the Tribe. Tribes can tax and regulate both Indian and non-Indian activity or people within reservations and can bar them from their reservations.[6] A major implication of Tribal sovereignty in research involving AI/AN people is that Tribal governments can legally prohibit or regulate research within their reservation, and even bar researchers from entering it.

IHS is committed to Tribal sovereignty and to the self-determination and cultural integrity of AI/AN communities. Four IHS policies and procedures regarding research reflect that commitment.

All research must be approved by the governments of the Tribal communities involved in the research.[7] Furthermore, all publications from that research must be reviewed by the Tribal government.[8]

By federal regulation 45 CFR 46, every IRB must have at least one member whose primary interest is "nonscientific." In the IHS IRBs, the "nonscientific" member[s] must be enrolled members of Tribal communities. (In most IHS IRBs, the proportion of members who are American Indian or Alaska Native exceeds 50 percent.)

IHS IRBs examine the negotiations both between the researcher and *potential volunteer*, and between the researcher and *Tribal community*. This policy means that IHS IRBs apply the basic ethical principles — respect, beneficence, and justice — to Tribal communities as well as to individuals who participate in research studies.

IHS IRBs encourage researchers to give, and Tribes to ask for, a required set of elements of information (similar to the required set of elements in 45 CFR 46 for individual volunteers' consent), to ensure that the Tribes' consent is truly informed.[9]

CORE VALUES OF TRIBAL COMMUNITIES

To understand the core values of many, if not all, AI/AN Tribal communities, and of many members of those communities, one must understand their histories. The histories of Native peoples have been far from ideal after they and initially European and then Euroamerican and Eurocanadian peoples encountered each other. The estimates by many respected authorities, using modern methods of demography, of the total Native population in 1492 in what is now the United States range from 1.8 million to 18 million, with most estimates between 2 and 5 million. The nadir (about 1890 to 1910) of the

AI/AN population was 228,000, representing a remnant of only 5 to 11 percent of the estimated 1492 population.[10]

The problematic nature of the encounters between Native peoples and eventually dominant societies was not just demographic, but also cultural, and the history of these encounters has direct bearing on the current issue of using stored tissues for research purposes. In the following quotation, Richard Grounds, an assistant professor of anthropology and member of the Yuchi and Seminole Tribes, discusses the complex reactions of members of the Yuchi Tribe of Oklahoma to the proposed uses of tissue samples by the North American Regional Committee of the Human Genome Diversity Project (HGDP).[11]

> Yet it will be harder to dismiss what the Native [Yuchi] voices of caution [about the HGDP] represent. They are the current expression, the echo, of the long memory of the oppression and genocide perpetrated by Euroamerican society upon Native peoples. The great disparity in levels of trust between Native American and non–Native American societies regarding such a project derive from fundamentally different historical experiences. The issue is not as simple as the good intentions of the members of the HGDP. Throughout Yuchi history, I can think of no major case of momentous interaction with Euroamerican society which unequivocally resulted in a generally positive outcome for Yuchis. Betrayal and loss characterize the major historical events, from the so-called "Removal" in which many Yuchis were brought in chains from Georgia to Indian Territory (now Oklahoma) in the 1830s, to "Allotment" which broke up communally held lands at the turn of the twentieth century, through the implementation of the boarding school system throughout the first half of the twentieth century. Even though many of the participants in those activities carried positive intentions, many negative consequences for the cultural life of the community continue to be felt today.[12]

The demographic and cultural nadir was not hidden while it was happening. For instance, the ubiquitous museum collections of Northwest Coast Indian artifacts — from Moscow to Los Angeles — began in 1875, with the most intense period being the next forty years. The reason was the extensively shared perception among Europeans, Americans, and Canadians that

> time was essential, that civilization was pushing the primitive to the wall, destroying the material culture and even extinguishing the native stock itself. . . . This sense of urgency, this notion of a scientific mission, was a constant theme of nineteenth- and early twentieth-century anthropology. . . . Stewart Culin [then curator of American archaeology and gen-

eral ethnology at the University of Pennsylvania, and later at Brooklyn's Institute of Arts and Sciences, wrote in 1900 that] "the Indian — as a savage — is soon to disappear" and "there soon will be nothing left upon the reservation." [13]

In a quite recent qualitative study about the Mesquaki Tribe in Iowa, a young traditionalist described how his/their culture has endured:

> Our culture is a living thing. We don't do the ceremonies exactly the way they were done a hundred or two hundred years ago. We may be doing some things different. Some people who don't come to the ceremonies might say we do it wrong, but we do the best we can. We are trying to keep alive what the creator gave us. I was taught that the tribe has always had conservatives and progressives. We have always had to decide how much of the whiteman's ways we will use. Sometimes we don't bend fast enough, and we hurt ourselves. Other times maybe we give up our old ways too fast, and that hurts us too. The ones who want us to be more modern drag us along, and the ones who are more traditional save what we have. And we are still here.[14]

Two aspects of this quotation are striking. First, his affirmation "we are still here" implies that being "here" was, and is, in doubt. Second, traditionalists and progressives discuss and make decisions with care and intensity because the *community's survival* — and thus each individual's survival as a Mesquaki person — is the real subject. Given the expectation of the imminent cultural and physical extinction of North American Indians — an experience lived within the lifetimes of some Tribal elders alive today — it is not surprising that a strong core value and concern of Native communities is their physical and cultural survival. A core activity is *self-determination* to ensure that survival.

There is also a striking fact related to this essay. Neither this core value nor this core activity of Native communities is generally known — much less taken account of — by most researchers or health professionals in charge of, or using, specimens taken from Native peoples in the course of medical care or research.

The relevance of the context just described to the use of stored specimens in research is discussed in the next section. I argue that much of the IHS approach applies to research involving non-AI/AN communities and peoples. But one aspect of the context is not generally applicable: Tribal sovereignty. Tribes have *legal* standing to force researchers to seek approval by the Tribe. In the United States most groups other than states do not have anything similar to the legal jurisdiction of AI/AN Tribes. The rest of the essay discusses the *ethical* standing of communities — AI/AN Tribes and others — regarding the use of stored specimens in research.

Communities

To discuss the applicability of the IHS approach, we first need to define the word "community." In their discussion of "communitarianism" as a community-based theory of biomedical ethics, Tom Beauchamp and James Childress define "community" as follows: "Some communitarians refer almost exclusively to the political state as the community, whereas others refer to smaller communities and institutions with defined goals and role obligations. Some include the family as a basic communal unit, within which being a parent and being a child involve specific roles and responsibilities. . . . Understanding a particular system of moral rules . . . requires an understanding of the community's history, sense of cooperative life, and conception of social welfare."[15]

As another example, the final draft of the Canadian *Code of Conduct for Research Involving Humans* defines groups ("collectivities") in article 13.1. Collectivities are "population groups with social structures, common customs, and an acknowledged leadership."[16] They include nations, cultural groups, small indigenous communities, and some neighborhood groups. The definition is also explicitly intended to include families.

By contrast, in a book on communitarian bioethics, Ezekiel Emanuel defines "community" in terms of function rather than structure, and his definition includes more groups. This definition is stated in political science concepts: "A political community is a group of citizens mutually committed to one another in the ongoing process of deliberation in elaborating their shared conception of the good life and [in] specifying laws and policies. . . . Communities are often formed on the basis of a newly acknowledged common commitment to some vision of human life."[17]

My definition of "community" is shorter than but substantively similar to Emanuel's. This simple definition reflects years of work and discussion in the IHS: "community" is born from strong mutual concern or necessity.[18] This definition (and the one by Emanuel) covers AI/AN Tribes, as well as advocacy groups such as the National Breast Cancer Coalition that are defined not by a common "culture" of the members but by their common concerns and necessities. Such advocacy groups have special interests in the research proposed, often because the members themselves have or had the condition being investigated or because it is in their family. Note that this definition does not imply that communities are homogeneous in their values.

Having defined "community" for the purposes of this essay, we can now address the question, "Do communities have sufficient ethical standing to have a voice in controlling the use of stored specimens from their members in research?" That question can be broken down into three sequentially detailed questions. (1) Do the values and concerns of communities differ from the values and concerns of professional researchers and of health care providers? (2) Are professional researchers and health care providers themselves able to represent well those other values and concerns of communities? (3) Are the unique values and concerns of communities sufficiently compelling for communities to have an active voice in the research process?

DIFFERENT VALUES AND CONCERNS ABOUT HEALTH AND RESEARCH

Many ethnic, lay, and advocacy communities have values and concerns that differ from those of professional researchers and providers, as shown by the following examples.

1. Physical and cultural *survival* is a core value and pressing concern, as discussed above.

2. Many health professionals believe that people with a disability automatically have a lower *quality of life* than people without disability. In contrast, many people with disabilities self-rate themselves on standard questionnaires as having the same quality of life as people with "objectively" "normal" health status. Some professionals interpret this unexpectedly (to the professionals) high self-rated quality of life as due to lowered expectations of people with a disability — or even to "widespread . . . imputations of explicitly psychiatric symptoms like euphoria, or asognosia [*sic*] (indifference to disability) to those offering such accounts" of happiness and high quality of life.[19] This interpretation seems unlikely. Many people with a disability who have a high quality of life do realize their physical limitations, but they have different values than the professionals who observe them — values in which relationships are more important than physical prowess. Consider the following quotation of a person with multiple sclerosis (MS): "Now I know that I have MS I am much more tolerant and have become less tense. I do not worry if I cannot do anything — and there are quite a few things I cannot do. I think I am getting on fine. I am living at peace with it [MS]. I think I am a better person. In a way my life is richer than it ever was. I am surrounded by *love, care and attention by my husband, family, neighbors and friends.*"[20] An implication for research

and health care of this difference in values is that treatments or programs that would improve "objective" physical functioning at the expense of personal relationships might be unacceptable to many people with disabilities.[21]

3. People with disability have *diverse values and concerns*. Consider people with another disability: "patients [on renal dialysis] and spouses to a remarkable degree regard themselves as 'back to normal' or comparable to normals which means that they successfully fight loss of socio-economic position, and many manage to retain or even improve the occupational status of husband or wife or both."[22] One implication is that values and concerns vary within large groups such as "people with a disability," or "minorities," or "Native people."

4. Professionals may not know well what patients and laypeople view as important in *decisionmaking*. For instance, a set of elements of information about screening for being a carrier of a recessive gene for cystic fibrosis (CF) was given to consumers with a family history of CF, to consumers without a family history of CF, and to professionals and staff in CF and genetic clinics; they determined the order in which they wanted the questions answered. The consumers with family history had the same order for the questions as consumers without family history; professionals and staff of the CF and genetic clinics answered differently than both consumer groups.[23] As another example, separate focus groups of patients who had breast cancer, members of families with breast cancer, the general public, and nurses and doctors were asked to review and discuss a draft consent form for donating tissue left over from biopsy or surgery for possible cancer to research tissue banks. Among other findings, the patient, family, and public groups were more concerned than the professionals about involving family members in the decision (e.g., they wanted to take the consent document and information home for a few days before deciding); changing their minds; getting feedback about the utility of the tissue bank (what research findings were made); taking "extra tissue"; and risking the potential loss of medical insurance.[24] At least one implication for general research is that consent forms developed by professionals may not match, or may be out of sync with, the concerns and decisionmaking processes of the potential volunteers.

5. Many professionals may not understand *stigmatization* due to diagnoses. For instance, epilepsy is a biomedical disease to most professionals; even so, many professionals and medical sociologists have known that others in society stigmatize people with that condition. But listening carefully to people with epilepsy suggests that professionals' and sociologists' knowledge is not accurate. Many people with epilepsy *self-stigmatize* themselves — feel shame —

often without or before having experienced any discrimination or external stigmatization.[25] An implication is that researchers should proactively counteract potential self-stigmatization.

6. Professional bioethics may be *ethnocentric* with its emphasis on autonomous decisionmaking using full knowledge. Less acculturated Mexican Americans and Korean Americans, by contrast, have a family-centered method of making decisions.[26] The Patient Self-Determination Act (PSDA) requires discussing with each patient entering a hospital his or her preferences for direct care instructions by means of a living will or a designated agent to make health care decisions (with a durable power of attorney) should he or she become decisionally incapacitated. However, many traditional AI/AN people believe that a straightforward discussion with a patient about those options can actually harm the individual: discussing negative information turns it into reality.[27] The implication is that many ethnic groups in the United States may have values and concerns that differ from those of the majority culture or professional bioethicists.

7. Professional experts understand *risk and safety* differently from many nonprofessionals. To the former, risk is a straightforward scientific calculation of probability of occurrence times the *physical* damage. Psychometric studies have shown that many laypeople perceive environmental risks by weighing two factors. One factor is a spectrum from known to unknown risk — with "unknown risk" being not known to those exposed, with delayed effects, or new to science. The other factor is a spectrum from less to more dreadful, with "more dreadful" being global, catastrophic, with fatal consequences, not equitable, with high risk to future generations, and involuntary.[28] As an example, the World Health Organization (WHO) noted that the safety of contraceptives is understood as toxicity vs. efficacy by research scientists, while to many women it is protection against sexually transmitted diseases (STDs) and infertility, fewer side effects, and being under the control of users.[29] The implication for research in general, and for research with tissue specimens in particular, is that we all impute values to "risk," and the values imputed often differ between professionals and laypeople.

8. The *value imputed to tissue specimens themselves* also varies between professional and laypeople. One professional view was graphically exemplified by the term one well-known IRB physician used to describe human tissues left over from medical procedures: "garbage." Many laypeople appear to have a different view, at least for some types of tissue. For instance, an IRB asked postpartum women who had just delivered in its hospital if they wanted to give consent for the research use of their anonymized placentas; the majority

said yes.[30] The point is that some tissues, such as placentas, may have more value to some people — may still represent or be associated with the person — than other tissues.[31] One implication is that the federal regulations designed to protect human subjects and govern the use of tissue specimens — 45 CFR §46.101(b)(4) — are ethnocentric; exempting from IRB review (and thus from consent) the research use of all specimens, so long as they are anonymous, is based on the *professional* — not lay — values about "discarded" human tissues.

9. *Research using specimens involves core culture, beliefs, values, and religion* held by many members of many communities. Consider the Maori of New Zealand:

> Within my own culture, Maori tribes collectively have shared values about that which is *tapu* (sacred) and that which is *noa* (common). Hair, blood, mucus, the main sources used by westerners to collect DNA, are all *tapu*. . . . Western science goes to great lengths to de-humanize the humanness or life-force of human genes; hence, terms such as "specimens," "materials," "properties," and "collections" . . . ignore the essence of life contained within. For Maori, a gene has *mauri* (a life force) as do many other things, such as rocks of special significance, sacred sites, and placenta (afterbirth). . . . It is contrary to indigenous tradition to "objectify" a gene or human organs as these are living and sacred manifestations of the ancestors; they are a life-force that continues to exist *ex-situ*.[32]

While the history of the United States and Canada includes religious freedom and tolerance, it also includes not respecting non-Christian religions and core cultures of their Native peoples.[33] Many people do not recognize the points of conflict between a particular activity such as research and a religion dissimilar to that of the majority's culture;[34] they may not realize how a conflict may be transformed to permit the religion and activity to coexist.[35] Yet some genetic researchers have discussed common issues with ethicists and religious leaders from major religions with good results for both groups. One implication is that for research using tissue specimens to be accepted by minority communities, researchers should acknowledge possible religious concerns and should discuss common issues with the religious leaders of those communities.[36]

REPRESENTING THE DIFFERENT VALUES
AND CONCERNS OF COMMUNITY

Lay and community values and concerns differ so much from those of research or health professionals that they are not able to represent communities well. Some community values and concerns are not perceived by many professionals, such as survival, self-stigmatization, and the process of decision-making. Other values and concerns are contrary to those of some outside professionals, such as the understanding of "risk," unusual perspectives on bioethics, and the significance of religious beliefs. Yet others oppose the self-interest of some research professionals, such as placing considerable value on some tissues that the professionals view as basically worthless. One should not expect researchers or professionals to represent community values and concerns that are contrary to, or even worse that directly oppose, their own values or self-interest.

ARE COMMUNITY VALUES AND CONCERNS
SUFFICIENTLY IMPORTANT?

One way to answer this question is to describe the specific values and concerns that three communities with active participation in the research process have brought to the table. The three communities are disease activist groups, AI/AN Tribes, and NASA astronauts.

Until recently, the planning process for research on AIDS or breast cancer did not include people from the communities affected by those diseases. In the mid-1980s first individual researchers and then researchers and regulators in NIH, FDA, and universities accepted AIDS activists from the gay community in the planning, reviewing, and conducting of AIDS research.[37] The National Breast Cancer Coalition was accepted as a formal partner to plan, review, and conduct breast cancer research in the mid-1990s.[38]

Both activist communities wanted to change the existing research agenda and methods that had been determined primarily by the research community. They wanted more research for prevention and practical treatments, more outreach to minorities with the condition, more appropriate use of placebos, better access to protocols, better recruitment and retention of subjects, and more effective research use of tissues. Thus, both communities had a positive stance toward research, wanting to *expand the benefits of research* to the affected people.

Many Tribes have a different set of values, a negative stance toward research; they want to *restrict research, to prevent harms* to their communities. Many people in AI/AN — and other — communities have a "great[er] disparity in levels of trust"[39] about research in general than the relative trust of many people of the majority community. I have sometimes been a lightning rod for that distrust; the reasons for the distrust I heard were generally as stated by Dr. Grounds in the quotation given earlier. Many African Americans also distrust research for historical reasons that include abuses by the Tuskegee syphilis — and other — research, government-sponsored involuntary sterilizations, indifferent or worse behaviors and attitudes of segregated and some other health care systems, problematic sickle cell screening, and so forth.[40]

Let me be clear: research has helped AI/AN Tribes. From determining effective treatment for the scourge of trachoma (which causes blindness) in the 1930s, to developing effective treatment for TB in the 1950s, to determining which Hemophilus vaccine would be effective in AI/AN infants and young children, advances in biomedical knowledge based on research involving specific Tribes have directly benefited all Tribes and many other peoples everywhere.

Research about stigmatizing conditions could harm Tribes and AI/AN individuals, however, such as determining the prevalence of an "alcoholism" gene using saved anonymous tissue specimens from a specific Tribe, or from several Tribes or even just "American Indians and Alaska Natives." The subject of such research is the Tribe or the larger AI/AN *group itself*. The Tribe or AI/AN group may be *directly* harmed, even if individuals remain anonymous or not identified. *Individual* members of the Tribe and all other AI/AN individuals, moreover, also can be harmed by at least two additional problems: one is external stigmatization by other people who read or hear about the research; the other is self-stigmatization by AI/AN individuals themselves when they read or hear about the research.[41]

Stigmatization of Tribes by research is not just hypothetical; it has occurred recently. Consider these examples:

1. A state health department investigated an outbreak of syphilis in a reservation. After local newspapers publicized it, Tribal children were called derogatory names at school and Indians were prohibited from using rest rooms in some nearby gasoline stations.[42]
2. Researchers announced the results of a study on alcoholism in an identified western Native community at their news conference held in the eastern United States. The publicity had immediate adverse effects, both in the community and on the community's credit-worthiness as it tried to raise funds in Wall Street.[43]
3. The Navajo Nation asked researchers of the 1993 epidemic of Hantavirus Pulmonary Syndrome (HPS) not to name any Navajo locales in their publications. Two of the first research articles listed the names of Navajo sites where HPS cases or animals infected with hantavirus had been found.[44] Many Navajo people saw this as an invasion of privacy, all the more distressing because they had already experienced both national TV, newspapers, and magazines showing their funerals and public discrimination (e.g., a summer basketball

camp for high school athletes at a nearby large university "disinvited" the contingent of Navajo teenage athletes who had already been invited).

NASA astronauts have a third set of values and concerns, *to facilitate feasibility of the research and increase its acceptability* to the astronauts, to ensure its success. Some space missions have research as their primary objective;[45] other missions have research projects as only add-on secondary activities. Research with astronauts in space has several special aspects: (1) astronauts have more knowledge than most researchers about what research is feasible in space; (2) the research must be acceptable to the astronauts before the flight, because they must both be trained as the "operator" of the experiment and learn the requirements as a research subject; and (3) even in a research mission, they can cancel or change the research when the situation changes regarding safety, other essential features, or personal concerns or consent. The astronauts thus have become proactive partners in the research; for instance, when the primary objective of a space mission is not research, astronauts limit the protocols to practical research about their well-being (e.g., the formation of kidney stones) and exclude basic science research (e.g., collecting urine to monitor electrolyte balance). The astronauts both volunteer as subjects and function as research facilitators to enable the research to succeed both scientifically and practically.[46] (Native communities also have knowledge not possessed by most researchers that may be essential to the success of the research in that community.)

The sets of values and concerns of these three participating communities make, to many people, a convincing *prima facie* claim of importance: their values and concerns are *right*. Is the claim of importance also supported by the *consequences* of community participation?

A comprehensive analysis of the impact of AIDS activists is that they benefited both the conduct of research and their community, although not without some harms along the way.[47] It is too soon for such an analysis of breast cancer activists such as the National Breast Cancer Coalition,[48] but their public accomplishments are impressive. Since starting in 1991, the Coalition has helped obtain more funding and support for breast cancer research; increased the interest to participate in research by potential volunteer participants; actively recruited volunteer participants in research and helped retain them in research; helped organize specimen banks for genetic research into cancer, helped them to be acceptable to laypeople who are potential donors, and helped recruit donors; and improved the design of protocols, especially practical day-to-day aspects, so that the interface of researcher with volunteer participant is more user-friendly, potentially resulting in improved rates of both recruitment and retention in the research.

A comprehensive analysis of participation in research by Native communities has not been done. But communities that changed their set of values and concerns when circumstances changed offer partial evidence. For example, the Maori distrusted and wanted to restrict research — which was under the control of researchers of the majority society. After two Maori Research Centers that included Maori as directors were established at major universities, the Maori helped expand research by the centers to maximize its benefits and facilitated and increased its acceptability.[49] Another example is a seven-year-long participatory research project of community-based cancer prevention in Hawaii; it transformed the attitudes toward research of the 18,000 Native Hawaiians in the community from "feeling exploited or 'used as guinea pigs'" by researchers to enthusiastic participants and even co-investigators.[50] My own experience in IHS is similar. For more than two decades, AI/AN Tribes have reviewed and approved (or disapproved) research, with good results for both the researchers and Tribes.

On both (rights-based) deontological and (preliminary) consequentialist grounds, then, communities have ethical standing to have an active voice in research, in order to (1) maximize possible benefits of research to individuals and communities; (2) minimize possible risks and harms to individuals and communities; and (3) facilitate, improve the quality of, and increase the acceptability of desirable research. What are the desirable attributes of that voice, of community participation?

Community Participation in Research

Although the specific content of unique values and concerns varies among communities, some of the values and concerns that differ from researchers and professionals have already been discussed and include the following:

the physical and cultural survival of the community;
the qualities of life valued in the community;
the process of decisionmaking used by the community;
the problem of external stigmatization;
the possibility of self-stigmatization;
ethics and bioethical concerns;
the understanding of risk;
values imputed to some types of tissue specimens;
religious beliefs and practices;

the medical and social impact of certain methods of research;

the medical and social impact of the future research agenda;

the minimization of harms to the community;

distrust of researchers based on earlier experiences; and

the desire to facilitate more realistic, valuable, and acceptable research.

Bioethicists have addressed the ethics of community participation in research to only a limited extent. Emanuel discusses communal rights as being "for the purpose of realizing certain elements of a particular conception of the good life."[51] Although he does not describe community participation, his description of the desirable physician-patient relationship could be analogized to the researcher-community relationship: "The physician-patient relationship is a deliberative interaction in which the physician and patient articulate, as friends, worthy ideals to be realized through medical care. . . . [Medical] services should ensure the continuation of the common life as well as the possibility for individuals to realize the capacities of self-development unique to political participation."[52]

Annette Baer's discussion about families could also be analogized to communities.[53] She claims that individualistic contractarianism — the basis of most modern Euroamerican ethics — presupposes that the contractors have approximately equal power and reasonably complete understanding about the subject of the contract. When people in a relationship have unequal power and knowledge, however, the principles of consent and justice may not be sufficient, and may even be irrelevant, at least for families. She asserts that the major ethical task is to define and then to achieve the desired relationship between unequal players, defining each player's responsibilities within that context.[54] The relevance of Baer's work is that power and knowledge are also not equally shared in health care and biomedical research.

In biomedical ethics, and especially in research ethics, explicit, truly informed consent by the individual patient or research subject — the person with less knowledge and power — is one means to bridge the power and knowledge disparity.[55] Another way of bridging the difference is for researchers to affirm the importance of community participation in shaping the research study before the research is done. To do this, researchers need to work to establish a *desirable relationship with the people in the community* who may participate in the research.

FOUR ATTRIBUTES OF DESIRABLE RESEARCHER-COMMUNITY RELATIONSHIPS

The Council for International Organizations of Medical Sciences (CIOMS),[56] the Human Genome Diversity Project (HGDP),[57] the Canadian

Code, and researchers and community people[58] have all stated that *research ethics applies to communities* and not just to individuals. Desirable researcher-community relationships would embody appropriate ethical principles. One major principle of research ethics is respect for research subjects, with its corollary being the consent of the persons participating in research studies. The American regulations for research and the Canadian *Code* provide descriptions of the content of consent for research volunteers.[59] Research ethics also includes the principles of beneficence and nonmaleficence and of justice.[60] The HGDP[61] and Canadian *Code*[62] describe how researchers should and could *apply those principles to communities.*

The desirable relationship would recognize not just "scientific risk" but also the *view of "risk"* by Native and other communities, which includes the present and future well-being of their community. For example, the Canadian *Code* takes a "subject-centered" perspective[63] and notes "subject-centered" risks: "research may affect a person's or a group's identity and self-esteem" (pp. 1–3). "What is there to be afraid of when one becomes a 'research subject'? Many things. In general, one is afraid . . . of being humiliated for one's personal history; or of having one's cultural or group identity mocked" (pp. 1– 4).

A third attribute concerns *community permission.* The *Code*'s section "Research with Collectives" states that: "the researcher must seek to protect the members of the collectivity, and the collectivity itself, from harm" (p. 13-2); and "when undertaking research with a family, community or other collectivity, the researcher may not begin until permission has been obtained from the appropriate authorities for that collectivity" (p. 13-3).

The fourth attribute is to *engender trust and confidence.* Both CIOMS[64] and HGDP[65] recognize that when communities are distrustful due to historical lack of power (i.e., lack of self-determination) exercising more self-determination will help engender trust. In particular, both the Canadian *Code* and HGDP state that communities should *actively participate in planning, reviewing, and conducting research.*[66] Bioethicists agreed: "Prior and ongoing community consultation should be an integral part of the planning and design of clinical trials of nonvalidated therapies" in AIDS research.[67] Experienced researchers of Native health care proposed similar views: "Researchers and biomedical practitioners increasingly will work as consultants in partnerships with Aboriginal communities or through a co-managed research and health care delivery process aimed at developing community-based health policy that meets local needs and is environmentally sound, sustainable, and culturally appropriate."[68] An additional action that will help engender trust is to have the communities *review and approve the research publications.*[69] (This is not relevant to all communities; disease advocacy groups seldom preview research articles.)

SOME LIMITATIONS OF COMMUNITY PARTICIPATION

While positive attributes of community participation have been well described, possible limitations of community participation have not been as widely discussed.[70] One general limitation is that active participation by communities is valuable, but is not an automatic or universal panacea. Community participation, like all human activities, can be more or less beneficial, depending on the *content* of that participation.[71] That content, in turn, relies on both careful talking and careful listening — by both the researchers and the communities.

Some researchers may oppose community participation in their own research, citing scientific limitations such as the science being "too technical" or the involvement of laypersons as representing a threat to "academic freedom"; many such claims seem both scientifically and ethically dubious. However, one alleged problem is valid, and it pertains to data safety and monitoring boards (DSMBs) that oversee major randomized controlled trials (RCTs). Having community people on a DSMB may be quite beneficial for some research; in a case I am familiar with, the community representatives helped maintain the trust of the community not only by their presence but also by suggestions they made for managing an important Adverse Event Report. But for the DSMB to work, all members must maintain confidentiality about early findings of the RCT (e.g., possible but not statistically significant trends). Some potential community members may find that responsibility impossible to meet, especially if their friends, relatives, or they themselves have the same life-threatening condition being studied by the RCT.[72] (Note that potential physician DSMB members will have the same problem if they have patients with the same life-threatening condition being studied.)

VIEWS OF THE IHS RESEARCH PROGRAM

The IHS research program developed its set of desirable attributes of research with communities without reading the documents cited in this essay, and even before most of these documents were published. Interestingly, the approach independently advocated by IHS was similar to those advocated by CIOMS; Levine, Dubler, and Levine; Waldram, Herring, and Young; the HGDP; and the Canadian *Code*.

For instance, the IHS research program explicitly applied the three principles of respect, beneficence/nonmaleficence, and justice to Tribal communities: [73]

> *Respect*: the researcher must give Tribes full information and obtain their informed consent, and not identify them in results without their explicit consent. Tribes can refuse to participate or withdraw without pressure. When reviewing such research, IRBs should include Tribal members with expertise about community concerns.
>
> *Beneficence/Nonmaleficence*: the researcher must maximize benefits to Tribal communities by reporting research results to them and minimize community risks by protecting their privacy to prevent stigmatization. The researcher and Tribe should plan the research together.
>
> *Justice*: the researcher should not try to enroll Tribes in risky research with little benefit to their members or themselves, but should offer to include them in research studies that give them a fair chance of participating in research that will be potentially beneficial to them.

The IHS also independently developed recommendations about the degree and type of community participation. Table 1 gives the IHS research program's description of the spectrum of activity by communities in which research takes place, starting with the most passive and going to the most active; the program's recommendations have been that all research be at least at level 2, but preferably level 5 or 6.

The similarity of recommendations for research with communities, independently developed by the IHS research program and by many other experienced authorities, suggests that the ethical position is valid. In all recommendations, the *partnership* of researcher and community is critical for the desirable relationship between researchers and communities.

Conclusion

The values underlying this essay are that (1) research can be a valued activity, (2) appropriate research (including appropriate research on tissue specimens) should be nurtured, and (3) research is dependent upon the goodwill of the society that funds it and the communities and volunteer participants with and in whom it takes place.

Research is not an activity by autonomous researchers on passive "subjects"; if it were, researchers would not be concerned about recruitment and retention. Rather, research is an activity interdependent with community-

TABLE 1. *Relationship of Activity and Responsibility by the Group and Researchers*

Six conceptual levels of the researcher-community relationship are arranged along a continuum, from the researcher *using* a group and its people that are *passive*, to full *partnership* involving the group and the researcher, to the group itself *initiating* part of the research.

1. "Bleed and run,"[1] "safari," or "helicopter" research: the researchers drop into the group, do the research or obtain the specimens, and then leave with the tissues and data for good. The group and its members are passive.
2. The researcher comes back to report the research results to the group, which still remains relatively passive when it receives the report.[2]
3. The group negotiates with the researchers so that they arrange for more services as a *quid pro quo* for doing the research in or with the group.
4. The researchers increase the competence and capacity of the group or of some of its members (i.e., improve the capabilities of the group to deliver services or do research). The group exercises that expanded competence and capacity.
5. The group and researchers are partners in the design, execution, analysis, and reporting of the research. (The group's resources and ideas often make the research succeed.) The group and its members are quite active and pro-active.
6. The group determines its research priorities and initiates the research. It calls in researchers as needed to be partners/consultants in the design, execution, analysis, and reporting of the research. The research is the group's.

Source: Modified and adapted from William L. Freeman, "Making Research Consent Forms Informative and Understandable," *Cambridge Quarterly of Healthcare Ethics* 3 (1994): 510–521.

[1] North American Regional Committee, HGDP, "Proposed Model Ethical Protocol," p. 1438.
[2] Effective reporting of research results about conditions important to the community quickly moves the community to an active role, stage 5 or 6; Louis Tekaronhiake Montour and Ann Celia Macaulay, "Diabetes Mellitus and Atherosclerosis: Returning Research Results to the Mohawk Community," *CMAJ* 139 (August 1988): 201–202.

partners and individual volunteer-participants. A partnership of researchers with active communities and volunteer participants can

> help promote the mutual achievement of each other's goals;
> help minimize harms and maximize benefits to volunteer participants,
>   both individual people and communities;

help increase the scientific validity of the research;

help increase the acceptability and practical feasibility of the research;

help educate *communities* about the value to them of appropriate research and what "appropriate" means;

help educate *researchers* about the value to them of appropriate community participation and what "appropriate" means; and

nurture both the research enterprise and the society and communities in which it takes place.

This essay gives a bioethical rationale for community participation and describes some characteristics of that participation. Some concerns and values of many ethnic, lay, or activated advocacy communities are so distinct from those of researchers and health professionals that those communities must themselves represent their concerns and values and not rely on representation by others. One community's stance may be positive, to expand and focus the benefits of research; another community's stance may be negative, to protect itself from harm, especially stigmatization and self-stigmatization; yet another's stance may be mutually facilitative, to ensure the acceptability and practical feasibility of the research methods and thus the scientific validity of the research. In practice, most community participation has all three elements.

Many individuals and organizations (both researchers and laypeople, from both within and outside Native, minority, and other communities) have recognized that communities have a legitimate major active role in proposing, planning, approving, conducting, and publishing and disseminating research. The similarity of the independently developed recommendations (by the IHS research program, CIOMS, Levine et al., Waldram et al., the HGDP, the Canadian Tri-Council Working Group, and many others) supports the claim of appropriateness of community participation in research. The draft *IHS Guidelines* simply extend to the research use of tissue specimens the basic IHS policy that requires approval by the Tribal governments of all research and that promotes partnerships of Tribes and researchers.

Acknowledgments

This essay does not necessarily represent the views of the Indian Health Service. Work on the essay was supported by the Obermann Center for Advanced Studies, University of Iowa. Most work was done while I was a fellow at its Faculty Research Seminar on Ethical and Legal Implications of Stored Human Tissue Samples, June 10–21, 1996. I thank Professor Emeritus Dr. C. Esco Obermann, who funded the Obermann Center and before that helped develop the GI Bill during and after World War II. I have received direct benefit from both his efforts.

Notes

1. Although "AI/AN" is used throughout, the guidelines and this essay may be appropriate for Native Hawaiian, Canadian First Nations, and Inuit, Maori, and other Native peoples.

2. The Snyder Act of November 2, 1921, authorized recurring expenditure of funds "for the benefit, care, and assistance of the Indians throughout the United States" (Ch. 115, 42 Stat. 208 [codified as amended at 25 U.S.C. §13]).

3. For more information about the IHS, its programs, and the health status of AI/AN people it serves, see *Trends in Indian Health — 1996* and *Regional Differences in Indian Health — 1996*, both by the Division of Program Statistics, Office of Planning, Evaluation, and Legislation, Indian Health Service, DHHS, 1997 (and published yearly).

4. National Commission for the Protection of Human Subjects of Biomedical and Behavioral Research, *The Belmont Report: Ethical Principles and Guidelines for the Protection of Human Subjects of Research* (Washington, D.C.: Department of Health and Human Services, 1979).

5. Charles F. Wilkinson, *American Indians, Time, and the Law* (New Haven, Conn.: Yale University Press, 1987).

6. "The [Supreme] Court recognized that tribal power can extend to activities of [non-Indians] . . . if there is a tribal interest sufficient to justify tribal regulation. . . . Tribal jurisdiction within reservations can also be based on transactions between non-Indians or tribes or on non-Indian activities that directly affect Indians or their property" (Rennard Strickland, Charles F. Wilkinson, et al., eds., *Felix S. Cohen's Handbook of Federal Indian Law: 1982 Edition* [Charlottesville, Va: Michie, 1982], pp. 256–257).

7. IHS, "Chapter 7 — Research Activities," in *Indian Health Manual* (Rockville Md., 1987). Chapter 7 is currently undergoing updating; the basic policy will remain, however. The IHS policy of requiring approval by the Tribal government began at least twelve years before the 1987 version of chapter 7. See the "Subjects" subsection in the "Materials and Methods" section of John L. Coulehan, Susan Eberhard, Louis Kapner, et al., "Vitamin C and Acute Illness in Navajo School Children," *New England Journal of Medicine* 295 (October 28, 1976): 973–977.

8. The requirement about Tribal review publications is not intended to be a restriction on academic freedom, and to my knowledge has never been used for that purpose. Tribal review of publications is discussed in a position paper obtainable from me.

9. American Indian Law Center, Inc., *Model Tribal Research Code*, 2nd ed. (Albuquerque, N.M.: American Indian Law Center, Inc., 1994).

10. C. Matthew Snipp, *American Indians: The First of This Land, a Census Mono-graph Series for the National Committee for Research on the 1980 Census* (New York: Russell Sage Foundation, 1989), the first and third chapters.

11. For a brief description of the HGDP, and for its approach to research with Native communities, see North American Regional Committee, Human Genome Diversity Project (HGDP), "Proposed Model Ethical Protocol for Collecting DNA Samples," *Houston Law Review* 33 (Winter 1997): 1433–1473. The goals of the HGDP are quite controversial among some Native or indigenous peoples. See Patricia Kahn, "Genetic Diversity Project Tries Again," *Science* 266 (November 4, 1994): 720–722; "Genome Diversity Alarms," *Nature* 377 (October 4, 1995): 372; Declan Butler, "Genetic Diversity Proposal Fails to Impress International Ethics Panel," *Nature* 377 (October 5, 1995): 373; Tim Beardsley, "Vital Data: Trends in Human Genetics," *Scientific American* 274 (March 1996): 100–105; and especially the issue of *Cultural Survival Quarterly* 20 (Summer 1996) which has detailed articles presenting all sides. However, I am not aware of major disagreement with those parts of the "Proposed Model Ethical Protocol" discussed in this essay.

12. Richard A. Grounds, "The Yuchi Community and the Human Genome Diversity Project: Historic and Contemporary Ironies," *Cultural Survival Quarterly* 20 (Summer, 1996): 64–68.

13. Douglas Cole, *Captured Heritage: The Scramble for Northwest Coast Artifacts* (Norman: University of Oklahoma Press, 1995), p. 287.

14. Douglas E. Foley, *The Heartland Chronicles* (Philadelphia: University of Pennsylvania Press, 1995), p. 120.

15. Tom L. Beauchamp and James F. Childress, *Principles of Biomedical Ethics*, 4th ed. (New York: Oxford University Press, 1994). In public health, the definition of community is "[a] group of individuals organized into a unit, or manifesting some unifying trait or common interest; loosely, the locality or catchment area population for which a service is provided, or more broadly, the state, nation, or body politic" (John M. Last, *A Dictionary of Epidemiology*, 3rd ed. [New York: Oxford University Press, 1995], p. 33).

16. The Tri-council Working Group of the Medical Research Council, Natural Sciences and Engineering Research Council of Canada, and Social Sciences and Humanities Research Council wrote the *Code of Conduct for Research Involving Humans*, hereafter cited as *Code*. All quotations are from the May 28, 1997, final draft, found at www.ethics.ucs.ubc.ca/code/sec-01.html.

17. Ezekiel J. Emanuel, *The Ends of Human Life: Medical Ethics in a Liberal Polity* (Cambridge, Mass.: Harvard University Press, 1991), p. 167.

18. The wording of this definition was first suggested to me by Roger Gollub, M.D., M.P.H., epidemiologist for the Albuquerque Area, IHS.

19. Ian Robinson, "Personal Narratives, Social Careers and Medical Courses: Analyzing Life Trajectories in Autobiographies of People with Multiple Sclerosis," *Social Science of Medicine* 30 (1990): 1173–1186.

20. Robinson, "Personal Narratives," p. 1180 (emphasis added).

21. That may help explain why many people with deafness whose hearing could be physically improved by an operation to implant cochlear-assist devices refused the operation; the improvement in hearing would be an experience that they could

not share and that might isolate them from their own community, friends, and lovers.

22. Uta Gerhardt, "Patient Careers in End-stage Renal Failure," *Social Science and Medicine* 30 (1990): 1211–1224 (p. 1212).

23. Melanie F. Myers, Barbara A. Bernhardt, Ellen S. Tambor, and Neil A. Holtzman, "Involving Consumers in the Development of an Educational Program for Cystic Fibrosis Carrier Screening," *American Journal of Human Genetics* 54 (April 1994): 719–726.

24. Prospect Associates, *National Action Plan on Breast Cancer, Model Consent Form for Biological Tissue Bank Focus Group Report* (Rockville, Md.: Prospect Associates, 1997).

25. Graham Scambler and Anthony Hopkins, "Generating a Model of Epileptic Stigma: The Role of Qualitative Analysis," *Social Science and Medicine* 30 (1990): 1187–1194.

26. Leslie J. Blackhall, Sheila T. Murphy, Gelya Frank, Vicki Michel, and Stanley Azen, "Ethnicity and Attitudes toward Patient Autonomy," *JAMA* 274 (September 13, 1995): 820–825.

27. Joseph A. Carrese and Lorna A. Rhodes, "Western Bioethics of the Navajo Reservation: Benefit or Harm?" *JAMA* 274 (September 13, 1995): 826–829. Letters to the editor and the response by the authors presented ways to accomplish the basic intent of the PSDA — to help the providers understand the values of the patient — without violating Navajo values; see *JAMA* 275 (January 10, 1996): 107–110.

28. Paul Slovic, "Perception of Risk," *Science* 236 (April 17, 1987): 280–285.

29. Anna C. Mastroianni, Ruth Faden, and Daniel Federman, eds., Committee on the Ethical and Legal Issues Relating to the Inclusion of Women in Clinical Studies, Division of Health Science Policy, Institutes of Medicine, *Women and Health Research: Ethical and Legal Issues of Including Women in Clinical Studies* (Washington, D.C.: National Academy Press, 1994), p. 192.

30. Robert Veatch, reported in a public presentation.

31. People in some Tribes have traditional beliefs that the placenta, umbilical cord, and umbilical cord blood are sacred and must be handled in a special manner. IHS hospitals give such tissues back to the patient or family upon request.

32. Aroha Te Pareake Mead, "Genealogy, Sacredness, and the Commodities Market," *Cultural Survival Quarterly* 20 (Summer, 1996): 46–51.

33. The Office of Indian Affairs, Circular No. 1665, April 26, 1921, reads in part: "The sun dance, and all other similar dances and so-called religious ceremonies are considered 'Indian Offences' under existing regulations, and corrective penalties are provided," as quoted in *Felix S. Cohen's Handbook of Federal Indian Law* (reprint of 1942 edition; Albuquerque: University of New Mexico Press, 1971), pp. 175–176. That circular was supplemented in 1923 and was not rescinded until the Office of Indian Affairs issued Circular No. 2970 on January 3, 1934. The history in Canada is similar. For instance, the Canadian government outlawed the community religious ceremonial called potlatch and similar gatherings in the Northwest Coast in 1885. See Douglas Cole, *An Iron Hand upon the People: The Law against the Potlatch on the Northwest Coast* (Seattle: University of Washington Press, 1990).

34. As an example of conflict, the goals of the HGDP are to "lead to advances

in understanding the biological development and the history of our species and, ultimately, in understanding and treating many diseases with genetic components" (North American Regional Committee, HGDP, "Proposed Model Ethical Protocol," p. 1433). Understanding the development and history of our species may seem benign. But when a project was proposed to obtain blood samples from several AI/AN groups in one region to do genetic tests to define the peopling of the Americas (presumably over the Bering Strait more than thirty centuries ago), the Tribal elders refused; their concern apparently was about that "benign" goal. Non-Natives might better understand the opposition of the elders by imagining analogous research in the majority society. The elders and the Native groups already know how they came to be — a religious belief about their origins that has nothing to do with migration over the Bering Strait. Imagine that the research was to do genetic tests on blood from Euroamericans to prove that there was no King David. If there was no King David, there were no descendants of King David, no "root of Jesse," and thus no religious pedigree to Jesus of Nazareth. Would not there be similar opposition in our majority science-respecting society to such "benign" research?

35. "One of the new roles of the sacred practitioners in Native American communities today is to figure out how to maintain [their sources] of sacred knowledge in the midst of modern life" (Peggy V. Beck, Anna Lee Walters, and Nia Francisco, *The Sacred: Ways of Knowledge, Sources of Life* [Tsaile, Ariz.: Navajo Community College Press, 1990], p. 137).

36. "[Researchers] may have difficulty identifying all the culturally relevant authorities. Certainly, recognized Native American tribal governments will always be at least one appropriate authority. But many cultures also have non-governmental authorities of importance. These may be elders, religious leaders, traditional leading families or clans, or other people recognized within the culture as having authority. . . . Even for populations with formal governments, the 'informal authorities' will often be of such cultural significance that their permission should also be obtained" (North American Regional Committee, HGDP, "Proposed Model Ethical Protocol," p. 1446).

37. For the ethics underlying this activism, see Carol Levine, Nancy Neveloff Dubler, and Robert J. Levine, "Building a New Consensus: Ethical Principles and Policies for Clinical Research on HIV/AIDS," *IRB: A Review of Human Subjects* 13 (January–April [1–2], 1991): p. 1–17. For a brief history, see Jeffrey Levi, "Unproven AIDS Therapies: The Food and Drugs Administration and ddI," in Kathi E. Hanna, ed., Division of Health Sciences Policy, Committee to Study Biomedical Decision Making, Institute of Medicine, *Biomedical Politics* (Washington, D.C.: National Academy Press, 1991), pp. 9–37. See also Steven Epstein, *Impure Science: AIDS, Activism, and the Politics of Science* (Berkeley: University of California Press, 1996).

38. Jane Erikson, "Breast Cancer Activists Seek Voice in Research Decisions," *Science* 269 (September 15, 1995): 1508–1509.

39. Grounds, "The Yuchi Community," pp. 64–68.

40. See Annette Dula, "African American Suspicion of the Healthcare System Is Justified: What Do We Do about It?" *Cambridge Quarterly of Healthcare Ethics* 3 (1994): 347–357; Annette Dula and Sara Goering, eds., *It Just Ain't Fair: The Ethics of Health Care for African Americans* (Westport, Conn.: Praeger, 1994).

41. Self-stigmatization has been especially observed in genetic testing. Some people who screen positive for being a carrier of a recessive gene (e.g., sickle cell trait) markedly change their self-image and self-worth even though they have no disease.

42. A. Russell Gerber, Leland C. King, Gerald J. Dunleavy, and Lloyd F. Novick, "An Outbreak of Syphilis on an Indian Reservation: Descriptive Epidemiology and Disease-control Measures," *American Journal of Public Health* 79 (January, 1989): 83–85.

43. The events and possible lessons are discussed in *American Indian and Alaska Native Mental Health Research* 2 (Spring 1989).

44. Stuart T. Nichol, Christina F. Spiropoulou, Sergey Morzunov, et al., "Genetic Identification of a Hantavirus Associated with an Outbreak of Acute Respiratory Illness," *Science* 262 (November 5, 1993): 914–917; and James E. Childs, Thomas G. Ksiazek, Christina F. Spiropoulou, et al., "Serologic and Genetic Identification of Peromyscus Maniculatus as the Primary Rodent Reservoir for a New Hantavirus in the Southwestern United States," *Journal of Infectious Diseases* 169 (June 1994): 1271–1280.

45. Some research used significantly invasive procedures, such as recording central venous pressure by an indwelling catheter through a vein in the arm to near the heart that was inserted the night before launch and kept in place to the end of the first flight day: Jay C. Buckley Jr., F. Andrew Gaffney, Lynda A. Lane, Benjamin D. Levine, et al., "Central Venous Pressure in Space," *Journal of Applied Physiology* 81 (July 1996): 19–25. Such risky research is important for safer space flight: Mary Ann Bassett Frey, "Space Research Activities during Missions of the Past," *Medicine and Science in Sports and Exercise* 28 (Suppl.) (October 1966): S3–S9.

46. This aspect of NASA research is discussed by the National Bioethics Advisory Committee's report about the protection of human subjects of research conducted by the federal government departments and agencies (in preparation).

47. Epstein, *Impure Science: AIDS, Activism, and the Politics of Science*.

48. Erickson, "Breast Cancer Activists." More information about the National Breast Cancer Coalition can be obtained from the Internet at www.natlbcc.org; or P.O. Box 66373, Washington, D.C. 20035, telephone (202) 296-7477.

49. Personal communication, Arohia Durie, Ph.D., and Mason Durie, M.D. Maori values and concerns are similar to those of AI/AN Tribes. See Mason Durie, *Whaiora: Maori Health Development* (Oxford, England: Oxford University Press, 1994).

50. Doris Segal Matsunaga, Rachelle Enos, Carolyn C. Gotay, Richard O. Banner, Ho'oipo DeCambra, et al., "Participatory Research in a Native Hawaiian Community: The Wai'anae Cancer Research Project," *Cancer* 78 (Suppl.) (October 1, 1996): 1582–1586.

51. Emanuel, *The Ends of Human Life*, p. 170.

52. Emanuel, *The Ends of Human Life*, p. 249. See also Ezekiel J. Emanuel and Linda L. Emanuel, "Four Models of the Physician-Patient Relationship," *JAMA* 267 (April 22–29, 1992): 2221–2226.

53. Annette C. Baer, *Moral Prejudices: Essays on Ethics* (Cambridge, Mass.: Harvard University Press, 1994).

54. "[In] medical ethics . . . the discussion used to be conducted in terms of pa-

tients' rights, of informed consent, and so on, but now tends to get conducted in an enlarged moral vocabulary, which draws on what [Carol] Gilligan [author of *In a Different Voice*] calls the ethics of *care* as well as that of *justice*" (Baer, *Moral Prejudices*, p. 19).

55. Alexander Capron lists several functions of informed consent: minimize harm; promote autonomy and self-determination; improve research, by fostering greater thoughtfulness by researchers and increasing accuracy of data collected by volunteers; regularize relationships, from a researcher's exclusive power over research subject to a relationship that includes elements of equality; and protect privacy. See A. M. Capron, "Protecting of Research Subjects: Do Special Rules Apply in Epidemiology?" *Law, Medicine and Health Care* 19 (Fall–Winter 1991): 184–190. Capron also notes that informed consent by the individual helps protect the person from physical, mental, or emotional *harm*, but not from *moral wrongs*.

56. CIOMS, "International Guidelines for Ethical Review of Epidemiological Studies," *Law, Medicine and Health Care* 19 (Fall–Winter 1991): 247–258; see p. 254 ("Preventing harm to groups") and p. 256 ("Representation of the community").

57. North American Regional Committee, HGDP, "An Overview of the Ethical Issues and the Collecting Process," in "Proposed Model Ethical Protocol," pp. 1436–1438.

58. "International Workshop on Ethical Issues in Health Research among Circumpolar Indigenous Populations," June 2–3, 1995, Inuvik, Northwest Territories, Canada; the conference was co-sponsored and attended by the Canadian Society for Circumpolar Health, the International Union for Circumpolar Health, the American Society for Circumpolar Health, the Nordic Council for Arctic Medical Research, the Nordic Society for Arctic Medicine, and the Danish/Greenland Society for Circumpolar Health. See also the "Tenth International Circumpolar Conference on Health," May 19–23, 1996, Anchorage, Alaska. There have been many other meetings with similar statements.

59. For the United States, the content is listed in the 45 CFR §46.116. For Canada, the content is listed in Tri-council Working Group, *Code of Conduct for Research Involving Humans*, section 5, p. 5-1. The two lists are almost identical.

60. *The Belmont Report*, Tri-council Working Group, *Code of Conduct*, pp. 2-1 to 2-2.

61. North American Regional Committee, HGDP, "Proposed Model Ethical Protocol," pp. 1454–1456. The "Protocol" discusses several ethical principles, including respect for the community's culture, informed consent by both individuals and communities, maximizing benefits and minimizing risks to communities, and justice (under the title "appropriateness").

62. The Tri-council Working Group's section 13 on collectivities discusses those principles. *Respect*: "Treat the host family, community or collectivity with respect and dignity" (p. 13-1). *Consent*: "Researchers have the responsibility to explain the nature and goals of the research in terms that make clear the benefits and harms to the collectivity. . . . so that the collectivity's . . . decision to participate in the research constitutes an informed decision" (p. 13-3). *Beneficence*: "In proposing research so that it will best meet the needs of a collectivity, the researcher should ensure that the collectivity has the opportunity to participate in the design of the project" (p. 13-4). *Non-*

maleficence: "The researcher must seek to protect the members of the collectivity, and the collectivity itself, from harm" (p. 13-1).

63. "It is essential when ethically assessing the participation of human subjects in given research projects *to take a subject-centered perspective, in contrast to a researcher or even a society-centered perspective.* . . . It was the practical failure . . . to adopt and act upon a subject-centered perspective that permeated the abuses of human research subjects" (Tri-council Working Group, *Code of Conduct*, p. 2-7 [emphasis in original]).

64. "The importance of group identity, and of treating social communities with dignity and respect, is increasingly recognized. Human beings gain security, happiness, and enjoyment by forming [social] networks. . . . Respect and beneficence for populations requires [*sic*] researchers to observe choices made by local communities, and to avoid any activity which stigmatizes, demeans, harms, or disintegrates human populations, intentionally or unintentionally" (Larry Gostin, "Ethical Principles for the Conduct of Human Subject Research: Population-Based Research and Ethics," *Law, Medicine and Health Care* 19 [Fall–Winter 1991]: 191–201). Harms or wrongs to both individual and populations include lack of self-determination or autonomy.

65. For instance, HGDP's North American Regional Committee opposes obtaining a sample from even truly informed volunteers from a subject group that does not itself give consent: "The HGDP intends to study populations, not individuals [. . . that often] are politically or economically marginal in their countries. They have faced discrimination, oppression, and even genocide. . . . Such methods [i.e., not requiring each group's consent] would themselves be another form of attack on the autonomy of the population" (North American Regional Committee, HGDP, p. 1443).

66. For the Tri-council Working Group, see "beneficence" in note 62 above. The HGDP states: "Ideally, researchers . . . should be closely connected with the populations that provide those samples, connected not as 'scientist' and 'subject', but as partners" (p. 1468); "The community's participation may be particularly helpful in planning at least two aspects of the research: its goals and its methods" (p. 1469).

67. Levine, Dubler, and Levine, "Building a New Consensus."

68. James B. Waldram, D. Ann Herring, and T. Kue Young, *Aboriginal Health in Canada: Historical, Cultural, and Epidemiological Perspectives* (Toronto: University of Toronto Press, 1995), pp. 270–271.

69. "The researcher needs to provide the collectivity with an opportunity to react and respond to the findings before the completion of the final report, in the final report and in all relevant publications that arise from the research" (Tri-council Working Group, *Code of Conduct*, article 13.12).

70. Steven Epstein discusses both the benefits and limitations of active community participation in AIDS in *Impure Science*.

71. Thomas H. Murray, "Individualism and Community: The Contested Terrain of Autonomy — Communities Need More Than Autonomy," *Hastings Center Report* 24 (1994): 32–33.

72. LeRoy Walters (personal communication) pointed out this issue to me. See also David L. DeMets, Thomas R. Fleming, Richard J. Whitley, James F. Childress, et al., "The Data and Safety Monitoring Board and Acquired Immune Deficiency Syndrome (AIDS) Clinical Trials," *Control Clinical Trials* 16 (December 1995): 408–421.

73. William L. Freeman, "Making Research Consent Forms Informative and Understandable: The Experience of the Indian Health Service," *Cambridge Quarterly of Healthcare Ethics* 3 (1994): 510–521.

IHS Guidelines for the Collection and Use of Research Specimens [August 3, 1997, Draft]

SUMMARY

Research with blood or tissue specimens is both valuable and problematic for many American Indian and Alaska Native [AI/AN] communities. Research and other entities that use, store, or distribute specimens from or with IHS involvement must comply with these Guidelines.

- Researchers who save specimens must inform each volunteer participant in the original consent process about the saved specimens, and the nature of future tests and uses. Blanket consents for future testing of specimens are not fully informed consents.
- To protect people and communities from harms of research, each proposed future use of saved specimens must first be approved by Tribes and Institutional Review Boards (IRBs). Such approval also maintains people's trust in care and research.
- Each proposed use must be within the limits and conditions of the original consent. Those conditions apply to each stored specimen whether or not the person from whom it was obtained has died or the specimen [has been] made anonymous.
- There are particular concerns with genetic or DNA testing, storing or testing tissues with special cultural meaning or value (e.g., placenta, umbilical cord blood), and controversial uses (e.g., patenting human specimens or material derived from them).
- The specimens must be stored with security, and handled and disposed of with respect.

DETAILS

I. Objectives

The objectives of these IHS Guidelines for specimens are simultaneously to:

- support fully informed Tribal and IRB review and approval of research that will save specimens for future research, or that will use saved specimens;
- support fully informed consent by each potential volunteer participant of the research that obtains specimens to be saved;

- support future use of specimens that is based both on the merits and soundness of the science, and by the concerns and health priorities of the Tribe(s) involved; and
- support the proper obtaining, retention, and use of saved specimens that observe the limits and intent of the informed consent by the people from whom the specimens were obtained, and of the approval by the IRB(s) and Tribal government(s).

II. The IHS Guidelines

(1) All researchers who obtain or use, and all entities that store specimens obtained with IHS involvement must follow these Guidelines. The IHS will distribute these Guidelines, inform researchers, tissue banks, and reviewers of them, and distribute a set of sample consent forms for obtaining specimens to be saved.

(2) If blood or tissue will be obtained directly from participants under a research protocol, both the protocol and its consent form must specify both the tests to be done under the protocol, and if any specimens will be saved.

(3) If any specimens will be saved, both the protocol and consent form must state the nature of future "secondary uses," and the process to seek approval of the future uses. If the following may be done in the future, the protocol and consent must mention:
- DNA tests, or other genetic tests, or growth of perpetual cell lines;
- blood or tissues from the placenta or umbilical cord, other tissues with strong social meaning or value, or other aspects about which the AI/AN community involved may be concerned. (In many AI/AN communities, such aspects include: patenting specimens or derivatives; length of time that specimens will be saved; physical security of the specimens and who has access to them; and how the specimens — that are part of a person's body — will be disposed.)

(4) The researchers of the original protocol must not permit others to engage in, and must not themselves engage in, secondary use of specimens until they comply with all steps. "Secondary use" includes the following:
- tests or other uses not explicitly mentioned, either by name or as a class, in the original protocol and consent; or
- giving or loaning specimens to anyone else. (This does not include other laboratories doing allowed tests for the original researchers; it does include laboratories retaining specimens or doing their own tests.)

(5) Researchers of the original protocol, and of a new protocol receiving specimens, must track and comply with the limits on the use of each

specimen imposed by the consent of the person from whom it was obtained, even if the specimen is anonymous or if the person from whom the specimen was obtained has died.

(6)   All proposed secondary uses of specimens must be reviewed and approved for scientific value by an independent group. The original protocol that stores specimens must include such review and approval in its procedures. Stored specimens are a nonrenewable resource that should be depleted only by research with sufficient scientific value; specimens must not be hoarded (e.g., to benefit a researcher's career), but must be shared if it benefits the person, Tribe, or society. Those two obligations are especially important for specimens not easily obtained (e.g., by surgery or biopsy).

(7)   All proposed secondary uses of specimens must be reviewed and approved by the Tribal government(s) with jurisdiction. The original protocol that stores specimens must include such review and approval in its procedures.

(8)   All proposed secondary uses of specimens must be reviewed and approved by each participating institution that holds, sends, or receives the specimens, by its SPA IRB or its Multiple Project Assurance of Compliance (MPA) procedures. The researcher of the new protocol must send the consent form(s) under which the specimens were originally obtained with the request for IRB review.

(9)   Many "anonymous" specimens have clinical or demographic information about the people from whom the specimens were obtained. IRB review must assess if *true anonymity* is achieved and maintained (i.e., that identification of some people cannot occur due to combination of demographic or clinical data or linkage to other databases).

(10)   All proposed uses of specimens must be evaluated to determine if they are within the original truly informing consent and related to the original study [see table 1]. *Within the original truly informing consent* means that the consent form cited the uses as a class (e.g., "kidney function tests") or by name. *Related to original study* means the stated purposes for which the specimens were obtained. Proposed uses are exempt from IRB review if they are within the original consent *and* related *and* anonymous; however, the determination that they meet all three criteria is by the institution's MPA procedure or SPA [Single Project Assurance] IRB, not by the researcher. All other proposed uses within the original consent require "expedited" or full IRB review.

(11)   If some or all proposed uses *are not within the truly-informing consent form*, they usually are so for one of three reasons.

TABLE 1. *Proposed Uses within the Original Truly Informing Consent*

Related to original study	Anonymous	Standard conditions for the new research protocol or plan
yes	yes	Scientific merit review and approval (i.e., "review, then either approval or veto, of the protocol"); and each institution's review and approval; and notification of Tribe; and publications identify the community only with Tribal consent.
yes	no	Scientific merit review and approval; and IRB review and approval of the protocol's modification; and notification of Tribe; and researchers not contact individuals without their consent; and publications identify the community only with Tribal consent.
no	yes *or* no	Scientific merit review and approval; and IRB review and approval; and formal Tribal review and approval; and individual informed consent, unless excepted by the IRB for non-anonymous specimens; and publication not identify individuals without their consent; and publications identify the community only with Tribal consent.

- The original consent form did not mention future use at all. (Such forms were frequent in previous research or clinical care.)
- The original consent form gave blanket consent, and thus was not truly-informing by today's standards (also in older research or clinical care).
- The future use is beyond a reasonably detailed truly-informing consent. Future possible uses or protocols are so varied that a table of standard conditions is not feasible. Every proposed use must be approved by all Tribe(s) and IRB(s) involved to protect against the risks of research, and by an independent scientific review group.

(12) Many new tests require pre-test counseling, as do genetic tests. If the

protocol will do new tests with clinical relevance to people from whom the specimens were obtained, and if the specimens are identifiable, the researchers must specify how and when they will obtain the informed consent of each person to receive — or to not receive — the test results. (Many new tests are not CLIA [Clinical Laboratory Improvement Act] approved; generally the results of non-CLIA approved tests are not given directly to participants.)

(13) The entities retaining specimens, and the PI [principal investigator] and co-investigators of every protocol that obtains, stores, tests, or uses the specimens must sign a copy of one of the following. The signed agreements extend these Guidelines to laboratories, specimen banks, and researchers that receive, hold, test, or secondarily use any specimens; the original researcher must obtain the same written agreement from them. The originals are sent to the IRB(s) and Tribe(s) involved. If the new protocol is receiving specimens for secondary use, copies of the signed forms are sent to the original researcher.

(a) *For use of specimens that are anonymous*:
The undersigned investigator agrees to the following with respect to datasets and specimens involved in this project:
1. I will not use the specimens and their data I receive for any purpose other than those stated in this protocol and approved by the Tribe(s) and IRB(s);
2. I will not release the specimens or data I receive to any person or study;
3. I will not attempt in any way to establish the identity of the subjects of the specimens or data received that are anonymous.

(b) *For use of specimens that are not anonymous*:
The undersigned investigator agrees to the following with respect to datasets and specimens involved in this project:
1. I will not use the specimens and their data I receive for any purpose other than those stated in this protocol and approved by the Tribe(s) and IRB(s);
2. I will not release the specimens or data I receive to any person or study;
3. I will not attempt to contact any individual or family other than as stated in this protocol, without prior approval by the IRB(s) and Tribe(s) involved.

(14) Storage of all specimens must provide physical security from unauthorized or inappropriate access. The disposal of specimens must be respectful.

(15) Researchers of a new protocol to use existing specimens have the same obligations as do the researchers of the original protocol. Those obligations generally include:
- presenting the results of the research to the Tribe(s) involved; and
- seeking Tribal review of publications.

(16) Research teams must insure "institutional memory" to comply with requirements after the PI has left. Research teams should also have written agreements with their institutions to define control and responsibility over the storage and disposition of the specimens. The Tribe(s) and IRB(s) involved may need to know those agreements.

(17) IRB(s) and Tribal government(s) may notify funding agencies, supporting institutions, and publishers or editors of violations of these Guidelines that are not resolved.

(18) These Guidelines must be re-examined, and may be modified, as experience develops.

III. Background and additional information

The secondary research use of blood or tissue specimens is increasing in frequency and sophistication. Such use may benefit participants and communities whose specimens are tested. If blood or tissue specimens are *anonymous*, and if they exist before the research use, then 45 CFR 46 §101(b)(4) permits research on them without the informed consent of the people from whom they were obtained, because such research appears to pose no risk to those people no matter how sensitive the tests.

A community may be harmed even though the specimens are anonymous for the individual, if they retain the community's identification or are known to have come from the community. The community at risk may be specific Tribes, a group of Tribes (e.g., "Northwest Tribes"), or an ethnic group (e.g., "American Indians"). When IHS is or was involved in the collection or storage of specimens, they are not anonymous for community because they are known to be from AI/AN people. For this policy, then, "anonymous" specimens means "anonymous only for the individual"; they are identifiable for at least the large AI/AN community.

For anonymous specimens, it is impossible for the researcher to obtain the identity of people either directly (e.g., by name) or by a combination of data elements, with either only the data at hand, or with other information (e.g., from medical records) or other people (e.g., who have access to medical records). For specimens to be anonymous, the researcher must not have, and has no access to even with possible cooperation by others, any data that alone or in combination identify one or more people from whom the specimens were obtained.

A special consideration applies once the specimens are *in research*, i.e., either obtained directly from volunteer participants under a research protocol, or were stored specimens that had been gathered originally as a process of care and now obtained under a research protocol. Subsequent activities are a *modification* of the research protocol *if* they were not stated in the originating protocol. (Such activities include, but are not limited to: giving or lending the specimens to another researcher, using them for tests other than those of the obtaining protocol, seeking a patent.) All modifications of a protocol must be reviewed and approved by the original IRB(s) by either expedited or full IRB review; see §46.103(b)(4) and 46.110. The IRB(s) must also determine if the proposed new use or release of specimens is within the limits of the original informed consent.

IHS has five additional *special considerations*, circumstances, and concerns.

- Confidentiality and anonymity are more difficult to maintain in small rural communities, as are most IHS sites, than in large urban areas.
- Because clinical care data in the IHS are computerized, true anonymity is difficult to achieve, due to possible combinations of computerized *clinical* data elements.
- AI/AN communities have been stigmatized by recent research, which reinforces the fears and distrust that many AI/AN and other people have about research.
- Many AI/AN people have special cultural values and concerns related to the use of blood and other tissues.
- Tribal governments legally control research done within their jurisdiction. IHS Guidelines must work with each Tribe's Codes and Procedures to control research.

There are three basic approaches to obtaining the informed consent of people participating in research or care that saves specimens.

- One is a broad consent that gives general permission to save specimens. It maximizes future testing and flexibility, which benefits future progress in science; however, it does not recognize possible harms to communities or individuals by tests for stigmatizing conditions. For example, a protocol and consent form that leftover blood will be saved for "future tests about diseases of importance to AI/AN people" is a blanket consent. It covers too much, from alcoholism to otitis media, from non-stigmatizing conditions to highly stigmatizing conditions. As such, participants could not know what the risks and benefits might be. More restrictive wording is better, e.g., "future tests about infections important to AI/AN children" of specimens saved in a vaccine trial. These Guidelines do not take this approach of a blanket consent.

- Another is a detailed consent. At the time the specimen is obtained, each participant decides whether to permit saving a specimen, what tests can and cannot be done, and whether to be contacted about results of future tests. The approach maximizes participant control; however, the control is exercised when participants lack relevant information. The Guidelines do not take this approach, because future tests are too varied to list, and the risks and benefits of tests to be developed are not known.
- The Guidelines take a third approach: the *community* reviews and approves each future use when it is proposed; each *participant* decides about being contacted with result of future tests when they are proposed, and their risks and benefits more clearly known, under pretest counseling. The community (Tribal government) review is a check against misuse of the specimens. Participant decisions about future tests are made when maximal information is available.

Please give comments, suggestions, or critiques to:

William L. Freeman, M.D., M.P.H.

PART III
Special Issues in the Use of Stored Tissue Samples in Forensic and Military Settings

The Use and Development of DNA Databanks in Law Enforcement

John W. Hicks

Information on the incidence and nature of crimes forms the basis upon which forty-two states have enacted legislation requiring that individuals convicted of specified offenses submit to DNA typing. The DNA Proficiency Act of 1995 authorizes the Federal Bureau of Investigation to establish a national index of DNA identification profiles for use by law enforcement agencies. The federal legislation calls for the FBI to publish standards that assure the reliability of DNA test results and the compatibility of the data. These standards are to be developed upon recommendations from a DNA Advisory Board comprised as specified in the law. The FBI system is named CODIS (the Combined DNA Index System).

The need for CODIS is clear. A 1993 crime victimization survey estimated that there were 485,290 incidents of rape and/or sexual assault and only 104,810 of these incidents were reported to police. There were 38,420 arrests for forcible rape and 22,004 convictions. In 24.4 percent of the estimated incidents, the perpetrator was not known to the victim.[1] Other studies have indicated that as many as 63 percent of persons released from incarceration are re-arrested within three years on other offenses, with violent offenders having a greater likelihood of recidivism.[2]

Personal identification is therefore a critical issue in law enforcement. While inked fingerprints are the traditional (and remain the best) means of identification, latent fingerprint impressions are only occasionally recovered from the scenes of violent crimes. Blood and other body fluids as well as hair and other biological tissues are the most common evidence recovered from such scenes. DNA technology provides a powerful new identification tool for investigators to help solve crimes.[2-6]

The CODIS System

The CODIS system will eventually contain four national files of DNA records: a population file, a forensic file, a convicted offender file, and a missing persons file. These files, contributed by all CODIS participants, will exist on the national CODIS computer located at the FBI in Washington, D.C. In addition, these file types will exist on state and/or local systems.

The national population file includes all DNA records derived from population studies conducted by CODIS subscribers. These population DNA records are the basis for the statistical assessment of the significance of the DNA match in casework. Due to limited resources, the number of individuals represented in the population studies of any one laboratory is limited. At the discretion of the local laboratory, these DNA records are electronically forwarded to the state or national population files. The DNA records are anonymous.

The advantage of the national population file over the population file maintained at a local laboratory is that a significantly larger number of DNA records are available for statistical analysis. In this way, nationally standardized and validated methods of assessing the statistical significance of a DNA match are available on a larger number of population DNA records to various local laboratories. This is effective in fostering greater confidence in the estimate of the relative rarity of a DNA profile in a case.

THE FORENSIC FILE

The local, state, and national forensic indexes will contain the unaccounted-for DNA profile(s) from unknown suspect cases. These indexes will also contain the DNA profiles derived from the crime scene or other lawfully obtained evidence in cases where a DNA match has been made and investigators have identified a suspect.

Crime scene evidence is limited to the evidence that is received by investigators. Examples are bed linen or other items legally obtained in the crime scene search; evidence from the victim, such as vaginal, oral, or anal swabs, or swabs of body fluid stains on the victim; the clothing and possessions of the victim; and objects obtained as a result of a consensual search or search warrant.

The forensic index is the key to the effectiveness of CODIS. CODIS will conduct regular searches of the forensic index at all three levels (national, state, and local) for DNA matches. There are three possible match outcomes in the search of the forensic indexes.

First, an intercase match may link two or more cases, none of which have suspects. This information, upon verification of the laboratories originating the DNA profiles, will be provided to the criminal investigators. The investigators, having received this new lead information, will then coordinate investigative activities in a way that may lead to the identification of a serial offender. Second, an intercase match between a case without a suspect and one with a suspect will result in a previously unavailable and important lead for investigators of the unknown suspect case. The third type of intercase match involves two or more cases, all of which have a (the same) suspect. This information would be of particular interest to prosecutors and the courts in the adjudication of each case, especially when the cases are in separate jurisdictions. Without this link, each case could proceed separately or not go forward at all. By linking the cases, additional evidence is available that will lead to stronger prosecutions. In some cases, the courts may sentence the serial offender using different sentencing standards than if the offender was considered a first-time/onetime offender.

THE CONVICTED OFFENDER FILE

The convicted offender index will exist at state and national levels. The only local offender indexes supported will be those authorized by state authorities responsible for the administration of its convicted offender DNA program. The state offender index will only be supported in those states that have enacted legislation enabling them to maintain an index of DNA identification records of convicted offenders or otherwise lawfully permitted maintenance of such an index under state authority.

The national CODIS convicted offender index will only contain those DNA records that originated from the state offender indexes. As in all CODIS files, the originator of the DNA record retains responsibility and ownership of its DNA records. The state determines which offender DNA profiles will be forwarded to the national convicted offender index. Also, the state retains the responsibility for, and will have the capability of expunging, its convicted offender DNA records from its state index and from the national index.

After the DNA record from crime scene evidence in an unknown suspect case is forwarded to state and national CODIS forensic files, it will be searched against the convicted offender indexes. A match in the convicted offender index will result in a potentially significant new lead for the police investigating the unknown suspect case.

However, further laboratory work is required in cases where the convicted offender profile was furnished by a laboratory other than the one conducting the DNA examination of the unknown suspect case. In these cases, the local laboratory obtains a blood sample from the convicted offender and conducts its own DNA analysis of the blood sample. This requirement eliminates the need to coordinate witness travel from a distant laboratory in support of the prosecution of the case, as well as verifying the DNA analysis of the convicted offender.

The DNA records of convicted offenders include the specimen identification number, the DNA profile (DNA identification characteristics), and the information related to the analytical conditions of the DNA analysis. No personally identifying information or other information unrelated to the identification purposes of the index is included with the DNA record. Personally identifying information concerning convicted offenders is retained within the custody and control of the sponsoring state agency and is not in the state or national convicted offender indexes.

THE MISSING PERSONS FILE

This index will not be implemented until the completion and implementation of the population, forensic, and convicted offender files. The missing person index will exist at the local, state, and national CODIS levels. It will contain the DNA profiles of recovered persons whose identities are sought by investigators. An example of a living missing person is the recovered small child who is unable to provide information concerning his or her identity. A deceased missing person may be a murder victim or an unidentified individual who dies from natural causes.

The missing person index will also contain known (or reference) DNA records of close relatives of missing persons, in addition to those of the missing person (from DNA from the missing person before their disappearance, when available). The DNA records from the relatives of the missing person will only be retained with the voluntary consent of the individual or under court order.

Using sophisticated computer analysis that takes into account sound genetic principles of inheritance, searches for matches of missing persons and their relatives will be conducted. Confirmed matches will result in the solution of otherwise very difficult missing person cases. Upon conclusion of a missing person investigation with a match or through other investigative means, the DNA profiles of living missing persons and their relatives will be expunged from the CODIS indexes. Also, close relatives of missing persons can direct the removal of their DNA record from the system at any time, except in those cases where removal would violate a court order. The DNA records from living missing persons and the relatives of missing persons will not be used in the search for criminal suspects.

For CODIS to work, all forensic laboratories must use compatible DNA test systems so that data can be compared. The tests must also be performed at a high technical standard to assure reliable results in which others can be confident. Federal legislation was passed in September 1994 to promote uniform standards for forensic DNA testing and to provide federal funding support to state and local law enforcement agencies to establish or expand their DNA testing capabilities. The law will be implemented through the Bureau of Justice Assistance and the FBI in the U.S. Department of Justice.

Effective law enforcement often depends on how well investigators gather, analyze, and manage information, whether that information be obtained through interview of subjects and witnesses or through the meticulous forensic analysis of the crime scene. The CODIS system makes maximum use of the forensic DNA data recovered from violent crime scenes to facilitate cooperation and mutual support among law enforcement agencies and to enhance their effectiveness.

A Case Example

Rosie Gordon was eleven years old. Her body was found less than five miles from the sidewalk where her bicycle stood. Rosie had been abducted two days earlier in the mid-afternoon from the street in front of her home in a middle-class suburban community outside Washington, D.C.

Based on the circumstances of her disappearance and death, behavioral specialists from the National Center for the Analysis of Violent Crime in Quantico, Virginia, developed a criminal profile of the perpetrator and suggested that investigators in the township where Rosie lived and investigators in adjacent townships scour incident reports for the prior three years. They searched these reports for details similar to Rosie's case: daylight abduction, young female victim, residential neighborhood, possible sexual molestation. Four cases were identified through this process that met the criteria developed by the profiles. The four victims had been released by their abductor after being sexually assaulted. DNA testing was used to establish that semen recovered from the four victims in those incidents came from the same man. Investigators had been unable to develop a viable suspect in any of the four cases in spite of extensive interviews. Until the DNA testing was performed, the linkage of the four cases had not been established.

A task force was formed to coordinate the investigations, and a comprehensive review of the investigative details which had been gathered and cataloged for each case was conducted. In one of the cases, a partial vehicle license number had been recalled by the victim and in another case the victim described an unusual tattoo on her assailant's forearm. Other details were pieced together from the four cases, which ultimately led to the identification of Randall Breer, an individual with a record of prior arrests in a New England state for sex-related offenses.

Breer was charged and subsequently convicted of abduction and rape in the four cases and is serving four life sentences in prison. He has not admitted involvement in Rosie Gordon's death. While investigators believed there were similarities between her case and the circumstances in the cases of the four young girls, there was insufficient evidence to formally charge him in the Gordon case.

One can only speculate on the outcome of the Rosie Gordon case and similar cases that preceded her abduction if DNA technology and the CODIS system had been available at that time. Perhaps Breer would have been identified and arrested in connection with the first molestation based on his DNA record being entered into CODIS at the time of his conviction in New England. The second, third, and fourth young girls might never have been victimized by Breer. Even if he had not had an earlier conviction and DNA record on file, CODIS might have alerted investigators to the series activity in the third or fourth related cases. Once they were alerted, a coordinated effort might have identified Breer more quickly and, if he was responsible for Rosie Gordon's abduction, prevented her death.

Notes

1. U.S. Department of Justice, Bureau of Justice Statistics, *Sourcebook of Criminal Justice Statistics — 1994* (Washington, D.C.: U.S. Government Printing Office, 1995).

2. Jean McEwen and Philip Reilly, "A Review of State Legislation on DNA Forensic Data Banking," *American Journal of Human Genetics* 54 (1994): 941–958.

3. John Hicks, "DNA Profiling: A Tool for Law Enforcement," *FBI Law Enforcement Bulletin* 57 (1988): 1–5.

4. John Hicks, *DNA Technology and Forensic Science* (Cold Spring Harbor, N.Y.: Cold Spring Harbor Laboratory, 1989).

5. U.S. Congress, Office of Technology Assessment, *Genetic Witness: Forensic Uses of DNA Tests* (Washington, D.C.: U.S. Government Printing Office, 1990).

6. National Academy of Sciences, *DNA Technology in Forensic Science* (Washington, D.C.: National Academy Press, 1992).

Storing Genes to Solve Crimes:
Legal, Ethical, and Public Policy Considerations

Jean E. McEwen

Although the activity of DNA storage had its inception in the context of genetic research and clinical medicine, these applications of the technology are quickly becoming eclipsed by the storage of DNA in the arena of criminal forensics. By June 1, 1996, forty-two states had enacted statutes that authorize or require states to establish forensic DNA databanks, and several other states had similar bills pending.[1] These laws typically require specified categories of criminal offenders to provide blood (and sometimes also saliva) samples at the time they are sentenced or prior to their release from prison. State crime labs will then extract DNA from these samples and, using a standardized set of enzymes and probes, create for each offender a unique DNA identification "profile." These data will then be digitized and entered onto computer, and the samples themselves will be placed in storage. If in the future a crime is committed that involves biological evidence (such as semen or blood) but few other leads, investigators will be able to analyze the evidence sample and compare the resulting DNA profile against the reference profiles created from the samples of known offenders that are already in the databank — much in the same way as is done with conventional fingerprint records.[2-4]

By June 1, 1996, across the country, samples from almost 300,000 offenders had cumulatively been amassed, with more than 80 percent of those samples in Virginia, California, Washington, North Carolina, and Alabama. Although fewer than 65,000 of these samples had been analyzed, the rate at which crime labs will be able to process the samples collected for their databanks should increase markedly over the next few years, as the technology becomes less expensive and better automated and as more DNA analysis resources are made available. The DNA Identification Act, a federal law passed in 1994, will make $25 million in matching grants available to states for DNA-related activities over a five-year period as long as the states adhere to certain uniform quality assurance and other standards.[5] This law also formally authorizes the Federal Bureau of Investigation to establish a national computer network called CODIS (Combined DNA Index System) to facilitate the exchange of DNA data between crime labs in different states.[6]

The CODIS network, when fully operational, should be an effective law enforcement tool. By June 1, 1996, "cold hits" through DNA databanks had been achieved in at least 28 cases (where DNA extracted from unknown evidence samples found at crime scenes was tested and found to match that of a known offender whose DNA profile was already on file). In addition, in at least 45 other instances, involving more than 100 crime scenes, DNA databanks had been used to establish associations between two or more open cases (where DNA data derived from the testing of unknown evidence samples and entered into databanks were linked to the same as-yet-unidentified person).

Forensic DNA databanks hold special promise for rape and sexual assault cases, where biological evidence from the perpetrator (semen) is often available but where victims often cannot positively identify their perpetrators through independent means.[2-4] DNA databanks may also be useful in some homicide investigations or other violent crime cases where nonbiological leads are limited but where biological evidence from the perpetrator (such as blood, fingernail scrapings, or hair shed in the course of a struggle) is found at the scene. DNA databanks may have considerably less utility in the investigation of *nonviolent* crimes, but even in such cases they may have some utility (for example, where saliva is present on a stamp or flap of an envelope used in the commission of a "white collar" offense).

Controlling the Expansion of DNA Databanks

While it is a relatively straightforward task to identify the types of crimes most susceptible to resolution through a DNA databank, determining the types of criminal offenders who should be required to provide samples for DNA databanking is more difficult. Most of the earliest DNA databanking laws, enacted in the late 1980s and early 1990s, were quite circumscribed in scope, directed almost exclusively at persons convicted of rape or other violent sexual assaults.[7] The rationale for this relatively narrow focus was based on Bureau of Justice Statistics data showing that rapists released from prison are 10.5 times more likely than other released prisoners to be subsequently arrested for rape and that released prisoners who have served time for other sexual assaults are 7.5 times more likely to be arrested later for a like offense.[8] Since rape and sexual assault are the two types of crimes for which DNA databanking can be expected to have its greatest utility, this approach reflected an attempt to target the laws to those whose criminal pasts suggested the greatest propensity to commit these crimes.

The past several years, however, have seen a steady expansion in the scope of state DNA databanking laws to cover not only persons convicted of violent sex crimes, but also those convicted of other offenses (including, in some states, even some misdemeanors). Some of this expansion can be justified in cost-benefit terms; for example, due to the phenomenon of "crossover" crime, it is not uncommon for persons convicted of such offenses as burglary, robbery, and assault subsequently to be arrested for sex crimes or other violent crimes that may involve biological evidence.[8] In addition, persons convicted of sex-related misdemeanors may actually be active recidivist rapists who merely happened to be apprehended in an early or uncompleted stage of their criminal activities. However, some states' laws are drafted so broadly as to cover even offenses that are neither violent nor sex-related. Virginia's law, for example, covers *all* convicted felons — even those convicted only of white-collar crimes.[9] This will soon result in the amassing of samples from hundreds of thousands of people, the vast majority of whom are unlikely ever to commit an offense involving biological evidence that would be suitable for comparative analysis through a DNA databank (or in which a databank would be *needed* to solve the case).

The scope of DNA databanks is gradually expanding along other dimensions, as well.[7] For example, most states are now requiring samples not only from persons convicted of covered offenses after the statute's effective date, but also from those already serving prison sentences. States increasingly are also enacting laws (or amending existing laws) to cover certain juvenile offenders, mentally institutionalized offenders, and persons initially charged with covered offenses who have plea bargained to or are ultimately convicted only of lesser offenses. For example, South Dakota requires samples from persons who have merely been *arrested* for (not necessarily convicted of) a covered offense,[10] and some other states are considering amending their laws also to do this.

This rapid expansion in the coverage of DNA databanking laws has occurred despite the recommendation of the National Academy of Sciences in its 1992 report, *DNA Technology in Forensic Science*, that states proceed to adopt a "go-slow" approach to setting up databanks.[2] Although several states' databanking statutes have been challenged in court on constitutional grounds, none, to date, has been invalidated. Courts have consistently (although not always unanimously) rejected arguments that such laws violate the Fourth Amendment's protection against unreasonable searches and seizures, reasoning that requiring samples from persons who have been convicted of crimes bears a rational relationship to a legitimate state interest in facilitating future criminal investigations.[10] Courts have also uniformly upheld databanking laws over arguments that the laws variously violate the *ex post facto* clause, due process, equal protection, the Eighth Amendment prohibition against cruel and unusual punishment, the Sixth Amendment guarantee of assistance of counsel, and First Amendment religious freedom guarantees.[11-12]

However, the ongoing trend toward broadening the ambit of state DNA databanking laws has many civil libertarians worried that as the technology improves a "surveillance creep" will occur, with an ever-widening segment of the population required to provide samples.[13-14] For example, as it becomes easier and less expensive to create DNA identification profiles using trace quantities or saliva or hair, rather than blood, such samples may well become the preferred materials for building some states' databanks — just as urine and hair are becoming, in many places, the preferred samples for drug testing among the prison population. Should this occur, so that samples can be collected just by rubbing a swab inside a subject's cheek or pulling out a hair, the ease and inexpense of collecting samples could provide an impetus for requiring samples from still more people. Using saliva or hair could also lessen the Fourth Amendment concerns associated with DNA databanks because the physical intrusion (although not the *nonphysical privacy* intrusion) involved in taking samples of this type would likely be regarded as minimal.[15] As a result, courts might begin to insist on a less close nexus between the stated purpose of forensic databanks and the categories of persons covered, providing another impetus for the further expansion of databanks.[16-17]

Instructive here is the experience of Britain, where legislation enacted in 1995 authorized for the first time the nonconsensual collection and storage of "nonintimate" DNA samples (saliva or hair) from every person charged with any recordable offense, regardless of whether or not DNA is relevant to the offense in question.[18] Some 675,000 people per year are expected to be asked for samples under this law, which is expected to result in 5 million stored profiles by the end of the century.[19] Strikingly, on the same day this law went into effect, police in Wales began asking all 2,000 male inhabitants of a particular neighborhood "voluntarily" to provide samples of blood for DNA analysis, in an attempt to find the perpetrator in a high-profile case that involved the murder and rape of a teenage girl.[20] In another case just a few weeks later, police conducted a dawn raid on more than 1,500 homes in a selected area and took samples from hundreds of suspected burglars.[21] This case marked the first direct *mass* use of the new police powers *forcibly* to take DNA samples and demonstrates that unrestrained expansion in state authority to take DNA samples for databanks can have pervasive civil liberties effects.

The United States has a considerably stronger tradition of privacy than does Britain, and it is unlikely that a U.S. court would uphold such a mass roundup of suspects for the collection of DNA samples. Moreover, at least for the immediate future, the relatively high cost of analyzing samples will probably provide at least a degree of restraint on the continued expansion of databanks. Nevertheless, public pressure to extend state DNA databanking requirements to broader segments of the population seems likely — fueled in part by the early successes of existing databanking and by rising fears of crime. In a 1995 Harris poll of 1,000 American adults, 56 percent said they thought it would be acceptable for states to build databanks with the DNA profiles of *all newborn babies*.[22]

While the prospect of a population-wide forensic DNA databank seems unlikely (at least for the immediate future), the history of conventional fingerprinting requirements in the United States suggests that over time many persons who have had no involvement with the criminal justice system will find themselves in DNA databanks. When the FBI's Identification Division was first established in 1924, its sole purpose was to provide a central repository of criminal fingerprint records for law enforcement agencies nationwide. However, in 1933, a Civil Identification Section was established, and the number of fingerprint cards in the FBI's files rose to 10 million by 1939. Around World War II the number of civil fingerprint submissions expanded further, with the FBI's files swelling to hold more than 42.8 million prints by 1942. Today conventional fingerprints are required in connection with routine security clearances for countless state and federal employees and, at the state level, as a condition of obtaining licenses and employment in a myriad of regulated industries. A projection by the Office of Technology Assessment estimates that by the year 2000 the FBI will be receiving 100,000 fingerprint card submissions per day, of which 50,000 will be for *non–criminal justice* applications.[23]

Will DNA databanks follow a similar course? Are we heading down a slippery slope, where DNA databanks, initially aimed at a narrow "pariah" group of violent repeat sex offenders but already expanding in their scope, will soon encompass large numbers of people without any criminal records? Given the many potential applications of DNA identification testing technology that can be imagined outside of the law enforcement context, there is reason to believe that they may. For example, samples could be required from persons suspected of being illegal aliens, or even from all new immigrants, in an effort to identify those making false claims of familial relationships. Welfare recipients could be asked for samples in order to maintain their eligibility for benefits, as part of an effort to curb fraud and abuse. Samples from persons enrolled in substance abuse treatment programs could also be taken and banked — either to guard against claims of sample switching in connection with drug or alcohol testing or on an assumption that such persons are more prone than others to engage in future criminal acts.

On the one hand, having on file a reference DNA profile for a large portion of the populace would undoubtedly lead to the apprehension of many perpetrators who, but for their inclusion in the databank, might never have been brought to justice. It could also be argued that only the guilty should have reason to object to having their DNA identification data in a bank. But it is doubtful whether popular support for the crime-fighting benefits of DNA databanks can justify their indefinite expansion in a country that prides itself on individual privacy and personal autonomy. Indeed, the unchecked expansion of DNA databanks could fundamentally alter the relationship between individuals and their government, with important implications for civil liberties.

Stored DNA Identification Data and the Problem of Relatives

In addition to raising civil liberties implications, forensic DNA databanks raise significant privacy issues. However, in assessing the privacy concerns associated with databanking, one must differentiate between the storage of the blood or other biological *samples* and the storage of the DNA *data* derived from their analysis.[24]

Although the DNA identification *data* derived from the analysis of samples collected for forensic DNA databanks involve certain privacy concerns, these concerns, relative to those associated with DNA test results in *medical* contexts, are at least for the present quite limited. This is because the DNA identification profiles most crime labs are storing in their databanks are based on restriction fragment length polymorphism (RFLP) technology, a technique which focuses only on "junk" areas of the DNA. These areas do not code for structural proteins and thus, apart from their ability to uniquely identify individuals, are genetically uninformative.[2-4] DNA profiles contain no information relating to predisposition to or presence of genetic disease or to any other physical or behavioral characteristics or traits and in this sense are in most respects, from a privacy standpoint, no different from conventional fingerprints. In fact, to the extent that DNA profiles, unlike conventional fingerprints, cannot differentiate between identical twins, they are actually somewhat *less* informative.

There is, however, one respect in which banked DNA identification profiles are *more* informative than conventional fingerprints — a difference with potentially important civil liberties ramifications. Unlike conventional fingerprints, DNA profiles derived from the analysis of crime scene evidence, when run through a databank, are uniquely capable of implicating biological *relatives* of the perpetrator, whose profiles, while not *identical* to the perpetrator's profile (the evidence profile), may be *similar*. This could occur, for example, where the perpetrator of a crime had not previously provided a sample for a databank, but where a close relative *had* done so. Such a case would almost surely invite follow-up investigation (in search of leads to other family members and ultimately to the perpetrator), but in the process innocent individuals who had the "misfortune" to share some of the perpetrator's genetic markers could be targeted. In extreme cases, following up all leads thus generated could lead to the harassment of whole families or racial groups through a sort of "genetic guilt by association."

This potential for a databank search to lead to biological relatives of the perpetrator before leading to the perpetrator may arise in part from a recommendation contained in the 1992 National Academy of Sciences report that an initial match obtained through a search of a databank should be confirmed by testing with additional probes a new sample obtained from the person so identified — with only the statistical frequency for the additional probes presented as evidence at trial.[2] Although the purpose of this recommendation is ostensibly to prevent any selection bias inherent in searching a databank, its practical effect may be to make labs inclined initially to search (or, more accurately, screen) their databanks with a minimal number of probes (those that are the least discriminating or "polymorphic"), saving the most polymorphic probes for confirmation and presentation in evidence at trial. This, in turn, will increase the likelihood of generating multiple suspects after the initial databank screen, all or most of whose DNA will eventually turn out not to match the evidence sample but who in the interim will have been subjected to surveillance and possibly required to give more blood for testing. Even if only *one* lead is generated from the initial screen, that lead may be merely to a relative of the perpetrator whose DNA matches the evidence sample across the first probes tested, but will not match on further testing.

This "problem of relatives" may be exacerbated by the fact that cases in which resort must be made to a DNA databank to identify a suspect will tend to be cases in which DNA evidence is more crucial to establishing the identity of the perpetrator than it is in many other cases, where such evidence may be merely corroborative. Where DNA evidence is pivotal, the pressure on police to go out and draw the blood of potential suspects with as little loss of evidence as possible may be substantial.

The potential for databank searches (or at least preliminary databank *screens*) to generate whole lists of potential (and probably genetically related) suspects rather than conclusively pointing to a single person will also increase as the number of persons in databanks increases and as labs begin to share DNA data on an interstate basis more frequently. The problem is also likely to be magnified as states move increasingly toward the use of polymerase chain reaction (PCR) technology for analyzing databank samples, because the DNA data generated with most PCR-based systems, at least at present, tend to be less discriminating than those derived using RFLP techniques.

The potential for unfairly targeting multiple (innocent) suspects could be minimized if crime labs retained the samples collected for their databanks after analyzing them; to the extent that the original samples are available for retesting, it would presumably be unnecessary to draw new samples from tentative suspects for confirmatory analysis. But this approach has a disadvantage in that it tends to perpetuate the indefinite retention of samples — a practice which, as discussed more fully below, raises significant informational privacy concerns.

Stored DNA Identification Data and the Future

Apart from the fact that an initial search of a DNA databank may, at least indirectly, lead to the targeting of innocent persons who merely happen to share some of the perpetrator's genetic characteristics, the DNA data being generated for databanks today are, as discussed earlier, for the most part no more sensitive than conventional fingerprint records. This could change in the future, however, as advances continue in our understanding of the human genome and in DNA testing technology itself.

First, while it is true that the RFLP analysis methods being used for today's DNA identification profiles focus on areas of the DNA that have no *known* function, it is possible that today's "junk" DNA will become tomorrow's "treasure."[25-26] Next, and perhaps more importantly, a number of crime labs are beginning to move away from RFLP technology toward PCR-based methods for analyzing their databank samples. Because these techniques, unlike RFLP techniques, focus directly on genes and not merely on "spacer" material, they are likely to contain some data about predisposition to genetic disease or other personal matters that a trained individual examining the profile could at least theoretically glean. Although the meaning and extent of such information is not yet well understood, it is already known, for example, that the DQ-alpha locus (one of the most commonly examined loci for forensic PCR analysis) resides within a gene that controls a range of immunological processes and is associated with diseases.[2] Should DNA base sequencing someday become the preferred method of analysis for banked DNA samples, information about the precise genetic code of large parts of the genome could conceivably be generated. The amount of information about people that could potentially be discerned from examining the data in a forensic DNA databank would then go well beyond information relating to individual identification.

Even the limited data contained in today's (primarily RFLP-based) DNA identification profiles could, at least potentially, be of interest to persons outside the law enforcement community (such as child support officials and immigration authorities) seeking to track people's whereabouts or familial relationships for reasons unrelated to the investigation of crime. Moreover, continuing advances in the science of informatics will make it increasingly difficult to control the flow of banked DNA data. For example, techniques of computer matching (the comparison of two or more sets of electronic records to search for people included in both or all sets) could be used to correlate and monitor not only the activities of individuals but also their familial relationships. And, of course, if forensic DNA databanks were ever to connect with medical record databases, an enormous amount of personal information about individuals could be derived — all at the click of a button.[27-28]

For all of these reasons, the privacy implications of stored DNA data go beyond those associated with conventional fingerprint records. Nevertheless, as discussed below, even these privacy implications pale in comparison to those associated with stored DNA *samples*.

Samples Collected for Forensic DNA Databanks: Should They Be Saved?

Samples collected for forensic DNA databanks from which DNA has been extracted (or may be extracted in the future) contain a potential *wealth* of genetic information, some of which may be highly personal, sensitive, or stigmatizing to individuals. This information may concern predisposition to genetic disease (or the presence of a genetic condition), various other physical characteristics, and potentially, in the future, even some behavioral traits. Moreover, such information may be of interest to a range of persons and institutional entities, ranging from insurance companies and employers to school systems, adoption agencies, or other government agencies.[26-28]

The extent of the risk that samples collected for forensic DNA databanks will be disseminated to such third parties without authorization has occasionally been overstated. For example, an insurance company seeking to learn an applicant's predisposition to genetic disease could easily request a blood sample from the applicant and test it directly, without seeking recourse to samples housed in a state crime lab. Nevertheless, the risk that samples will be tested (perhaps many years later) for reasons unrelated to those for which they were collected, and that the resulting data will be used for questionable purposes, is by no means purely theoretical. For example, some people are concerned that if genes should someday be found that predispose people to engage in violent behavior (and tests be developed to determine who has them), states will seek to have the samples retested for this purpose.[29] Such testing could arguably be justified as having a law enforcement justification and thus as being consistent with the databank's intended purpose — but its implications for society could be far-ranging.

The National Academy of Sciences, in recognition of the privacy risks that the retention of banked samples may entail, recommended that crime labs that maintain databanks destroy the samples after analyzing them, although it acknowledged that a short retention period may be warranted during a databank's initial start-up phase, while the technology is evolving.[2] On the other hand, the American Society of Human Genetics (ASHG) Ad Hoc Committee on Individual Identification by DNA Analysis endorsed the practice of saving samples, while emphasizing the importance of implementing adequate rules of disclosure and access.[30] These conflicting approaches reflect the difficulties involved in balancing a range of competing interests.

On the one hand, it should not be necessary to save samples collected from convicted offenders specifically for databanks in order to ensure their availability as evidence in a subsequent prosecution. As the National Academy of Sciences recommendations make clear, it is only the match between the evidence sample and the *confirmatory* sample drawn from a suspect identified through a search of a databank that should be introduced at trial.[2] On the other hand, saving samples ensures that they will be available to defendants in future cases who may seek to contest the validity of the databank search through which they were first identified. As discussed earlier, it also permits confirmation within the lab of a tentative match to a suspect obtained from a preliminary databank screen before the suspect so identified is asked to provide more blood for testing.

Many crime labs believe that the indefinite retention of samples is needed to ensure that the samples will be available for retesting as new and improved (PCR-based) technologies come on line.[31] Labs understandably want to prevent their databanks from becoming "locked into" an outmoded technology and eventually becoming obsolete. But this concern raises the separate question of whether the large-scale collection and analysis of samples for databanking at the present time may simply be premature (or at least highly inefficient). It is difficult to argue against a policy of going forward to collect and analyze at least those samples taken from the most violent habitual offenders, in the interest of public safety. However, any rush to launch a massive data-bank program using still evolving technologies may ultimately prove ineffi-cient since, if labs wish to remain "state of the art," they will only need to reanalyze the samples once more stable technologies emerge.[31] Importantly, it was the observation that databanks launched too hastily could, in the end, find themselves locked into a "dinosaur" technology that was a major impetus be-hind the National Academy of Sciences' recommendation that states adopt a more measured, incremental approach to establishing databanks.[2]

Existing Safeguards for Databank Privacy

Whatever the arguments for and against the long-term retention of sam-ples, it appears that crime labs, at least currently, plan to keep their samples indefinitely (except in situations where expungement is required, as when the conviction in connection with which the sample was drawn has been reversed on appeal).[31] This raises the question of whether existing legal protections adequately protect the informational privacy interests of those required to provide samples for databanks.

Much variation exists among states in terms of the levels of protection they provide for the privacy of the DNA samples collected for databanks (and the DNA data derived from their analysis).[7] However, the federal DNA Identifi-cation Act incorporates several privacy provisions that should provide at least a measure of protection. That law requires crime labs, as a condition of par-ticipating in the CODIS network, to limit the disclosure of stored individu-ally identifiable DNA samples and data to criminal justice agencies for law enforcement identification purposes (and for use in judicial proceedings if otherwise admissible and to criminal defendants in connection with the cases in which they are charged). It also provides criminal fines of up to $100,000 for the knowing, unauthorized *obtaining* of DNA *samples* and for the know-ing, unauthorized *obtaining or disclosure* of individually identifiable DNA *data*.[5] It remains to be seen, however, how effective the DNA Identification Act will be in protecting privacy. Significantly, the law entrusts its enforcement to the FBI and other law enforcement agencies, despite the recommendation of the National Academy of Sciences that primary oversight should reside with an independent agency.[2]

Although the FBI, in developing the protocols for the CODIS network, has been quite proactive in developing data encryption capabilities and other computer security software, preventing internal security breaches will present an ongoing challenge. The General Accounting Office, in a 1993 report on the National Crime Information Center (NCIC) network (on which CODIS has been patterned), found that the NCIC was vulnerable to misuse even from individuals with *authorized* access. The report listed numerous instances of illegal NCIC file breachings by individuals in twenty-three states, including both the intentional disclosure of information to private investigators in exchange for money and the alteration or deletion of information in NCIC records.[32] Given the arguably even greater sensitivity of the genetic information that will be housed in DNA databanks, constant vigilance will be essential to minimize the possibility of abuse.

Research on Stored Forensic Samples: The Behavioral Genetics Question

Although the DNA Identification Act places strict limitations on the dissemination of individually identifiable DNA samples (and data), it permits the disclosure of *anonymous* samples (from which all individual identifiers have been removed) for a "population statistics database," for identification research and protocol development purposes, or for quality control purposes.[5] The explicit authorization in this law for the creation of a population statistics database using anonymous DNA samples raises the question of whether this database itself must be used only for law enforcement purposes (to calculate the statistical frequencies associated with the probes used for forensic analysis) or, alternatively, whether anonymous samples may be used for other types of research. This question has gained currency because Alabama's databanking statute, enacted in 1994, expressly authorizes such use; it provides that Alabama's population statistics databank may be used "to provide data relative to the causation, detection, and prevention of disease or disability" and "to assist in other humanitarian endeavors including, but not limited to, educational research or medical research or development.[33]

Genetics researchers would not find the repositories of samples collected from convicted offenders for forensic DNA databanks particularly useful in *finding* genes, because this endeavor typically relies on familial linkage analysis (the comparison of samples from affected and unaffected individuals *within families*). However, once a gene of interest has been found and a test has been developed to determine who has it, banked DNA samples could be used to provide researchers with much other information. For example, such samples could be used for studies of allele frequencies (to estimate how many people

in a given population carry a gene of interest) or genotype-phenotype correlations (to determine how many people who have the gene exhibit the trait).
Thus, samples collected for forensic DNA databanks could provide a rich
source of useful epidemiological information for the understanding of many
genetic disorders and for the protection of public health.[34]

Banked samples from convicted offenders collected for forensic databanks
could someday come to be seen as an *especially* valuable resource for *behavioral* geneticists — such as those interested in studying the possibility of a genetic predisposition to violence, pedophilia, or alcoholism.[7] By studying large
numbers of samples taken from violent habitual felons, investigators might be
able to learn whether certain genetic mutations are more commonly found
among chronic recidivist criminals. But the specter of having samples initially
collected for identification purposes someday being used for behavioral genetics research — especially for research on the genetics of violent behavior — is
disquieting.[29, 35] Indeed, some people believe that any research giving credence
to the notion that a relationship — however indirect — exists between genes
and crime is ethically suspect, representing only thinly veiled racism or the
"old eugenics" wrapped in the respectable garb of modern science.[36–37]

The real question, of course, is not whether or not behavioral genetics research of this type is ethically *defensible*, but, rather, whether such research
should be done with stored samples from convicted offenders originally collected for a very different purpose *without the specific informed consent of those
who provided them.* This, in turn, raises important questions regarding both
the proper interpretation of existing federal guidelines for the protection of
human subjects in research and broader policy considerations.

On the one hand, the federal guidelines governing the protection of human
subjects in research recognize an exception to the usual requirement of informed consent in situations that involve only the study of already existing
samples that either are publicly available or have been completely stripped of
all identifiers.[38] In addition, another section of the guidelines, which sets out
enhanced protections applicable to biomedical and behavioral research involving prisoners, provides that prisoner research on the possible causes, effects, and processes of incarceration and of criminal behavior is permissible
so long as the study presents "no more than minimal risk and no more than
inconvenience to the subjects."[39] On the other hand, the Office of Protection
from Research Risks (OPRR) of the National Institutes of Health (NIH) has
taken the position that "the fact that genetic studies are often limited to the
collection of family history information and blood drawing should not . . .
automatically classify them as minimal risk."[40]

A similar view is reflected in a 1995 consensus statement on informed consent to research on stored tissue samples in *nonforensic* contexts; this document emphasizes that even though using stored samples for genetic research does not require the active participation of those from whom the samples were derived, it implicates a range of important interests relating to both personal privacy and individual autonomy.[41] While it might be urged that persons who commit crimes "give up" some of their privacy and autonomy interests as an incident of being convicted, the guidelines expressly recognize prisoners as a potentially "vulnerable population." Indeed, it is precisely *because* they are vulnerable, due to their incarceration, that the guidelines provide certain *enhanced* protections for research using prisoners as subjects.

Although genetic research on anonymous stored samples collected from convicted offenders for databanks may thus technically be permissible under existing federal guidelines, permitting the use of such samples in research (especially behavioral genetics research) without the informed consent of those from whom they were drawn is problematic from a public policy standpoint. The removal of identifiers arguably cannot completely solve the problem, because even anonymous behavioral genetics research can have an effect on those who provided the samples and on their families and kinship or racial groups.[42] For example, such research may tend only to reinforce stigmas already associated with some behavioral traits, leading to intangible, but nonetheless real, harms. Some behavioral genetics research (especially research on genetics and violence) may also tend to divert societal attention and resources away from efforts to deal with the environmental or economic roots of such problems — again indirectly causing harm.

An interesting question also exists as to whether samples collected specifically for forensic DNA databanking (that is, for the generation of identification-related data) can ever be *made* truly anonymous, as is required under the federal guidelines to make stored samples exempt from the requirement of informed consent. The guidelines state that for the exemption to apply the information must be recorded "in such a manner that subjects cannot be identified, directly or through identifiers, linked to the subjects."[38] But the fact that DNA is in effect an inherent identifier raises the question of whether, realistically, absolute anonymity of DNA samples can ever be guaranteed — at least in the unique context of *forensic* DNA storage. This is because once a sample has been analyzed for a forensic DNA databank, a unique reference profile associated with that sample will in fact exist — both physically (in the lab that generated the profile) and in digitized form (on the databanking computer network).

As long as the databanking network remains secure, and as long as no individual identifiers are directly affixed to DNA profiles stored in the lab, the risk seems negligible that an anonymous sample made available for unrelated research could be traced to its source solely with reference to its unique identifying characteristics (that is, by profiling the anonymous sample and comparing the results with the DNA profiles created for the databank). However, should DNA identification data over time move into wider circulation, ensuring anonymity may become more difficult. Some people, for example, have envisioned a day in which DNA identification profiles effectively replace today's Social Security number and become a "national identifier."[26-27] While this is perhaps futuristic, it is not entirely farfetched. DNA profiles can easily be reduced to a convenient bar-coded form, and the inherent immutability of DNA would make changing or forging one's DNA profile virtually impossible. Should the day ever come when *everyone's* DNA profile is on file with the government (or some other large institution), the very notion of an "anonymous" sample of one's DNA could become obsolete.

Acknowledgments

The research for this work was supported by Boston College Law School, the New England School of Law, the Eunice Kennedy Center for Mental Retardation, and a grant from the Ethical, Legal, and Social Implications Program of the Human Genome Project (Department of Energy Grant DE-FG02−91ER61237).

Notes

1. Ala. Code §§36-18-20, et seq. (1994); Alaska Stat. §44.41.035 (1996); Ariz. Rev. Stat. Ann. §31−281 (1993); Ark. Acts 922 (1995); Cal. Penal Code §§290.2, 3060.5, Cal. Govt. Code §76104.5 (1994); Colo. Rev. Stat. Ann. §17-2-201(5)(g)(1) (1988); Conn. Gen. Stat. Ann. §54−102g (1994); Del. Code Ann. tit. 29, §4713 (1994); Fla. Stat. Ann. §943.325 (1994); Ga. Code Ann. §24-4-60 (1992); Haw. Rev. Stat. §706−603 (1992); Ill. Ann. Stat. ch. 730, ¶ 5/5-4-3 (1992); Ind. Code Ann. §10-1-9 (1996); Iowa Code Ann. §13.10, Iowa Admin. Code §§61−8.1(13), et seq. (1991); Kan. Stat. Ann. §21−2511 (1991); Ky. Rev. Stat. Ann. §§17:170, 17:175 (1992); Me. Rev. Stat. Ann. tit. 25, §1571 (1996); Md. Ann. Code art. 88B, §12A, Md. Code Ann. Cts. & Jud. Proc. §10−915 (1994); Mich. Comp. Laws Ann. §750.520m (1994); Minn. Stat. Ann. §§299C.155, 609.3461 (1993); Miss. Code Ann. §45-33-15 (1995); Mo. Ann. Stat. §§650.050, 650.055 (1991); Mont. Code Ann. §44-6-101 (1995); Nev. Rev. Stat. Ann. §176.111 (1989); N.J. Stat. Ann. §§53:1−20.17, et seq. (1994); N.H. House Bill 1584 (1996); N.Y. Exec. Law Art. §§995, et seq. (1994); N.C. Gen. Stat. §§15A-266, et seq. (1993); N.D. Cent. Code §§31-13-02, et seq. (1995); Ohio Rev. Code

Ann. §§109.573, 2151.315, 2901.07 (1995); Okla. Stat. Ann. tit. 22, §§751.1, 991a, tit. 57, §584, tit. 74, §§150.27, et seq. (1996); Or. Rev. Stat. §§137.076, 181.085 (1991); 35 Pa. Cons. Stat. §§7651.101, et seq. (1996); S.C. Code Ann. §§23-3-600, et seq. (1995); S.D. Codified Laws Ann. §§23-5-14, et seq. (1990); Tenn. Code Ann. §§38-6-113, 40-35-321 (1991); Tex. Code Ann. §§411.141, et seq. (1995); Utah Code Ann. §§53-5-212.1, et seq. (1994); Va. Code Ann. §19-2-310.2 (1993); Wash. Rev. Code §§43.43.752, 43.43.754 (1990); W. Va. Code §§15–2B-1, et seq. (1995); Wis. Stat. Ann. §§165–76, 165.77, 973047 (1993).

2. National Academy of Sciences, National Research Council, Commission on Life Sciences, Board of Biology, *DNA Technology in Forensic Science* (Washington, D.C.: National Academy Press, 1992).

3. United States Congress, Office of Technology Assessment, *Genetic Witness: Forensic Uses of DNA Tests* (Washington, D.C.: United States Government Printing Office, 1990).

4. J. Ballantyne, G. Sensabaugh, and J. Witowski, eds., *DNA Technology and Forensic Science*, Banbury Report 32 (Cold Spring Harbor: Cold Spring Harbor Laboratory Press, 1989).

5. DNA Identification Act, 1994, 42 U.S.C. §§14131, et seq., §§379kk, et seq.

6. Technical Working Group on DNA Analysis Methods (TWGDAM), "The Combined DNA Index System (CODIS): A Theoretical Model," in L. T. Kirby, ed., *DNA Fingerprinting: An Introduction* (New York: Stockton Press, 1989), pp. 279–317.

7. J. E. McEwen and P. R. Reilly, "A Review of State Legislation on DNA Forensic Data Banking," *American Journal of Human Genetics* 54 (1994): 941–958.

8. United States Department of Justice, Office of Justice Programs, Bureau of Justice Statistics, *Recidivism of Prisoners Released in 1983* (Washington, D.C.: Government Printing Office, 1989).

9. Va. Code Ann. §19-2-310.2 (1993).

10. S.D. Codified Laws Ann. §§23-5-14, et seq. (1990).

11. E.g., *Jones v. Murray*, 962 F.2d 302 (4th Cir. 1992), cert. denied, 113 S. Ct. 472 (1992); *Ryncarz v. Eikenberry*, 824 F. Supp. 1493 (E.D. Wash. 1993); *Sanders v. Coman*, 864 F. Supp. 496 (E.D. N.C. 1994); *Vanderlinden v. Kansas*, 874 F. Supp. 1210 (D. Kan. 1995); *Washington v. Olivas*, 856 P.2d 1076 (Wash. 1993); *Gilbert v. Peters*, 55 F.3d 237 (7th Cir. 1995); *Rise v. Oregon*, 59 F.3d 1556 (9th Cir. 1995).

12. E.g., *Ewell v. Murray*, 11 F.3d 482 (4th Cir. 1993), cert. denied, 114 S. Ct. 2112 (1994); *People v. Calahan*, 649 N.E.2d 588 (Ill. App. 1995); *State ex rel. Juv. Dept. v. Orozco*, 878 P.2d 432 (Or. App. 1994); *People v. Wealer*, 636 N.E.2d 1129 (Ill. App. 1994), cert. denied, 642 N.E.2d 1299 (Ill. 1994).

13. G. M. Doot, "The Secrets of the Genome Revealed: Threats to Genetic Privacy," *Wayne Law Review* 37 (1991): 1615–1645.

14. A. DeGorgey, "The Advent of DNA Databanks: Implications for Information Privacy," *American Journal of Law and Medicine* 16 (1990): 381–398.

15. D. L. Burk, "DNA Fingerprinting: Possibilities and Pitfalls of a New Technique," *Jurimetrics Journal* 28 (1988): 455–471.

16. E. S. Lander, Testimony before United States Congress, House Committee on the Judiciary, Subcommittee on Civil and Constitutional Rights, *FBI Oversight and Authorization Request for FY 90*, 102nd Cong., 1st sess. (March 22, 1989).

17. P. L. Bereano, "The Impact of DNA-Based Identification Systems on Civil Lib-

erties," in P. R. Billings, ed., *DNA on Trial: Genetic Identification and Criminal Justice* (Cold Spring Harbor: Cold Spring Harbor Laboratory Press, 1992), pp. 119–128.

18. Criminal Justice and Public Order Act of 1994, part IV, §55 (amending Police and Criminal Evidence Act of 1984, §63).

19. D. Campbell, "April Start for DNA Criminal Database," *Guardian*, March 17, 1995, p. 11.

20. F. Barbash, "Search for Killer Draws Blood: All Men in Welsh Neighborhood Face 'Voluntary' DNA Test," *Washington Post*, April 14, 1995, p. A1.

21. J. Bennetto, "Police Raid 1500 Homes in DNA Offensive against Burglary," *Independent*, May 5, 1995, p. 2.

22. Harris Poll, reported by H. Taylor, *Gannett News Service*, May 28, 1995.

23. United States Congress, Office of Technology Assessment, *The FBI Fingerprint Identification Automation Program: Issues and Options* (Washington, D.C.: Government Printing Office, 1991).

24. P. R. Reilly, "Reflections on the Use of DNA Forensic Science and Privacy Issues," in J. Ballantyne, G. Sensabaugh, and J. Witowski, eds., *DNA Technology and Forensic Science* (Cold Spring Harbor: Cold Spring Harbor Laboratory Press, 1989), pp. 43–54.

25. D. L. Burk, "DNA Identification Testing: Assessing the Threat to Privacy," *University of Toledo Law Review* 24 (1992): 87–102.

26. J. C. Hoeffel, "The Dark Side of DNA Profiling: Unreliable Scientific Evidence Meets the Criminal Defendant," *Stanford Law Review* 42 (1990): 465–538.

27. E. D. Shapiro and M. L. Weinberg, "DNA Data Banking: The Dangerous Erosion of Privacy," *Cleveland State Law Review* 38 (1990): 455–486.

28. Y. H. Yee, "Criminal DNA Data Banks: Revolution for Law Enforcement or Threat to Individual Privacy?" *American Journal of Criminal Law* 22 (1995): 461–490.

29. B. Scheck, "DNA Data Banking: A Cautionary Tale," *American Journal of Human Genetics* 54 (1994): 931–933.

30. American Society of Human Genetics (ASHG), Ad Hoc Committee on Individual Identification by DNA Analysis, "Individual Identification by DNA Analysis: Points to Consider," *American Journal of Human Genetics* 46 (1990): 631–634.

31. J. E. McEwen, "Forensic DNA Data Banking by State Crime Laboratories," *American Journal of Human Genetics* 56 (1995): 1487–1492.

32. United States General Accounting Office, *National Crime Information Center: Legislation Needed to Deter Misuse of Criminal Justice Information* (Washington, D.C.: United States General Accounting Office, 1993).

33. Ala. Code §§36-18-20, et seq. (1994).

34. A. G. Motulsky, "Societal Problems of Forensic Use of DNA Technology," in J. Ballantyne, George Sensabaugh, and J. Witowski, eds., *DNA Technology and Forensic Science* (Cold Spring Harbor: Cold Spring Harbor Laboratory Press, 1989), pp. 3–12.

35. N. L. Wilker, S. Stawski, R. Lewontin, and P. R. Billings, "DNA Data Banking and the Public Interest," in Paul R. Billings, ed., *DNA on Trial: Genetic Identification and Criminal Justice* (Cold Spring Harbor: Cold Spring Harbor Laboratory Press, 1992), pp. 141–149.

36. P. L. Bereano, "DNA Identification Systems: Social Policy and Civil Liberties Concerns," *International Journal of Bioethics* 1(1990): 146–155.

37. J. S. Alper and J. Beckwith, "Genetic Fatalism and Social Policy: The Implications of Behavior Genetics Research," *Yale Journal of Biology and Medicine* 66 (1993): 511–524.

38. CFR, Title 45, §46.101(b)(4).

39. CFR, Title 45, §46.301, et seq.

40. National Institutes of Health, Office of Protection from Research Risks, *Protecting Human Research Subjects: Institutional Review Board Guidebook* (Washington, D.C.: Government Printing Office, 1993).

41. E. W. Clayton, K. K. Steinberg, M. J. Khoury, E. Thomson, L. Andrews, M. J. Ellis Kahn, L. M. Kopelman, and J. O. Weiss, "Informed Consent for Genetic Research on Stored Tissue Samples," *JAMA* 274 (1995): 1786–1792.

42. E. W. Clayton, "Panel Comment: Why the Use of Anonymous Samples for Research Matters," *Journal of Law, Medicine, and Ethics* 23 (1995): 375–377.

DNA Banking in the Military: An Ethical Analysis

Kenneth Kipnis

On December 16, 1991, the Department of Defense (DoD) issued a memorandum authorizing the establishment of a DNA registry and specimen repository within the Armed Forces Institute of Pathology (AFIP).[1] The proposed registry and repository were to be developed to improve the military's "remains identification" capabilities. While dog tags had been issued since 1906, and fingerprints and dental X-rays had long been used to identify the bodies of those killed in battle, the immense destructiveness of modern warfare and the imperative to bury the fallen in marked graves called for the most effective — the most technologically sophisticated — approaches. The severity of damage to a soldier's body had too often precluded positive identification by traditional means. The new program promised a solution.

About a year later, on January 5, 1993, the assistant secretary of defense for health affairs (ASD[HA]) promulgated the initial policies for the new program.[2] According to this second memorandum, biological samples would be obtained from all enlisted men and women, with priority being given to those in high-risk occupational fields. In practice, military technicians would draw blood from enlistees and use it to fill four one-inch diameter circles printed on absorbent paper. Fingerprints, signatures, and identifying data would be taken at the same time. In addition, cells would be swabbed from inside the cheek and the swabs placed in vials of isopropanol preservative. Both the swab and two of the four blood spots would be labeled, indexed in the registry, and stored in the DNA repository for retrieval and analysis if needed later on. (The other two blood spots would go into the enlistee's medical record.)

Even if all that remained of a dead soldier was a small fragment, personnel working in the registry would be able to use the latest and most sophisticated technologies to match DNA recovered in the field against the indexed samples of soldiers listed as missing within the event or engagement. Except perhaps for identical siblings, if a fragment came from someone who had served in the military the AFIP would, in theory, be able to obtain a positive identification. The methods already existed to do this in 1991, and there was every reason to believe that these technologies would become easier, cheaper, and more reliable as the program got under way.

Technically, the repository was envisioned as a DNA bank, storing only the labeled blood spots and vials that would be indexed in the registry's computers for easy retrieval. Each sample was to be carefully "linked" to the enlistee who had provided it. In contrast with the registry and repository, a DNA database is a more sophisticated and expensive system that obtains, records, and indexes the latent genetic information derivable from tissue samples. For example, those who commit crimes — particularly sex offenses — often leave behind DNA. Much as they have done with fingerprints, governments are beginning to establish forensic DNA databases, hoping to match cellular materials found at crime scenes with DNA profiles derived from the tissue samples of convicted felons.[3] The technologies needed to establish standardized DNA databases are becoming cheaper and more discerning. If these were computerized and linked to other records, they could serve scientific, medical, legal, and other purposes. But as these databases become larger and more sophisticated, the phrase "unlinked DNA" will gradually become oxymoronic. For it could someday be as easy to trace an "anonymous" DNA sample to its source as it now is to return a misplaced driver's license to its owner.

Importantly, the DoD's memoranda and policy statements did not call for a database. Remains identification requires the analysis of DNA only when an enlistee is reported missing,[4] and, even then, only when potentially matching body parts, otherwise unidentifiable, are brought in from the field.[5] By June 1995, over 1 million DNA specimens were stored in the repository and indexed in the registry. Since new samples were to be added at an estimated rate of 200,000 per year, and since the program contemplated a seventy-five-year storage period for the specimens, the collection was expected eventually to reach about 18 million, the largest in the world.[6]

The Emergence of Conflict

On January 26, 1995, at Kaneohe Marine Corps Air Station on Oahu, a detachment from the First Radio Battalion was mustered for what appeared to be a routine physical examination. These marines were scheduled to leave Hawaii for training in California and then go to sea for a six-month "float." Implementing the remains-identification program, the staff at the medical clinic was taking blood specimens and mouth swabs. Asked for the samples, Lance Corporal John Mayfield III wanted to know what the DNA would be used for and who would have access to it. The clinic staff did not know. A second marine, Corporal Joseph Vlacovsky, also asked about the purposes of DNA collection. There was no explanation. Independently, both men refused to cooperate. About two weeks later the commanding officer of their battalion — Lieutenant Colonel Richard Monreal — issued a written order to Mayfield and Vlacovsky that they turn over samples of their DNA at 0800 hours on February 9, 1995. Neither complied.[7]

Willful disobedience of a lawful command of a superior commissioned officer is a most serious infraction in the marines. Under wartime conditions it is punishable by death.[8] Charged with that offense, Mayfield and Vlacovsky were the first members of the armed forces to face court-martial for refusing to provide the DNA samples required under the new policy. If they were found guilty, punishment could include six months in military prison, a demotion to private, a reduction in pay, a bad-conduct discharge, and the loss of all of veterans' benefits, including college financing under the GI Bill. Eric Seitz, the attorney for the two men, cross-filed a class action in the Federal District Court with the intention of shutting down the entire DNA banking program.

As the legal issues percolated through the federal courts and the military system of justice, the case began to attract attention, first in Hawaii and then nationally. The two local daily newspapers — the *Honolulu Advertiser* and *Honolulu Star-Bulletin* — followed the proceedings and ran editorials as the saga proceeded. The *Los Angeles Times*, *Washington Post*, and *New York Times* covered the story, as did National Public Radio. There was also television coverage. The publicity depicted two marines, both in their twenties and with otherwise impeccable records, conscientiously refusing to obey a direct order to turn over their DNA to an agency of the United States government. This image raised broad and potentially consequential concerns about the scope of enlistees' obligations to obey orders and, reciprocally, the boundaries of the armed forces' authority to issue them. Reports came in describing less publicized refusals in California, Washington, Illinois, and the Western Pacific. It is the purpose of this essay to identify and address some of the issues raised by these events.

DoD Policies and Practices

Since both Mayfield and Vlacovsky wanted to know what might be done with their DNA apart from remains identification, it is useful to begin by asking what the Pentagon's policies and practices were at the time of their refusal. The initial policy promulgated in the second ASD(HA) memorandum considered whether the collection could be used for expanded purposes: "Requests for access to the Registry or Specimen Repository for purposes other than remains identification purposes shall not, ordinarily, be approved. In extraordinary cases, when no reasonable alternative means of obtaining a specimen for DNA profile analysis is available, a request for access to the DoD Registry and Specimen Repository shall be routed through the appropriate Secretary of the Military department, or his designee, for approval by the ASD(HA)."

The policy did not specify what counted as an extraordinary case or an unreasonable means of obtaining specimens: these determinations were left to the discretion of the ASD(HA). Accordingly the question Mayfield and Vlacovsky were asking on January 26, 1995 — What might be done with my DNA? — had no substantive answer. Requests for expanded use would be subject to a judgment call. Absent further refinements of the policy, no one could say in 1995 what uses could be authorized as the calendar approached 2070, when the policy required destruction of their samples.

At least four circumstances could raise concerns that additional uses of the DNA bank either were or might come to be contemplated. First, the Pentagon had decided on a seventy-five-year storage period when it issued its 1993 policy. Except for samples from long-missing soldiers, that time span substantially exceeded what was required for casualty identification. Vlacovsky, for example, would be about 100 years old at the time his DNA was discarded. To be sure, remains are sometimes recovered decades after a conflict. But the problem of identifying very old body fragments could be solved by retaining the small number of samples from enlistees reported missing. If the sole purpose of the program was to identify those killed in the line of duty, it was anomalous and worrisome that the DoD intended to keep all the samples well after enlistees had completed their military obligations.

Second, the quantity of DNA collected was substantially greater than what was needed for the purpose of remains identification. While positive identifications can be achieved using tissue samples smaller than a pinhead, the four one-inch blood spots contained many hundreds of times that amount. The need for a robust system did not fully explain why the DoD was taking so much.

Third, there was a history of carelessness in the DoD's record of experimentation on enlistees. Even while preparations for the court-martial were under way, a presidential advisory committee — the Advisory Committee on Human Radiation Experiments (ACHRE) — was conducting public hearings on government-sponsored research on human subjects between 1944 and 1974. The committee's *Final Report*,[9] released in October 1995, took issue with DoD research on the effects of atomic explosions on soldiers. During weapons testing in the 1950s, for example, data were gathered from infantry positioned near blasts and from pilots ordered to fly through atomic clouds.[10] Despite well-documented research agendas in some instances, the *Final Report* complained about chronic vagueness in the DoD's conceptual boundary separating experimentation on enlistees from mandatory training exercises intended to "provide reassurance."[11] For example, in describing studies contracted to the Human Resources Research Organization (HumRRO), the committee writes:

> There is no question that HumRRO activities were research involving human subjects; the projects involved an experimental design in which soldier-subjects were assigned either to an experimental or a control condition. Available evidence suggests, however, that the Army did not treat HumRRO as a discretionary research activity but as an element of the training exercise in which soldiers were participating in the course of normal duty. The HumRRO subjects were apparently not volunteers. Dr. Crawford [who had been in charge of some of these studies] in 1994 said of the HumRRO subjects, "Whether they were requested to formally give their consent is pretty unknowable because in the Army or any other military service people generally do what they're asked to do."[12]

Fourth and finally, the DoD was beginning to think about genetics research and development for military purposes and, indeed, was considering the use of the repository's DNA samples as a part of that effort. In June 1993 the surgeon general of the U.S. Army directed the establishment of the "DoD Consolidated DNA/Genetics Process Action Team" to identify current and future "assets and needs for genetic services applications and technologies in the Department of Defense."[13] Of particular importance was the applicability of genetics to operational medicine. Since soldiers often face unusual exposures (e.g., radiation, disease agents, chemicals, extreme atmospheric pressures, high noise levels), and since the physiological response to an exposure often has a genetic component, it was thought that genetic research and DNA analysis might ultimately permit the selection and assignment of soldiers on the basis of genetic resistance to specific risks. While the Process Action Team may not have considered it, it is evident that if protective DNA sequences were identified it might then be possible to introduce these genes into soldiers lacking natural resistance. Prior to the court-martial, Mayfield and Vlacovsky worried that research of this sort was being contemplated and that their DNA might be used for such purposes.

Research and development in operational genetic medicine requires a substantial DNA bank, and in 1995 the most important asset of that type was the DOD Specimen Repository and Registry. When, in March 1996, the Process Action Team submitted its "Pat" Report,[14] a central focus was on "Genetics in Operational Medicine." The team recommended establishing investigational registries for military operations. Alluding to the need for recoverable baseline data, the report observed that "one does not need to know exactly what one is going to test for, or even to have validated tests, in order to justify establishment of a DNA specimen repository." More to the point here, the report observed: "It may also be possible to expand the use of the current DoD DNA Specimen Repository, if done in an appropriate fashion and with protection for privacy concerns. . . .The DNA Registry was established solely for identification purposes. For this reason, access to this databank [*sic*] for purposes other than casualty identification requires both extraordinary circumstances and the approval of the Assistant Secretary of Defense for Health Affairs (ASD/HA)." Though the report was not submitted to the army's surgeon general until March 1996, the inclusion of this language lends credibility to the concerns that Mayfield and Vlacovsky were expressing a year earlier.

In sum, the DoD's 1995 policies governing the program did not include substantive limitations on the purposes that could be served by expanded access to the registry and repository. In terms of the length of storage and the quantities of genetic materials obtained, the program could allow the use of the stored samples for substantially expanded purposes without compromising its remains-identification function. Further, the DoD had conducted ethically flawed research on human subjects in the past and, more specifically, had been careless in distinguishing between investigational activities requiring consent and other activities that did not. Finally, the DoD's Process Action Team was recommending the initiation of programs of genetic research and development and had identified the repository and registry as potentially valuable assets. The procedures for authorizing such expanded usage were already in place.

It is to be emphasized that, as far as can be determined, the ASD(HA) did not authorize, plan, or consider expanded use. Further, neither the possibility of such use nor the military's interest in it can alone establish that the DoD exceeded its authority or was in any way at fault in implementing its program. It is to these issues that we now turn.

Liberal Democracy and the Military

At a primitive level, it is possible to understand the conflict between the two young men and the military as a clash between radically different frames of reference. The more familiar of the two paradigms is what might be called a "liberal democratic" perspective. For many, the seizure of personal biological samples from a politically vulnerable population is a moral outrage manifestly redolent of Nazi medical experiments. Courses in medical ethics routinely teach that, except where there are certain psychological deficits, it is unethical to perform medical procedures or research on adults in the absence of informed consent: here there was neither consent nor disclosure. At a broader level, liberal democratic governments are supposed to respect the fundamental rights of all citizens: they do not permit the summary state seizure of bodily tissues. Even within the criminal justice system, there must be a judicial warrant and a showing of probable cause before blood can be taken from suspects.[15] From this viewpoint, not even the military should be able to seize the DNA of enlistees without the compelling justification required for violation of a fundamental right.

Those with experience in the armed forces are familiar with a second, very different frame of reference: what we might call a "military" point of view. Put bluntly, if your ass belongs to Uncle Sam, then so does the DNA it contains. Clearly the military cannot function if soldiers are free to choose which orders they will obey. Mayfield and Vlacovsky were given written orders signed by their commander. While soldiers may have a duty to disobey orders to commit war crimes, nothing like that was at issue. On the contrary, remains identification is an important responsibility of the armed forces. Since the orders issued to Mayfield and Vlacovsky were in furtherance of a consummately reasonable purpose, the soldiers should have done what they were ordered to do and should be disciplined for their refusal.

Between these two extremes is a complicated story. Military culture has a poorly understood but profound effect on the ethical practice of medicine. To trace the scope and justification of the enlistee's distinct status, one must take into account the United States Constitution at one end of the military hierarchy and the acceptance of induction into the armed services at the other.

The preamble to the Constitution explicitly delegates to the federal government the responsibility to "provide for the common defense." In delegating this responsibility, the Constitution, *ipso facto*, also delegates those other legal powers that are essential in discharging that responsibility. Although the question of which powers are so justified is a central issue in military jurisprudence, this "military necessity" provides the justifying basis for an officer's distinctive legal authority over enlistees, an authority that significantly dilutes familiar constitutional rights. Within military courts, the standard used to determine an order's legality is extremely broad: "All activities which are reasonably necessary to safeguard and protect the morals, discipline and usefulness of the members of a command and are directly connected with the maintenance of good order in the services are subject to the control of the officers upon whom the responsibility of the command rests."[16]

The implications of this standard are profound, especially in the practice of medicine. The responsibility of the DoD to maintain an armed force can reasonably entail the powers required to ensure the readiness of that force; the authority, for example, to require volunteer soldiers to submit to medical procedures intended to ensure reliable combat readiness. Intrusions that would plainly count as battery in civilian life — such as compelled physical examinations — are routine and acceptable in the armed services. It will be assumed in what follows that this authority is proper, both constitutionally and in relation to defensible political and ethical theories.

While these considerations provide a basis for military command authority, it is the act of enlistment, solemnized in an oath, that grounds the soldier's reciprocal duties. In the United States volunteers promise to uphold and defend the Constitution: the soldier's foundational obligation. Consent is critical at the point of entry into the military system but has little place once the enlistee is within the system, provided that orders are justified by military necessity. (We will ignore the complications created by wars in pursuit of unjust causes and those that are unjustly prosecuted.) The ethical commitment to accept the special responsibilities of military life can entail the duty to accept interventions intended to prevent and correct impairments in one's ability to discharge those responsibilities. Thus vaccinations, foot care, cooperation with physicians, and so forth are unconditionally mandatory for soldiers as they are not in civilian life.

Because of their unique jurisprudential and ethical status, soldiers ordinarily enter the clinical setting with antecedent legal and ethical obligations to comply with physicians' orders. Reciprocally, military physicians characteristically focus upon the presenting patient *qua* soldier, attending primarily to the health-related requirements attaching to the role. Only secondary importance will attach to the desires and wishes of the human being occupying the role. There need be no conflict here, for good soldiers fuse their identities with the group and, accordingly, want for themselves what good soldiers need. Where there is substantial tension between the soldier's health-related requirements and the needs and wants of the enlistee, a military physician may perceive this as evidence of unsuitability for military life. Accordingly, enlistees often rely on civilian doctors when personal medical problems arise.

Military Necessity and the DoD Program

Given the scope of "military necessity" and its relevance to the understandably trimmed contours of a soldier's liberty, it is difficult to challenge the DoD's authority to require enlistees to cooperate with remains identification procedures. This essay does not attempt the task. The dog tag is hardly controversial. And, in particular, the history of Vietnam-era MIAs prominently suggests that our ability to remove names from the lists of the missing can be critically important to loved ones, to other soldiers, and to the polity as a whole.

Nor is it useful to focus on the venipuncture, the physical intrusion occasioned by the program. Although trespasses across the boundaries of the body are ordinarily of great legal and ethical significance (e.g., rape and battery), the military routinely and justifiably orders medical examinations and treatments requiring such contact. And even if such physical intrusions were objectionable in themselves, it might be possible to obtain ample tissue without wrongful contact. The FBI successfully matched DNA derived from dried saliva on a postage stamp used by the Unabomber with DNA from an envelope used by Theodore Kaczynski.[17]

Nonetheless, this case would not have arisen had the military provided reliable assurance that the banked samples would be used for remains-identification purposes only, that the specimens would be destroyed or returned when the donors became ineligible for combat service, and that other uses of the DNA would require the prior voluntary informed consent of the donor. The ethically interesting issue is whether the military has the authority, based upon current standards, to require soldiers to provide DNA samples for unspecified purposes *beyond* those implicated in remains identification.

It is useful to compare a genetic code with intellectual property. For a broad range of things we can call our own — inventions, corporate logos, and novels, for example — we enjoy legal rights and powers that are protected by the law of patents, trademarks, and copyrights. Suppose, for example, that I write poems on scraps of paper and send them to people I know. Although the inscriptions have passed into the possession of the designated recipients, exactly what legal entitlements have changed hands? Do the recipients own the poems as well as the paper? Can they copyright the poems, preventing others from publishing them, including me? Are the recipients, like the clients of ghost writers, permitted to publish "my" poems over their names? While the law of intellectual property provides us with some guidance about the transfer of title to literary works, the legal standards associated with the ownership of a genetic code are *terra incognita* by comparison. Now consider that, in sending out my poem, as I lick the envelope and stamp, a specimen of my genetic material also becomes part of the package. Like an inscription on paper, the DNA can be read and interpreted, and the readings and interpretations can be published. But we have not decided what legal protections these sequences, unlike poems, are to receive.[18]

If, like the whorls of a fingerprint latent on something touched, one's DNA were without meaning or value apart from identification purposes, few would care about title or privacy protections. But, unlike fingerprints, the base-sequences of DNA can provide information of profound importance. First and most importantly, because of genetic susceptibilities to health-related conditions, one's DNA can be read, borrowing some of George Annas' words, as a probabilistic future medical diary written in a code we have not fully cracked.[19] We have already associated discrete DNA sequences with hundreds of medical conditions and many more are to come. Thus, in principle, anyone with linked DNA and the right technology would have access to health-related information about the sources: more information, in some cases, than the sources will have about themselves. With ordinary medical records, the physical files belong the doctor or hospital, but the information they contain belongs to the patient. If the health-related information latent in DNA is to receive the same protection as personal medical records, then custodians of genetic materials must be limited in their legal powers to extract and distribute it. Such restrictions are not generally in place.[20]

Second, the information derivable from linked DNA also reveals comparable information about the source's blood relatives: especially children, siblings, and parents. Analysis can be used to establish or disprove paternity and the presence of certain diseases and susceptibilities. The impact of disclosure can be extensive as well as profound. Third, there is the possibility of stigmatization and discrimination on the basis of disclosed genetic information, particularly in employment and insurance.[21] Fourth and finally, when useful sequences of genetic code are identified and developed into commercial products, those providing these valuable materials should, it seems, ordinarily have a claim to a portion of the wealth that their DNA has been used to generate. No such conventions currently exist.[22]

To be sure, only limited personal information can now be gleaned from DNA analysis, and the process is complex and expensive. But as we move toward cheaper and more revealing methods, the military's vast indexed collection of DNA samples, as already noted, will become an enormously attractive asset for study and exploitation. If genetic data and identifiers were to flow freely — to researchers, to other government agencies, to insurance companies, to the press, to potential employers, and so on — the potential costs to enlistees in the loss of privacy, long after their service obligations had lapsed, could be great indeed. These potential risks and burdens of genetic data collection and dissemination, while not trivial, might bear no relationship to "military necessity": the constitutional responsibility for national defense that is at the heart of the justification for military discipline and at the foundation of the soldier's distinctive ethical obligations. Lacking a mechanism for reporting expanded use to donors, there might be no way — apart from conscientious refusal at the outset — to prevent misuse before irreparable damage was done. In the absence of any reliable assurance that the samples would be used only for remains-identification purposes, it was not unreasonable for the two marines to assume that the Department of Defense was going to do whatever it wanted.

The Limits to Military Usage

Despite the obscurity of the transaction between the two marines and the Department of Defense, there are at least two types of limitation on expanded use that are relevant. The first involves the use of tissues in research. The principles here have been clear since the Nuremberg trials following World War II. For the victors of 1945, it was salient evidence of the justice of the Allied cause that the vanquished had, in the name of research, committed crimes against humanity. The Nuremberg Code emerged in 1947 from international outrage at compelled participation in medical experimentation.[23] Its first principle began: "The voluntary consent of the human subject is absolutely essential." After the World Medical Association's 1964 Declaration of Helsinki (revised in 1975) and the 1979 *Belmont Report*,[24] it gradually became axiomatic that, ethically, investigators must obtain the voluntary informed consent of competent research subjects before it is permissible to do research upon them. Consent forms (disclosing in advance the procedures and risks and requiring the signature of the research subject) and institutional review boards (to review proposed research and the mechanisms for obtaining consent) are now routine protections when research on human subjects is contemplated.

But in this case there was no meaningful consent (the marines were ordered to submit to DNA sampling), there was no information (the military was silent about the purposes to be served in the future use of these samples), and none of the routine protections were reliably in place. Given the broad applicability of the ethical standards that have long governed research both internationally and in the United States, these limitations on the use of tissue samples would be applicable even when the research is militarily necessary.

The second limitation flows from the scope of military necessity as a justification for the dilution and waiver of civilian liberty. What residual rights remain? We have already mentioned a duty (and hence a liberty) to disobey orders to commit war crimes. But constitutional rights to privacy also survive induction. Officers may not, for example, open first-class mail addressed to enlistees, nor, except for inspections, can they search personal possessions without probable cause. In one case involving health-related information, in *United States v. Spencer*, a military court held[25] that an order directing an enlistee to produce civilian medical records was overly broad and illegally interfered with the defendant's private affairs. There is an obvious parallel between the health-related information contained in protected medical records and the health-related information derivable from linked DNA. Comparable invasions of privacy can occur along either route.

While, ordinarily, military orders enjoy a presumption of legality, the court there said that lawfulness *cannot be presumed* when an order invades the privacy or personal rights of individuals in the absence of a showing of just or sufficient cause. It is useful here to distinguish between the taking of tissue samples for remains-identification purposes only — arguably a sufficient justification — and the taking of tissue samples for unspecified purposes — arguably an insufficient justification. It is the latter that is at issue here. Where the trimming of constitutionally backed liberties is not justified by military necessity, "relative" conscientious refusal (i.e., refusal to obey an order on the grounds that it conflicts with a institutional obligation) would appear to be both ethically justifiable and organizationally useful.

The ethical justification is founded on the oath taken upon induction: to "uphold and defend the Constitution of the United States of America." It would seem that, when the lawfulness of an order cannot be presumed, the paramount obligation "to uphold and defend the Constitution" can then entail a duty to disobey such an order if obedience would plainly betray fundamental, albeit militarily diluted, constitutional rights. The military's need for a sound remains-identification program may have been compelling, but the need for unlimited access to the stored tissue samples was not. Although the two soldiers may have had a general duty to obey the orders of those in command, they may have had a higher conflicting military obligation here. In disobeying orders, Mayfield and Vlacovsky may have been uncommonly good marines.

Conscientious refusal can be organizationally useful as well. At the court-martial, soldiers who had been called as witnesses testified that the defendants' public refusals had, in their opinions, strengthened the military by encouraging improvements in the new program. In that case, the DoD should have thanked the two soldiers rather than prosecuted them. For it is easy to sympathize with the military's choice to implement the program as quickly as possible, even if further refinement was going to be needed. There were actual and potential hot spots in the early 1990s — Kuwait, the former Yugoslavia, Somalia, Rwanda, and Haiti. There was a way to obviate the need to bury yet another unknown soldier. One would not want an armed force that refused to move forward until it had certainty that all potential difficulties had been taken into account. It is often better to take the calculated risk that only manageable problems will arise as programs take off and that adjustments can be made on the fly. But if one chooses to set out in a possibly faulty craft, it is wise to anticipate that corrections will be needed and imprudent to discourage the expression of misgivings.

As it happened, just two weeks before the court-martial began, the Office of the Assistant Secretary of Defense for Health Affairs issued new protections that, in effect, addressed the defendants' doubts about the DNA banking program.[26] Allowing that "misgivings have been heard from a few," this third memorandum narrowed the scope of the program. Samples would henceforth be destroyed in fifty years (instead of seventy-five) or at the request of the sample source following completion of service in the military. Most important, substantive exclusionary limitations were explicitly placed on expanded use. The use of the tissue samples was limited to (1) remains identification, (2) quality assurance, (3) uses to which the sample source or surviving next-of-kin consents, and (4) court-ordered uses where the sample is necessary for the investigation or prosecution of a crime punishable by one year or more of confinement, provided that such use is approved by the assistant secretary of defense for health affairs in consultation with the Department of Defense general counsel. While it is possible that these new rules could be revoked or abrogated in the future, and worrisome that such departures might not be visible and subject to public debate, this third memorandum goes a long way toward resolving the issues raised by Mayfield and Vlacovsky.

Yet, in authorizing "uses to which the donor . . . consents," the refinements were raising precisely those "voluntariness" problems that the Advisory Committee on the Human Radiation Experiments had identified. ACHRE's *Final Report* had found that the DoD needed improvements in its protection of military personnel serving as volunteer research subjects.[27] They urged that the military sharpen its distinction between research-related activities where the enlistee's involvement is discretionary and other military activities where participation is mandatory. They recommended that officers and investigators be educated in applicable human subjects regulations. They pressed for the establishment of registries of all enlistees who had volunteered for human studies. And they recommended that commanding officers be excluded from activities intended to recruit research participants and that an independent ombudsperson be present. Although, historically, the military has not been very concerned about the liberty interests of soldiers, the DoD may have to be more thoughtful whenever it undertakes research on enlistees.

The court-martial was a bench trial; the judge, a lieutenant commander in the navy. On the second day, April 16, 1996, the two marines were found guilty of willfully disobeying an order. Notwithstanding the seriousness of the offense, their punishment consisted of a letter of reprimand and confinement to base for one week. Some weeks later, after their tours of duty had expired, Lance Corporal John Mayfield III and Corporal Joseph Vlacovsky left the United States Marines with honorable discharges and all their GI benefits.

Acknowledgments

Work on this paper was supported by the Obermann Center for Advanced Studies at the University of Iowa. Much of the research was done while I was a fellow at its Faculty Research Seminar on Ethical and Legal Implications of Stored Human Tissue Samples, June 10–21, 1996. Additionally, as the case discussed in this essay proceeded, I was involved as an expert witness for the defense. I am greatly indebted to the defendants, John Mayfield III and Joseph Vlacovsky, and to their attorney, Eric Seitz, for assistance. Claire Gorfinkel and Leanne Logan also contributed to this essay.

Notes

1. Deputy Secretary of Defense Memorandum 47803, "Establishment of a Repository of Specimen Samples to Aid in Remains Identification Using Genetic Deoxyribonucleic Acid (DNA) Analysis," December 16, 1991.

2. Assistant Secretary of Defense (Health Affairs) Memorandum and Policy Statement, "Establishment of a Repository of Specimen Samples to Aid in Remains Identification Using Genetic Deoxyribonucleic Acid (DNA) Analysis," January 5, 1993.

3. Jean E. McEwen and Philip R. Reilly, "A Review of State Legislation on DNA Forensic Data Banking," *American Journal of Human Genetics* 54 (1994): 941–968; see also Barry Scheck, "DNA Data Banking: A Cautionary Tale," *American Journal of Human Genetics* 54 (1994): 931–933.

4. The registry was also conducting ongoing, randomized, blinded analyses of samples for quality assurance purposes.

5. Work is under way on microchip-equipped, handheld devices that, in minutes, can use DNA analysis to reassociate commingled body fragments in the field: remarks of Lieutenant Colonel Victor Weedn, June 13, 1996, at the Obermann Center for Advanced Studies, University of Iowa.

6. Declaration of Lieutenant Colonel Victor Weedn, Medical Corps, United States Army, filed in *Mayfield v. Dalton*, United States District Court for the District of Hawaii, June 29, 1995.

7. Dean Chadwin, "The Gene War," *Honolulu Weekly*, September 6, 1995, pp. 6–9.

8. Uniform Code of Military Justice, chapter 47, subchapter X, section 809, article 90: Assaulting or Willfully Disobeying Superior Commissioned Officer.

9. Advisory Committee on Human Radiation Experiments, *Final Report: Advisory Committee on Human Radiation Experiments* (Washington, D.C.: U.S. Government Printing Office, 1995).

10. Advisory Committee on Human Radiation Experiments, *Final Report*, chapter 10, "Atomic Veterans: Human Experimentation in Connection with Atomic Bomb Tests," pp. 454–505.

11. Advisory Committee on Human Radiation Experiments, *Final Report*, p. 484.

12. Advisory Committee on Human Radiation Experiments, *Final Report*, p. 463.

13. Department of Defense, Armed Forces Institute of Pathology Pamphlet, "History and Mission of the DoD DNA Registry and DNA Specimen Repository," April 1995.

14. Process Action Team for a Consolidated Military Genetics/DNA Program, "Final Report of the Process Action Team for a Consolidated Military Genetics/DNA Program," prepared for Lt. Gen. Alcide M. LaNoue, Marine Corps, USA (March 29, 1996): pp. 19–20. This report, to the surgeon general of the U.S. Army, does take up some of the ethical issues raised by military genetics. I owe a debt of gratitude to the office of Congressman Neil Abercrombie of Hawaii for energetic assistance in obtaining a copy of the report.

15. *Schmerber v. California*, 384 U.S. 757 (1966).

16. *U.S. v. Martin*, 1 USMCA 674, 5 CMR 102, 1044 (1952).

17. "Court Documents Show Evidence Tying Suspect to the Unabomber," *New York Times*, June 14, 1996.

18. See, for example, Joan Stephenson, "Pathologists Enter Debate on Consent for Genetic Research on Stored Tissue," *JAMA* 275 (February 21, 1996): 503–504; and Vickie L. Hannig, Ellen Wright Clayton, and Kathryn M. Edwards, "Whose DNA Is It Anyway? Relationships between Families and Researchers," *American Journal of Medical Genetics* 47 (1993): 257–260.

19. George J. Annas, "Privacy Rules for DNA Databanks: Protecting Coded 'Future Diaries,'" *Journal of the American Medical Association* 270 (November 17, 1993): 2346–2350.

20. George J. Annas, Leonard H. Glantz, and Patricia A. Roche, "Drafting the Genetic Privacy Act: Science, Policy, and Practical Considerations," *Journal of Law, Medicine, and Ethics* 23 (1995): 361.

21. Kathy Hudson et al., "Genetic Discrimination and Health Insurance: An Urgent Need for Reform," *Science* 270 (October 20, 1995): 391–393.

22. *Moore v. Regents of the University of California*, 793 P.2d 479 (Cal. 1990).

23. George J. Annas and Michael A. Grodin, eds., *The Nazi Doctors and the Nuremberg Code: Human Rights in Human Experimentation* (New York: Oxford University Press, 1992).

24. National Commission for the Protection of Human Subjects of Biomedical and Behavioral Research, *The Belmont Report: Ethical Principles and Guidelines for the Protection of Human Subjects of Research* (Washington, D.C.: U.S. Government Printing Office, April 18, 1979).

25. *United States v. Spencer*, 29 M.J. 740 (AFCMR 1989), at 743.

26. Assistant Secretary of Defense (Health Affairs), memorandum, "Policy Refinements for the Armed Forces Repository of Specimen Samples for the Identification of Remains," April 2, 1996.

27. Advisory Committee on Human Radiation Experiments, *Final Report*, pp. 823–825.

Stored Biologic Specimens for Military Identification: The Department of Defense DNA Registry

Victor Walter Weedn

Identification of remains, in times of war as well as in times of peace, is an important and humanitarian mission of the Department of Defense (DoD). Recognizing the need for DNA identification to bolster traditional methods of identification, the Department of Defense DNA Registry was established in 1991.

The DoD DNA Registry is a Division of the Office of the Armed Forces Medical Examiner (OAFME), a Department of the Armed Forces Institute of Pathology (AFIP), and serves to support the OAFME's identification efforts. The DoD DNA Registry consists of the Armed Forces DNA Identification Laboratory (AFDIL) and the Armed Forces Repository of Specimen Samples for the Identification of Remains. The DNA collection program will eventually replace the military's duplicate panograph program that was created in 1986 for identification purposes.

The Need for DNA Identification

A cost of doing business for the U.S. military is the identification of war dead; indeed, this is a national priority. The OAFME, however, is involved in more identification efforts in time of peace than in time of war.

Prior to and during the Civil War, soldiers were identified through visual recognition. The soldiers soon realized that they might not be identified should they fall in battle. Their comrades in arms, who might recognize them, might themselves fall in battle or flee the battlefield. Their bodies might become difficult to recognize due to disfiguring injuries or postmortem decomposition.

Soldiers at the time began to purchase metal tags inscribed with their names so that they might be identified after death. They wanted to ensure that if they made the ultimate sacrifice, proper respects would be paid. Service-members feel similarly today.

The "dog tag" was the primary method of identification for World Wars I and II. However, dog tags are mere personal effects that confer little more than presumptive identification that may not withstand scrutiny. They can come loose from a body. They may be exchanged as a sign of friendship. Indeed, cases of the wrong dog tag on a body have occurred.

345

The military has since moved to positive methods of identification, particularly dental and fingerprint comparisons. There are, however, certain limitations to these identification methods; they simply are not applicable in all cases. Although the military sends a ten-finger fingerprint card to the FBI for filing on all servicemembers, between 15 and 30 percent of those fingerprint cards are discarded as smudged or otherwise of unacceptable quality. Therefore, fingerprint comparison cannot be accomplished for a significant portion of the U.S. military population. Similarly, due to the success of water fluoridation programs, servicemembers increasingly have fewer and even no dental restorations upon which to base dental comparisons. Moreover, remains may be fragmented. A fragmented body may have no teeth or fingers. Many body parts, such as an amputated leg, will never be identified by dental or fingerprint means — yet this tissue will contain abundant amounts of DNA.

In all mass disasters a percentage of victims simply cannot be identified by the traditional fingerprint or dental methods. In Operation Desert Storm, the following statistics pertain to the 298 remains processed at the Dover Port Mortuary in 1991: 30 percent of the servicemembers had no fingerprint records on file, 14 percent of the remains had no printable fingers, 12 percent of screening dental panographs were uninterpretable, 8 percent of the remains had no dentition present, and 26 percent of the remains were fragmented.

The first case during Operation Desert Storm in which an identification could not be made by dental or fingerprint comparison was the result of a motor vehicle accident. The victim had teeth, but his medical and dental records were not located. A duplicate panograph (screening pan oral dental radiograph) was retrieved from the central repository in Monterey, California, but, unfortunately, it was overexposed and uninterpretable. The individual had fingers, but no fingerprint record was on file with the FBI. This individual was eventually visually identified by his brother, who viewed the mutilated remains. This experience was emotionally traumatic and would not have been necessary if the military's DNA identification program had been fully operational at the time.

The next set of cases in which dental or fingerprint identifications could not be made involved a friendly fire incident. A Hellfire missile hit and destroyed an armored personnel carrier, killing three of seven occupants. The recovered bodies were fragmented and partially incinerated and included neither heads or arms. The three bodies were identified through their blood group types A, AB, and O, a highly fortuitous event unlikely to happen again given the circumstances.

The modern battlefield is highly lethal. With the greater destructive power of weaponry, bodies are increasingly fragmented and incinerated, thus making identification increasingly problematic.

American society has also changed. Families have come to expect that their loved ones will be identified and returned and have demanded that the remains be identified with certainty. The public is aware that DNA testing is available and brings greater capacity to make identifications than ever before. Expectations have accordingly been raised.

Establishment of the DoD DNA Registry

AFDIL was developed during Operation Desert Storm in 1991 and has since been involved in many identification efforts for the military. Two early examples demonstrate the utility of the military's DNA identification capability.

CASE 1

A navy pilot was lost over Iraq in early January 1991. Two months later, approximately one pound of tissue — thought to be his entire mortal remains — was recovered. As insignificant as this small portion of decomposed tissue seemed to be, it was the federal government's responsibility to make an identification, if possible. A positive identification of this piece of tissue would permit the conclusion that the pilot had died as a result of enemy action and was not being held as a prisoner of war. AFDIL performed amplified fragment length polymorphism (AmpFLP) analysis on the tissue, as well as on tissue samples from his (possible) wife and children, which resulted in an exclusion; it was not the pilot in question.

Of course, such cases always assume correct parentage. Nonpaternity is a major reason for a DNA databank of reference samples from servicemembers themselves. Testing of the tissue was also accomplished using mitochondrial DNA (mtDNA) sequencing. As there are many thousands of copies of mtDNA for every one copy of nuclear DNA, it is easier to obtain results from degraded samples. But mtDNA is inherited strictly maternally. So in this case the reference samples from the wife and children were not helpful. His mother and siblings were not available for sampling, as he was an adopted child. Again, this is a reason for a repository of DNA samples from servicemembers themselves; many servicemembers have no families or have family members who cannot be located.

In this case, the possible family provided the pilot's electric shaver that he left at home, from which hair clippings were obtained for mitochondrial analysis. Again, it was determined that this was not tissue of the individual it was thought to be. After extensive DNA testing and reviewing the circumstances concerning the loss of the pilot, the AFDIL declared the pilot killed-in-action with his body not recovered (KIA-BNR)

CASE 2

After Operation Desert Storm, the U.S. military participated in cleanup efforts in the theater of operations. While servicemembers were disposing of ordinance, an explosion ensued, killing three. One body was intact, quickly identified, and returned to his family. The other two bodies consisted of 238 pounds of commingled, fragmented, and partially incinerated remains. Only one fragment was itself identifiable, a small portion of maxilla containing three molars with dental restorations. After the remains arrived at the Dover Port Mortuary, collections of DNA specimens took a day and a half; in the subsequent thirty-six hours, performance of HLA DQ-Alpha dot/blot testing permitted identification of tissues as one or the other body.

Such difficult identifications are not uncommon. The DoD DNA Registry has been responsible for approximately 200 identifications during peacetime since its inception. The OAFME is particularly involved in many aircraft mishaps, in which the remains are typically severely fragmented and partially incinerated.

Testing for current remains identification can be performed efficiently and in high volume. This involves the testing of nuclear or chromosomal DNA. For most small accidents, results are reported within approximately twenty-four hours.

Another identification mission of AFDIL is the DNA testing of skeletal remains from Southeast Asia, Korea, and even World War II. This testing involves mtDNA sequencing, which is slow, laborious, and expensive. Currently approximately ten mtDNA cases are analyzed each month.

Just as AFDIL has the ability to perform such specialized nuclear DNA and mitochondrial DNA analysis for the Department of Defense, it also conducts testing on a limited number of requests from outside agencies. In this capacity AFDIL has performed DNA identifications for many high-profile cases, including work with the Federal Bureau of Investigation on the victims of the Branch Davidian incident at Waco, Texas; assistance to the National Transportation Safety Board for the aircrew of the U.S. Air flight #427 mishap, near Pittsburgh, Pennsylvania; the identification of victims from the TWA flight #800 mishap off Long Island, New York; and the confirmation of the identification of Tsar Nicholas II for the Russian government.

DoD DNA Collections

A DNA specimen will be obtained and stored from all United States servicemembers for use as a reference specimen. Although DNA identifications can be made using reference specimens from family members, DoD collects DNA specimens from servicemembers themselves. This repository of specimen samples from servicemembers is necessary because of instances of nonparentage, adoption, family unknown, family whereabouts unknown, mutational events, reluctance to approach families when identity is in doubt, and the need to perform testing as expeditiously as possible.

The DoD is collecting specimens from new personnel from all the services: army, air force, navy, and marine corps. DNA specimen collections commenced in June 1992. Additionally, collections from the residual forces (servicemembers already in the military at the inception of the program) are under way. Specimens are received at a rate of 1,000–5,000 per day. By 2002 samples should be collected from all U.S. servicemembers. A DNA collection is now required for current military members before deployment or movement into hostile fire zones.

The collection kit used by the military was developed during Operation Desert Shield in anticipation of Operation Desert Storm, but collections were not made at that time. The military's DNA collection and storage system was specifically designed to prevent error from sample switching or mislabeling to the maximal extent possible. Redundancy was built into the system. The collection kit has been lauded as an innovative and cost-effective DNA collection and storage system, which is now sold commercially. Many state DNA sex offender databanks employ a system modified from that developed by the military. Other countries have also looked to the U.S. Armed Forces as a model system.

DNA specimens are collected as blood stains, from either a finger-stick or venipuncture, and an oral swab. The DNA collection kit costs approximately three dollars and is all-inclusive, including the pencil to fill out the form. The servicemember fills in his or her name, Social Security number, date of birth, and branch of service. On the reverse side of this card, a fingerprint is taken, a bar code is affixed, and the signature of the servicemember is obtained, attesting to the validity of the sample. The bloodstain is made on filter paper attached to the card; the same type of filter paper is used for collection of blood from neonates for phenylketonuria (PKU) testing. An oral swab (buccal scraping) is also collected as a back-up source of DNA material. The sample is fixed in isopropanol and sent with the card to the repository.

A double-shipping barrier pouch with a swab and a bloodstain card is used to ship the specimens to the repository; another card is placed in a metal foil pouch with the health record. The bloodstain cards are shipped and stored with desiccants to ensure proper drying of the blood specimen.

At the repository, cards are vacuum-sealed with a desiccant in a seven-layer metal foil barrier pouch and then frozen at $-20°C$ in large walk-in freezers. A 16 by 31 foot freezer can hold approximately 1.4 million specimens.

A computer system has been developed to track the specimens. A specimen processor first reads the bar code on the bloodstain card and checks to ensure a match with the bar code of the oral swab. The specimen processor then enters the Social Security number and the first three letters of the last name, and the computer system looks for a match from a DoD personnel file. After verification of the data on the card with the information automatically re-trieved, a new label is generated for the storage pouch. The bloodstain card and a desiccant are placed in the newly labeled pouch, and then the pouch is vacuum-sealed and archived. The computer system maintains a record of where specimens are filed and which have been retrieved.

To ensure the retrievability and the integrity of stored specimens, a quality assurance program has been instituted. Every month, 100 samples are ran-domly selected and tested to check that the cards are properly placed and that DNA can be recovered and typed from the cards or swabs or both.

Privacy Considerations

From the conceptual origins of the program, DoD recognized the privacy concerns involved in the collection and storage of DNA specimens. These con-cerns are addressed through a set of protections and safeguards that include local precautions, DoD policy, pertinent law, program scrutiny, and public visibility. These protections include security, restrictions on access to the spec-imens and any resultant information, and limitations of purpose. The speci-mens and any test results are treated as a part of the medical record — as confidential information. The Armed Forces Repository of Specimen Samples for the Identification of Remains was created for the express, limited, and humanitarian purpose of human remains identification.

Local precautions involve security measures, restrictions on access to the materials, and education of personnel who are involved in DNA operations. The security measures include physical security of the premises as well as se-curity of the repository accessioning computer system.

DoD policy protections are embodied in a series of documents.

DECEMBER 16, 1991, AUTHORIZATION

This document authorizes the assistant secretary of defense for health affairs to establish a DNA Registry to consist of a laboratory and a repository of reference specimens of servicemembers.

JANUARY 5, 1993, POLICY GUIDANCE

This document sets forth the overall parameters of the program, including restrictions on use and need for security and confidentiality.

MARCH 9, 1994, IMPLEMENTING INSTRUCTIONS

This document sets forth detailed operating procedures to the services and a general time frame for implementation.

JUNE 14, 1995, SYSTEMS NOTICE

This document, required by the Privacy Act, is published in the *Federal Register* and gives legal constructive notice to the world that DNA specimens are taken and how this "system of records" is used. The Systems Notice makes known the responsible individual and address for inquiries. The army's "Blanket Routine Uses," which make allowance for various uses of most systems of records, do not apply to this system and no exemptions are claimed; thus these records have far greater protections than other sensitive records.

APRIL 2, 1996, POLICY REFINEMENTS

This document promulgates certain policy refinements to previous policy. First, the routine period of retention of specimen samples was set at fifty years, in accordance with that of other health records, a technical correction to the previously announced destruction schedule of seventy-five years. Second, servicemembers are given the opportunity to request the destruction of their individual specimen samples, "upon completion of their military service obligation or other applicable DoD relationship." Third, the potential use to which these specimen samples may be put is clarified. The 1993 policy guidance states that the DNA collections could be used for "other purposes" under "extraordinary circumstances" only "when no reasonable alternative means for obtaining a specimen for DNA profile analysis is available" and approved by the assistant secretary of defense for health affairs. The policy refinements state that the collected specimens may be used for (1) identification of remains, (2) internal quality assurance purposes, (3) consensual uses, and (4) other uses compelled by other applicable law, as when compelled by a proper judicial order or authorization for a felony when no other specimen is available and upon approval of the ASD(HA) after consultation with DoD general counsel.

Fourth, and last, the title of the repository was changed to "The Armed Forces Repository of Specimen Samples for the Identification of Remains" to improve public understanding of the purpose of the repository.

JULY 18, 1996, ACCELERATED PROGRAMS DIRECTIVE

This document mandates the acceleration of DNA collections such that all specimen samples are collected by the turn of the millennium, January 1, 2000.

OCTOBER 11, 1996, ELIMINATION OF HEALTH RECORD
SPECIMEN SAMPLE IMPLEMENTING INSTRUCTIONS

In accordance with the Policy Refinements directive, this documentation specifies the implementing instructions for the elimination of the specimen sample in the military medical record. New cards are no longer to be placed in the medical record, and medical record pouches are to be pulled from medical records and destroyed within one year.

Significantly, these instructions also called for the dissemination of explanatory information to collection sites to facilitate understanding by servicemembers of the purpose of the DNA specimen sample collections.

NOVEMBER 4, 1996, EARLY DESTRUCTION
IMPLEMENTING INSTRUCTION

In accordance with the Policy Refinements directive, this document specifies the implementing instructions for the early destruction of specimen samples at the request of servicemembers. The system calls for documented verification of the destruction process within six months of a valid request. Only servicemembers who have completed their obligation and are not eligible for recall may request early destruction of their specimen sample.

MARCH 17, 1997, ACCOMMODATION OF
RELIGIOUS PRACTICES DIRECTIVE

This directive permits service branches to exempt mandatory DNA collections to accommodate religious practices.

OTHER PROTECTIONS

Other policies are being developed, which include a revision of the Systems Notice and an initiative to drop the oral swab specimen as a cost-cutting measure.

A proposal by Representative Joseph Kennedy (D-Mass.) was introduced in 1996 that would codify the limitations of purpose established in the Policy

Refinements; it was passed by the U.S. House of Representatives, but defeated by the Senate.

In addition to specific military regulations, and policy guidance, other applicable federal laws provide protections and safeguards for the archived specimens and resultant information. The primary relevant federal legislation pertaining to the collections program is the federal Privacy Act of 1974, which is the current federal standard promulgated, after due deliberation by Congress, on privacy. It is this Privacy Act that requires the public notice of the collections and their purpose in the *Federal Register* as a "Systems Notice." Moreover, DoD treats the collected DNA specimens as part of the medical record, and thus they fall under statutes that protect the confidentiality of the medical records.

During the early implementation of the program and before the promulgation of many of the current policy documents, an oversight committee, created by the ASD(HA), assisted the development and coordination of policy recommendations and provided programmatic oversight. Currently, in addition to AFIP administration, oversight is provided by AFIP's Board of Governors, which is chaired by the ASD(HA) and includes the three military service surgeons general and top officials of the Veterans Administration and the Department of Health and Human Services, as well as the AFIP's Scientific Advisory Board (composed of many nationally recognized civilian and military scientists and administrators). Thus, the DNA Registry and the DNA collections program are monitored by the military's civilian secretariat and by the civilian scientific community.

Perhaps as significant as legal protections and administrative oversight is the substantial visibility of the DNA collections program, which ensures public scrutiny of all aspects of the program. The Armed Forces Repository of Specimen Samples for the Identification of Remains has become a model program for large DNA repositories. This is in part due to its previous appellation, the "DoD DNA Specimen Repository"; perhaps if it had been initially designated the "DoD Blood Reference Center," it might have been less likely to be considered any different than other archives of biological material. The visibility and public knowledge of this program will continue to be fostered by the Department of Defense in meeting this all-important mission of casualty identification.

It should be noted that the DNA Registry keeps no sensitive information that can be used as the basis for genetic discrimination. The sensitive information that is kept is the name, Social Security number, race and ethnic group, and the latent genetic information in the DNA. Without testing, the information in the DNA is not available. Specimens are only stored; they are not tested unless needed for identification or for certain quality assurance purposes.

In the event of testing, the information gleaned is meaningless for anything other than identification. As in the case of fingerprints, there is a lot of potential information, enough to individuate every man, woman, and child, but it is meaningless for anything other than identification. AFDIL typically performs analysis of noncoding repetitive regions of DNA that are useful for identification, but have no clinical significance. For example, the identification of an HUMTHO 7,8 type genetic locus has no prejudicial implications — it could not be used by employers or insurers as a basis for discrimination; nor does it confer any psychological or social stigma.

Challenges to the DoD DNA Registry

The DNA collections program is a mandatory program. Individuals cannot opt out of it, as they have consented to serve in the armed forces with all the requirements placed on military servicemembers. Accountability of all servicemembers is necessary for the military to accomplish its overall mission. Similarly, many other requirements in the military are compulsory, such as urine drug testing, fingerprinting, dental panographs, HIV testing, physical examinations, and physical fitness tests, all of which are needed by the armed forces to maintain national defense readiness.

To date, two marines and one air force servicemember have been charged with refusal to provide DNA specimens. Each has been tried by court-martial for willful failure to obey a direct order of a superior officer and accordingly been convicted and punished. Well over 1.3 million specimens had been collected before these refusals. Significant press coverage accompanied the inception of this program. As investigative reporters sought stories of apprehension and concern from servicemembers, what they found instead was great support for the program among military personnel.

Contemporaneously with the court-martial proceedings, the two marines filed a federal class action suit in the federal District Court in Hawaii claiming that the program was unconstitutional and invaded their privacy rights. The court rejected all of the plaintiffs' claims, denied the class certification, and granted the government's motion for summary judgment.[1]

Significant portions of the court's opinion include the following. With regard to the constitutional claim of *invasion of privacy*:

The taking of blood samples and oral swabs for the purpose of remains identification presents, on its face, a far less intrusive infringement of Plaintiffs' Fourth Amendment privacy rights than the blood testing in either *Schmerber*, *Skinner*, or *Von Raab*. The blood test at issue in *Schmerber* involved a seizure of evidence to be used in a possible criminal prosecution. In *Skinner* and *Von Raab*, blood, urine, and breath tests were used to detect the illegal or illicit use of drugs or alcohol, the confirmation of which could be grounds for disciplinary action or criminal sanctions. . . . (p. 6)

Plaintiffs concede that the military's stated purpose for the DNA registry — remains identification — is a benign one. But they argue that the military *could*, at some point in the future, use the DNA samples for some less innocuous purpose, such as the diagnosis of hereditary diseases or disorders and the use or dissemination of such diagnoses to potential employers, insurers and others with a possible interest in such information. Plaintiffs have presented no evidence that the military has used or disclosed, or has any plans to use or disclose, information gleaned from the DNA samples for any purpose other than remains identification. A challenge to such hypothetical future use, or misuse, as the case may be, of the samples in the DNA repository does not present a justifiable case or controversy. . . . (p. 7)

The court finds that the military has demonstrated a compelling interest in both its need to account internally for the fate of its service members and in ensuring the peace of mind of their next of kin and dependents in time of war. The court further finds that when measured against this interest, the minimal intrusion presented by the taking of blood samples and oral swabs for the military's DNA registry, though undoubtedly a "seizure," is not an *unreasonable* seizure and is thus *not* prohibited by the Constitution. . . . (p. 8)

With regard to the *breach of contract claim* that the marines did not enlist with knowledge of the DNA collections program:

In fact, the enlistment documents that Plaintiffs concede they signed make amply clear that military enlistees may be subjected to a plethora of laws, regulations, and requirements that would not normally apply to civilian employees of the Government. The documents also indicate that such laws, regulations and requirements can change at any time. (p. 9)

The enlistment documents promise no limits on the military's ability to take blood or tissue samples or perform other medical tests on enlistees, whether for purposes of assessing physical fitness, detecting the use of illegal drugs, or otherwise. Indeed, Plaintiffs were undoubtedly subjected to such tests in connection with their enlistment. The sampling performed in connection with the DNA registry is not so qualitatively different so as to require a separate, more specific form of consent than that required for other testing. . . . (p. 9)

With regard to federal regulations which require *informed consent for research*:

The DoD DNA Registry does not meet the regulatory definition of "research." (p. 10) . . . there is no evidence that Plaintiffs or their fellow service members are being subjected to any kind of experimentation or research. Once a blood sample and oral swab are taken and stored, the individual service member's relationship with the registry becomes dormant. The sample is not retrieved and scrutinized unless and until the service member is believed to have died in action. Even then, the military's inquiry is limited to determining whether the DNA in the sample matches that in the remains believed to be those of the service member. The service members whose DNA samples are kept in the registry are no more human guinea pigs than are the millions of service members whose dental records were kept on hand by the military to provide for remains identification in past wars.

The court finds that the DoD DNA Registry and related blood and tissue sampling does not violate 32 CFR Part 219. . . . (p. 11)

With regard to the plaintiffs' motion to *represent all military servicemembers* who are compelled to provide blood and other tissues for DNA identification:

Plaintiffs have failed to show that any service members other than themselves actually oppose the program. Accordingly, the court DENIES Plaintiffs' Motion to Certify Class. (p. 12)

The Ninth Circuit Court of Appeals heard the case on appeal and vacated the judgment of the district court, remanding the case with instructions to dismiss for mootness since both appellants had left the active duty military.[2]

Conclusion

Despite the strong privacy concern, the military servicemembers generally strongly support this program. Servicemembers who make the ultimate sacrifice will want their remains recovered, identified, and returned to their families for proper respects to be paid — so that others may know that they gave their life for their country. The degree of concern over the privacy issue that this identification program poses is indicated by (1) the few (three) service-members who have refused to have DNA collected and (2) the few (three) servicemembers who have requested the early destruction of their DNA specimen sample.

There are innumerable scattered and diverse stores of biologic material in existence, all of which contain DNA and some of which are larger than the Armed Forces Repository of Specimen Samples for the Identification of Remains. Examples of other potentially DNA-bearing archives include hospital pathology microscopic slides and tissue blocks, blood banks, sperm banks, organ and tissue banks, and research tissue stores. DNA is far more widespread and available than commonly believed; DNA is present in specimens collected for drug testing, in the tubes of blood drawn for clinical laboratory testing, from the clothes that people wear, and from envelope seals and stamps licked by the sender. The protections and safeguards of these other sources of DNA are far less than those of the DoD program.

From the very beginning of this program, the Department of Defense has been very specific as to the mission of DoD DNA Registry, which is the identification of those who have made the ultimate sacrifice for our nation. It is the goal of this organization never again to bury the remains of an American serviceman or servicewoman under the inscription "Here Rests in Honored Glory an American Soldier Known But to God."

Acknowledgments

The views expressed are mine and do not necessarily reflect the views of the Department of Defense or the Department of the Army.

Notes

1. *Mayfield v. Dalton*, 901 F. Supp. 300 (D. Hawaii, 1995).
2. No. 95–16626, filed March 27, 1997, Honolulu.

Contributors

Jeannette Anderson, R.N., M.A., is the clinical coordinator of the Regional Genetic Consultation Service in Iowa. She has also served as the nurse coordinator of the Iowa Neonatal Metabolic Screening Program at the University of Iowa.

Mary Ann G. Cutter, Ph.D., is an associate professor of philosophy, University of Colorado, Colorado Springs. She headed the Committee on Genetics and Insurance, Colorado Governor's Commission on Life and the Law, which drafted a state law limiting access to genetic information by the health, group disability, and long-term care insurance industry.

William L. Freeman, M.D., M.P.H., is the director of the research program in the Indian Health Service and chairs the National IHS Institutional Review Board. He has recently been on the staff of the National Bioethics Advisory Commission.

Jane Getchell, Dr.P.H., is associate director and chief of the Disease Control Division of the University of Iowa Hygienic Laboratory. She is certified as a high complexity clinical laboratory director by the American Board of Bioanalysis.

Karen Gottlieb, Ph.D., J.D., is currently a senior research associate at the National Center for State Courts. Her research interests include the use of genetic and epidemiologic evidence in the courts, genetic medical malpractice, and the interplay of feudal law and inbreeding on the island of Sark.

Henry T. (Hank) Greely, J.D., is a professor of law and professor, by courtesy, of genetics at Stanford University, where he specializes in health law and policy and in legal issues in genetics. He co-directs the Stanford Program on Genomics, Ethics, and Society and serves on the North American Committee of the Human Genome Diversity Project, whose ethics subcommittee he chairs.

John W. Hicks, M.P.A., is deputy director of the Alabama Department of Forensic Sciences, director of the state's DNA database program, and a member of the national DNA Advisory Board established under federal law in 1995. In 1988 he was appointed by the director of the Federal Bureau of Investigation (FBI) to coordinate a national program for the implementation of DNA identification technology in law enforcement.

Muin J. Khoury, M.D., Ph.D., is a geneticist in the National Center for Environmental Health at the Centers for Disease Control and Prevention (CDC). He is especially interested in the connections between medical genetics, epidemiology, and public policy.

Kenneth Kipnis, Ph.D., is a professor of philosophy at the University of Manoa. He has written broadly on legal philosophy and professional ethics, most recently publishing pieces on ethicists as expert witnesses and on parental refusals of pediatric care for religious reasons.

Bartha Maria Knoppers, Ph.D., J.D., is a professor of law and senior researcher at the Center for Public Law Research at the University of Montreal. She is also the president of the Ethics Committee of the Human Genome Organization, a member of the UNESCO International Bioethics Committee, and a co-editor of *Legal Rights and Human Genetic Material*.

Susan C. Lawrence, Ph.D., is an associate professor in the Department of History and a member of the Program in Biomedical Ethics and Medical Humanities at the University of Iowa. She is currently working on the history of human dissection and its relationship to the evolution of anatomy texts for medical students.

M. Therese Lysaught, Ph.D., is an assistant professor in the Department of Religious Studies at the University of Dayton. She is a member of the Recombinant DNA Advisory Committee of the NIH and works in the areas of genetics and theological medical ethics.

Jean E. McEwen, J.D., Ph.D., is an associate professor at Boston College Law School and also serves as adjunct lecturer in law and bioethics at New England School of Law. She has written on a variety of issues in law and genetics and has a particular research interest in the ethical, legal, and public policy implications of DNA databanks.

Geraldine M. McQuillan, Ph.D., is a senior infectious disease epidemiologist at the National Center for Health Statistics. Her research areas of interest include hepatitis viruses, HIV prevalence in the United States, and immunization status for vaccine preventable diseases.

Jon F. Merz, J.D., Ph.D., is an assistant professor in the Center for Bioethics at the University of Pennsylvania. His research interests include privacy and confidentiality in medicine and research, reproductive rights and policy, research ethics and regulation, informed consent, issues raised in the foregoing areas by genetics technologies, and right-to-die law and policy.

Lisa Milhollin (now Lisa Johnson), B.A., received her degree from the University of Iowa in 1997 and is currently a first-year medical student at the University of Iowa College of Medicine.

Jeffrey C. Murray, M.D., is a professor of pediatrics; biological sciences; literature, science, and the arts; and pediatric dentistry at the University of Iowa. His area of interest in research is in applying techniques of human molecular genetics to the identification of genes involved in birth defects, such as cleft lip and palate, and he is involved in presenting the educational aspects of the ethical, legal, and social components of the human genome project to high school and lay audiences.

Curtis R. Naser, Ph.D., is an assistant professor of philosophy at Fairfield University in Connecticut and teaches in the Program in Applied Ethics. He works with several IRBs and focuses his research on the ethics of research involving human subjects.

Ryan Peirce, B.A., received his degree from the University of Iowa in 1997 and is currently a first-year medical student at the University of Illinois.

William Rhead, M.D., Ph.D., is a professor of pediatrics, University of Iowa College of Medicine. He is a biochemical geneticist, a metabolic disease specialist, and the clinical consultant to the Iowa Newborn Screening Program.

Eric J. Sampson, Ph.D., is director, Division of Environmental Health Laboratory Sciences, National Center for Environmental Health at the Centers for Disease Control and Prevention (CDC). His area of interest includes laboratory measurements for epidemiologic studies in environmental health, chronic diseases, newborn screening, nutrition, and public health emergencies.

Pamela Sankar, Ph.D., is an assistant professor of bioethics at the University of Pennsylvania. She has graduate degrees in both anthropology and communications, and her primary research interests include biomedical culture and medical confidentiality practices.

Amy E. T. Sparks, Ph.D., is a research scientist and the director of the In Vitro Fertilization and Reproductive Testing Laboratory at the University of Iowa Hospitals and Clinics. Her research interests include gamete and embryo micromanipulation and cryopreservation.

Karen K. Steinberg, Ph.D., is chief, Molecular Biology Branch, National Center for Environmental Health at the Centers for Disease Control and Prevention (CDC). She was instrumental in developing a nationally representative sample of immortalized cell lines for the study of genetic risk factors for common disease, and she has developed a CD-ROM, *The Genetic Basis of Cancer*, to explain the genetic basis of heriditary and sporadic cancers and the social, legal, and ethical implications of genetic testing for health care workers.

Jan Susanin, B.S., is supervisor of the Iowa Neonatal Metabolic Screening Program at the University of Iowa Hygienic Laboratory.

Dorothy E. Vawter, Ph.D., is the associate director of the Minnesota Center for Health Care Ethics. Her research interests include organ and tissue donation, research with human subjects, cross-cultural health care ethics, and medical futility and other challenges to professional integrity.

Victor Walter Weedn, M.D., J.D., is a state medical examiner and director of Region II of the Alabama Department of Forensic Sciences. He was formerly a lieutenant colonel (promotable) in the U.S. Army and the founder and for seven years the program manager of the Department of Defense DNA Registry at the Armed Forces Institute of Pathology.

Robert F. Weir, Ph.D., is a professor in the Department of Pediatrics and the School of Religion and the director of the Program in Biomedical Ethics at the University of Iowa College of Medicine. He is the author of *Abating Treatment with Critically Ill Patients* and numerous articles on topics in bioethics, including informed consent in the context of DNA banking.

Index

Abercrombie, Neil, 343n

Abman, S. H., 29n

Accurso, F. J., 29n

Acuff, K. L., 29n

advance directives, xiii, 236–266; for decisions about stored tissues, 254–266; for decisions at end of life, 251–253, 275; nonstatutory types, 251–252; statutory types, 251–252

Advisory Committee on Human Radiation Experiments (ACHRE), 332, 341, 342n

Al-Hasani, S., 80n

Allen, B. D., 79n

Alper, J. S., 30n, 328n

American Association of Blood Banks, 46, 59n, 64n

American College of Medical Genetics, 12, 15, 17–18, 30n, 31n, 88n, 242

American Fertility Society, 70, 80n, 81n, 189–190

American Indian and Alaska Native (AI/AN) communities, 267–301, 287n

American Society for Reproductive Medicine, 66, 68, 70–77, 79n

American Society of Human Genetics, 11–12, 15, 17, 23, 30n, 31n, 84, 88n, 245, 247, 320

Ames, Michael M., 141n

Amit, A., 79n

Ammann, Arthur J., 65n

amplified fragment length polymorphism, 347

anatomy, 119–32

Anatomy Act of 1832 (England), 119, 122, 127–128, 132

Anderson, Jeannette, 3

Anderson, Sanford, 59n

Andrews, Lori, 16, 29n, 31n, 87n, 88n, 106n, 176n, 217n

Annas, George J., 30n, 84, 88n, 141n, 148, 156n, 164, 176n, 177n, 217n, 241, 250, 261n, 262n, 338, 343n

anonymized tissue, xii, 5, 18–27, 84–86, 100, 103–104, 160–165, 175, 222, 237–238, 242–245, 247–248, 255, 260, 262, 275

anonymous tissue, xii, 19, 84, 160–165, 175, 237–238, 242–243, 245, 255, 296, 298–299, 322–325, 330

Appadurai, Arjun, 135n

Arabian, Justice, 131

Areman, Ellen M., 61n

Aries, Philippe, 138n

Armed Forces DNA Identification Laboratory, 345

Armed Forces Institute of Pathology (AFIP), viii–ix, 329–344, 345–357

Armed Forces Repository of Specimen Samples for the Identification of Remains, 345, 352–353

Aronson, R. A., 29n

Asch, R. H., 79n, 80n

Assessing Genetic Risks, 15

Austin, M. A., 87n

Avery, S. M., 81n

Azem, F., 79n

Azen, Stanley, 289n

Badawi, A. F., 87n

Baer, Annette, 281, 291n

Baird, D. T., 80n

Ball, D., 177n

Ballantyne, J., 326n, 327n

Ballin, Ami, 59n

Balmeceda, J. P., 79n

Banner, Richard O., 291n

Barak, Y., 79n

Barbash, F., 327n

Bayliss, U., 29n

Beardsley, Tim, 288n

Beauchamp, Tom L., 179n, 272, 288n

Beaudet, A. L., 30n
Beaune, P., 87n
Beck, Peggy V., 290n
Beckwith, Jonathan, 30n
Beecher, Henry, 179n
behavioral genetics, 322–324
Bell, D. A., 87n
Belmont Report (1979), 339, 343n
Bendixen, Kae, 140n
Bennetto, J., 327n
Bentley, James, 135n
Bereano, P. L., 326n, 327n
Bernard, Claude, 169, 178n
Bernhardt, Barbara A., 289n
Bertolini, Francesco, 61n
Bertrand, E., 79n
Biafono, Ellen M., 59n
Bignon, J., 87n
Billings, Paul R., 30n, 61n, 327n
Birtwistle, N. J., 232n
Blackhall, Leslie J., 289n
Blair, Roger, 137n
Blank, Robert H., 262n
Bleich, J. David, 135n
blood samples, vii, ix, xiii, 3–10, 32, 54,
    82–86, 96, 160, 186, 198, 233, 236, 239–
    240, 259, 311, 332, 349, 355
Boerwinkle, E., 87n
Bogdan, Robert, 140n
Bogert, G. T., 197n
Bolton, V., 80n
Bonnicksen, Andrea L., 262n
Botkin, Jeffrey R., 30n
Boulton, M. I., 80n
Bowman, M. C., 81n
Boyer, R. E., 196n
Boyse, Edward A., 61n, 62n
Braude, P., 80n
Brindsden, P. R., 81n
Brody, Baruch, 150, 156n
Brody, J. V., 179n
Brown, J. R., 79n
Brown, Louise, 183
Brown, N. N., 87n
Browning v. Norton–Children's Hospital,
    129

Broxmeyer, Hal E., 61n
Buckley, Jay C., Jr., 291n
Bugawan, T. L., 86n
Burk, D. L., 326n, 327n
Burke, J. F., 232n
Burns, J. K., 217n
Butler, Declan, 288n
Bynum, Caroline Walker, 115, 135n
Bynum, W. T., 136n

cadavers, xiii, 111–134, 172
Campbell, D., 327n
Candy, C. J., 79n
Caplan, Arthur, 216, 232n
Capron, Alexander, 170, 179n, 180n, 292n
Carey, Eben J., 139n
Carey, W. F., 30n
Carrese, Joseph A., 289n
Caskey, C. T., 30n
Cassiman, J. J., 87n
Caulfield, T., 227, 231n
Cavalli-Storza, Luca, 105, 106n
cell lines, vii, x, xiii, 83, 91, 97, 130–131,
    182, 233, 237–238, 240, 295
Cenee, S., 87n
Center for Advanced Reproductive Care,
    66, 81n
Centers for Disease Control and Preven-
    tion (CDC), vii, x–xi, xiii, 82–86, 239–
    241, 247
Chadwick, Ruth, 111, 134n, 138n
Chadwin, Dean, 343n
Chalmers, T., 179n
Chapler, F. K., 80n
cheek cells, vii, ix, 82, 91, 96, 236, 239, 329,
    349, 352, 355
Cherniawsky, K., 227, 231n
Chestnut, D. H., 80n
Childress, James, 272, 288n, 293n
Childs, James E., 291n
Cho, Mildred, 216
Clague, A. E., 87n
Clayton, Ellen Wright, 20–22, 25, 31n,
    88n, 99–102, 104, 108n, 157n, 164, 171,
    176n, 178n, 217n, 240, 243–245, 247–
    248, 261n, 328n, 343n

Code of Conduct for Research Involving Humans (Canada), 272, 282

Cohen, B., 233n

"cold hits," 311

Cole, Douglas, 288n, 289n

Cole, F. J., 139n

College of American Pathologists, 246–247, 261n

Collins, Francis S., 29n

Combined DNA Index System (CODIS), viii, xiv, 305–310, 311, 321

commercial DNA banks, 17

commercial interests, 211–212, 220, 224, 238, 242, 250, 263, 294, 338

Committee on Assessing Genetic Risks (Institute of Medicine), 15–22, 26

commodification, 226–235

confidentiality, x, 143–154, 161, 198–216, 233–234, 237, 244, 262, 300

consent documents, xiii, 19, 49, 75, 76, 83, 189, 194, 198–225, 233–235, 239–240, 245, 249, 256, 263, 294–301, 339

cord blood banks, 35–39

Cord Blood Registry, 62n, 63n

Coriel Institute, 96

Corrigan, E., 81n

Cosme, J., 87n

Council for International Organizations of Medical Sciences (CIOMS), 281, 283, 286, 292n

Council of Europe, x, 229, 232n

Council of Regional Networks of Genetic Services (CORN), 15–18, 21–29

Council on Ethical and Judicial Affairs (American Medical Association), 48, 52, 64n

Craig, Bruce, 135n

Crauford, D., 177n

Crigger, Bette-Jane, 105n

Crowther, S. M., 232n

Cruzan, Nancy, 254

cryopreservation (of embryos), xii–xiii, 66–79

Culin, Stewart, 270

Cunningham, F. Gary, 62n

Cutter, Mary Ann G., xiii, 143–154

Daston, Lorraine, 139n

Daukes, Sidney H., 139n

David, M. P., 79n

Davies, A. R. W., 232n

Davis v. Davis, 73, 81n, 184–185, 191, 196n

Dawson, K., 71, 81n

Declaration of Helsinki (1964), 339

Decorte, R., 87n

Decruyenaere, Marleen, 177n

Deeg, H. Joachim, 61n

DeGorgey, A., 326n

Deliliers, G. Lambertenghi, 60n

Del Zio v. Presbyterian Hospital, 183–184, 196n

DeMets, David L., 293n

Department of Defense (DoD), viii, xiv, 239, 329–344, 345–357

Depierre, A., 87n

Devreker, F., 79n

diagnostic use, 15, 17–18, 26–27, 194, 236–238, 242, 244, 255, 263

Diamond, Jared, 135n

Dicke, Arnold, 147, 155n

Dickson, D., 232n

discrimination, 13, 143–159, 274–286

DNA, vii, 82–84, 89, 266, 330, 338, 346, 357

DNA analysis, 3–10, 28, 82–86, 89, 143–154, 161, 250, 305–310, 311–312, 331–334, 337–338, 347–348, 354

DNA banking, x–xi, 4–5, 17, 198–216, 226–235, 247, 329–344

DNA banks, 82–86, 198–216, 309–344

DNA databases (or databanks), viii–ix, xiv, 4–5, 17, 22–24, 82–86, 89–105, 146, 193, 195, 237, 239, 305–310, 311–325, 330, 349

DNA Identification Act (1994), viii, 311, 321, 326n

DNA Proficiency Act (1995), 305

DNA Registry, viii–x, 163, 260, 329–344, 345–357

DNA repositories, 96–97, 182, 191, 345–357

DNA samples, vii–x, xiii–xiv, 5, 54, 82–86, 89–102, 160–162, 182, 186, 236–238, 249–250, 264–266, 316, 319, 321, 329–330, 332, 349, 352

DNA Technology in Forensic Science, 313
Dondero, T. J., 30*n*
Doodeward v. Spence, 128, 140*n*
Doot, G. M., 326*n*
Douglas, Mary, 123
Downing, B., 81*n*
Dracker, Robert A., 63*n*
Dresser, Rebecca, 262*n*
Dubler, Nancy N., 180*n*, 290*n*, 293*n*
Dula, Annette, 290*n*
Dunleavy, Gerald J., 291*n*
Dunn, Peter, 62*n*
Durie, Arohia, 291*n*
Durie, Mason, 291*n*
Dwire, Angela, 156*n*
Dworkin, Gerald, 179*n*
Dworkin, R. B., 217*n*

Eckfeldt, J. H., 87*n*
Edelstein, Ludwig, 178*n*
Edwards, Kathryn, 164, 171, 178*n*, 343*n*
Elias, Sherman, 30*n*, 262*n*
Ellsworth, D. L., 87*n*
Emanuel, Ezekiel, 261*n*, 272, 281, 288*n*,
    291*n*
Emanuel, Linda, 261*n*
Ende, Milton, 59*n*
Ende, Norman, 59*n*, 60*n*, 61*n*
Engel, A., 87*n*
Engel, D., 80*n*
Engelhardt, H. Tristram, Jr., 179*n*
Englert, Y., 79*n*
English, Denis, 61*n*
English, Veronica, 81*n*
Enos, Rachelle, 291*n*
epidemiological studies, vii, x, xii–xiii,
    82–86, 160, 164–165, 238–239, 322
Epstein, Steven, 290*n*
Erikson, Jane, 290*n*
Erlich, H. A., 86*n*, 87*n*
ethical, legal, and social implications
    (ELSI): as branch of the National
    Human Genome Research Institute,
    17, 25, 83, 240, 245, 248, 325; as com-
    mittee of Human Genome Organiza-
    tion, 93–94, 107*n*

Eurocord Transplant Group, 34
European Blood and Marrow Transplant
    Group, 34
Evers-Kiebooms, Gerry, 177*n*

Faden, Ruth R., 29*n*, 179*n*, 289*n*
Fanos, J. H., 30*n*
Farrell, P. M., 29*n*
Faure, Bernard, 135*n*
Federal Bureau of Investigation (FBI),
    viii, x, xiv, 305–310, 311, 346, 348
federal regulations, 19, 84, 160–163, 199,
    243–244, 247–248, 263, 269, 272, 276,
    287*n*, 299–300
Federman, Daniel, 289*n*
Feinleib, Manning, 162, 165, 177*n*
Fernandez, M. N., 60*n*
Ferrari, Giovanna, 136*n*
filter-paper cards (for dried blood spots),
    3–5, 17, 21–29
Final Report (ACHRE), 332, 341, 342*n*, 344*n*
Findlen, Paula, 139*n*
Finke, Harry J., 137*n*
Fitzgerald, Garret, 216
Fleming, Thomas R., 293*n*
Fodor, S. P. A., 176*n*
Foley, Douglas E., 288*n*
forensic science, viii, x, xiii, xiv, 17–18,
    193, 195, 305–310, 311–325, 330
Fossum, G. T., 79*n*
Foundation for the Accreditation of He-
    matopoietic Cell Therapy, 47, 64*n*
Fox, Lynda M., 154*n*
Francisco, Nia, 290*n*
Frank, Gelya, 289*n*
Frankel, T., 197*n*
Frederick, J. L., 79*n*
Freeman, William, xiv, 156*n*, 232*n*, 249,
    267–301, 294*n*
French, Roger, 136*n*
Frey, Mary Ann Bassett, 291*n*
Fried, Charles, 177*n*, 179*n*
Fullarton, J. E., 31*n*, 88*n*

Gaffney, Andrew, 291*n*
Gannal, J. N., 139*n*

Garner, F., 81*n*

Geary, Patrick, 135*n*

Geerts, L., 79*n*

Geertz, Clifford, 135*n*

Geller, Gail, 29*n*

genetic information, 12, 16, 82–86, 143–154, 157–159, 162, 337

Genetic Privacy Act (proposed), 16, 18, 20, 23, 141*n*, 160, 176*n*, 241–242, 250

genetic studies, vii, x, 82–86, 89–102, 198–225, 226–235, 238, 243, 246, 255, 258, 262, 264, 333

genetic testing, 143–154, 157–159, 305–310

George, J. R., 30*n*

Gerace, R. L., 29*n*

Gerber, A. Russell, 291*n*

Gerhardt, Uta, 289*n*

Getchell, Jane, 3

Gilbert, J. P., 179*n*

Gindoff, P. R., 80*n*

Glantz, Leonard H., 30*n*, 176*n*, 217*n*, 241, 250, 261*n*, 343*n*

Glass, Kathleen Cranley, 233

Gluckman, Eliane, 59*n*, 60*n*, 61*n*, 62*n*, 64*n*

Godard, B., 228, 231*n*, 233

Goering, Sara, 290*n*

Gold, R. L., 217*n*

Golde, David, 185

Goldgar, D. E., 217*n*

Gollup, Roger, 288*n*

Gook, D. A., 80*n*

Gordon-Grube, Karen, 138*n*

Gorfinkel, Claire, 342

Gosden, R. G., 80*n*

Gostin, Larry O., 31*n*, 293*n*

Gotay, Carolyn C., 291*n*

Gottlieb, Karen, xiii, 182–196

Grady, G. F., 30*n*

Grant, K., 80*n*

Greely, Henry, xiii, 89–105, 106*n*, 142*n*

Green, Mark, 177*n*

Greenwald, R. A., 180*n*

Gregg, R. G., 29*n*

Grierson, A., 81*n*

Grimes, Ronald L., 141*n*

Grizzard, William S., 61*n*

Grodin, Michael A., 343*n*

Grody, Wayne, 164, 170, 176*n*, 177*n*, 244–245, 247, 260, 260*n*

Grounds, Richard, 270, 288*n*

Guidelines for Collection, Processing and Storage of Cord Blood Stem Cells (New York), 45

Gunning, Jennifer, 81*n*

Guttman, Ronald, 137*n*

Gwinn, M., 30*n*

Hadro, T., 217*n*

Hagelberg, Erika, 142*n*

Hahn, S. J., 81*n*

Hall, J. L., 80*n*

Hallman, D. M., 87*n*

Hamer, F. C., 79*n*

Hammond, K. B., 29*n*

Hanna, Kathi E., 290*n*

Hannes, M., 79*n*

Hannig, Vicki, 164, 171, 178*n*, 343*n*

Hannon, W. H., 30*n*

Hardiman, Roy, 138*n*

harm, 20, 25, 160–176, 268, 278–281, 284–286, 299

Harper, Peter S., 181*n*

Harris, David T., 59*n*, 61*n*, 63*n*, 64*n*

Hassemer, D., 29*n*

Hayney, M. S., 87*n*

health insurance companies, 143–154

Hecht, Deborah, 191

Hecht v. Superior Court of Los Angeles County, 190–191, 196*n*, 197*n*

Hellman, Deborah S., 179*n*

Hellman, Samuel, 179*n*

Heman, D., 87*n*

hematopoietic stem cells, 33–35

Herring, D. Ann, 293*n*

Hicks, John, xiv, 305–310, 310*n*

high speed genetic testing, 161

Higuchi, R., 87*n*

Hippocrates, 167, 178*n*

Hirtle, M., 227–228, 231*n*

Hoeffel, J. C., 327*n*

Hoffman, G., 29*n*

Hofmeyr, G. L., 62*n*
Holmes, Edward, 216
Holtzman, Neil, 13, 30*n*, 31*n*, 88*n*, 261, 289*n*
Hopkins, Anthony, 289*n*
Horn, G. T., 86*n*
Horne, G., 79*n*
Horowitz, Mary, 59*n*
Horton, Jay, 17–18, 23, 31*n*, 217*n*, 232*n*, 260*n*
Hsieh, L. L., 87*n*
Hudson, Kathy, 155*n*, 343*n*
Hull, M. G. R., 81*n*
Human Genome Diversity Project (HGDP), xi–xiii, 89–102, 195, 281–283, 286, 288*n*, 292*n*, 293*n*
Human Genome Organization (HUGO), x, 91, 229
Human Genome Project, 82, 89–92
Human Resources Research Organization, 333
Hussain, Wajid, 135*n*

Indian Health Service, 267–301, 287*n*
Indian Self-Determination Act of 1975, 268
informed consent, ix, xii, 10, 15–29, 32, 39–50, 52–54, 83, 89–102, 112, 129–131, 133, 153, 160–165, 168, 192, 198–225, 236–266, 268, 275, 281–290, 294–301, 323–334, 330–332, 336, 339–342, 356
institutional review boards (IRBs), 19–20, 24, 102–103, 160, 166, 168, 175, 239, 243, 249, 268–270, 275–276, 294–301
Integrated Molecular Analysis of Genomes and their Expression (IMAGE) Consortium, 97
International Cord Blood Transplant Registry, 33
in vitro fertilization, 66–79, 184
Iowa Neonatal Metabolic Screening Program, 3
Isoyama, Keiichi, 62*n*
Issaragrisil, S., 60*n*

Jackson, Percival, 136*n*
Jaffe, Erik S., 137*n*
Jansen, R. P. S., 80*n*
Jeffrey, R., 79*n*
Jinks, D. C., 87*n*
Jiraisi, Nancy, 136*n*
Johnston, W. I. H., 80*n*
Jonas, Hans, 170, 179*n*
Jones, H. W., Jr., 72, 80*n*, 81*n*
Jonsen, Albert, 166, 178*n*, 179*n*
Just, J. J., 87*n*

Kaback, Michael M., 30*n*
Kaczynski, Theodore, 337
Kadlubar, F. F., 87*n*
Kahn, Ellis M. J., 176*n*, 217*n*, 328*n*
Kahn, J. A., 79*n*
Kahn, M. J. E., 31*n*, 88*n*, 106*n*
Kahn, Patricia, 105*n*, 197*n*, 288*n*
Kane, William, 190–191
Kant, Immanuel, 179*n*
Kantamneni, J. R., 81*n*
Kaserman, David, 137*n*
Kennedy, Joseph, 352
Kettle, L. M., 79*n*
Khoury, Muin J., 31*n*, 82, 88*n*, 106*n*, 176*n*, 217*n*, 328*n*
King, Leland C., 291*n*
King, M. C., 87*n*
King, Y. K., 79*n*
Kinsella, T. D., 228, 231*n*
Kipnis, Kenneth, xiv, 329–344
Kirby, L. T., 326*n*
Knoppers, Bartha, xiii, 106*n*, 107*n*, 217*n*, 226–235, 231*n*, 232*n*, 249
Knox, Linda, 216
Kodish, E., 217*n*
Kogler, Gesine, 62*n*, 64*n*
Kohli-Kumar, Mudra, 60*n*, 64*n*
Kohn, M. A., 30*n*
Kolata, Gina, 177*n*
Kopelman, Loretta M., 31*n*, 88*n*, 106*n*, 176*n*, 217*n*, 328*n*
Kselman, Thomas A., 135*n*
Ksiazek, Thomas G., 291*n*

Kuller, Jeffrey A., 59 n, 63 n
Kurtzberg, Joanne, 59 n

Laberge, C., 217 n, 228, 231 n, 232 n, 233
Laessig, R. H., 29 n
Lammers, Stephen E., 180 n
Lander, E. S., 326 n
Lane, Lynda A., 291 n
Laporte, Jean-Philippe, 60 n
Lappe, Marc A., 177 n
Last, John M., 288 n
Laurent, P., 87 n
Law, Jane Marie, 135 n
Lawrence, Susan, xii–xiii, 111–134, 136 n,
    139 n, 140 n
Laxova, A., 29 n
Lebel, R. R., 217 n
Ledger, W., 79 n
Lee, Robert, 134 n
Lennon, G., 107 n
Lessing, J. B., 79 n
Levi, Jeffrey, 290 n
Levine, Benjamin D., 291 n
Levine, Carol, 180 n, 290 n, 293 n
Levine, Robert J., 180 n, 262 n, 283, 286,
    290 n, 291 n, 293 n
Levitt, Daniel, 61 n
Levy, Harvey, 14, 30 n
Lewis, B. D., 29 n
Lewkonia, R. M., 228, 231 n
Lewontin, R., 327 n
Lieberman, B. A., 79 n
Lind, Stuart E., 64 n
Linderkamp, Otwin, 62 n
linkable (or identifiable) tissues, 19, 22,
    25, 27, 160–176, 202, 209–210, 214–215,
    223, 233, 237–238, 243–244, 247, 260,
    262, 296, 298–299, 329–344
Lipp, Martin R., 142 n
Lipshutz, R. J., 176 n
Litman, M., 226, 231 n
"living will," 251
Livolsi, V., 217 n
Logan, Leanne, 342
Lowe, C. R., 81 n

Lucier, G. W., 87 n
Lynch, Richard, 246
Lyotard, Jean-Francois, 149–150, 156 n
Lysaught, Therese, xii, 3–29

MacDonald, Michael M., 136 n
Macilwain, Colin, 105 n
MacNamee, M. C., 81 n
Maddox, John, 103 n
Marcus, S., 81 n
Marshall, Eliot, 106 n
Mastroianni, Anna C., 289 n
Matson, P. L., 79 n
Matsunaga, Doris Segal, 291 n
Matthews, C. D., 79 n
Matthews, Paul, 119, 129, 136 n
Mauer, K., 87 n
Maulitz, Russell, 139 n
Mayfield, John, III, 330–335, 340–342
Mayfield v. Dalton, 342 n, 357 n
McCabe, Edward, 31 n, 87 n, 245, 261 n
McCane, Byron R., 135 n
McCarrick, P. M., 30 n
McCullough, Jeffrey, 61 n, 63 n, 65 n
McCullough, Larry, 155 n
McEwen, Jean, xiv, 18, 29 n, 30 n, 155 n,
    217 n, 310 n, 311–325, 326 n, 327 n, 342 n
McGurdy, Paul R., 62 n
McKinnon, R. A., 87 n
McKusick, Victor A., 86 n
McPeak, B., 179 n
McQuillan, Geraldine M., 82
Mead, Aroha Te Pareake, 289 n
Meagher, Emma, 216
Mearns, E. A., 217 n
Menozzi, P., 106 n
Meny, Geralyn M., 61 n, 62 n
Mertelsmann, Roland, 61 n
Merz, Jon, xiii, 198–225, 217 n, 232 n, 249
Michel, Vicki, 289 n
Milhollin, Lisa, 3
military settings, viii–ix, xiv, 17, 329–344,
    345–357
Miller, H. W., 87 n
Miller, Michael W., 177 n

Miller, R., 87n
Milleron, B., 87n
Millikan, R. D., 87n
Mischler, E. H., 29n
Model Ethical Protocol (of HGDP), 89, 94–95
Modell, E., 79n
Mohr, L., 79n
Molne, K., 79n
Monreal, Richard, 330
Moore, John, 130, 186, 194
Moore, S., 80n
Moore v. the Regents of the University of California, 130, 183, 185–186, 188, 191, 196n, 197n
moral status of embryos, 66, 70–71
Morgan, Derek, 134n
Morris, C. P., 29n
Morris, Michael, 177n
Morzunov, Sergey, 291n
Moss, Arthur J., 62n
Mosteller, F., 179n
Mottla, G. L., 81n
Motulsky, Arno G., 31n, 88n, 327n
Mullis, K. B., 86n
Mulvihill, J. E., 180n
Mumford, S. E., 81n
Murphy, Sheila T., 289n
Murphy, Terence R., 136n
Murphy, Timothy F., 177n
Murray, Jeffrey, x, xii, 3
Murray, Thomas H., 30n, 156n, 217n, 293n
museums, 125–126, 131
Myers, Melanie F., 289n

Naser, Curtis, xiii, 160–176
National Academy of Sciences, 313, 317, 320, 326n
National Action Plan on Breast Cancer, 200
National Bioethics Advisory Commission, 260
National Breast Cancer Coalition, 272, 277, 279

National Center for Human Genome Research (now the National Human Genome Research Institute), 17–23, 25, 83, 157n, 240, 248
National Center for the Analysis of Violent Crime, 309
National Commission for the Protection of Human Subjects of Biomedical and Behavioral Research, 287n
National Crime Information Center, 322
National Health and Nutrition Examination Study (NHANES), vii, 82–86, 163, 239–241
National Heart, Lung and Blood Institute, 34
National Human Genome Research Institute, 240
National Institutes of Health, 17, 83, 91
National Museum of the American Indian Act, 132
National Research Council, 92
Native American Graves Protection and Repatriation Act, 132
Native Americans, xiv, 132, 267–301
Natowicz, Marvin, 155n
Nebert, D. W., 87n
Nelson, E., 227, 231n
Nelson, P. V., 29n
neonatal blood spots, vii, x, xii, 3–29, 236, 238–239, 256, 258, 349
newborn screening, xi, 3–29
Newman, B., 87n
Newton, C. R., 87n
Nichol, Stuart T., 291n
Nijs, M., 79n
North American Regional Committee (of HGDP), 94, 101, 105, 106n, 270
North American Task Force for Development of Standards for Hematopoietic Cell Transplantation, 46
Novick, Lloyd F., 291n
Nuremberg Code (1947), 339

Obasaju, M., 79n
Obermann, C. Esco, 287

Obermann Center for Advanced Studies, x, 59, 216, 286–287, 342

Obermann Faculty Research Seminar, x, 161, 216, 286–287, 342

Office of Protection from Research Risks (OPRR), 20, 160, 248, 323

Office of the Assistant Secretary of Defense for Health Affairs, 329, 331, 341, 342 n, 344 n, 351

O'Neill, Onora, 177 n

Ord, T., 79 n

Ordoras, J. M., 87 n

Osborn, S. M., 80 n

Ostrer, Harry, 155 n

ownership of tissue, x, 23–24, 66, 112, 130, 133, 137 n, 152–153, 182–196, 198–216, 226–235, 238, 240, 263, 335, 337

Pahwa, R., 60 n

Palca, Joseph, 180 n

Pappaioanou, M., 30 n

Pardoe, Colin, 141 n

Park, Katherine, 139 n

Parker, Lisa S., 181 n

Parsons, Talcott, 179 n

pathology, vii, xi, 113, 126, 129, 160, 194, 236, 238, 243–248, 259, 357

Patient Self-Determination Act, 252, 275

Payne, D., 79 n

Pease, A. C., 176 n

Pease, E. H. E., 79 n

Peirce, Ryan, 3

Pelias, Mary Z., 180 n, 181 n

Pellegrino, Edmund, 166, 178 n, 180 n

Perera, F., 87 n

Peyser, M. R., 79 n

Phillips, John, 242, 245

Piazza, A., 106 n

polymerase chain reaction (PCR), 6, 82, 318

Porter, Roy, 136 n

Powers, Madison, 29 n

preembryos, vii, 66–79, 182, 186, 236, 239

Preston, Jennifer, 155 n

Printz, M., 87 n

privacy, ix–x, xiv, 32, 143–154, 234, 236–237, 246, 262–263, 311–325, 339–342, 351, 354–357

Privacy Act (1974), 351, 353

property rights, xiii, 23, 93–94, 119–120, 128, 130, 133, 182–196, 226–235, 238, 335, 337

property transfer: as abandonment, 187–188; as bailment, 188–190; as gift, 190–192; as trust, 192–194

prospective studies, xii, 18, 100, 237–238, 243–245, 255

public health, 3–8, 25, 82–86

Puga, A., 87 n

Quaid, Kimberly A., 177 n

Randal, Judith, 59 n

Ranieri, E., 29 n

Rapid Action Task Force (of ASHG), 245, 247, 249, 261 n

Reilly, Philip, 17–21, 29 n, 30 n, 155 n, 165, 170, 176 n, 217 n, 261 n, 310 n, 326 n, 327 n, 342 n

religious beliefs, 114–117

"required request," 58

research ethics boards, 227

restriction fragment length polymorphism (RFLP), 316–318

retrospective studies, xii, 18, 100, 238, 243, 245–246

Rhead, William, 3

Rhodes, Lorna A., 289 n

Richards, B., 87 n

Richards, M. B., 142 n

Richardson, Ruth, 118, 121, 136 n

Roberts, C. J., 81 n

Roberts, K. B., 139 n

Roberts, Leslie, 106 n

Robertson, E. F., 30 n

Robertson, G., 226, 231 n

Robertson, John, 75–76, 81 n

Robinson, Ian, 288 n

Roche, Patricia A., 30 n, 176 n, 217 n, 241, 250, 261 n, 343 n

Rodesch, C., 79*n*
Rogers, P., 81*n*
Rosner, Fred, 135*n*
Rothman, Kenneth, 164, 177*n*
Roughead, William, 136*n*
"routine inquiry," 58
Rubenstein, Pablo, 59*n*, 60*n*, 61*n*, 62*n*, 63*n*
Rubinstein, David C., 177*n*
Rupp, Jan C. C., 136*n*
Rural Advancement Foundation International, 105*n*
Russell, Mary D., 135*n*
Ryall, R. G., 29*n*
Ryan, M. K., 180*n*

Sacher, Ronald A., 61*n*
Saiki, R. K., 86*n*
Salopek, Paul, 105*n*
Sampson, Eric J., 82
Sankar, Pamela, xiii, 198–225, 217*n*, 232*n*, 249
Satcher, David, 86
Saunders, D. M., 76, 81*n*
Saxer, Victor, 135*n*
Sayers, H. M., 65*n*
Scambler, Graham, 289*n*
Scarf, Maggie, 176*n*
Scheck, B., 327*n*, 342*n*
Schiewe, M. C., 80*n*
Schoysman, R., 79*n*
Schrader, C. S., 80*n*
Schull, Jack, 92
Seashore, M. R., 29*n*, 30*n*
secondary research uses, x, 5, 17–20, 22, 28, 237–239, 255, 295–296
Segal-Bertin, G., 79*n*
Seitz, Eric, 331, 342
Sensabaugh, G. F., 87*n*, 326*n*, 327*n*
Shapiro, E. D., 327*n*
Shaw, L. W., 179*n*
Sheehy, Gerard, 135*n*
Sherry, G., 29*n*
Shettles, Landrum, 183
Shurin, S., 217*n*

Siebzehnubel, E., 80*n*
Simpson, J. L., 30*n*
Skegg, P. D. G., 136*n*
Slociv, Paul, 289*n*
Smale, David A., 136*n*
Snipp, C. Matthew, 288*n*
Society for Assisted Reproductive Technologies, 68, 79*n*
Sokol, R. J., 29*n*
Sordal, T., 79*n*
Sparks, Amy, xii, 66–79, 79*n*, 80*n*, 81*n*
sperm banks, 194–195
Spiropoulou, Christina F., 291*n*
Standards for Blood Banks and Transfusion Services, 46
Standards for Hematopoietic Progenitor Cell Collection, Processing and Transplantation, 47
state laws, 3–8, 15, 23, 143–154, 154*n*, 155*n*, 258, 263, 305–310, 311–325, 325*n*, 326*n*
Stawski, S., 327*n*
Steinberg, Karen, xiii, 31*n*, 82–86, 88*n*, 106*n*, 176*n*, 177*n*, 217*n*, 328*n*
Stephenson, Joan, 261*n*, 343*n*
stigmatization, 20, 274–275, 278–280, 284–286, 300, 354
Stillman, R. J., 81*n*
Stocking, George W., 141*n*
Stone, S. C., 79*n*
Storage of Genetics Materials Committee (of ACMG), 242, 247, 249, 261*n*
stored body parts, xiii, 111–134
Stovall, D. W., 79*n*, 81*n*
Strickland, Rennard, 287*n*
Stucker, I., 87*n*
Study to Understand Prognoses and Preferences for Outcomes and Risks of Treatment (SUPPORT), 254
Sugarman, Jeremy, 52, 54, 65*n*
Sunde, A., 79*n*
"surveillance creep," 314
Susanin, Jan, 3
Sykes, B. C., 142*n*
Syrop, Craig H., 79*n*, 80*n*, 81*n*

Tambor, Ellen S., 289n
Tanouye, Elyse, 177n
Task Force on Genetic Information and Insurance, 144, 155n
Taube, S., 217n
Taylor, J., 87n
Teacher, John, 139n
technologically assisted reproduction, xi, 66–79, 187
Therrell, B. L., 31n
third-party access, ix–x, xiii, 13, 198, 262–266, 319, 338
Thomas, D. P., 179n
Thomas, S. M., 232n
Thompson, C. L., 87n
Thomson, D. M., 87n
Thomson, Elizabeth, 31n, 88n, 106n, 176n, 217n, 328n
tissue banks, xi, 153, 260, 274, 295, 357
tissues: as religious relics, 114–117; as waste, vii, 32, 113, 122, 183, 275
Tomlinson, J. D. W., 139n
Tong, Rosemary, 156n
Tracy, R., 87n
Trainor, Kevin M., 135n
Tri-council Working Group, 288n, 292n, 293n
Trounson, A., 71, 79n, 81n
trust (as repository), 24, 182–196, 200
Turnbull, Paul, 141n
Turner, C. W., 62n
Tyler, A., 177n

Ubel, Peter, 216
umbilical cord blood, vii, xii, 32–59, 182, 256, 294–295
Uniform Anatomical Gift Act, 51, 122, 135n, 138n, 141n
United Nations Education, Social, and Cultural Organization (UNESCO), x, 229, 232n
United States v. Spencer, 340, 344n
University of Iowa Hygienic Laboratory, 3–5
University of Pennsylvania, 200, 217

van den Berg, M., 79n
Van den Berghe, Herman, 177n
Vanderpool, Harold, 180n
Vanderzwalmen, P., 79n
van Roosendaal, E., 79n
Van Voorhis, B. J., 67, 79n, 80n, 81n
Varney, Helen, 63n
Vawter, Dorothy, xii, 32–59, 65n
Veatch, Robert, 171, 179n, 180n, 289n
Venner, Charles, 187–188
Venner v. Maryland, 187
Verhey, Allen, 180n
Verhoef, M. J., 228, 231n
ViaCord, 60n
Vincent, R. D., 80n
Vizenor, Gerald, 141n
Vlacovsky, Joseph, 330–335, 340–342
von Beroldingen, C. H., 87n
von Staden, Heinrich, 123, 138n, 139n

Wade, J. C., 80n
Wagner, John E., 59n, 60n, 61n, 62n, 64n
Wagner, Joshua, 105
Waldram, James B., 293n
Walker, Vickie, 137n
Wallace, R. Jay, Jr., 179n
Walsh-Vockley, C., 30n
Walters, Anna Lee, 290n
Walters, LeRoy, 179n, 293n
Wang, X. J., 79n
Watson, J. D., 87n
Webb, R., 80n
Weber, Barbara, 216
Weedn, Victor, xiv, 342n, 345–357
Weeks, Christine, 216
Weinberg, M. L., 327n
Weinman, George H., 137n
Weir, Robert, x, xiii, 17–18, 23, 31n, 217n, 232n, 236–266, 260n, 261n, 262n
Weiss, Gary, 180n
Weiss, Joan O., 31n, 88n, 106n, 176n, 217n, 328n
Wertz, Dorothy, 12, 30n
Whitley, Richard J., 293n

Whittingham, D. G., 80n
Wilcken, B., 29n
Wiley, Joseph, 59n, 63n
Wiley, V., 29n
Wilfond, B. S., 29n, 30n
Wilker, N. L., 327n
Wilkinson, Charles F., 287n
Williamson, R., 177n
Winchell, Danette, 156n
Winkel, C. A., 79n
Winski, John B., 132, 141n
Witowski, J., 326n, 327n

Wood, C., 81n
Wood, M. J., 79n
World Health Organization, 275

Yaron, Y., 79n
Yee, Y. H., 327n
York v. Jones, 81n, 189
Young, T. Kue, 293n
Yovel, I., 79n

Zimmerman, Larry, 141n
Zix-Kieffer, I., 60n